The Labor Market for Health Workers in Africa

The Labor Market for Health Workers in Africa

A New Look at the Crisis

Agnes Soucat, Richard Scheffler, with Tedros Adhanom Ghebreyesus, *Editors*

THE WORLD BANK
Washington, D.C.

ISBN (paper): 978-0-8213-9555-4
ISBN (electronic): 978-0-8213-9558-5
DOI: 10.1596/978-0-8213-9555-4

Library of Congress Cataloging-in-Publication Data

The labor market for health workers in Africa: A new look at the crisis/[edited by] Agnes Soucat, Richard Scheffler.
    p. ; cm.
  Includes bibliographical references.
  ISBN 978-0-8213-9555-4 — ISBN 978-0-8213-9558-5
  I. Soucat, Agnes L. B. II. Scheffler, Richard M. III. World Bank.
  [DNLM: 1. Health Manpower—Africa South of the Sahara. 2. Health Personnel—education—Africa South of the Sahara. 3. Health Personnel—organization & administration—Africa South of the Sahara. W 76]
  362.10967—dc23

2012013536

Contents

Boxes

Figures

Tables

Foreword

The outcome of the multiyear partnership between the Global Center for Health Economics at the School of Public Health, University of California Berkeley; the Africa Region Health, Nutrition and Population Unit of the World Bank; and the Human Development Department at the African Development Bank has produced an academically rigorous book that provides a new understanding of the Human Resource Crisis in Africa. The tools and concepts in it have many applications to offer across low- and middle-income countries, making this book one that will be used around the globe.

The Human Resources for Health Specialists of the World Bank and African Development Bank have made many visits to Berkeley to work with Professor Scheffler and our graduate students, and to learn from one another. Numerous workshops were held at Berkeley and in various African countries, bringing the various editors and authors together with African practitioners and academics. This partnership and the research highlighted within the jointly produced book also led to the development of the Global Health Labor Markets course, which was taught at Berkeley and attended by human resource researchers and policy makers from 15 low- and middle-incomes countries. Indeed, this partnership is a role model for what can be accomplished by academic institutions working with the World Bank and the African Development Bank. We are pleased and proud of this book, which will be a landmark in the field of human resources for health around the globe.

Stephen M. Shortell, Ph.D., M.P.H., M.B.A.
Dean, University of California, Berkeley,
School of Public Health

As African countries race toward the finish line to reach the Millennium Development Goals by 2015, this book comes at the right time for us, policy makers who are looking for ways to scale up health services and improve the performance of our health workers. Over the last few years, we have tested various models in Africa to help us understand how to create fiscal space, rapidly scale up the number of health workers, and get them to work in rural areas. We found that perhaps the most important ingredient in financing health services is flexibility and innovation. In Rwanda, for example, we established performance-based financing to better link the deployment and remuneration of health workers to their actual performance in delivering services. This book provides tremendous value to us, in providing an inventory of what works, providing tools to scale up health worker production and improve the distribution and performance of health workers, and negotiate the ins and outs of health markets in Africa. It provides lessons learned in Africa on the most recent country analysis, using state-of-the-art tools and new empirical results. I am sure this book will be useful to academicians, heads of human resources departments, researchers, the global international health community, and the community at large, who are helping African governments design better policies for human resources development.

Kampeta Sayinzoga
Permanent Secretary and Secretary to the Treasury
Ministry of Finance and Economic Planning, Rwanda

Preface

Addressing the challenge of decent healthcare and education for low-income families is critical to building the human capital that African countries need to sustain economic growth in the years ahead. Within this broad goal, specific challenges linked to Human Resources for Health (HRH) in Africa must be addressed to achieve stronger health systems, universal access to health services, and greater improvements in actual health outcomes. Today, it is widely recognized among Ministries of Health and development partners that the overall availability, distribution, and performance of health workers in Africa must be rapidly improved.

Since HRH first gained prominence on the international development agenda in 2002, African governments have made significant headway in obtaining critical data and evidence on HRH that was previously lacking. With several partners, the World Bank has been supporting governments in their efforts to develop this evidence base and subsequently their strategies, policies, and programs on HRH. The emerging consensus is that in order for policy solutions to work, they must take into account the unique and rapidly evolving dimensions of national health labor markets in Africa.

Once dominated by governments, health labor markets today often involve multiple private and nongovernmental players. Identifying why there is a problem with numbers, distribution, or performance in a public labor market thus requires moving beyond the traditional focus on production or education only. The funding and management capacity available to competing employers and the behavior of health workers, which is motivated by different working and living conditions and incentives, both merit greater attention.

This book draws on the lessons, knowledge, and data gathered by the World Bank's Africa Region Human Resources for Health Program. For the first time, the various complexities of HRH labor markets are addressed comprehensively in one volume. Given the increasing demand in countries for strong health workforces that can help achieve universal health coverage, we hope this book will be beneficial to researchers, policy makers, and practitioners who are trying to develop evidence-based HRH interventions to achieve this end.

Ritva Reinikka
Director, Human Development
Africa Region
The World Bank

Acknowledgments

This book is an outgrowth of the World Bank's Africa Region Human Resources for Health Program, which is funded by the Government of Norway and aims to advance knowledge on Human Resources for health for policy making. Christophe Lemiere (Senior Health Specialist) and Christopher H. Herbst (Health Specialist) of the World Bank (WB) led the project team.

The book was developed in close collaboration with individuals from the African Development Bank (AfDB), the University of California, Berkeley, and policy makers from Africa. Agnes Soucat (Director of Human Development, AfDB), Richard Scheffler (professor of Economics, University of California, Berkeley), and Tedros Adhanom (Minister of Foreign Affairs and former Minister of Health, Ethiopia) jointly edited the book.

The specific chapters were devised during working sessions held in 2011 at the University of California, Berkeley. Chapters were prepared by, or in close collaboration with, individuals from academia, research centers, and development organizations. The WB-AfDB-Berkeley team collaborated closely with individuals from Harvard University, Cornell University, Johns Hopkins University, the University of Maryland, and the University of East Anglia. Research centers involved include Oxford Policy Management (OPML) Group and CHR Michelesen Institute (CMI).

Chapters were also written by, or in collaboration with, individuals from the World Health Organization, USAID's Capacity Plus, and the International Finance Corporation (IFC).

The team is grateful to a large number of individuals who provided reviews, comments, or inputs on various drafts of the book. They include Peter Berman, Ok Pannenborg, Richard Seifman, Maureen Lewis, Jean Jacques de St. Antoine, Timothy Johnston, Magnus Lindelow, GNV Ramana, Gaston Sorgho, Akiko Maeda, Edson Coreija, Mario Dal Poz, and Tom Hall. The team would also like to thank Donald Kaberuka (President of the AfDB), Ritva Reinnika (Director Human Development, The World Bank), Trina Haque (Sector Manager, HNP–West and Central Africa, The World Bank), Olusoji Adeyi (Sector Manager, HNP–East and Southern Africa, The World Bank), as well as Stephen M. Shortell (Dean of School of Public Health, University of California, Berkeley) for their overall support during the process of writing this book.

Finally, without the generous financial support from the Government of Norway, this book would not have been possible. The Africa Region Human Resources for Health (HRH) program continues to benefit from Norway's support, greatly expanding the knowledge base on HRH with increasing implications for, and achievement of, results on the ground.

CHAPTER 1

Labor Market Analysis of Human Resources for Health

Agnes Soucat and Richard Scheffler

Health systems in Sub-Saharan Africa have changed profoundly over the last 20 years. The economic crisis of the 1980s and 1990s rattled public health care systems, which were largely holdovers from the colonial and postcolonial eras. The later wave of structural adjustments and public sector reforms wrought further change. As African economies opened to market-based approaches, the private sector became a sizable source of health care service. Today about half the health expenditures in Africa are private, and private providers play a major role in the delivery of outpatient services.

Democratization and better access to information have put pressure on African governments to expand health care access and improve quality of services. Service delivery is now often at the center of political platforms. In 2002 free primary education and basic health care were part of electoral programs in Uganda. More recently the debate in Ghana's 2009 elections centered largely on health insurance.

Economic growth in the past decade has given African governments the fiscal space to grow their health budgets. Increases in government health spending and official development assistance for health raised demand for health workers in the region (OECD DAC 2009). Too often, however, the supply of qualified workers remains rigid, leading to inflationary pressures on wages and shortages of health workers. When more and more funding is available for the same pool of health workers—and the public sector, private sector, and donors compete for a limited number of qualified health workers—pressure on wages grows. Policy makers recognize that the human resources problem in the region is hampering the expansion of services needed to reach the Millennium Development Goals (WHO 2006).

Sub-Saharan Africa's labor market for human resources is changing rapidly. The notion that African labor markets comprise small pools of public sector workers characterized by low productivity, poor performance, and inadequate financing is false. Africa's labor markets are complex, with resources from governments, donors, the private sector, and households. Health workers are no longer exclusively civil servants: they may also be private sector employees or independent contractors, or some combination of all three, working through both formal and informal arrangements.

The private sector is an emerging force in the health worker labor market on both the demand and supply sides. On the demand side, more financing from economic growth and official development assistance is passing through nongovernmental organizations. On the supply side, burgeoning private medical and nursing schools in some countries testify to the private sector's growing contribution to the health worker labor market. This contribution and its interplay with the public sector is redefining how Africa produces, distributes, and manages health workers.

The Labor Market for Health Workers in Africa: A New Look at the Crisis sheds light on the status of health worker need, supply, and distribution across Africa. It analyzes regional and country data to answer six key questions: What are the specific levels of human resources for health in Africa? What are the differences in human resources for health across countries? What are the changing roles of the public and private sector in the health worker market? What motivates health worker performance? How do you train health workers? How do you produce them?

This book uses the analytical tools of labor markets and views the human resource crisis in health from an economic perspective. It relies on new information and innovative approaches in Africa. This chapter describes the framework for labor market analysis used in this book and summarizes the subsequent chapters. It also sets out the contributors' main conclusions and recommends steps to better understand health labor markets in Africa and other low- and middle-income countries.

The Health Labor Market Framework

The Labor Market for Health Workers in Africa: A New Look at the Crisis employs a labor market framework of analysis to examine the building blocks of the labor market and how they interact. Figure 1.1 is a schematic overview of the labor market framework applied in this analysis.

The analysis of the health labor market starts with an assessment of need (see figure 1.1, box A), which is the traditional public health method for determining health worker supply. This book proposes a new methodology to determine need that incorporates contextual factors within each country (chapter 2). This new and improved method is a starting point for estimating the need for health care workers.

A needs-based analysis alone does not consider the full labor market for health workers. From a demand-side perspective, three major sectors that demand health workers also shape health worker labor markets: public, private, and donor (box B). Governance structures also influence

Figure 1.1   Framework of the Health Labor Market

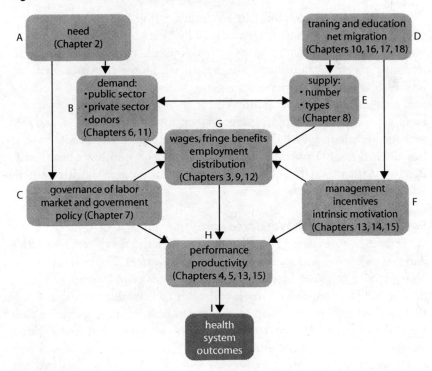

the health worker market by setting rules and establishing the role of public policy in enabling the market to function (box C).

From a supply-side perspective, the training, education, migration, and attrition of health workers influence the market by determining the pool of available workers for each country (box D).

The effects of training, migration, and attrition are reflected in the supply of qualified health workers (box E). A country's production of qualified health workers, offset by those who move abroad or leave practice, determines its ability to match supply with demand. Training also impacts the intrinsic motivation of health workers, which, along with management incentives, influences performance (box F).

Health worker need, demand, supply, training, and governance combine to determine employment conditions, including wage levels; fringe benefits; and institutional, geographic, and specialty distributions (box G). Taken together these factors define performance and productivity (box H) and, ultimately, health system outcomes (box I).

Structural Overview

This book has four sections. Part I establishes the framework and tools needed to analyze health labor markets in Africa and low- and middle-income countries in other regions. Part II presents empirical evidence on the supply and distribution of the health workforce in Africa, drawing lessons from these experiences. Part III details how performance can be analyzed, measured, and improved. It examines the productivity of health workers, incentives for performance, intrinsic motivation, and key management issues. Part IV presents information on the production of health workers. It looks at education, barriers to becoming a health student in Africa, and financing for higher education in health care in African countries.

Part I. Tools for Health Workforce Analysis

Chapter 2, "Needs-Based Estimates for the Health Workforce" (Scheffler and Fulton), opens the discussion of needs assessment. The chapter begins by explaining the World Health Organization's needs-based approach for determining the benchmark ratio of health care workers. It expands on this method with other health workforce indicators and contextual data from a variety of African countries. With this improved needs-based approach it provides new estimates for health worker needs and workforce benchmarks. Chapter 2 develops a framework that can be used not only in Africa but also in low- and middle-income countries in other regions.

Chapter 3, "A Labor Market Approach" (Andalón and Fields), presents an innovative approach to examining health labor markets in Africa. Using analytical tools for understanding labor markets from an economic perspective, it identifies key challenges of the health worker crisis in Africa: production, underutilization, distribution, performance, and financing. This chapter explains why the number of employed health workers in African countries is lower than what is "needed" to meet a given policy objective. It suggests that more empirical data, a full labor market analysis, and social cost-benefit criteria are necessary before policy recommendations can be confidently offered.

Chapter 4, "Productivity of Health Workers: Tanzania" (Mæstad and Mwisongo), sets out a new approach to analyzing productivity and explores the limitations of this analysis using different measures of productivity. The strengths and weaknesses of each are detailed. The authors suggest that health worker productivity in Tanzania is poor, on average about 22 percent of what is technically possible.

Chapter 5, "Health Worker Performance" (Brock, Leonard, Masatu, and Serneels), presents a model of health worker performance that examines inputs, outputs, and policy levers that influence health worker performance. The analysis is anchored by an examination of rural Tanzania, which offers context and lessons on the barriers to health worker performance. The health worker performance model examines three aspects of health worker motivation: adherence to medical protocols, confidence, and absenteeism. This new way of thinking about performance is key to labor market analysis in Africa and other low- and middle-income settings.

Chapter 6, "Fiscal Issues in Scaling Up the Health Workforce" (Soucat, Vujicic, Sy, and Sekabaraga), focuses on public sector budgeting and how government fiscal policy affects staffing levels. It uses data and information from Kenya, Rwanda, and Zambia on the wage bill and employment practices to illustrate labor market rigidities in African countries. It argues that contrary to population perception, wage bill ceilings do not hamper expansion of the health workforce; rather, outdated policies that fail to account for the changing role of the public and private sectors restrict expansion.

Chapter 7, "Politics and Governance in Human Resources for Health" (Mitchell and Bossert), describes how government and political structures affect labor markets and how these structures can be improved.

There is a trend toward labor market–oriented systems with greater regulation in private markets. The chapter points out the dangers of poor performance in a health labor market not adequately regulated. The authors draw on examples from Ethiopia, Ghana, Rwanda, and Zambia.

Part II. Distribution of Health Workforce

The analysis of the distribution of the health workforce begins with chapter 8, "How Many Health Workers" (Ahmat, Bilal, Herbst, and Weber). This chapter presents the best available data on the total supply of health care workers in Africa. It illustrates how poor the data collection is and how collection differs between countries. Estimating health worker numbers is a difficult task because the data are not uniform across countries and estimates vary. Even with data problems, it is clear that health work strategies differ in African countries.

Chapter 9, "Rural-Urban Imbalance of Health Workers in Sub-Saharan Africa" (Lemière, Herbst, Dolea, Zurn, and Soucat), examines the key issue of rural and urban imbalances, offering tools to analyze distribution equity. It presents case examples from Benin, Chad, the Democratic Republic of Congo, Kenya, Mali, Mauritania, Mozambique, Niger, and Senegal. The authors highlight the barriers to appropriate and adequate urban and rural distributions in Africa. There appears to be an adequate supply in most urban areas and a severe shortage in rural areas.

Chapter 10, "Migration and Attrition" (Özden and Sewadeh), focuses on the migration of health workers in Africa. It notes that approximately a fourth of physicians trained in Africa now work in Organisation for Economic Co-operation and Development countries. The top four destinations for African-trained doctors are the United Kingdom, the United States, Canada, and Australia. This chapter discusses migration rates across African countries and the key reasons for migration, drawing lessons from a survey of Ghanaian physicians living abroad. The chapter finds that training, remuneration, and career opportunities all contribute to a high rate of physician emigration.

Chapter 11, "Public and Private Practice of Health Workers" (Ensor, Serneels, and Lievens), examines the economic issues that influence health workers' choice between the public and private sectors, using qualitative and quantitative studies from Ethiopia, Ghana, and Rwanda. The authors note that while most African countries have opened their health care markets to private sector providers, policies in these countries are still tailored toward an exclusively public sector model. The chapter presents a case study of dual practice from Ethiopia, offering insights about the conditions that result in widespread dual practice across the continent.

Chapter 12, "The Equity Perspective" (Gwatkin and Ergo), examines the health worker labor market by discussing different concepts and definitions of equity, and the ambiguity of this concept. It analyzes health workforce equity in Ethiopia, Ghana, Mozambique, Rwanda, and Zambia, illustrating a fundamental dilemma: equity across geographical areas is an important concept but it is limited. Many poor populations live in areas with adequate supplies of health workers but remain underserved. Workforce equity is a serious problem in all African countries.

Part III. Performance of the Health Workforce

The analysis of health worker performance opens with chapter 13, "Incentives for Provider Performance" (Soucat, Gertler, Basinga, Sturdy, Vermeesh, and Sekabaraga). The chapter explores a new model for financing health workers' pay for performance and shows that many African countries are testing pay-for-performance measures. It presents the analytical framework for pay for performance and provides a detailed case example of its application and results in Rwanda.

Chapter 14, "Intrinsic Motivation" (Leonard, Serneels, and Brock), provides an innovative behavioral framework for examining intrinsic motivation, applying it to choice of health occupations in Africa. It looks at how norms are determined and how health worker motivation can be analyzed and improved. The chapter uses a case example from Rwanda to examine motivation. The evidence surprisingly suggests that health worker motivation is very poor.

Chapter 15, "Facility-Level Human Resource Management" (Lemière, Mahoney, and Nyoni), focuses on best practices in human resources management, including management skills, autonomy of decision makers, and incentives. It provides an analytical framework for management and performance and applies it to Tanzania. Finally, it looks at the barriers to improving human resources management in Africa and the lack of good evidence on the topic.

Part IV. Education and Training of Health Workers

The chapters in part IV examine health worker training and education in Africa. Chapter 16, "Health Worker Education and Training" (Tulenko, Gasakure, and Neusy), shows how preservice education affects productivity, stock shortfalls, and distribution of health workers. The authors note that there is little or no connection between the employers and trainers of health care workers, leading to a disconnect between training and service. The chapter explores the factors behind high student attrition, barriers to adequate financing, and the lack of flexibility in training health workers. It provides country examples from Ethiopia and Malawi.

Chapter 17, "Becoming a Health Worker Student" (Righetti, Strasser, Materu, and Herbst), focuses on enrollment of health care workers in health science education programs. It examines three defining factors of student enrollment in health science training programs: academic preparation, financial barriers, and institutional capacity. It looks at enrollment patterns in 14 African countries and data on the application and admission to medical training programs.

Chapter 18, "Paying for Higher Education Reform in Health" (Preker, Beciu, Robyn, Ayettey, and Antwi), presents a detailed analysis of the cost estimates of scaling up health worker education and applies the analysis to Ghana. It sets out the investment and recurrent costs of expanded training and explores financing sources that countries can pursue to meet the additional costs. The chapter provides financing scenarios for educating health care workers in Ghana. This country-specific analysis can be applied to other African countries as well.

Conclusion

As the chapters in this book make clear, Africa is not homogenous. Country realities differ, sometimes greatly. Not every country has a shortage of health workers. Wages vary, as do worker preferences and public policies. What does this book tell us about the human resources for health crisis in Africa today?

• Some African countries have made tremendous progress developing innovative approaches to managing human resources for health. South Africa developed an approach to selecting and training students that led to a rise in health workers in rural and impoverished communities. Ethiopia launched a massive effort to increase the number of health workers to deliver services that contribute to the Millennium Development Goals. It has trained and hired more than 30,000 health extension workers to deliver a basic package of promotive and preventive interventions, including family planning and malaria prevention and treatment. It is also tripling the production of medical officers and doctors trained to address maternal mortality and most illnesses that require referral or hospital care. Ethiopia is also analyzing incentives to reduce emigration of qualified health workers and distribute workers to rural areas.

Ghana increased remuneration of both doctors and nurses. Early data suggest that the pay increases reduced migration but have not affected performance. The Ghana experience raises interesting questions about the fiscal consequences of the salary increase and the pressure it places on the government to boost wages of other public sector employees.

Rwanda implemented the broadest reform of human resources observed in low-income countries. A substantial and growing portion of health worker remuneration now depends on performance contracts between the government and autonomous facilities. Rwanda decentralized its health care framework, and all facilities are now fully autonomous and can hire and fire health workers. The country's innovative approach supports cooperatives of community health workers who are under contract with the government.

- The traditional manpower planning framework is outdated and should be revised to include the parameters influencing the health labor market. Typically, analysts and policy makers rely on a manpower planning and management approach to forecast needs, plan production and deployment, and manage health workers in a centralized manner. This approach almost always focuses on the public sector and supply side exclusively, underestimating the demand for health labor generated by private resources from households and growing aid for health. It largely ignores the market forces that influence wages and the incentives environment that health workers operate in. Too often this framework relies on models from countries outside Africa, with different political, institutional, and societal contexts. This outdated manpower framework must be replaced with a more dynamic health labor market framework that builds on a broad range of international experience in public sector reform.

- Policy makers and analysts should distinguish between deficiency and shortage, which are often confused in policy debates. Deficiency—often wrongly labeled shortage—exists when there is a gap between needs and actual numbers of health workers. This is a problem in all African countries. Africa remains the region with the fewest health workers in relation to total population.

True shortage occurs when there is a gap between the funding for health workers and the number of available health workers. Shortage leads to inflationary pressures on wages and crowding out of the public sector, including poaching of health workers. Unlike health worker deficiency, not all African countries experience health worker shortages. True shortage is an issue only in Ethiopia, Malawi, Mozambique, and Zambia. By contrast, Kenya and Nigeria have large numbers of unemployed health workers. Deficiency and shortage call for different policies tailored to the specific situation and political economy of the country in question.

• Health worker deficiency is a rural problem. Few countries are responding to the lessons learned from international experience about the need to develop specific approaches for the training of rural health workers. Ethiopia developed a health extension program comparable in size and ambition to the effective and well-documented family health program in Brazil. Brazil's program has more than 200,000 community health workers that form the backbone of rural health service delivery. Thailand's program for developing a pipeline of rural doctors is emulated by only Ethiopia and South Africa. Most medical schools in Sub-Saharan Africa are still located in capital cities, though there is progress in moving nursing schools to rural areas. Very few African countries have a truly effective policy that creates incentives for health workers to practice in rural areas; workers in urban areas usually earn more than their rural counterparts. Governments and donor communities should focus on rural deficiency and stimulate the production of health cadres most likely to serve the rural poor.

• Many African countries pay little attention to the emerging private sector. More than half of the health expenditures in Africa are private, and private nursing schools have blossomed throughout Sub-Saharan Africa. The provider/purchaser split is already a reality in countries like the Democratic Republic of Congo, Mali, Rwanda, and Zambia. Yet many countries report only their public sector health workers to the World Health Organization. Many governments only finance public schools and do a poor job of regulating private schools and clinics. Ethiopia's accreditation of private nursing schools is a good example of how to address nurse deficiencies and shortages. Rwanda's approach of contracting faith-based organizations engages private providers in the delivery of essential services to the poor. Uganda and Zambia are experimenting with similar programs. Overall the African health labor market is similar to the European market: a diverse mix of institutional models with various degrees of private sector participation in providing and financing services.

• The performance of health workers is mostly unknown but the few rigorous studies available (Rwanda and Tanzania) paint a bleak picture. Performance is typically associated with skills and training and indeed these factors are critical. Effort is also essential, however, and in some cases determines performance more so than skill. Health workers often do less than what they are capable of doing. Innovations such as performance-based financing, which Burundi and Rwanda are scaling up, can make a difference by aligning financial incentives to producing relevant, quality services. Incentives are not the only answer, and it is important to cultivate intrinsic motivation by selecting students with altruistic or rural backgrounds and encouraging professional and/or public ethos through training curricula.

• Migration is often blamed for the ills of African health systems, but available studies show a more nuanced picture. Cohort studies in Ethiopia show a relatively low initial desire to migrate, which grows over time. Health workers with higher income and urban backgrounds are more likely to migrate, suggesting that poverty is not the main driver. Instead, the opportunity to pursue higher income may be the primary driver. Higher income plays a role in retaining health workers, as in Ghana. Emigration and rural-urban imbalance seem to be two faces of the same phenomenon. Recruiting health workers from rural areas and offering training tailored to local diseases (rather than diseases more common in richer countries) are promising strategies.

• The issue of fiscal space for wages is a red herring in the health worker debate. A more binding constraint is likely the insufficient funds available for investment in growing the supply of qualified health workers. Available evidence shows that wage bill ceilings are not the problem in most cases: in the majority of African countries there is no wage ceiling issue.

Several countries have dramatically expanded their fiscal space for health worker wages. Most have increased resources for health, channeling a large part to health worker remuneration. Countries are innovative in tackling wage issues, often breaking the rigid rules of postcolonial integrated civil service, as in Ghana and Rwanda. But not enough financing is channeled to the supply side and health worker education. Governments should reestablish the balance and make more resources available for investments that relax supply constraints by fostering public-private partnerships for nursing and medical education.

- Overall we know very little about the supply and distribution of health workers in Africa. The information deficit is staggering, even for the most basic indicators. This dearth of data limits the impact of policy. For most African countries we do not know the number of qualified health workers in the country at a given time, let alone how health worker density evolves in contexts where populations are rapidly growing. We know even less about health worker distribution at subnational levels and between the public and the private sectors. We know close to nothing about health workers' gender, income, and socioeconomic background. And, we know very little about their specific motivations and the incentives that influence their behaviors. A major investment is required to generate the evidence needed to support effective policies.

- Finally, health worker issues are country-specific. Each country should diagnose its own health labor market issues taking advantage of the tools presented in this book. Producing more health workers and paying them more is not always the right answer. There is no one-size-fits-all policy.

    National governments and the donor community should systematically support country-specific analyses of the labor market to understand the binding constraints on both demand and supply sides. The analysis should include wage analyses; discrete choice experiments; institutional analyses; cost and efficiency analyses; analyses of supply constraints; analysis of health worker performance, including measurements of skills and efforts; and impact evaluations of the policies implemented. Only then can countries respond effectively to the human resource crisis.

References

OECD. DAC report on Aid Predictability: Survey on Donors' Forward Spending Plans. 2009.

WHO (World Health Organization). 2006. *World Health Report 2006*. Geneva: WHO.

PART 1

Tools for Health Workforce Analysis

CHAPTER 2

Needs-Based Estimates for the Health Workforce

Richard M. Scheffler and Brent D. Fulton

A trained health workforce is at the center of the health system, and without one, medical equipment, supplies, facilities, and medication will be inefficiently used. Accurately estimating the number of required health workers in Sub-Saharan Africa is important given limited regional resources, and these estimates will help governments and donors allocate health care budgets prudently. A needs-based approach can estimate health workforce requirements by assessing the extent that the existing health workforce meets health care needs. This chapter uses a needs-based approach to estimate empirically health worker requirements to meet various health care needs in 18 Sub-Saharan countries. Health worker requirements vary greatly, and depend on the specific health care need that is used to generate the requirement, and the population distribution of the individual country.

A Conceptual Needs-Based Approach to Estimating Health Workforce Requirements

Well-trained cadres of health workers are essential to maximize the effectiveness of a country's health care system and improve the health status of its people (Chen and others 2004). For health care planners and government officials, estimating the required number of health workers for specific health care needs is an important part of strengthening health systems and achieving the health-related Millennium Development Goals (Crisp and Gawanas 2008). This chapter presents a conceptual framework—the needs-based approach—to estimate human resources (specifically doctors, nurses, and midwives) for health requirements for various health care measures, and applies the framework empirically to 53 countries, including 18 in Sub-Saharan Africa.

How can we estimate needs-based requirements for health workers? We can do so by showing the relationship between a country's health workforce and its specific health care service use or health outcome goals, which serve as proxy measures for need. The approach begins by selecting health care services or health outcome measures. Examples include the proportion of births attended by a skilled health worker, breast cancer screening, infant and maternal mortality, and the burden of disease for conditions such as HIV/AIDS, tuberculosis, and malaria. The number of health workers required to achieve goals on the selected measures is then estimated using data from multiple countries or from multiple regions within a country.

Using this needs-based approach, the World Health Organization (WHO) found that countries that did not have at least 2.28 doctors, nurses, and midwives per 1,000 residents were, on average, unable to achieve 80 percent coverage of births by a skilled birth attendant (2006). WHO selected the 80 percent threshold partly because it wanted to set a minimum desired coverage level, and partly because the benefit of additional health workers on the birth coverage rate began to diminish near this threshold.

To estimate the number of health workers that a country requires, however, a model should incorporate additional health care measures and factors that affect worker productivity. This chapter thus improves on the WHO method in two ways. First, WHO estimated the number of required health workers using a single health care measure: birth attendance by a skilled health worker. This chapter examines multiple health care measures to show how the number of workers required to achieve a specific goal is sensitive to the measure used. Second, the relationship between health workers and health measures varies across countries because of differences in worker productivity. These differences stem from dissimilar health care systems, financing mechanisms, worker training, geographic characteristics, and population distributions, as well as variations among such other factors as medical facilities, equipment, supplies, and pharmaceuticals. WHO did not account for these produc-tivity differences in its analysis.

To demonstrate elements of this more nuanced approach, this analysis includes two country-level population distribution factors—urbanization and land area per capita—to show how human resources for health requirements vary by country. Extending this approach would include the other factors that affect worker productivity just mentioned.

Applying the Needs-Based Approach

The approach is applied to 53 countries, including 18 in Sub-Saharan Africa, using data from the *World Health Survey 2002*. WHO sponsored this survey, which randomly sampled about 4,000 adults per country. Respondents were asked about their own and family members' health status and health care use and expenditures, as well as demographic infor-mation, including whether the respondent lived in an urban or rural set-ting. Health workforce supply estimates are from WHO (2006).[1] To be consistent with that publication, the analysis defined health workers as doctors, nurses, and midwives. Country population estimates are from the U.S. Census Bureau's 2002 Global Population Profile.

The resulting statistics for the full sample of 53 countries and 18 Sub-Saharan countries are based on a country as the unit of analysis, and are not weighted for population differences, consistent with WHO (2006; table 2.1). Except for vaccinations and vitamin A supplement, health care service use was generally lower for Sub-Saharan Africa than for the full sample. Also, for all 53 countries the average number of health care workers was 4.25 per 1,000 population, while the Sub-Saharan average was 1.73.

To examine the relationship between the size of the health workforce and measures of health care service use and outcomes, 12 health care services and two health outcomes were analyzed (see table 2.1). The basic analysis included the number of health workers per 1,000 popula-tion, and further analyses included the percentage of the country's population living in an urban area and the country's land area per capita, because these characteristics may be related to an individual's access to health care services (see annex 2A for more detail on methods). The results illustrate which health care services and health outcomes were statistically related to the size and composition of the health workforce, and whether the required number of health workers varied according to a country's population distribution.

Table 2.1   Country Health Care Service, Health, and Population Distribution Statistics

	All countries (n = 53)		Sub-Saharan countries (n = 18)	
	Mean	Standard deviation	Mean	Standard deviation
Health care services				
Birth attended by health worker (1 yes, 0 no)[a]	0.83	0.23	0.74	0.23
Birth attended by doctor (1 yes, 0 no)[a]	0.67	0.34	0.46	0.30
Birth attended by nurse or midwife (1 yes, 0 no)[a]	0.77	0.27	0.73	0.27
Pelvic examination in last three years (1 yes, 0 no)[b]	0.37	0.28	0.17	0.14
Pap smear test in last three years (1 yes, 0 no)[b]	0.55	0.27	0.44	0.14
Mammography in last three years (1 yes, 0 no)[c]	0.16	0.17	0.05	0.04
HIV testing offered when pregnant (1 yes, 0 no)[d]	0.25	0.25	0.19	0.16
Received health care when needed it (1 yes, 0 no)	0.96	0.04	0.94	0.04
Received any vaccination (1 yes, 0 no)[e]	0.71	0.20	0.76	0.11
Received DPT vaccination (1 yes, 0 no)[e]	0.91	0.09	0.93	0.05
Received measles vaccination (1 yes, 0 no)[e]	0.77	0.14	0.82	0.10
Received vitamin A capsule or similar supplement (1 yes, 0 no)[e]	0.46	0.25	0.61	0.21
Health outcomes				
Health rating (1 very good or good, 0 otherwise)	0.60	0.14	0.64	0.11
Health satisfaction (1 very satisfied or satisfied, 0 otherwise)	0.61	0.13	0.59	0.14
Health workforce				
Doctors per 1,000 population	1.30	1.34	0.21	0.27
Nurses and midwives per 1,000 population	2.95	2.84	1.52	1.68
Health workers per 1,000 population	4.25	3.98	1.73	1.85
Population distribution				
Land (square kilometers) per capita	0.04	0.08	0.08	0.12
Urban (percent of total population)	49.80	24.50	38.00	21.33

Sources: WHO 2002; CIA's *The World Factbook* (land area); U.S. Census Bureau, Global Population Profile: 2002 (population).

Note: DPT = diphtheria, pertussis (whooping cough), and tetanus.

a. Asked of women who were pregnant in the last five years (since January 1998).
b. Asked of women ages 18–49.
c. Asked of women ages 40–69.
d. Asked of women who were pregnant in the last two years (since January 2001).
e. Asked of children under five years old.

Relationship between Health Workers and Health Measures

The number of health workers per 1,000 population was positively related to many of the health care service measures. These included births attended by a health worker (doctor, nurse, or midwife), births attended by a doctor, births attended by a nurse or midwife, a pelvic examination in the last three years, a Pap smear test in the last three years, a mammography in the last three years, HIV testing offered during pregnancy, and health care received when needed (tables 2A.1 and 2A.2). No relationship was found between the number of health workers and whether a child received vaccinations.[2]

To illustrate one specific relationship, figure 2.1 shows the percentage of births attended by a health worker as a function of the number of health workers per 1,000 population, for all 53 countries. Each dot represents a country, and the curved line shows the predicted percentage of births attended by a health worker. Similar to WHO (2006), this analysis found that coverage varied significantly among countries with similar numbers of health workers per 1,000 population, emphasizing the need to incorporate additional variables into the model.

Countries where about 90 percent or more of births were attended by a health worker had a wide range of such workers per 1,000 population,

Figure 2.1   Percentage of Births Attended by a Health Worker versus Number of Health Workers per 1,000 Population, by Country

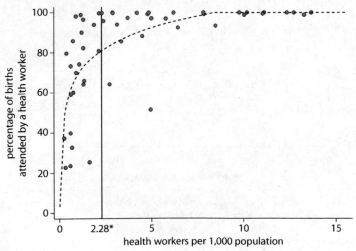

Source: Bivariate regression result in table 2A.1 (row 1).
Note: The vertical line indicates the WHO threshold of 2.28 health workers per 1,000 population.

largely because the additional health workers are providing nonbirth–related care (see figure 2.1). Of the 23 countries that fall below the WHO threshold of 2.28 health workers per 1,000 population, 14 (or 61 percent) did not achieve 80 percent coverage for births, which was less than the 85 percent found by WHO (2006; see figure 2.1).

Figure 2.2 shows the predicted percentage of people in the 18 Sub-Saharan countries that would receive health care on the basis of different numbers of health workers per 1,000 population. The health care services have a statistically significant relationship with the number of health workers, after accounting for each country's population distributions (that is, urbanization and land area per capita). The predictions were based on Sub-Saharan countries' average population distributions: the proportion of the population living in urban areas (38 percent) and land area per capita (0.08 square kilometers).

These results suggest that a country would require various numbers of health workers to achieve particular levels of use of specific health care services. For example, to achieve 80 percent coverage of births by a health worker, a country would require 1.7 health workers per 1,000 population

Figure 2.2   Predicted Percentage of Population Receiving Health Services Based on the Number of Health Workers per 1,000 Population, 18 Sub-Saharan Countries

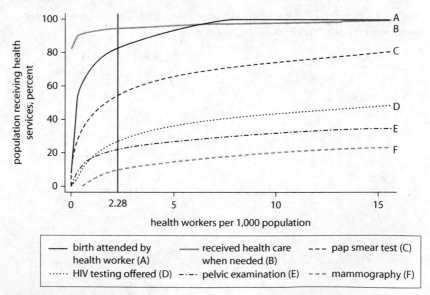

Source: Multivariate regression results in tables 2A.1 and 2A.2.
Note: The vertical line indicates the WHO threshold of 2.28 health workers per 1,000 population.

(see figure 2.2, line A). This level would, however, achieve much lower percentages on the other measures, such as Pap smear tests (line C), HIV testing offered during pregnancy (line D), pelvic examinations (line E), and mammographies (line F). If health worker productivity increased, each line would shift upward (box 2.1).

To illustrate how the required number of health workers varies based on a country's population distribution, figure 2.3 shows the estimated number of health workers per 1,000 population required to achieve 80 percent coverage of births for the 18 Sub-Saharan countries. The average is 1.7, ranging from 0.7 in the Republic of Congo to 4.3 in Namibia. The required number varies by country because of differences in the proportion of the urbanized population ($p < .1$) and in land area per capita (although this was not a statistically significant result). These factors partly explain why countries with about the same number of health workers per 1,000 population had different shares of births covered by a health worker (see figure 2.1). The average proportion of people living in urban areas for the 18 countries is 38 percent, ranging from 10 percent in Malawi to 92 percent in the Democratic Republic of Congo. Based on the analysis, the share of births attended by a health worker is predicted to increase by 0.3 percentage points for every percentage point rise in the population that lives in an urban area ($p < .1$).

The variation among countries in figure 2.3 shows that the average required number of 1.7 health workers per 1,000 population is a poor

---

Box 2.1

Service Delivery and Health Worker Productivity

The World Health Organization selected the 80 percent coverage rate for births partly to set a minimum desired coverage. As seen in figure 2.2, however, the predicted coverage of HIV testing offered during pregnancy (line D), pelvic examinations (line E), and mammographies (line F) come nowhere close to this standard, even when the number of health workers is significantly higher than the World Health Organization's 2.28 health worker threshold. Other factors, such as supplies and equipment, are likely to be the key constraint, rendering these tests and examinations virtually useless (for lack of treatment).

If investments addressed these constraints, health worker productivity could rise. In figure 2.2 this would shift each line upward, signifying countries' ability to use more health care services without increasing the number of health workers.

Figure 2.3   Estimated Number of Health Workers per 1,000 Population Required to Achieve 80 Percent Coverage of Births, 18 Sub-Saharan Countries

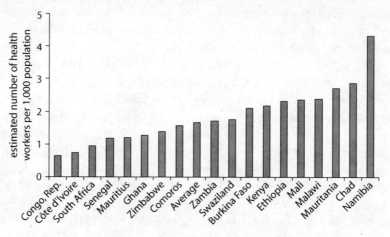

Source: Multivariate regression results shown in table 2A.2 (row 1).

estimate for many individual countries (box 2.2 discusses Chad, an out-lier example). In the same vein, WHO's 2.28 health workers per 1,000 is a poor estimate for many individual countries. As seen, therefore, includ-ing additional variables—such as geographic characteristics—that affect the relationship between the number of health workers and health care service utilization measures can improve estimates.[3] Such a needs-based analysis can also be applied below the national level, using regions or districts.

Limitations of—and Potential Improvements in—Needs-Based Analyses

The required number of health workers per 1,000 population is sensitive to the chosen health measure and varies across countries, based on their population distribution. Each country—or region within a country—needs to select a combination of relevant health measures and contextual factors to include in their models to estimate the health workforce requirement. The needs-based approach has four limitations (some can be overcome with additional data).

First, the government and private sector have to decide how best to spend their limited health funds. When the needs-based approach finds a shortage of health workers, this does not necessarily mean that additional

Box 2.2

Population Distribution and Human Resources for Health Requirements, Chad

In Central Africa, Chad is less urbanized (22 percent versus 38 percent) and has more land (0.14 square kilometers versus 0.07 square kilometers) per capita than the average of the 18 Sub-Saharan countries in WHO (2002). Low urbanization makes it more difficult for a health worker to attend a birth, and the country's coverage of births by a health worker was only 23 percent.

In 2004 (the year of the data in WHO 2006), Chad had 9.45 million people. It had 2,844 health workers (0.32 per 1,000 population), comprising 345 doctors (0.04 per 1,000 population) and 2,499 nurses and midwives (0.28 per 1,000 population). The 18 Sub-Saharan countries require an average of 1.7 health workers per 1,000 population to achieve 80 percent coverage for births. On this basis, Chad would require 16,000 health workers, implying a shortage of some 13,000 health workers (1.4 per 1,000 population).

Once Chad's urbanization and land area are included in the model, however, its requirements shoot up to 25,500 health workers (2.7 per 1,000 population), pointing to a shortage of about 22,500 (2.4 per 1,000 population).

funding should be spent to train and hire more health workers. It may be more cost-effective for funds to be spent on increasing the productivity of existing health workers, either through training and incentives or by increasing spending on other factors, such as medical facilities, equipment, supplies, or pharmaceuticals. For example, among the 18 Sub-Saharan countries, the average rate of HIV testing offered during pregnancy was only 19 percent. The binding constraint to achieving a higher testing rate may not be health workers, but lack of testing kits and antiretroviral medications. On the other hand, if a country determines that it is most cost-effective to scale up its health workforce, it may need to expand other parts of the health care system to use the new workers most efficiently.

Second, the needs-based approach estimates the required number of health workers per 1,000 population, but does not inform decision makers about optimal distribution of health workers in a country. So, the needs-based approach should use data from multiple communities within a country, when available, to estimate the required number at the community level.

Third, the lack of data on factors associated with health care services use (such as health facilities, equipment, supplies, and pharmaceuticals) and health outcomes (such as genetic factors, demographic characteristics, the environment, behavioral choices, education, and the above health systems factors) limits researchers' ability to offer more refined estimates of the number of required health workers. Most health workers do multiple tasks, so it would be ideal to measure productivity for particular tasks, and incorporate task shifting when it is cost-effective (Fulton and others 2011; Scheffler and others 2009). When these data are incorporated, more refined health worker requirement estimates can be made.

Fourth, the needs-based approach ignores economic factors such as health workers' wages and a country's economic capacity to train and employ them. Taking these factors into account leads to a demand-based approach that determines the number of health workers that a country can afford to train and employ (Scheffler 2008; Scheffler and others 2008).

Annex 2A   Supplemental Information on Data, Methods, and Results

Data

The primary data are from WHO (2002), which randomly sampled adults in 70 countries; about 4,000 adults per country were asked questions about their households. When the survey question had more than two possible responses, the analysis collapsed the responses into two responses, so that multiple measures could more easily be plotted on the same figure.

For example, the question that asked a woman when she last had a pelvic examination, the possible responses were: less than three years, four to five years, more than five years, and never. These responses were collapsed to indicate whether the woman had a pelvic examination in the last three years.

The analysis includes the following 53 countries by WHO region[4]:

- African Region (18): Burkina Faso, Chad, the Comoros, the Democratic Republic of Congo, Côte d'Ivoire, Ethiopia, Ghana, Kenya, Malawi, Mali, Mauritania, Mauritius, Namibia, Senegal, South Africa, Swaziland, Zambia, and Zimbabwe.
- Eastern Mediterranean Region (4): Morocco, Pakistan, Tunisia, and the United Arab Emirates.
- European Region (14): Bosnia and Herzegovina, Croatia, the Czech Republic, Estonia, Georgia, Hungary, Kazakhstan, Latvia, the Russian

Federation, the Slovak Republic, Slovenia, Spain, Turkey, and Ukraine.
- Region of the Americas (7): Brazil, the Dominican Republic, Ecuador, Guatemala, Mexico, Paraguay, and Uruguay.
- Southeast Asia Region (5): Bangladesh, India, Myanmar, Nepal, and Sri Lanka.
- Western Pacific Region (5): China, the Lao People's Democratic Republic, Malaysia, the Philippines, and Vietnam.

The survey suffers from two limitations related to any household survey. The first is whether the sample is nationally representative because of nonresponse, particularly within subpopulations such as pregnant women. Second, there may be biases when the adult respondent does not have full information about a member in the household who is included in the survey, such as children.

Methods

The analysis estimated two regression models for each of the 12 health care services (1–12 in table 2A.1) and health outcomes (13–14 in table 2A.1). The dependent variable in each model was the proportion of a country's respondents that received the health care service or achieved the health outcome.[5] The first model included the logarithm of the number of health workers (doctors, nurses, and midwives) per 1,000 population as the only independent variable.[6] The second model included additional variables to control for the percentage of the country's population living in an urban area and the country's land area per capita, because these characteristics may be related to an individual's access to health care services. To capture other factors specific to Sub-Saharan Africa, the second model also included a dummy variable indicating whether the country was in Sub-Saharan Africa.

In both models, the logarithm transformation of health workers was done because it allows for a nonlinear relationship between the number of health workers and the dependent variable, which may be the case because of diminishing marginal returns of an additional health worker. A quadratic specification was also tested for the multivariate models, which on average produced a similar R^2 statistic.

Results

Table 2A.1 presents the bivariate and multivariate regression results for the logarithm of the health worker variable for the 14 sets of models. The results for models 2 and 3 are for the logarithm of doctors and the

Table 2A.1 Health Care Services Use and Health Outcome Measures Regression Results for Health Workers

Dependent variable	Bivariate models: log (health workers per 1,000 population)			Multivariate models: log (health workers per 1,000 population)		
	Parameter estimate	Standard error	t-statistic	Parameter estimate	Standard error	t-statistic
1. Birth attended by health worker (1 yes, 0 no)[a]	0.329	0.05	6.54***	0.301	0.074	4.06***
2. Birth attended by doctor (1 yes, 0 no)[a]	0.390	0.05	7.85***	0.519	0.109	4.76***
3. Birth attended by nurse or midwife (1 yes, 0 no)[a]	0.244	0.07	3.31**	0.206	0.094	2.19*
4. Pelvic examination in last three years (1 yes, 0 no)[b]	0.433	0.06	7.72***	0.153	0.066	2.33*
5. Pap smear test in last three years (1 yes, 0 no)[b]	0.390	0.06	6.66***	0.314	0.086	3.65***
6. Mammography in last three years (1 yes, 0 no)[c]	0.268	0.03	7.84***	0.161	0.048	3.33**
7. HIV testing offered when pregnant (1 yes, 0 no)[d]	0.297	0.06	4.83***	0.258	0.089	2.91**
8. Received health care when needed (1 yes, 0 no)	0.049	0.01	5.39***	0.048	0.014	3.40**
9. Received any vaccination (1 yes, 0 no)[e]	−0.004	0.06	0.07	0.016	0.090	0.18
10. Received DPT vaccination (1 yes, 0 no)[e]	−0.030	0.03	1.19	−0.004	0.039	0.11
11. Received measles vaccination (1 yes, 0 no)[e]	−0.055	0.04	1.31	0.000	0.064	0.00
12. Received vitamin A capsule or similar supplement (1 yes, 0 no)[e]	−0.395	0.05	7.79***	−0.365	0.075	4.89***
13. Health rating (1 very good or good, 0 otherwise)	−0.108	0.04	2.87**	−0.096	0.058	1.64
14. Health satisfaction (1 very satisfied or satisfied, 0 otherwise)	0.000	0.04	0.00	−0.027	0.063	0.43

Source: Based on data from *World Health Survey 2002.*

Note: DPT = diphtheria, pertussis (whooping cough), and tetanus. All statistics are for logarithm of health worker variable, except model 2 is logarithm of a nurse or midwife variable. For multivariate models, control variables include land (square kilometers) per capita, percent urban, and an African region dummy variable. Number of observations ranged from 48 to 53.

a. Asked of women who were pregnant in the last five years (since January 1998).

b. Asked of women ages 18–49.

c. Asked of women ages 40–69.

d. Asked of women who were pregnant in the last two years (since January 2001).

e. Asked of children under five years old.

*p < .05   **p < .01   ***p < .001.

logarithm of nurses and midwives, respectively. The bivariate and multi-variate regression results had similar statistical significances, but the bivariate parameter estimate magnitudes tended to be larger. The parameter estimates for the health worker variable were statistically significant at the 0.05 level for the following eight dependent variables (models 1–8): births attended by a health worker (either a doctor, nurse, or midwife), births attended by a doctor, births attended by a nurse or midwife, a pelvic examination in the last three years, a Pap smear test in the last three years, a mammography in the last three years, HIV testing offered during pregnancy, and health care received when needed.

The models involving children receiving vaccinations did not have a statistically significant relationship with the number of health workers, but whether a child received a vitamin A capsule or similar supplement actually had a negative relationship with the number of health workers per 1,000 population, which requires further investigation. For the health outcome variables in the multivariate models, neither health rating nor health satisfaction was statistically associated with the number of health workers per 1,000 population.

The magnitudes of the parameter estimates have the following interpretation. A 1 percent increase in the number of health workers (hw) results in a $\beta/100$ unit change in the dependent variable (y). For example using model 1's bivariate result, if the number of health workers increased by 10 percent, the probability that a birth would be attended by a health worker would be predicted to increase by 0.0329, or 3.29 percentage points [$\Delta y = (\beta/100) \times \%\Delta hw$; $0.0329 = (0.0329/100) \times 10$].

Table 2A.2 shows the detailed regression results for the 14 multivariate models. The independent variables and statistics not shown in table 2A.1 are now discussed. The proportion of the population residing in an urban setting was positively associated with pelvic examination in the last three years, Pap smear test in the last three years, and mammography in the last three years (all $p < .05$), and approached being positively associated with HIV testing offered during pregnancy and having a birth attended by a health worker (both $p < .06$). A country's land area per capita was not statistically associated ($p < .05$) with any of the dependent variables, but it approached being positively associated with having a birth attended by a nurse or midwife and with a child receiving a vitamin A capsule or similar supplement (both $p < .08$). This result requires further investigation. The Sub-Saharan Africa binary variable was not statistically associated with any of the dependent variables, except it had a positive association for having a birth attended by a doctor ($p < .05$).

Table 2A.2 Health Care Services Use and Health Outcome Measures Multivariate Regression Results

Dependent variable	Health workers (log)	Land (sq km) per capita	Urban (% of total population)	Sub-Saharan Africa	Constant	N	R^2	F-statistic
1. Birth attended by health worker	0.301*** (0.074)	−0.352 (0.315)	0.003 (0.001)	0.106 (0.063)	0.558*** (0.065)	51	0.52	12.6***
2. Birth attended by doctor	0.519*** (0.109)	−0.410 (0.413)	0.001 (0.002)	0.258* (0.118)	0.683*** (0.103)	51	0.61	17.8***
3. Birth attended by nurse or midwife	0.206* (0.094)	−0.843 (0.455)	0.003 (0.002)	0.134 (0.085)	0.563*** (0.094)	51	0.26	4.1**
4. Pelvic examination <3 years	0.153* (0.066)	−0.072 (0.279)	0.006*** (0.001)	−0.098 (0.056)	0.026 (0.057)	51	0.73	31.6***
5. Pap smear test <3 years	0.314*** (0.086)	0.250 (0.366)	0.003* (0.001)	0.053 (0.074)	0.239** (0.075)	51	0.53	12.8***
6. Mammography <3 years	0.161** (0.048)	0.005 (0.205)	0.003** (0.001)	−0.027 (0.041)	−0.034 (0.042)	51	0.62	19.2***
7. HIV testing offered when pregnant	0.258** (0.089)	0.192 (0.376)	0.003 (0.002)	0.081 (0.076)	−0.036 (0.077)	51	0.43	8.6***
8. Received health care when needed	0.048** (0.014)	−0.008 (0.060)	0.000 (0.000)	−0.006 (0.012)	0.945*** (0.012)	51	0.36	6.6***

Independent Variables

table continues next page

Table 2A.2   Health Care Services Use and Health Outcome Measures Multivariate Regression Results *(continued)*

Dependent variable	Independent Variables				Constant	N	R^2	F-statistic
	Health workers (log)	Land (sq km) per capita	Urban (% of total population)	Sub-Saharan Africa				
9. Received any vaccination	0.016	−0.471	0.001	0.122	0.626***	49	0.07	0.9
	(0.090)	(0.377)	(0.002)	(0.076)	(0.077)			
10. Received DPT vaccination	−0.004	−0.172	0.000	0.028	0.934***	49	0.27	0.9
	(0.039)	(0.162)	(0.001)	(0.033)	(0.033)			
11. Received measles vaccination	0.000	−0.185	0.000	0.083	0.759***	49	0.08	1
	(0.064)	(0.265)	(0.001)	(0.053)	(0.054)			
12. Received vitamin A capsule or similar supplement	−0.365***	0.595	−0.001	−0.006	0.621***	49	0.59	16.0***
	(0.075)	(0.313)	(0.001)	(0.063)	(0.064)			
13. Health rating	−0.096	0.127	−0.001	−0.010	0.664***	52	0.15	2
	(0.058)	(0.249)	(0.001)	(0.050)	(0.051)			
14. Health satisfaction	−0.027	0.048	0.000	−0.036	0.623***	48	0.01	0.1
	(0.063)	(0.263)	(0.001)	(0.053)	(0.054)			

Source: Based on data from *World Health Survey 2002.*

Note: Results are parameter estimates and standard errors in parentheses.

*p < .05   **p < .01   ***p < .001.

The R^2 statistics for the health care services use models were 0.41 on average, with a range from 0.07 to 0.73. The R^2 statistics for the health outcome models were lower. The models that included vaccines and health outcomes did not have a statistically significant F-statistic ($p < .05$), emphasizing the need for additional variables.

Notes

1. The data year for the health workforce supply estimates varied by country. For the 53 countries of interest, most of the years were 2000–04.

2. The relationship between the number of health workers per 1,000 population and a child receiving a vitamin A capsule or similar supplement was negative, a finding that requires further investigation. For the health outcome variables, neither health rating nor health satisfaction was statistically associated with the number of health workers per 1,000 population, which is partly attributable to other factors that affect health, such as individual behaviors and the environment.

3. This can be extended to each country's health care system, financing mechanisms, and worker training, as well as other health care factors, such as medical facilities, equipment, supplies, and pharmaceuticals. Theory should determine the variables, along with their specifications, to include in the predictive model. When theory is not conclusive, different models can be tested empirically. One commonly used empirical goal is to minimize the mean of the squared error terms. A cross-validation method could be employed where the model is estimated for a subset of the sample, and predictions are made on the remaining sample. This procedure is repeated, for example, 10 times by excluding a different 10 percent of the sample each time (Hastie, Tibshirani, and Friedman 2001).

4. The *World Health Survey 2002* covered 70 countries, but not all its modules were fielded in 17 countries.

5. As in WHO (2006), the analysis also estimated human resource requirements using a dependent variable that was transformed with the arcsine function ($\sin^{-1}$), because proportions violate the variance homogeneity assumption across observations. Given that the results were very similar to the models with an untransformed dependent variable, the analysis presents the untransformed models, as the parameter estimates are easier to interpret.

6. When the dependent variable was whether the birth was attended by a doctor, the key independent variable was the logarithm of the number of doctors per 1,000 population. The analogous change was made when the dependent variable was whether the birth was attended by a nurse or midwife.

References

Chen, L., T. Evans, S. Anand, J.I. Boufford, H. Brown, M. Chowdhury, M. Cueto, L. Dare, G. Dussault, G. Elzinga, E. Fee, D. Habte, P. Hanvoravongchai, M. Jacobs, C. Kurowski, S. Michael, A. Pablos-Mendez, N. Sewankambo, G. Solimano, B. Stilwell, A. de Waal, and S. Wibulpolprasert. 2004. "Human Resources for Health: Overcoming the Crisis." *Lancet* 364 (9449): 1984–90.

Crisp, N., and B. Gawanas. 2008. *Scaling Up, Saving Lives: Task Force for Scaling Up Education and Training for Health Workers, Global Health Workforce Alliance.* Geneva: World Health Organization.

Fulton, B. D., R. M. Scheffler, S. P. Sparkes, E. Y. Auh, M. Vujicic, and A. Soucat. 2011. "Health Workforce Skill Mix and Task Shifting in Low-Income Countries: A Review of Recent Evidence." *Human Resources in Health* 9 (1).

Hastie, T., R. Tibshirani, and J. Friedman. 2001. *The Elements of Statistical Learning: Data Mining, Inference, and Prediction.* New York: Springer.

Scheffler, R. M. 2008. *Is There a Doctor in the House? Market Signals and Tomorrow's Supply of Doctors.* Palo Alto, CA: Stanford University Press.

Scheffler, R. M., J. X. Liu, Y. Kinfu, and M. R. Dal Poz. 2008. "Forecasting the Global Shortage of Physicians: An Economic- and Needs-Based Approach." *Bulletin of the World Health Organization* 86 (7): 516–23.

Scheffler, R. M., C. B. Mahoney, B. D. Fulton, M. R. Dal Poz, and A. S. Preker. 2009. "Estimates of Health Care Professional Shortages in Sub-Saharan Africa by 2015." *Health Affairs* 28: w849–w862.

WHO (World Health Organization). 2002. *World Health Survey 2002.* Geneva: WHO.

———. 2006. *The World Health Report 2006: Working Together for Health.* Geneva: WHO.

CHAPTER 3

A Labor Market Approach

Mabel Andalón and Gary Fields

Through the perspective of labor market economics, this chapter identifies five challenges of the health worker crisis in Africa: production, underutilization, distribution, performance, and financing.[1] Labor market economics clarifies the functioning of health worker labor markets in Africa as well as the dynamics that lead to specific labor market outcomes.[2] This perspective helps to explain why workers are paid what they are, why employers hire as many (or as few) people as they do, and why the number of employed health workers is what it is, and not necessarily what is "needed" to meet a given policy objective. Sound labor market analyses that collect empirical data together with social cost-benefit criteria are needed in most African countries before we can confidently offer policy recommendations to address these challenges (Fields 2007).

Five Challenges Associated with the Health Worker Crisis in Africa

One overarching problem that policy makers in African countries face is ensuring that they have enough human resources to meet a certain objective for delivering health care services. The number of health workers needed is referred to as the benchmark of needs, commonly derived from the needs-based approach (see chapter 2).

Although countries are advised to set their own benchmarks according to nation-specific health care policy objectives, cross-country comparisons are often based on the World Health Organization (WHO) benchmark of 2.28 well-trained health workers (doctors, nurses, and others). The ratio of 2.28 health workers per 1,000 population is estimated to be necessary to achieve 80 percent coverage of deliveries by skilled birth attendants, a health intervention clearly associated with the achievement of the Millennium Development Goals (WHO 2006).[3]

The ratio of health workers falls short of the WHO benchmark in 36 of 46 African countries. Of all African countries, only The Gambia, Mauritius, the Seychelles, and South Africa have 3.9 or more health workers per 1,000 inhabitants. Ghana, Nigeria, and Zambia had less than two, and many other countries actually had less than one (table 3.1). There were 1.9 health workers per 1,000 inhabitants in the whole African region, compared with 7.78 in the WHO region of the Americas in 2009 (see chapter 8).

Based on Africa's population in the early years of the first decade of the 2000s, meeting the WHO target of 2.28 health workers per 1,000 population would have required a 139 percent increase of health workers working in the field, from about 600,000 to 1,400,000 (WHO 2006). This huge gap between the observed density of health workers in African countries and the benchmark of needs—which we name a shortfall of health workers—is unlikely to have narrowed recently. A lack of health workers being produced, and less than full utilization of those produced, partly explains this shortfall.

Table 3.1   Number and Density of Health Workers per 1,000 Population, Selected African Countries

Country	Physicians		Nurses			Total density
	Number	Density per 1,000 population	Number	Density per 1,000 population	Year	per 1,000 population
Ethiopia	1,936	0.03	14,893	0.21	2003	0.24
Ghana	3,240	0.15	19,707	0.92	2004	1.07
Nigeria	34,923	0.28	210,306	1.70	2003	1.98
Rwanda	227	0.03	4,344	0.48	2005	0.51
Tanzania	822	0.02	13,292	0.37	2002	0.39
Uganda	2,209	0.08	16,221	0.61	2004	0.69
Zambia	1,264	0.12	19,014	1.74	2004	1.86

Source: Ministry of Health of Ethiopia 2007. The numbers for Rwanda are calculated based on Herbst (2007).

Production

The production challenge arises because Africa lacks people trained as health workers relative to a benchmark of needs (see chapter 16). The number of health workers trained in Africa plus the number of Africans trained elsewhere is the total prospective quantity of health workers. Although data on the total number of health workers trained in Africa are not readily available for most African countries, the best available estimates suggest that the total prospective quantity of health workers is below the benchmark.

Figure 3.1 represents the production challenge in a national labor market for health workers of a given African country, which for concreteness we will call AFR. Since we plot the monthly real compensation level (COMP, y-axis) as a function of the density of health workers (HW, x-axis), the WHO benchmark is the vertical line B. So, the density of health workers needed to achieve a particular health intervention is independent of the compensation level. The total prospective quantity of health workers is also a vertical line, in this case represented by P. The horizontal gap between the number of trained health workers, HW-All, and the HW-Benchmark of needs represents the production challenge: the number of additional professionals necessary to reach the WHO

Figure 3.1   The Production Challenge

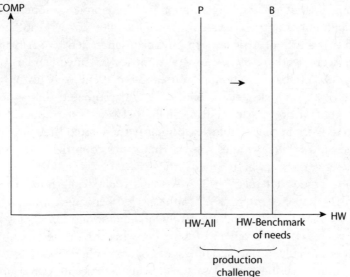

benchmark, assuming that African countries could devote whatever resources were needed to recruit all their trained health workers.

Scaling up the training of health workers in educational institutions would undoubtedly ameliorate production—reflected by a shift of the P line toward the HW-Benchmark of needs in figure 3.1—and raise the total prospective quantity of workers. Whether these newly trained health workers work in their field in Africa would, however, depend on the labor market conditions for health workers, there and elsewhere.

Underutilization

The difference between the number of persons trained as health workers in Africa and the number working (the employment level) is referred to as underutilization. This difference has several real and putative causes.

In areas of conflict or with high rates of HIV/AIDS, some trained health workers do not work simply because they die early. Available information for Lesotho and Malawi, for example, shows that 2.4 percent of medical doctors are lost each year due to premature mortality (Tawfik and Kinoti 2006). HIV's impact on health workers might, however, have peaked in the early years of the epidemic, as health workers have become more informed and prevention measures (and treatment) have become more widely available.

Of the health professionals trained in Africa, some are not working there because they are in other countries (see chapter 10). One study reported that, in 2004, almost a fourth of African-trained physicians were working in that role in Organisation for Economic Co-operation and Development countries (Bhargava and Docquier 2008). Another study found that a fifth of African-born physicians and a tenth of African-born nurses were working in developed countries (Clemens and Pettersson 2008). Of Zimbabwe's trained nurses, 34 percent were living abroad (WHO 2006). Dovlo and Nyonator (1999) estimated that more than 60 percent of doctors trained in Ghana between 1982 and 1994 emigrated to work in other countries, primarily the United Kingdom and the United States. These studies suggest that other countries' labor markets for these workers are better than Africa's.

Some argue that many health workers trained in Africa are unemployed. For labor economists, a health care worker is unemployed if he or she does not have a job and is actively looking for one. Unemployment is unlikely to be a big problem in Rwanda, where the government argues that it is difficult to find suitable staff (Sy and others 2008) or Malawi, where more than 64 percent of nurse posts are vacant (Government of

Malawi 2005). Available evidence does not allow us to be certain about unemployment in African countries. To the extent that there is unemployment, it is necessary to diagnose its magnitude, its type, and its causes (see annex 3A).

Some health workers might be working in nonhealth sectors or retiring early. But high-quality data on the numbers and locations of well-trained health workers who left the African health sector over the years (and have not returned) are unavailable, making it hard to calculate this aspect of underutilization, and the number of workers who could, in principle, be recruited from other sectors in Africa and in other countries.

Thus, labor market conditions in Africa and elsewhere affect trained health workers' labor market decisions, which ultimately determine the quantity of labor services at each level of compensation (box 3.1).

Distribution

Even though the density of health workers in some African countries is close to or even exceeds the needs benchmark, some population groups in those countries get less than their proportionate share of available services or resources—a problem of distribution. On the supply side, a shortfall for certain population groups may stem from health workers' desire to work in particular areas or serve particular types of patients. On the demand side, a shortfall may arise for groups lacking purchasing power. Although our discussion below revolves around the rural-urban dimension (see chapter 9), other distribution groups can be identified, such as region; tribe; gender; and income; as well as sector (public-private for-profit, private not-for-profit, or a mix of these); public health versus clinical care and treatment of high-risk versus other diseases.

Examples of Africa's rural-urban distribution issue abound. In 2004 about 20 percent of all public Ethiopian doctors worked in Addis Ababa, home to about 5 percent of the population (Hanson and Jack 2010). In 2006, 75 percent of Rwandan doctors worked in the city of Kigali, even though less than 20 percent of the population lived there (Ministry of Health of Rwanda 2006). In Zambia, the density of workers in both rural and urban areas is below the benchmark of needs, but in urban areas the density (1.71) is much higher than in rural areas (0.77) (Herbst and Gijsbrechts 2007).[4]

Reluctance to work in rural areas is related to personal characteristics, wages, and other job attributes. Health workers seem more likely to accept employment in areas that are similar to where they were born and raised.

Box 3.1

Labor Market Outcomes in Africa and Other Regions

Both the number of health workers employed in Africa—what economists call the employment level—and the market's compensation levels are the result of health labor market policies in the continent itself, in other sectors of the region, and in other countries, as well as the functioning of these labor markets. (Annex 3A gives a short description of nine basic concepts for understanding how labor markets for health workers function.) Data on wages, salaries, and other components of compensation packages for health workers can be found in McCoy and others (2008).

Box figure 3.1.1 illustrates how labor market characteristics in different countries lead to different employment and compensation levels. Curve S^{AFR} depicts a labor supply curve in Africa, expressing the number of people willing to work as health workers in Africa as a function of monthly compensation, everything else being constant. The supply curve is upward sloping because the number of people wanting to work as health workers in Africa increases as real compensation rises. Factors other than compensation, such as the conditions in other labor markets, affect the position of the labor supply curve.

Box Figure 3.1.1   Labor Markets in Africa and Other Regions

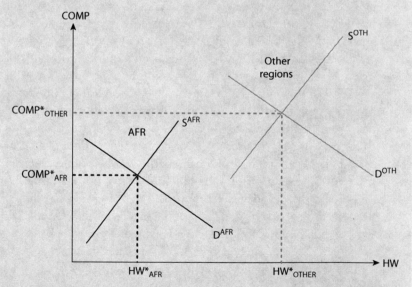

Curve D^{AFR} depicts a labor demand curve, expressing the number of people employers want to hire as a function of the real compensation paid to each worker,

(continued next page)

Box 3.1 *(continued)*

everything else constant. One reason that curve D^{AFR} is downward sloping is that, because the budget is relatively fixed, the ability of employers to hire more people decreases as real compensation increases. Aspects of the job other than compensation, such as job training, affect the position of the labor demand curve.

Because we assume that market equilibrating forces are free to operate, in equilibrium, the number of health workers currently working as health workers in Africa is represented by HW^*_{AFR} and the corresponding compensation level by $COMP^*_{AFR}$.

Box figure 3.1.1 also shows that Africa has fewer health workers (and so less health care) than other regions. In labor market economics this is because Africa is very poor. Africa's poverty makes it unable to create effective demand for health services: at any given compensation level, fewer health workers are demanded than if the continent were richer. So, Africa's demand for health workers lies to the left of that in other regions.

But because African countries lack means to train many health workers at any given compensation level, fewer health workers are available to work than if Africa were richer. So, the supply of health workers in Africa lies to the left of the supply of health workers in other regions. Africa thus has fewer employed health workers per capita than other, richer regions.

In Ethiopia residents of the capital city prefer to work in urban areas (Serneels and others 2007). Health workers with altruistic motivations, such as those trained in faith-based schools or those expressing willingness to work for the poor, more readily move from urban to rural areas for less money, or stay in rural areas (Serneels and others 2007, 2010).

Health workers' location decisions are also influenced by wages, other job attributes, and location-specific factors. In Rwanda, for example, health workers consider salaries and benefits (such as housing and access to health care), other job attributes (such as access to training, chances of promotion, and opportunities for holding a second job), and location-specific factors (such as access to good schools for their children and to infrastructure like electricity, water, quality housing, food markets, roads, and transport) (Serneels and Lievens 2008).

Building on the evidence of the factors relevant for workers when making location decisions, the methodology of contingent valuation has enabled the design of incentive schemes to attract or retain workers in disadvantaged areas. The schemes are based on the compensation that health workers have reported to be willing to accept to stay in or move to rural areas (Hanson and Jack 2010). For example, an incentive of US$1,000 was offered to people who agreed to move to rural areas in Liberia (Walsh 2007). Other countries (including Burkina Faso, Cameroon, Ghana, Malawi, Mali, and Zambia) have launched workforce strategies to improve compensation packages so that more people will work in rural areas (GHWA 2006).

Performance

The performance of health workers in Africa has been hypothesized to be unsatisfactory along three main dimensions. First, health workers are inefficient because they produce fewer health services than they potentially could given their skills and knowledge, because they do not have the means to do their jobs (see chapter 5). Second, the quality of the health services they produce is low relative to the medical protocols that should be followed for the interventions needed by the population served (see chapter 4). This can occur if health workers do not have appropriate skills and knowledge or decide not to follow the protocols. Third, health workers' behavior might be inadequate either because they have poor attitudes toward patients (see chapter 14) or because they engage in corruption and embezzlement.

One explanation for the low quality—and low quantity—of health workers' services in Africa is lack of equipment (such as hospitals or medicines) and other health support systems (such as health management, support workers, or information systems; Dieleman and Harnmeijer 2006). In Uganda essential drugs are out of stock more than half the time (Uganda MOH 2008). Hard evidence on the extent of this challenge in other countries is thin. Evidence on whether improving basic infrastructure and supplies in African countries affects the health services delivered is also limited (WHO 2006).

An alternative explanation is that health workers lack necessary skills and knowledge (Dieleman and Harnmeijer 2006), but the evidence is mixed. In many African countries with high maternal ratios and child mortality, basic treatment skills are deficient, particularly among doctors at the bottom of the competence distribution (Das, Hammer, and Leonard 2008). By contrast, studies in Tanzania (Leonard and Masatu 2007) and Rwanda (Basinga and others 2010) show that health workers are generally knowledgeable about the procedures that should be followed, but do not always follow them.

In areas where health workers' skills and knowledge are poor in Africa, either the quality of education itself is frequently low (Walsh 2007), or there is an inconsistency between the education received—often based on western models—and the country's epidemiological needs (Soucat and others 2007). Certificates issued by unaccredited institutions add to the problem (Walsh 2007). Further, some employers hire people with less than acceptable qualifications because of the difficulty in finding suitable candidates. As one doctor in Rwanda puts it: "There are health centers where the auxiliary health worker is head of the health center" (Lievens and Seerneels 2006, 37).

Given evidence on the association between years of training and knowledge of medical protocol among doctors (Leonard, Masatu, and Vialou 2007), in-service training programs are one strategy to upgrade health workers' knowledge and skills. Such programs can be adjusted to the nature of services delivered (rural or urban). For example, 30,193 new health extension workers in rural Ethiopia were trained in 2005–10 to offer an essential package of life-saving services that are particularly relevant in those areas, such as family planning, bednets, and immunization to its rural population (MoFED 2010). The effect of these tailored training programs on the knowledge of health workers and the quality of health care services delivered has still not been determined.

The inefficiency of health workers is associated with absenteeism and shirking. On any given day, 37 percent of health workers in Uganda are absent from work for no apparent reason (Chaudhury and others 2006). Some economists have proposed methods to address this failing, among others (box 3.2).

Some evidence shows that health workers in Africa have a bad attitude toward patients. According to one poor person in Tanzania: "[Health workers] treat us like animals; worse than dogs" (Narayan and others 2000, 76). Weak patient-management skills, corruption, and embezzlement are also identified as important behavioral problems of health workers in Africa, but we were not able to find any evidence supporting this argument.

Financing

The fifth component, financing, refers to the limited resources available in Africa for addressing the first four challenges. Verboom, Tan-Torres, and Evans (2005) estimated that bridging the global gap in health worker salaries by 2025 would require an increase for the average country of $10 per person per year. We regard this figure as much too low because

Box 3.2

Choice of Performance Levels: Economists' Views and Policies

To analyze performance's dependence on pay, labor economists developed the concept of "efficiency wages" (Stiglitz 1976). The idea is that employers who pay more than efficiency wages will be able to attract higher quality workers and induce existing workers to reduce absenteeism and shirk less.

Health worker performance, such as the number of work hours and the quality of treatment delivered, depends on pay and nonpay aspects. Thus, employers can influence worker performance by increasing pay or upgrading work conditions. Employers see benefits from improving pay and nonpay conditions of employment, but doing so is also costly. Policies to maximize health care outcomes need to be formulated accordingly.

Various policies have been implemented to address low performance. There is no evidence on the effectiveness of policies such as monitoring and accountability (Bjorkman and Svensson 2008; World Bank 2008), or professional norms. Performance-based financing (or pay for performance, see chapter 13) has been associated with a rise in health worker efficiency and a boost of enthusiasm and motivation (Basinga and others 2010; Rusa and others 2009). Whether the benefits of performance pay outweigh the costs, and therefore whether social welfare increases or decreases, has not yet been assessed (Scott and Jan 2011).

it does not adjust for the attrition caused by out-migration or the investment costs in training. It represents an additional 25 percent of current yearly spending on health services in countries with current shortfalls.

Eliminating the shortfall of health workers alone requires huge resources. Still, governments can base interventions on their ability to supplement the private sector headcount, maximizing the number of health workers with available funding (see chapter 6). Based on Africa's resources and past trends, a further 600,000 health workers could be employed over 2008–15, assuming a fixed labor-cost ratio, no wage change, and no skill-mix shift (World Bank 2007). Training these people in the period would require additional resources of about $14.2 billion (real 2006 US$). WHO data reveal that this is 36 percent of what is spent on health in Africa (WHO 2009).

Eliminating the rural-urban disparity in per capita health workers in Ethiopia, for example, would require an estimated health budget increase of 30–42 percent (Serneels and others 2007).

Conclusion

Taking a labor market economics perspective, this chapter discussed five challenges in the health worker sector in Africa: production, underutilization, distribution, performance, and financing. The chapter explained why workers are paid what they are, why employers hire as few people as they do, and why the number of employed health workers in African countries is lower compared to what is "needed" to meet a given policy objective.

Addressing any of the challenges is a laudable goal, but there are limited resources available in Africa for addressing multiple challenges. Using scarce resources on, for example, the quantity challenge in health means not using them on the performance challenge—or other sectors' development needs. If additional resources become available, countries should have a criterion for allocating these resources among the different development priorities. The framework we would advise is to compare the social benefits of each possible intervention with the social costs in order to identify the intervention with the highest net benefit to the country as a whole. More empirical data, a full labor market analysis, and social cost-benefit criteria are needed before policy recommendations can be confidently offered.

Annex 3A   Key Concepts from Labor Market Economics

- A *labor market* is the place where labor services are voluntarily bought and sold. A worker may sell his labor services to an employer in exchange for compensation. He may also decide to be self-employed—that is, to sell labor services to himself.

- Mainstream *labor market economics* analyzes the dynamics leading to a specific labor market outcome, which consists of the number of people working and the real compensation they receive for their work.

- The *fundamental building blocks* for analyzing the workings of any single labor market are labor supply, labor demand, and a compensation-determination process. Underlying these building blocks are several equilibrating forces.

- The *market labor supply* is the number of doctors, nurses, midwives, traditional healers, and other health workers wanting to work in the health professionals' labor market.

- The *market labor demand* is the number of health professionals with the necessary qualifications employers desire to hire and have the means to pay for. The country's public sector, private hospitals and clinics, faith-based organizations, self-employed, and patients themselves are all employers of health workers. The demand for health workers' labor is derived from the demand for what that labor produces (health services). The lower the demand for health services, the lower the demand for health workers will be.

- *Markets clear* when the amount of labor supplied equals the amount demanded. The market clearing quantity HW* has a corresponding compensation level COMP*. If the compensation is initially below COMP*, there is a "labor shortage" as there is more labor demanded than supplied. If the compensation level is initially above COMP*, there will be a "deficient demand unemployment," which results from the fact that employers lack the resources to hire all the health workers willing to work.

- There are three standard *equilibrating forces* in labor markets. First, workers are free to supply their labor to any given labor market or not. Second, employers can operate in the most advantageous location and hire the number of workers consistent with their ultimate goals given their available resources. Third, compensation will tend toward the market-clearing level.

- A compensation-quantity pair is an *equilibrium* if the market tends there, and, once there, the market tends to stay there. When equilibrating forces are free to operate, the labor market will be characterized by a *market-clearing equilibrium*, regardless of initial conditions. When the initial situation is characterized by unemployment or shortage, the equilibrating forces will eliminate them through changes in the behavior of employers and employees. When the compensation level is initially at the market-clearing level, neither employers nor employees have incentives to change the compensation level. Thus, the initial market-clearing pair will be an equilibrium.

- *Nonmarket-clearing equilibria* occur when standard equilibrating forces are not free to operate. Compensation might be kept above the market-clearing level because of trade unions, minimum wages, government pay policy, multinational corporations' pay policy, and/or labor codes. In this situation unemployment persists in equilibrium. In like fashion, compensation might be kept below the market-clearing level, resulting in an equilibrium characterized by a labor shortage.

Notes

1. We use the term health worker for simplicity. Other terms are health care professional, health service professional, and health service provider. Health management and support workers, such as clerks and cleaning people, are also important for the success of a health system, but that is not our focus. Health workers (as used in this chapter) account for two-thirds of the 59.8 million workers in health worldwide (WHO 2006).

2. For a comprehensive introduction to labor economics, see Ehrenberg and Smith (2012).

3. Allowing for uncertainty, countries with 2.02–2.54 per 1,000 inhabitants are regarded as failing to achieve 80 percent coverage for deliveries by skilled birth attendants.

4. Some authors suggest a distribution problem (also called geographic imbalance) when the proportion of health workers in urban areas is greater than in rural areas. This is not a problem if that proportion reflects their share in the total population—for example, if 20 percent of health workers are in urban areas because 20 percent of the population lives there.

References

Basinga, P., P. J. Gertler, A. Binagwaho, A. Soucat, J. R. Sturdy, and C. M. J. Vermeersch. 2010. "Paying Primary Health Care Centers for Performance in Rwanda." Policy Research Working Paper 5190, World Bank, Washington, DC.

Bhargava, A., and F. Docquier. 2008. "HIV Pandemic, Medical Brain Drain, and Economic Development in Sub-Saharan Africa." *World Bank Economic Review* 22 (2): 345–66.

Bjorkman, M., and J. Svensson. 2008. "Efficiency and Demand for Health Services: Survey Evidence on Public and Private Providers of Primary Health Care in Uganda." Paper prepared for AFT: PREM2, World Bank, Washington, DC.

Chaudhury, N., J. S. Hammer, M. Kremer, K. Muralidharan, and F. Halsey Rogers. 2006. "Missing in Action: Teachers and Health Worker Absence in Developing Countries." *Journal of Economic Perspectives* 20 (1): 91–116.

Clemens, M. A., and G. Pettersson. 2008. "New Data on African Health Professionals Abroad." *Human Resources for Health* 6 (1): 1–11.

Das, J., J. Hammer, and K. Leonard. 2008. "The Quality of Medical Advice in Low-Income Countries." Policy Research Working Paper 4501, World Bank, Washington, DC.

Dieleman, M., and J. W. Harnmeijer. 2006. *Improving Health Worker Performance: In Search of Promising Practices*. Geneva: World Health Organization.

Dovlo, D., and F. Nyonator. 1999. "Migration of Graduates of the University of Ghana Medical School: A Preliminary Rapid Appraisal." *Human Resources for Health Development Journal* 3 (1): 34–37.

Ehrenberg, R. G., and R. S. Smith. 2012. *Modern Labor Economics: Theory and Public Policy*. 10th ed. Boston, MA: Pearson Addison-Wesley.

Fields, G. S. 2007. "Labor Market Policy in Developing Countries: A Selective Review of the Literature and Needs for the Future." Policy Research Working Paper 4362, World Bank, Washington, DC.

GHWA (Global Health Workforce Alliance). 2006. *Strategic Plan*. Geneva: World Health Organization.

Government of Malawi. 2005. *Application for the Fifth Round, Global Fund to Fight AIDS, Tuberculosis and Malaria (GFATM): Health Systems Strengthening and Orphan Care and Support*. Lilongwe: Government of Malawi.

Hanson, K., and W. Jack. 2010. "Incentives Could Induce Ethiopian Doctors and Nurses to Work in Rural Settings." *Health Affairs* 29 (8): 1452–60.

Herbst, C. H. 2007. *Comprehensive and Accurate Information on Health Worker Stock, Profiles and Distribution: Reviewing the Experience of Rwanda to Obtain Such Information through a Facility Census*. Washington, DC: World Bank.

Herbst, C. H., and D. Gijsbrechts. 2007. *Adequacy and Accuracy of Information on Health Worker Stock, Profiles and Distribution in Zambia: Analysis of the Health Facility Census Data*. Washington, DC: World Bank.

Leonard, K. L., and M. C. Masatu. 2007. "Variations in the Quality of Care Accessible to Rural Communities in Tanzania." *Health Affairs* 26 (3): w380–w392.

Leonard, K. L., M. C. Masatu, and A. Vialou. 2007. "Getting Doctors to Do Their Best: The Roles of Ability and Motivation in Health Care Quality." *Journal of Human Resources* 42 (3): 682–700.

Lievens, T., and P. Serneels. 2006. *Synthesis of Focus Group Discussions with Health Workers in Rwanda*. Washington, DC: World Bank.

McCoy, D., S. Bennett, S. Witter, B. Pond, B. Baker, J. Gow, S. Chand, T. Ensor, and B. McPake. 2008. "Salaries and Incomes of Health Workers in Sub-Saharan Africa." *Lancet* 371 (9613): 675–81.

Ministry of Health of Ethiopia. 2007. *Human Resources for Health: Business Process Re-engineering*. Addis Ababa: Ministry of Health of Ethiopia.

Ministry of Health of Rwanda. 2006. *Annual Report 2006.* http://www.moh.gov. rw/index.php?option=com_docman&Itemid=13.

MoFED (Ministry of Finance and Economic Development) of the Federal Democratic Republic of Ethiopia. 2010. *Ethiopia: 2010 MDGs Report. Trends and Prospects for Meeting MDGs by 2015.* Addis Ababa: MoFED.

Narayan, D., R. Patel, K. Schafft, A. Rademacher, and S. Koch-Schulte. 2000. *Voices of the Poor: Can Anyone Hear Us?* New York: Oxford University Press.

Rusa, L., M. Schneidman, G. Fritsche, and L. Musango. 2009. "Rwanda: Performance-Based Financing in the Public Sector." In Performance Incentives for Global Health: Potential and Pitfalls, ed. R. Eichler and R. Levine, 189–214. *Washington, DC: Brookings Institution Press.*

Scott, A., and S. Jan. 2011. "Primary Care." In *Oxford Handbook of Health Economics*, ed. P. Smith and S. Glied. New York: Oxford University Press.

Serneels, P., and T. Lievens. 2008. "Institutions for Health Care Delivery, A Formal Exploration of What Matters to Health Workers, Evidence from Rwanda." CSAE Working Paper Series 2008–29, Centre for the Studies of African Economies, Department of Economics, Oxford University, Oxford.

Serneels, P., J. Montalvo, M. Lindelöw, and A. Barr. 2007. "For Public Service or for Money: Understanding Geographical Imbalances in the Health Workforce." *Health Policy and Planning* 22 (3): 128–38.

Serneels, P., J. G. Montalvo, G. Pettersson, T. Lievens, D. Butera, and A. Kidanu. 2010. "Who Wants to Work in a Rural Post? The Role of Intrinsic Motivation, Rural Background and Faith Based Institutions in Rwanda and Ethiopia." *Bulletin of the World Health Organization* 88: 342–49.

Soucat, A., O. Picazo, L. Rose, P. Serneels, M. Vujicic, G. Dussault, and K. Tulenko. 2007. *Human Resources for Health: Africa Concept Note.* World Bank, Washington, DC.

Stiglitz, J. E. 1976. "The Efficiency Wage Hypothesis, Surplus Labor, and the Distribution of Labour in LDCs." *Oxford Economic Papers* 28 (2): 185–207.

Sy and others. 2008.

Tawfik, L., and S. N. Kinoti. 2006. "The Impact of HIV/AIDS on the Health Workforce in Developing Countries." Background paper for *The World Health Report 2006.* Geneva: World Health Organization.

Verboom, P., E. T. Tan-Torres, and D. B. Evans. 2005. "Costs of Eliminating Critical Shortages in Human Resources for Health." Background paper for *The World Health Report 2006.* Geneva: World Health Organization.

Walsh, B. 2007. *Human Resources Issues in the Liberian Health Sector.* Monrovia: Norwegian Agency for Development Cooperation.

World Bank. 2007. *The Economic Context—Innovation, Value for Money and Sustainability in Task Force for Scaling Up Education and Training for Health Workers, GHWA*. Washington, DC: World Bank.

World Bank. 2008.

WHO (World Health Organization). 2006. *The World Health Report 2006: Working Together for Health*. Geneva: WHO.

———. 2009. *World Health Statistics 2009*. Geneva: WHO.

CHAPTER 4

Productivity of Health Workers: Tanzania

Ottar Mæstad and Aziza Mwisongo

Health worker productivity analysis can improve the use of scarce human resources for health in Africa. Productivity analysis identifies health facilities that organize their work more efficiently than others. These facilities can then serve as a basis for knowledge transfer among facilities. Productivity analysis also compares workloads across health facilities, identifying room for more efficient allocation of productive resources. This chapter provides an introduction to productivity analysis and presents a set of analytical tools, which are then applied to productivity data from Tanzania. Our analysis suggests that the health workforce is underused in many places, but overstretched in others.

High Workloads for Tanzanian Health Workers

The sun has already been up for a couple hours in Dar es Salaam, the largest city in Tanzania. At one of the city's health centers, eight nurses and clinicians are sitting on benches for their morning staff meeting. They share information about the two women who delivered during the night, the cholera patients, and the researchers who will spend the day at the center to learn more about how the health workers manage their workload.

A couple of days earlier we interviewed staff from this and other health facilities about how the health worker shortage affected their performance. What we heard gave reason to worry: "We are not doing our work properly because of the shortage of staff." "If the doctor decides to listen to everyone carefully and concentrates on each patient, at the end of the day that doctor will find he has attended only 20 patients, with 100 patients still in line." "As a result the doctors decide to rush in order to catch up with the large number of patients waiting." High workloads seem to make doctors reduce the quality of their work.

We were there to see with our own eyes. We spent the whole day on the waiting bench at the outpatient department, watching the flow of patients as they arrived, patiently waited, and quickly entered and left the doctor's office. What we saw astonished us: between 9:00 a.m. and 1:00 p.m., that office saw more than 90 consultations. During that time the doctor also left once or twice to see patients in the inpatient department. Each consultation lasted only two minutes on average, often only one. We were struck by the high productivity of the doctor, able to treat so many patients. At the same time our worries about the impact of the health worker shortage on the quality of health services was confirmed.

One year later, we were on our way to a small health center in rural Tanzania with our research team. We were about to start a large survey to look more systematically into the relationship between workload and health worker performance. After a three-hour drive we arrived at the center around 8:30 a.m. Two patients had just finished their consultations, but no more patients were in sight. During the next four hours, only two patients showed up. Again, we were astonished. Two health workers saw fewer than a handful of patients a day! We came back the next day and saw the same pattern.

These contrasting experiences raise important questions. Are Tanzania and other low-income countries using their small health workforces effectively? Is workload sufficiently accounted for when staff are allocated among health facilities? Are many health workers spending their days waiting for patients, while others are seriously overworked? Can reallocating health workers to places overcrowded with patients improve health outcomes?

These questions call for studies of health worker productivity (or efficiency). Health worker productivity analysis shows how much output (such as number of consultations) is produced per health worker at one health facility compared with others, shedding light on relative workload. The results may lead to more efficient allocation of productive resources, either through reallocation of health workers or through more targeted recruitment policies. Further, such analysis helps identify health facilities that organize their work more efficiently than others, which may serve as a basis for knowledge transfer among facilities. Finally, this analysis can be used to study productivity changes over time, both at health facilities and at the level of district or country.

This chapter introduces various approaches to productivity analysis.[1] It starts with a brief explanation of basic concepts and next discusses time and motion studies to analyze the extent that health workers spend their work time on productive activities. It then analyzes output-input ratios (total factor productivity) and the unit cost of production, discussing the importance of establishing relevant benchmarks to assess productivity and efficiency. To this end, it presents two methods for estimating the maximum level of output achievable for a given set of inputs (or equivalently, the minimum inputs needed to obtain a given output): data envelopment analysis (DEA), a linear programming technique; and stochastic frontier analysis (SFA), a statistical method similar to regression analysis, but more complex.

Our presentation of the various approaches to productivity analysis is accompanied by empirical illustrations based on survey data from Tanzania. The data suggest significant scope for productivity improvements—even with few health workers per capita—and thus considerable potential for strengthening health services and improving health outcomes given current resources.

Basic Concepts in Productivity Analysis

Our discussion uses standard concepts of productivity analysis, describing health care as a *production process* where *inputs* (such as staff and equipment) produce certain *outputs* (such as patient consultations). Productivity analysis is concerned with the efficiency of production: transforming inputs into outputs (see chapter 5). A *production frontier* describes the maximum attainable level of outputs at any given level of inputs. *Technical efficiency* is a measure of a health facility's ability to attain its maximum output given its inputs. Technical efficiency is usually scored between 0 and 1, where 1 indicates full efficiency as the facility operates on the production frontier. A score of 0.6 implies that the facility produces only 60 percent of its maximum output given its current use of inputs.[2]

A facility that is technically efficient might increase its output-input ratio by changing the size of its operations. *Scale efficiency* is a measure of the extent that a facility is optimizing its size. Since a health facility's scale of operations is often largely outside the management's control, we prefer, in this context, productivity measures that do not incorporate scale in efficiencies.

Total factor productivity is the ratio of outputs over inputs. When there are several inputs and outputs, they need to be combined into output and input indices to calculate total factor productivity. Changes in both technical efficiency and scale efficiency will affect total factor productivity.

Cost efficiency is a facility's ability to produce a given output at minimum cost, given the price of inputs. A facility that is technically efficient is not necessarily cost efficient because it may be able to produce the same output with an even cheaper combination of inputs. The ability of a facility to choose its input mix in order to minimize cost is called *input mix allocative efficiency*.

But cost-minimizing behavior is not usually expected in health facilities for two main reasons. First, the facility rarely has discretion in choosing inputs, and when it can, price signals may be weak. Second, decisions on input mix may deliberately follow criteria other than minimizing cost, such as maintaining certain service standards. Many studies of productivity in the public sector therefore confine their attention to technical efficiency. We, too, prefer this approach, though we discuss other techniques.

Time and Motion Studies

The original idea of time and motion studies—dating back to Frederick W. Taylor, Frank B. Gilbreth, and Lillian M. Gilbreth in the early 20th century—was to study the time use and number of motions for particular work tasks with the aim of increasing productivity, as well as reducing worker fatigue. "Taylorism" or "scientific management" was developed in the context of assembly lines, and has been criticized for its dehumanizing view of workers. The applicability of this approach to the study of health worker productivity is clearly limited, but it is still used.

Our interest in the time and motion concept lies in its ability to identify slack capacity: to what extent health workers spend their work time on unproductive activities (such as waiting for patients) rather than productive work. This may not be a typical approach to standard productivity analysis, but it is still useful in this context, as identifying slack capacity can lead to more efficient use of the health workforce.

A time and motion study in the health sector typically involves following health workers over an extended period (for example, one week) while noting at few-minute intervals the activities they perform (including nonproductive activities). The method is simple but resource demanding. Its costs can be reduced by increasing intervals between observations, since the surveyor may then follow several workers simultaneously. For example, if a surveyor records activities every sixth minute, the surveyor may be able to follow three health workers, recording activities for one worker every second minute.

One of the problems of time and motion studies is that workers may become more "productive" simply by being observed (the Hawthorne effect). This is not necessarily a serious problem, though, because if all workers change their productivity proportionately (admittedly, a huge if), we may still make unbiased comparisons across workers, health facilities, and over time.

Empirical Illustration

In light of the widespread shortage of health workers in Sub-Saharan Africa, one might assume that service providers have little or no slack capacity and that time and motion studies therefore have little to offer. Results from several studies in Tanzania suggest, however, a different picture.

One such study was conducted in 2006 on a sample of 158 health workers from two districts: Mwanga, where health worker density per capita was relatively high, and Meatu, where it was low (figure 4.1).

Figure 4.1   Productive and Unproductive Time Use, Meatu and Mwanga Districts, 2006

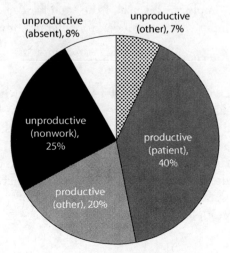

Source: Leon, Mwisongo, and Mcharo 2006.

Each worker was followed during an entire work day for five consecutive days, and their activities were recorded every sixth minute. Results show that workers spent only 60 percent of work time on productive activities and 40 percent on direct patient care; they spent 18 percent of their time waiting for patients. Another important finding showed that the share of nonproductive time increases sharply during the course of the day (Leon, Mwisongo, and Mcharo 2006). A similar study of 65 health workers from Zanzibar revealed almost identical results (Ruwoldt and Hassett 2007).

The findings suggest that the average slack capacity is significant and there is potential for increased outputs, especially in the afternoons.

Total Factor Productivity and Unit Cost Analysis

Total factor productivity is the ratio of outputs to inputs (Coelli and others 2003; Farrell 1957).

$$\text{Total factor productivity} = \frac{\text{Output index}}{\text{Input index}}$$

Health workers are the most crucial input in the health sector. Other major inputs include drugs, medical equipment (such as thermometers, stethoscopes, and gloves), and physical infrastructure (such as buildings and beds). The ultimate output is improved population health, but due to the difficulty of measuring changes in health outcomes, outputs are usually measured in terms of, for example, the number of patients treated, children immunized, or babies delivered.

Unit costs are simply the inverse of the total factor productivity measure, using total input costs as an index for total use of inputs:

$$\text{Unit costs} = \frac{\text{Total cost of inputs}}{\text{Output index}}$$

An important challenge for total factor productivity and unit cost analysis in the health sector is finding ways to aggregate different outputs into a meaningful output index. Even the smallest health facilities usually offer a broad range of services that require substantially different resource inputs and thus cannot be aggregated into a single output measure—the number of consultations, for example. Productivity analysis of firms that operate in competitive markets uses market prices of outputs as weights for aggregating multiple outputs, but such prices are seldom available in the health sector.

A different approach aggregates outputs into a standardized unit of output index using relative resource requirements for various types of outputs as weights. One example is the following index from Lindelöw, Reinikka, and Svensson (2003) for measuring aggregate outputs at lower level health facilities:

Standardized unit of output = (12 × deliveries) + (0.5 × immunizations) + (1 × number of outpatients) + (1 × antenatal care visits) + (1 × family planning consultations) + (5 × outreach patients). (Separate studies of resource use, perhaps including time and motion studies, are required to determine the index weights.)

Empirical Illustration

To illustrate the various approaches to productivity analysis, we will use the Health Worker Motivation, Availability, and Performance (MAP) dataset from Tanzania, even though the data were not collected for productivity analysis purposes.[3] The dataset, collected in 2007, includes data on outputs and inputs in outpatient departments of a stratified random sample of 126 health facilities in nine rural districts. We will confine our attention to one output—the number of outpatient consultations—and one input—the number of full-time health workers in the outpatient department.

Most of the 3,500 patients in the dataset presented with fever, cough, diarrhea, and other relatively mild symptoms. These conditions required the health worker to ask a set of questions and do certain physical examinations, without the need for much equipment (a thermometer and stethoscope generally sufficed). The health workers' time and effort thus accounted for most of the inputs.

The number of outpatient consultations was collected from facility records for two months before the survey. These data were available from 99 of the 126 health facilities. On average, the historic output levels matched the output levels on the day of observation very well. The number of health workers in the outpatient department was adjusted for part-time activity in other facility departments.

Total Factor Productivity. With only one output and one input, total factor productivity is simply the ratio between the two. The results are striking (figure 4.2 and table 4.1). In a large part of rural Tanzania the number of patients per health worker in the outpatient department appears quite low—the slack capacity at the first facility visited was not

Figure 4.2   Consultations per Health Worker in Outpatient Departments, Rural Tanzania

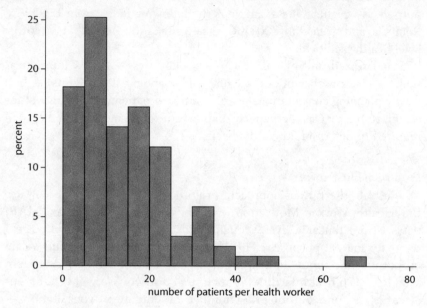

Source: MAP data set.

Table 4.1   Alternative Productivity Measures, MAP Dataset, Tanzania

	Mean	Median	5th percentile	95th percentile
Consultations per health worker ($n = 99$)	14.8	14	1.6	37.3
Total factor productivity ($n = 99$)	0.226	0.188	0.025	0.570
Unit costs of labor per outpatient (T Sh) ($n = 85$)[a]	1,072	719	250	2,679
Data envelopment analysis	0.308	0.243	0.025	0.820
Stochastic frontier analysis	0.477	0.498	0.096	0.781

Source: MAP data set.
Note: T Sh = Tanzanian shilling.
a. Of the 99 facilities with data on historic output levels, 14 did not provide salary data.

exceptional. In more than 40 percent of the health facilities, a health worker had fewer than 10 patients per day. Further, the number of consultations per health worker differed widely across facilities, from less than one patient to more than 60 patients per day. (The average time per consultation was less than six minutes.)

Total factor productivity is low. When we normalized the productivity of the most efficient provider to 1, our estimate of average productivity is 0.226. The low productivity is driven partly by a single provider with much higher productivity than the second most productive unit. But even if we eliminate this outlier, average productivity remains low at 0.325.

The results suggest a need to reconsider the allocation of health workers across health facilities (or outpatient departments) in order to improve health workforce utilization—but with a word of caution. Among the health facilities with fewer than 10 patients per health worker per day, 23 percent had only one health worker and another 44 percent had between one and two full-time health workers. Reallocating health workers in these circumstances would entail closing down some facilities. This may be sensible if other facilities are near (in fact, mission-based and government health facilities were sometimes located next to each other in our study area). Otherwise, reallocating health workers may reduce access to health care for parts of the population, making the tradeoff much more involved. Health facilities operating at a minimum staffing level are indivisible. This fact needs to be kept in mind in productivity studies of countries where small health facilities are scattered in sparsely populated areas.[4]

Unit Cost Analysis. Combining data on the number of health workers with data on gross salaries (table 4.1), the MAP dataset enables the calculation of unit labor costs per outpatient. We observe a 10-fold difference in unit costs between the 5th and 95th percentiles, suggesting again that productivity differentials are substantial. They are, however, not as large as indicated by total factor productivity, because some facilities with very few patients are staffed with less qualified staff on lower salaries.

Bjorkman and Svensson (2008) report similar results from a study of 50 lower level health facilities in Uganda. They identified a sevenfold difference in unit labor costs per outpatient, decreasing to a fivefold difference when they included other outputs and inputs using the above method.

Data Envelopment Analysis

If we are interested in *technical efficiency*, such as a health facility's ability to attain its maximum output at its current input, total factor productivity and unit cost analysis rarely suffice. Total factor productivity merges technical efficiency and scale efficiency into one measure, so it does not separate productivity loss resulting from inefficient sizes of health facilities.[5] Unit cost analysis suffers from the same problem, because it implicitly assumes that it is meaningful to compare unit costs of the most efficient health facility with those of other facilities. As explained above, unit cost analysis also captures aspects of input mix allocative efficiency that are not necessarily relevant for productivity analysis in the health sector. Finally, the simple approach to total productivity analysis and unit cost analysis, which uses a standardized unit of output index with fixed weights for aggregating outputs, makes strong and rigid assumptions about production technology. In practice, it is more likely that the appropriate weights differ depending on output-input mixes and the size of the health facility.

A measure of technical efficiency compares current output to the maximum achievable output as described by the production frontier. The frontier is, however, unknown and needs to be estimated. DEA and SFA offer two different approaches to estimate it.

DEA is a linear programming approach that estimates a production frontier based on the productivity of the best performers in the dataset (Charnes, Cooper, and Rhodes 1978; Coelli and others 2005). Figure 4.3 explains the method for one output and one input, with black dots representing observed output-input combinations of seven production units (such as departments or health facilities). We construct the production frontier by drawing a piecewise linear curve joining the output-input

Figure 4.3   Data Envelopment Analysis

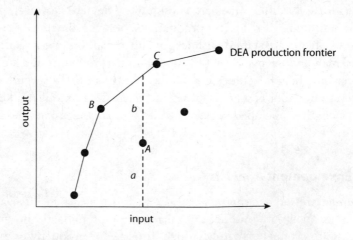

combinations of the most productive units. Five units are on the frontier, and are defined as technically efficient (in a simple analysis of output-input ratios, B would perform better than all others and would therefore be the only technically efficient unit).

We immediately realize that because the frontier is estimated from actual data, at least one health facility will always be scored as technically efficient. This does not imply that the facility has no room for improving efficiency; it only reminds us to interpret productivity estimates as relative and not absolute.

Two units fall below the frontier in figure 4.3. We measure the inefficiency of these units by comparing their output-input levels with those of their closest peers. If, for example, we want to know how much output facility A should be able to produce at the current input, we compare its output with a combination of the outputs of its peers, B and C. The production frontier on the segment BC thus defines what A should be able to produce. The technical efficiency of A is then $a/(a + b)$, while the "unused potential" $b/(a + b)$ is a measure of technical inefficiency.[6]

DEA allows us to compare health facilities with similar input/output levels to one another. In this way, more similar health facilities are compared with each other. Further, unlike other approaches to productivity analysis, DEA imposes very little structure on the production function. There is no need to specify weights up front to aggregate outputs and inputs—the only requirement is that if two output-input combinations are feasible, a third that combines the first two will also be feasible (convexity). The method is thus suitable when little is known about the production frontier. Finally, DEA assumes that the observed output-input combinations are feasible. This assumption is satisfied if the data present no measurement errors, which should not be taken for granted, especially in datasets from countries with weak systems for data collection and management.

Applied to the MAP data, the DEA method estimates higher average productivity than in the total factor productivity analysis, at 0.308 versus 0.226 (see table 4.1 and figure 4.4). The difference is explained by scale inefficiency, as some facilities are not optimally sized. Productivity estimates based on total factor productivity are therefore lower than the technical efficiency measured by DEA. The main results from the above discussion are still valid, though: productivity is low on average and highly variable across health facilities.

Figure 4.4   Productivity in Outpatient Departments, Rural Tanzania

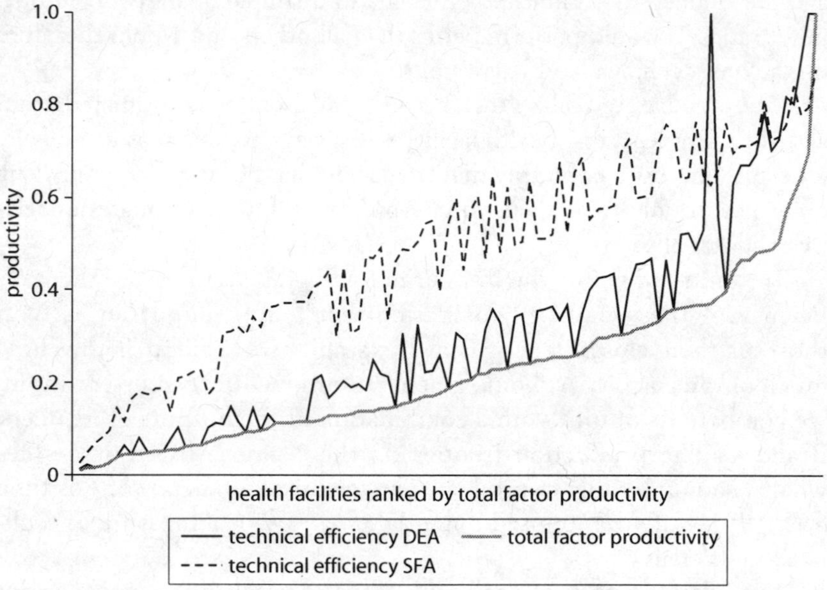

health facilities ranked by total factor productivity

——— technical efficiency DEA   ········ total factor productivity
--- technical efficiency SFA

Source: MAP dataset.
DEA = data envelopment analysis, SFA = stochastic frontier analysis.

Stochastic Frontier Analysis

SFA offers an alternative approach to estimating the production frontier, based on statistical analysis (Coelli and others 2005; Fried, Lovell, and Schmidt 2008). One advantage of SFA is that, unlike DEA, it can take account of measurement errors ("noise") in the data. With DEA all deviations from the frontier are taken as signals of technical inefficiency. Amid measurement errors and other sources of statistical noise, DEA therefore does not precisely estimate efficiency.

SFA takes account of statistical noise by assuming that the production frontier can be estimated from observed output-input combinations through a model of the type:

$$y_i = f(x_i) + v_i - u_i,$$

where y_i is observed output of provider i, x_i is observed input, $f(x_i)$ is the production frontier, v_i is a random error term that captures statistical noise (this term can be positive or negative), and u_i is a nonnegative constant measuring the degree of technical inefficiency.

In figure 4.5 the dots again illustrate observed output-input combinations of different providers. The SFA frontier fits the data but does not necessarily include all observed output-input combinations within the production possibility set, as illustrated by providers B and C. Their observed output levels exceed the production frontier, which is possible because the model allows for noise in the observed data. Now consider the technical efficiency of provider A. In the DEA model A's efficiency was measured relative to outputs of B and C. In the SFA model, technical inefficiency is measured as the distance u. In this case, the SFA model predicts less inefficiency than the DEA model for two reasons. First, the SFA production frontier is delinked from—and in this case falls below—the output-input combinations of B and C. Second, the SFA model allows for some random noise in the measurement of outputs, here illustrated by the distance v. Only the remaining gap—the distance u—expresses technical inefficiency.

The SFA method has three main disadvantages. First, it requires the analyst to make assumptions about the shape of the production frontier. A common approach is to assume a *translog* production function, a flexible specification. Second, the analyst needs to make assumptions about the distribution of the inefficiency term u. (Statistical software packages have, however, several standard options built in, making it easy to test the robustness to different assumptions.) Third, estimating and interpreting results is quite complex, especially with multiple outputs.[7]

Figure 4.5   Stochastic Frontier Analysis

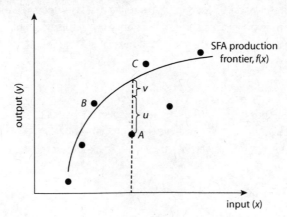

Applied to the MAP dataset, the SFA method estimates the mean technical efficiency at 0.477, significantly higher than DEA (0.308) (see table 4.1 and figure 4.4).[8] The SFA model apparently attributes a large share of the observed output-input differences to statistical noise. Even so, with an estimated average technical efficiency of less than 0.5 (with a standard deviation of 0.21), the overall conclusion remains the same as with the other approaches: productivity levels in outpatient departments in rural Tanzania are low and highly variable. Box 4.1 describes how a facility in Tanzania came out with varying methods for measuring productivity.

Box 4.1

Comparing Methods for Measuring Productivity

Ngori is a fairly large government health center a couple of hours away from the headquarters of a rural district in Tanzania. Its workload and productivity are about average among the facilities in the MAP dataset.

Three clinicians work in the outpatient department at Ngori, consulting 45 patients a day on average. The workload is moderate relative to Msasa health center, the busiest in the area, where two doctors consult 130 patients a day.

Total factor productivity at Ngori, compared with Msasa, is (45/3)/(130/2) = 0.23.

Since Ngori has more staff than Msasa, the two facilities are not directly comparable. With the DEA method, we may take this into account by comparing productivity at Ngori with one health center that is smaller and one that is larger. The smaller is still Msasa, and the larger is Chimamba hospital, which has five clinicians and 190 patients per day.

A linear projection, as used in DEA, implies that if it is possible to treat 130 patients with two clinicians and 190 patients with five, it should be possible to treat 150 patients with the three clinicians available at Ngori: 130 + (190 − 130)/(5 − 2) = 150.

DEA technical efficiency at Ngori is 45/150 = 0.30.

The difference between the DEA technical efficiency of 0.30 and total factor productivity of 0.23 is explained by scale inefficiency. An efficiently sized health center in this case will have two clinicians (as this is the size of the most

(continued next page)

Box 4.1 *(continued)*

productive unit, Msasa). Because Ngori is larger, it is not scale efficient. If there are good reasons for taking the size of Ngori as given, we might not emphasize such scale inefficiencies, making the relevant measure of productivity according to DEA 0.30.

Estimating a production frontier with the SFA method predicts that a health facility with three clinicians should be able to treat 85 patients a day. This is much less than suggested by the other methods, because SFA puts less emphasis on outliers with very high productivity (it assumes that outliers are created partly by measurement errors). SFA also predicts a measurement error for each facility, based on the overall pattern of the data. For Ngori SFA predicts that the true number of patients is 40 rather than 45.

SFA technical efficiency at Ngori is $40/85 = 0.47$.

Conclusion

Productivity analysis can contribute to better use of Africa's scarce human resources. Our analysis of data from Tanzania suggests that the health workforce is underutilized in many places while overstretched in others. We also found that average productivity in health facilities was low. Policy makers need to draw implications with great care, however, taking into account realities in the field, particularly given that some facilities are operating at a minimum staffing level.

The chapter offered a set of analytical tools suitable for productivity analysis. All the tools have advantages and disadvantages, and a choice needs to be made in each case depending on the purpose of the study (among other things). When several methods are applicable, the general advice would be to apply them all to test the sensitivity of efficiency estimates to the choice of method.

Productivity analysis has limitations that analysts need to keep in mind when interpreting results. It does not include any measure of output quality, and there may be systematic differences in case mix and the quality of inputs across health facilities. These facts may cause biases in the productivity estimates.

Further research should focus on getting high-quality input and output data from more countries to estimate productivity more reliably.

Acknowledgment

We are grateful to Sverre A. C. Kittelsen for valuable advice.

Notes

1. Coelli and others (2003, 2005) and Fried, Lovell, and Schmidt (2008) go into greater detail on productivity analysis.
2. This is called an *output-oriented* measure of technical efficiency. An *input-oriented* measure of technical efficiency expresses the extent that the use of inputs is minimized given the level of outputs.
3. See Mæstad, Torsvik, and Aakvik (2010) for a more complete description of the data and their collection.
4. For an example of total factor productivity analysis using the SOU approach, see Vujicic, Addai, and Bosomphra (2009).
5. Scale inefficiency may arise when the production technology exhibits decreasing or increasing returns to scale.
6. *Scale inefficiency* can also be measured with DEA methods, illustrated in the diagram as the distance between the maximum attainable output for A given by the production frontier, and the output that A would have achieved if A had had the same output-input level as B (the unit with the highest total factor productivity). The output level (2) will lie on a straight line from origo through B.
7. SFA analysis with several outputs is feasible by using distance functions. See Coelli and others (2003).
8. We estimated the translog production function $\ln y_i = \alpha + \beta \ln x_i + 0.5\gamma(\ln x_i)^2 + v_i - u_i$ and assumed half-normal distribution of the inefficiency term u_i.

References

Bjorkman, M., and J. Svensson. 2008. "Efficiency and Demand for Health Services: Survey Evidence on Public and Private Providers of Primary Health Care in Uganda." Paper prepared for AFT: PREM2, World Bank, Washington, DC.

Charnes, A., W. W. Cooper, and E. Rhodes. 1978. "Measuring the Efficiency of Decision Making Units." *European Journal of Operational Research* 2: 429–44.

Coelli, T., A. Estache, S. Perelman, and L. Trujillo. 2003. *A Primer in Efficiency Measurement for Utilities and Transport Regulators*. Washington, DC: World Bank.

Coelli, T., D. S. P. Rao, C. J. O'Donnell, and G. E. Battese. 2005. *An Introduction to Efficiency and Productivity Analysis*. New York: Springer Science.

Farrell, M. J. 1957. "The Measurement of Productive Efficiency." *Journal of the Royal Statistical Society, Series A (General)* 120 (3): 253–81.

Fried, H. O., C. A. K. Lovell, and S. S. Schmidt, eds. 2008. *The Measurement of Productive Efficiency and Productivity Change.* Oxford: Oxford University Press.

Leon, B., A. Mwisongo, and J. Mcharo. 2006. "Health Worker Productivity in Public Health Facilities in a Poorly Staffed as Compared to a Better Staffed Rural District in Tanzania Mainland: A Time and Motion Study." Unpublished manuscript.

Lindelöw, M., R. Reinikka, and J. Svensson. 2003. "Health Care on the Frontline: Survey Evidence on Public and Private Providers in Uganda." Africa Region Human Development Working Paper Series 38, World Bank, Washington, DC.

Mæstad, O., G. Torsvik, and A. Aakvik. 2010. "Overworked? On the Relationship between Workload and Health Worker Performance." *Journal of Health Economics* 29: 686–98.

Ruwoldt, P., and P. Hassett. 2007. *Zanzibar Health Care Worker Productivity Study. Preliminary Study Findings.* Capacity Project. Chapel Hill, NC: Intra Health International.

Vujicic, M., E. Addai, and S. Bosomphra. 2009. "Measuring Health Workforce Productivity: Application of a Simple Methodology in Ghana." Health Nutrition and Population Working Paper, World Bank, Washington, DC.

CHAPTER 5

Health Worker Performance

J. Michelle Brock, Kenneth L. Leonard, Melkiory C. Masatu, and Pieter Serneels

This chapter presents an overview of health worker performance, with the goal of understanding the role it plays in health systems by examining its inputs, outputs, and policy levers. The chapter acknowledges the importance of recognizing how much health workers do for their patients even when care is inadequate. While many constraints African countries face are common across the continent, some health sectors do better than others. Thus, even though most sectors in most African countries are below acceptable standards, they have as much to learn from each other as they do from other parts of the world. Even if there is little evidence on how to make health care in Africa adequate, there is substantial evidence on how to improve it.

Overview of Health Worker Performance

Whereas one of the main subjects of this book is the health worker shortage in Sub-Saharan Africa, this chapter develops a framework for understanding the performance of those health workers who currently practice. It suggests, as Rowe and others (2005), that low performance may be at least as important as shortages to explain poor outcomes. Rather than review the evidence of such failures, we develop a model to understand their sources. The first section of this chapter gives a snapshot of the health sector in Africa by examining a typical facility in rural Tanzania. It describes constraints to performance and provides insight into how to measure and understand this performance. Also, it outlines the importance of comparing different institutional frameworks of health care provision in Africa as a whole, and in different countries. The second section describes a conceptual model of health worker performance that helps us to understand its role in the health care system.

We begin by describing a typical rural health dispensary from the perspective of both the patient and the health worker. This overview is drawn from our extensive research in rural and urban areas of the Arusha region over the past nine years.[1]

A Typical Rural Health Facility in Tanzania

The patient's view. A typical health dispensary in rural Tanzania is staffed by a clinical officer or clinical assistant, and one or two nurses. Clinical officers traditionally have "ordinary level" education (four years of secondary schooling) and two years of medical training. Clinical assistants have an elementary school education and three years of medical training. National standards require dispensaries to have both a clinical officer and a clinical assistant, but due to chronic staffing shortages, no facilities meet these standards, and only half have a clinical officer on staff. The first posting for a clinical officer just out of school is often rural, so clinicians in rural areas have less experience than the average urban clinician.

Health facilities usually follow the rhythm of agricultural life, and because most people are busy in the early morning, the facilities rarely open until 10:00 a.m. or 11:00 a.m., closing around 2:00 p.m. or 3:00 p.m. They are busier on market days and when they hold specialty clinics. A nurse may greet arriving patients, but more frequently patients immediately queue outside the clinician's room. Facilities usually have two or three examination rooms and might have a large veranda that doubles as a waiting room. The facilities are not equipped to admit patients, but often have a couple of beds for observation. Few rural health facilities have running water or electricity. Water is often available nearby, usually at a pump.

Around 25 percent of clinicians are absent from rural posts on any given day (Klemick, Leonard, and Masatu 2009). When a nurse and a clinician are present, the nurse dispenses medicine, provides injections, and dresses wounds, with the main diagnostic tasks left to the clinician; if only a clinician, he or she will handle all these tasks. In practice, even if the only clinician is absent, the nurse takes over the duties of consulting patients, so a facility rarely closes. But because the nurse is not trained to do the clinician's job, absenteeism has consequences.

There is no triage, so a patient with an urgent case must negotiate a better place in the queue with the other patients. After waiting his or her turn, the patient enters the consultation room, greeted by a clinician sitting at a desk. Patients are supposed to carry their own medical records, as health facilities do not keep them. Since many patients do not carry them, the only health history available is drawn from the questions the clinician asks the patient.

In Tanzania many patients obtain medicines prescribed at no or low cost in the facility. Even when medicines are not available in the facility, they can be bought in local markets. So when patients value a clinician's diagnosis, they might visit a dispensary even if it does not have medicine. Similarly, patients might visit a facility with subsidized medicines, even if they have no faith in the clinician's diagnostic ability.

The average clinician asks four questions, and does one and a half physical examination procedures (such as taking the temperature). The average consultation takes just over six minutes. The lower quartile of clinicians asks two questions, performs no physical examination, and takes only three minutes to see a patient (from door opening to door closing) (Das, Hammer, and Leonard 2008). As nurses do not examine patients before they see clinicians, clinicians in this quartile do not know the patient's temperature, pulse, weight, or blood pressure when they diagnose their illness.

The health worker's view. Rural health facilities suffer more than urban facilities from the health workforce shortage, largely because most health workers posted to rural areas either do not accept the position or only stay a short period, after which they find jobs in urban settings.

Both anecdotal and empirical evidence point to various factors deterring health workers from staying in rural facilities.[2] These include economic disparities between rural and urban areas, poor communications in rural areas, a poor working environment, isolation from other economic opportunities, fewer possibilities for promotion and further training, and lack of good schools. The communication infrastructure, such as roads and telephones, is poor in rural areas. Some roads are passable only in the dry season, making it hard to travel to urban areas. Working conditions are also an important factor. For a health worker to perform well, the health facility needs to have basic medicines, equipment, and other supplies, and here, too, conditions are better in urban settings (though the government is trying to distribute amenities equitably).

Because civil servants' salaries are generally low (the wage of the average clinician in Tanzania is $150–$350 a month), most health workers have to find other income-earning activities, such as working part-time in a private health facility, opening a chemist shop, or engaging in petty business. These opportunities do not exist in rural areas, so the total earnings of rural workers are likely to be much lower than their urban peers.

The system of promoting civil servants, including health workers, is not functioning as expected—to the detriment of rural workers. Although a civil servant with satisfactory performance might expect to be promoted every two years, the reality is different. Most health workers are not promoted when due, and some work more than 15 years without promotion.[3] Because the authorities responsible for promotions are at the district or ministerial level, urban workers can access those authorities to enquire about delays, unlike their rural counterparts.

There are various professional development training programs for health workers at dispensaries and health centers. The majority target those practicing in a rural setting. In the public sector, workers are eligible for further training on government sponsorship after two years of post-degree work. If a health worker wants or needs further training, he or she has to register with the district medical officer, who in turn submits the name to the ministry of health for eligibility scrutiny. Those who qualify must take entry examinations, prepared by the ministry of health and administered at regional headquarters. But given the communication problems in rural areas, most rural health workers do not register with the district medical officer. Others fail to turn up to the examinations, either because they are unaware of the dates or because of travel difficulties. So, they miss out on professional development.

Finally, rural areas have very few good schools. The medical profession requires longer and arguably tougher training than other professions, including a sound education in primary school. Because many health workers would like their children to attend good schools, as they did, and because rural areas are hard pressed to offer them, they prefer to work in urban areas.

Comparative Analysis of Institutional Types

As the brief description from a health worker's perspective highlights, delivering proper health care to rural populations is difficult under the best of situations. Many problems that health workers face are inevitable features of health care in rural Africa. Some are surmountable; some are not. In outlining a view of health worker performance, it is important to be realistic about what can and cannot be done. One of the best tools for understanding the limitations and potential in the health care industry is comparing performance across sectors of the health care system. Sector refers to whether the health care facility is public, private, or not-for-profit. Note that rather than compare public sector workers' performance to an ideal standard of care, we compare them to other sectors where health workers face similar problems.

Absenteeism, for example, is very high across Africa, but it is also important to compare absenteeism between urban and rural settings, and private and public facilities. High rural and low urban absenteeism suggest an inherent difficulty in living and working in rural areas, while high rates in both settings point to a structural problem. Similarly, when absenteeism is as high in the private as in the public sector, it is hard to blame incentives for public sector performance; but when absenteeism in the public sector is significantly higher, incentives are much more likely to be important.

Very little of rural Africa has for-profit private health services. It is therefore more useful (despite caveats) to compare the public sector with the not-for-profit private sector—generally nongovernmental organizations—than with the for-profit private health care sector. The public and not-for-profit private sectors share a similar mission of service to the public sector, and most of them run systems of health facilities (dispensaries and hospitals) in rural and urban areas.

How to Measure and Understand Performance

One way to measure performance is to compare what is expected with what the practitioner was taught. We call this adherence—a measure of the delivery of necessary services according to patients' presenting symptoms. Another way to measure performance is to consider the practitioners' actual ability to provide the necessary service. We call this competence. While adherence compares each health worker to an ideal standard, competence compares what a health worker does for his patients relative to what he is capable of doing. In most cases adherence will be less than competence, as on average a health worker will perform below what he or she is maximally capable of. Using a sample of clinicians working in outpatient clinics in Tanzania, we can relate adherence and competence (figures 5.1 and 5.2; each shows the same data for the same sample, analyzed differently).[4]

Figure 5.1   Adherence and Competence: Analyzing the Employment Sector

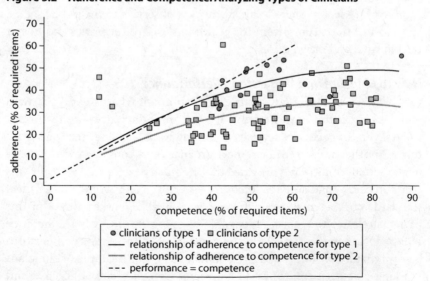

Sources: Leonard and Masatu 2007, 2010b.

Figure 5.2   Adherence and Competence: Analyzing Types of Clinicians

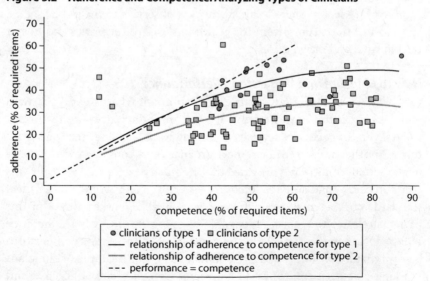

Sources: Leonard and Masatu 2007, 2010b.

The solid, 45-degree line shows where adherence is equal to competence—that is, where the clinician does what he knows how to do. Most of the observations are well below the line. The points near the line represent those who do, in practice, what they are able to demonstrate as their competence. The few clinicians with observations above the line represent cases where a clinician demonstrated low levels of competence, but provided care that was much better.

The two figures demonstrate several points about performance. First, adherence is very low. The average clinician does around 40 percent of the things he or she should do for patients. But as the best clinician in our sample does 60 percent of the necessary things, adherence is not a good absolute measure. Some of these clinicians are good and help their patients, while others are not good and do not help their patients. We do not know where to draw the line between good and bad, so it is better to analyze these clinicians looking for factors that increase adherence rather than expecting absolute adherence.

Second, competence is also very low, though higher than adherence. If training drives competence, these clinicians do not have enough. But where is the appropriate cutoff between adequate and inadequate competence? Although 100 percent competence may be a worthy goal, no clinician in the sample achieves it, making it a measure of limited use for comparing behavior.

Third, for most clinicians, competence and adherence show a significant gap (also referred to as the know-do gap.) The distance below the 45-degree line demonstrates how little these clinicians do relative to what they know how to do. This gap is a function of the effort they put into their work. Thus, effort—choosing to do what you know how to do—is an important input into the health care system.

Fourth, clinicians in the private not-for-profit sector have almost exactly the same average competence as clinicians in the public sector, but their adherence is higher (see figure 5.1, where sector A refers to the public sector and sector B refers to the private not-for-profit sector). This result is consistent with the interpretation that the private not-for-profit sector hires clinicians with the same capacity as the public sector, but gets them to perform better.

Fifth, for clinicians in the public sector, there is no significant relationship between competence and adherence. Except at the lower end of competence, the dashed line showing the average relationship is not upward sloping (see figure 5.1). This means that increasing competence does not increase adherence, so training would not improve quality for clinicians in this sector.

Sixth, if there were a way to move clinicians from the public to the private not-for-profit sector, quality of care would rise, even with no additional training (see figure 5.1). In this example, we have not detailed what would be involved in such a shift, but the graph demonstrates the potential for improvement from changes in the work environment.

Seventh, the type of clinician leads to significant differences in the relationship between adherence and competence (see figure 5.2). The definition of the clinician types in figure 5.2 comes from data other than those shown, but it is clear that clinician type 1 stands out significantly from the rest. Their competence is somewhat higher than other clinicians (labeled as type 2) and the relationship between adherence and competence is very different. They do not follow the 45-degree line exactly, but the gap between adherence and competence is much smaller.

These views offer multiple ways to address poor performance in African settings, without simply stating "performance is poor and must be improved everywhere." They allow us to think about the value of more training and effort. More important, they suggest that analyzing the differences between the two sectors or the qualities of clinicians of type 1 could offer important lessons (see box 5.1 on the literature measuring provider quality in developing countries).

Box 5.1

Measuring Provider Quality in Developing Countries

A large body of work evaluates clinician performance in the United States and abroad. In general, researchers study doctor effort by looking at clinician performance over a defined set of tasks. Authors commonly use randomized controlled studies, usually with an aim to determine which means might improve adherence to specific sets of protocol (Boekeloo and others 1994; Fairbrother and others 1999; Tierney, Hui, and McDonald 1986). But few studies use economic theory to inform the interventions (see Fairbrother and others 1999, for example). And while some hint at the behavioral underpinnings of their interventions, these issues have not been studied empirically (Soumerai and Avorn 1990).

(continued next page)

Box 5.1 *(continued)*

Authors that work on evaluating and improving provider quality in developing countries have made inroads into evaluating individual clinician quality—otherwise known as process quality—directly. Studies of process quality have been carried out in Indonesia (Santoso 1996), Paraguay (Das and Sohnesen 2007), India (Das and Hammer 2005), and Tanzania (Leonard and Masatu 2005, 2006; Leonard, Masatu, and Vialou 2007). The consensus is that quality is poor not only because of structural shortcomings but also because clinician competence is low. Santoso (1996) shows that health care providers in Indonesia are undereducated on the appropriate use of drugs for acute diarrhea, a leading cause of child morbidity and mortality. Das and Hammer (2005) determine that overall competence is low in their study region in India—and that clinicians who are highly competent relative to the sample merely have "the ability to identify life-threatening conditions and act accordingly." Compellingly, Leonard and Masatu (2005) find that despite low levels of competence, practice (process) quality is still lower than it could be; clinicians in Tanzania have the capacity to improve quality without additional training. Reliably measuring clinician performance allows us to investigate incentives and effort among individual clinicians.

While previous work identified important components of between-doctor variation, much variation in practice quality remains unaccounted for. Using vignettes and direct observation, researchers have studied the variation in quality by cadre, tenure, and type of organization. Das and Hammer (2005) find that the differences in competence between doctors in India are largely explained by training. In contrast, they also find that work experience in a neighborhood has little impact on competence. Training is also important in determining differences in the gap between knowledge and practice among Tanzanian clinicians (Leonard, Masatu, and Vialou 2007). But training differences between clinicians, while nontrivial, do not tell the entire story. Besides training, the study highlights the importance of the type of organization a clinician works for (public, nongovernmental, private). In their sample, organization type accounts for 50 percent of the dependent variable's variation. But considering these numbers together can be misleading: the authors are limited by their sample size and are forced to run a number of reduced form regressions, making the results' meaning unclear. Even so, it is apparent that a good deal of the variation in practice quality is explained by these differences between clinicians.

(continued next page)

Box 5.1 *(continued)*

Using data from Paraguay, Das and Sohnesen (2007) consider the possibility that clinicians make strategic effort choices. Such choices would imply that their motivation is intrinsic, tied to the characteristics of the patients they serve. Das and Sohnesen analyzed clinician behavior toward patients relative to both clinician and patient characteristics. For patients, the study focused on wealth, hypothesizing that clinicians would discriminate against patients based on income. Primary results suggest little difference in doctor effort across different patient backgrounds but large differences across physicians and facilities along the lines of doctor gender, contract type, facility type, and doctor salary. Importantly, clinicians did not vary effort according to the income of their patients. The authors conclude that clinicians do not discriminate against poor patients, but it is not clear whether the authors are capturing social preferences with this result.

A Framework for Health Worker Performance

This section offers a model of health worker performance[5] that allows us to think about the interaction of the multiple factors at work. Figure 5.3 shows a rough schematic presentation of the factors and decisions around health worker performance. The health system is driven by policy, but policy makers have only a few tools to improve the health system, called *policy levers*. From the perspective of health worker performance, these levers affect the supply of certain *health worker characteristics*, either by selecting different types of health workers to enter the system or by training health workers with different skills and personalities. These health workers supply *service inputs* into health care when they interact with patients. *Policy levers* act as tools to encourage (or discourage) health workers to supply certain service inputs. The quality of practitioners' interactions with patients can be described by a series of *service attributes*. Although policy can affect service attributes directly (setting fees, or building laboratories on site), most service attributes are determined by the provision of *service inputs* by health workers themselves. These service attributes are the factors that patients use to determine whether to seek care (and at which facility). The service attributes combined with demand determines *performance outputs* and *health system outcomes*. One of the more important performance outputs is health worker utility, particularly income or self-satisfaction, because anticipating utility determines the levels and service inputs that health workers will provide.

Figure 5.3   Model Schematic for Health Worker Performance

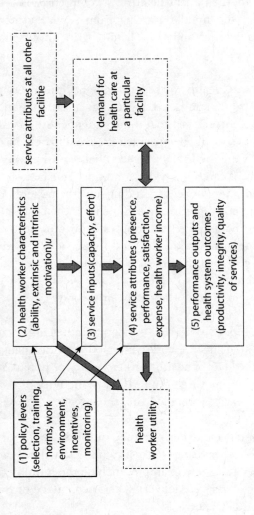

Broadly, the model shows that policy levers → health worker characteristics → service inputs → service attributes → performance outputs → health system outcomes.

The schematic representation and the model of health worker performance are easiest to explain by starting with the key element of any health care system: the patient-health worker interaction. Thus, we begin our discussion in the middle, moving from service attributes through health system outcomes and then from service inputs back to policy levers.

- *Service attributes.* Health workers provide health care to patients with at least four attributes: presence, performance, satisfaction, and expense. Presence represents the fact that if the patient chose to visit a particular provider, services would be provided (because the clinician is present). Performance is the medically assessed quality of the care, compared to some standard of care for a given condition. Satisfaction is how happy patients are with the services, including how the patient perceives quality, politeness, and responsiveness. Expense is the cost to the patient of the services provided. These attributes contribute to the demand for health care, in particular the demand for services at a given provider. The provision of health care also potentially generates revenue or income for the health worker, a feature which is not important to patients,[6] but can be important to health workers.

- *Performance outputs.* Whereas service attributes are measured at the level of the patient-health worker interaction, performance outputs are measured at the level of health worker, facility, or potentially the health system. We examine three types: the productivity of health workers, the quality of services provided, and the integrity of services provided.

- *Health system outcomes.* Performance outputs are important because they improve health system outcomes in society. There are many possible outcomes, but some examples include the number of immunizations, number of assisted deliveries, and percentage of the population covered with quality services.

- *Service inputs.* Provider effort and capacity are the service inputs, determining the attributes of a patient's visit. Effort is both whether the health worker provides a given service and how hard he or she works to diagnose and treat the patient. Capacity is the ability of a health worker to provide certain services, generally limited by training and the equipment available in the health facility. Whereas there may be an expectation that capacity, not effort, limits performance, overwhelming empirical evidence from developing countries points to inadequate effort. The Hawthorne effect demonstrates large changes in the quality of care in the hour following the arrival of a peer at the health facility (see box 5.2 later in the chapter). If quality can change simply because someone visits the health worker, it cannot be limited by training or equipment, because these things cannot change that quickly. Effort is not the only input into health care quality, but it is an important one in this context.

- *Health worker characteristics.* The characteristics of a health worker—including ability and intrinsic and extrinsic motivation—determine effort and capacity. Motivation directly affects effort. Further, the source of motivation will also have an important impact on the type of effort exerted, determining performance, satisfaction, and expense.

- *Policy levers.* The policy levers are selection, training, norms, work environment, incentives, and monitoring. The category of policy levers is a list of ways that policy makers can influence the outputs and outcomes given the motivation and abilities of health workers. Policy makers can design the education and recruitment of health workers so as to select those with the greatest ability or with certain motivational characteristics. Initial and continued training and established and encouraged norms can change the behavior of health workers: increasing their capacity to provide health care or motivating them to provide greater and more appropriate effort. Policy levers also affect the characteristics of health workers directly, through work environment, incentives, and monitoring.

A Model of Health Worker Performance

This section describes a model of health worker performance.

Service Inputs Lead to Service Attributes

This descriptive model follows directly from the framework presented above. We begin by examining the characteristics of a visit if a particular patient chose to visit a particular health worker. The visit remains hypothetical until the patient, comparing the service characteristics that would be available at all potential providers, decides to visit the health worker. The health worker chooses the services that he or she will provide based on the condition of the patient (and potentially other characteristics) as well as his or her own capacity to provide services. The choice of what services to provide generates three attributes of the visit: performance, satisfaction, and expense.

We focus on performance first. Performance is a combination of effort, competence, and whether a particular service is indicated (medically useful) for the patient. Performance is positive if the health worker is capable of performing the service and provides the effort to do so, and the item is indicated. Take the example of using a stethoscope to listen to a patient's breathing pattern. Capacity requires a stethoscope and the knowledge of how to use it. Its use is indicated if the patient's condition suggests listening to the heartbeat is medically useful. Effort is whether the health worker chooses to use the stethoscope. Performance is only positive when the stethoscope is present, the health worker knows how to use it, the condition indicates its use, and the health worker uses it. Providing items that are useless (not indicated by the patient's condition) but not dangerous does not increase or decrease performance.

Effort also produces satisfaction for patients and is judged by the patient. Just as each service contributes to performance if it is indicated by the patient's condition, each service contributes to satisfaction if patients with that condition value the service. Performance and satisfaction can, however, be different: the same service can contribute to performance but not satisfaction, satisfaction but not performance, or both. Bedside manner, politeness, and responsiveness are elements of satisfaction but not of performance. Satisfaction can also be contrary to performance. In some cases, what a patient wants is contrary to professional standards, and providing that service is both good for satisfaction and bad for performance.

For patients, an important feature of the services provided by a health worker is their expenditure on the services provided. The expenditure is determined by the services provided and the fee for those services. Note that the health worker cannot charge for the effort provided, only whether a service was provided. These expenses do not include nonmonetary costs (a patient's lost earnings) or travel costs. Fees are not a function of the capacity of the health worker and are frequently not a function of effort. For example, patients often pay a fixed fee for the consultation—which does not differ by the number of services provided—rather than for performance or satisfaction.

Finally, effort and capacity influence the health worker's income. The expenditure of patients is not the same as the income of health workers. In some cases, health workers earn the fees paid by patients, but they also have to pay costs to provide these services (the wholesale cost of medicines, for example). In some cases, even if there is no charge for a service, the employer may still compensate the health worker for providing the service. It is also possible that the employer will compensate a health worker only when he or she provides a service that is indicated for the patient's condition. Thus health worker income is a function of the fees charged, services' costs, and direct incentives from the employer. In deciding whether to provide a given service, the health worker is potentially concerned with the change in income from providing that service, not overall income. Thus, health workers may earn a high salary, but what matters for effort is the additional income from services provided.

Three common empirically measured service attributes (performance measures) can be drawn from this simple model: adherence to protocol, competence, and presence (absenteeism).

Adherence is the proportion of required items actually provided, among all required items, for a given patient, health worker, and work environment. Competence is the proportion of this same list that the health worker is able to provide. Adherence is a function of average effort for that type of patient and the competence of the provider. This two-part contribution to adherence allows us to examine the two important inputs into adherence separately. Increasing effort or capacity can improve adherence. More important, the value of increasing effort is a function of capacity, and the value of increasing capacity is a function of effort. When effort is low, increasing capacity has low returns; when capacity is high, the value of increasing effort is high.

To measure presence (absenteeism) we need to know whether the health worker would provide any services for a hypothetical visit. Thus, presence is a variable that measures whether the patient can expect to receive services if they were to visit the provider: a hypothetical measure of the probability of receiving care conditional on visiting a provider. Thus, if the health worker is always present (even if they provide very low effort), the expected presence is 1; if the health worker is present half of the time, expected presence is 0.5, whether the health worker provides high or low effort when they are there. Presence is the obvious counterpart to absenteeism. Just as with expected presence, absenteeism does not take into account the effort that health workers provide when they are there, nor does it take into account whether the patient visits the provider.

A health worker is absent if they are not available to see patients, whether there are patients or not.

Service Attributes Lead to Performance Outputs

As we introduce outputs, we are no longer discussing the attributes of hypothetical visits to providers. A visit can contribute to an output only if it occurs. Therefore, we need to know whether the patient will actually go to a particular provider when they suffer from a particular illness or condition. Note that patients do not demand particular services; they visit the provider when they are sick and are offered particular services. It is easiest to think of demand as a binary choice: the patient visits or the patient does not visit.

Demand. The demand for services provided at a particular facility is a function of patient satisfaction, expense, and presence (the probability that a health worker will be present for that particular visit), as well as these same characteristics at all other available facilities. Demand for services at one facility can go up because a health worker is more likely to be present, charges lower fees, or provides services that boost patient satisfaction. Demand can also rise because the other potential providers do a worse job on any of these. Note that all attributes that attract patients are hypothetical—what would happen if the patient visited— and do not indicate that the patient actually visits all other places. Thus, when effort leads to increased satisfaction (and does not greatly increase the expenses), it increases the probability that a patient will visit.

Productivity. Measured by the number of services provided by each health worker, productivity depends on the health worker's effort and the number of patients seeking care. The service is provided if the patient comes to the health worker and the health worker is present. A service is not provided if demand for the provider is zero or the health worker does not provide the service. The productivity of a health worker in a given work environment is the total number of each type of service provided over all patients—or the weighted sum of all services provided, where weight represents the importance (or cost) of each type of service provided. Note that productivity indicates only the number of services provided, not the number of quality services or even the number of indicated services provided. If a service has zero or negative weight on performance, it is still a service provided.

Quality of services. It is possible to measure the quality of a provider, facility, or health system by looking at the average performance for all services provided. Quality is similar to adherence, but measured over a wide range of services. The quality-weighted productivity of a health worker, facility, or system depends on the demand for services provided, as well as the average performance or quality of services provided by a health worker, facility, organization, or country, as demanded by patients. Looking at this measure by type of service and by practitioner and work environment is productive.

A given sector's overall performance is the performance for all services provided (available and demanded), divided by the number of services provided. When the performance for each service is high, overall performance will be high. If the demand for services with high performance is high and the demand for services with low performance is low, overall performance will be high, even if the performance for existing services is average. Demand and performance interact to determine overall performance.

Integrity. Integrity reflects the extent that health workers provide services that are in their patients' best interest. Because performance also reflects the patients' best interest, we choose a definition that contains different information about the services provided. The integrity of the services provided by a health worker is a function of the expense of indicated and provided services, divided by the expense of provided services. In other words, the integrity of the visit is measured by the proportion of total expenses incurred that are indicated for the patient's condition. Note that this is the profession's view of value, not the patient's. Patients might value services that are not indicated and not value some services that are indicated.

This definition is connected to adherence, but instead of the proportion of indicated items actually provided, it reflects the number of indicated items out of the total number of items provided, as well as the cost of those services. Whereas adherence increases if health workers perform more indicated services, integrity increases when fewer unnecessary services are provided. Integrity also reflects each item's expense, suggesting a motivation for providing more effort than is indicated: earning fees. A visit to a health worker characterized by indicated services has greater professional value, potentially reflecting a health worker with greater integrity. Note that this measure does not reflect the average cost of the visit (which matters to patients) but the proportion of the average expense that is professionally indicated.

Health Worker Characteristics Lead to Service Inputs

The health worker maximizes utility when deciding what effort to provide to a patient. In the short run, his or her capacity is predetermined. Effort has a direct cost, and its benefits come from the attributes of a visit to a health worker (performance, satisfaction, and expense) as well as the income earned from the visit. Recall the important features for health workers, all determined by effort: performance, satisfaction, expenditure, and income.

The benefit of exerting effort is a function of these four attributes and the weight health workers put on each. How much health workers care about performance, patient satisfaction, their own income, and patient fees (expenditure) varies, reflecting the tastes of health workers. In addition, how much health workers care about performance can vary by the service provided and the work environment. Thus a health worker can be described by his or her preferences for performance as well as for service- and environment-based performance.

How much health workers care about patient satisfaction varies by the patient's characteristics, and therefore some health workers prefer satisfaction and some prefer identity-based satisfaction.

Income earned from providing a service can vary considerably across patients, but how much health workers care about income varies only by health worker.

How much health workers care about patient expenses can vary by patient type and health worker, producing preferences for expenditure and identity-based expenditure. Note that if health workers care about expenditure, they prefer lower expenditure for their patients—expenditure is not the same as income.

Thus the health worker potentially gains utility from each service to the degree that it increases performance, satisfaction, and income, and decreases expenditure. But providing services has a cost—the opportunity cost of effort. When the health worker decides only whether to provide a service, he or she will exert effort if the gains from visit attributes exceed the cost of effort.

The health worker provides effort only once, so if any source of motivation is large enough, the health worker will provide effort. For example, if the net fee earned from a service is worth more than the cost of effort for that service, a health worker who is not motivated by performance or satisfaction will provide the service. At the same time, a health worker who cares about performance or satisfaction will provide the service even if he or she earns no income from it. Thus, sources of motivation are, in many cases, substitutes; either source of motivation can lead to effort, but motivation from both sources does not necessarily lead to increased provision.

When a service is indicated, but does not lead to patient satisfaction (and when providers do not care about patient expenses), the service is provided only if the health worker cares about performance or is compensated by their employer for providing that service. When a service is not indicated, but leads to patient satisfaction (and when providers do not care about patient expenses), the service is provided only if the provider cares about patient satisfaction or revenue.

Health worker utility and patient demand. The model only describes what the health worker would do when visited by a particular type of patient. To understand a health worker's motivation, we must also consider whether the patient seeks the service and what other activities the health worker must perform. For example, by considering demand, we see that patient satisfaction can be an important indirect source of motivation for health workers who are motivated entirely by earned income; without patients, they have no income.

Performance and patient demand. This simple model of one patient's visit introduces an interesting conundrum for the health worker motivated only by performance. When performance also leads to patient satisfaction, the health worker will augment patient load by performing activities that raise performance and by not performing activities that do not raise performance. Since the health worker earns utility from performance, he or she can choose an optimal workload by raising fees when he or she has too many patients.[7] The health worker will earn greater utility from performance as well as greater income, even if he or she is not motivated by income.

The conundrum arises if performance does not automatically lead to patient satisfaction. The health worker motivated by performance can experience lower utility by increasing effort slightly. Improved performance leads to a smaller workload and fewer opportunities to earn utility from providing high performance care. Why? Because this type of health worker does not earn utility from knowing that they would provide high quality care if they had patients; they earn utility from actually providing high quality care to patients who visit. Thus, even if health workers care nothing for satisfaction and income, they may find their utility increases by "giving-in" to patients' demands in order to earn utility from providing high-quality care to a larger number of patients. This will be particularly true when effort for a service provides no contribution to performance, but contributes to satisfaction, encouraging the patient to visit and allow the health worker to provide other services that do increase performance. So, a health worker who cares only about performance may be motivated to prescribe unnecessary drugs, even when they know these drugs do not improve performance.

Health worker utility for many patients. Health workers do not make decisions about each hypothetical patient independent of other patients they are seeing. What they would do if a patient was their only patient is likely to be different from what they do when they have many patients. We limit the question by thinking of the activities a health worker faces in a given period, which could be a day or even a week. The health worker decides how much effort to exert (which services to provide) taking into account the total effort that he or she will exert over the period. Each unit of effort has a benefit in the individual visit, independent of other visits, but the cost of effort depends on how many other visits there are.

As effort's cost depends on all the activities of the health worker, we can introduce the intuitive concept that health workers have a limited amount of time—or get tired after seeing many patients. Thus, the cost of effort for one patient rises if the health worker sees more patients. When a health worker sees two patients a day and provides low effort, it is because there is no good reason to provide effort. When a health worker sees 60 patients a day and provides low effort, it is because the cost of working harder for each of the 60 patients would be overwhelming, even if desired.

Increasing motivation can have multiple impacts on effort. When a health worker has low overall motivation, he or she provides low effort. Any rise in motivation is thus likely to have two impacts. First, it will encourage the health worker to provide more services to each patient. Second, it will increase his or her willingness to see more patients. The second effect arises because, at low effort, little additional motivation can overcome the cost of effort; the cost of working harder is not very high. At high effort, however, increases in motivation from other sources are less likely to improve the quality of care for individual patients or to raise the number of patients that a health worker is willing to see. This is because additional units of effort are very costly to health workers who already provide high effort.

More important, increases in incentives are likely to be tied to particular services. The health worker's employer can choose to implement a reward for a type of service by changing the compensation for that service. This will cause the health worker to provide more of this service, increasing effort. At the same time, it raises the cost to the health worker for all other services because it increases total effort. If the health worker was providing another service to patients because it raised performance, and the health worker cared about performance, more direct incentives may cause the health worker to decrease the other service.

This task shifting is particularly important in health care because no employer can pay a health worker for every necessary service, so increasing raising incentives for a subset of services will have important consequences if health workers have no other source of motivation.

Also, for a health worker motivated entirely by performance, raising incentives for particular services will increase income, but not motivation. He or she earns income from already doing the right things, and is not more likely to do them because of this incentive. So, for performance-motivated health workers, incentives do not help, and can even damage performance for such workers.

As chapter 14 on intrinsic motivation shows, empirical evidence points to a crowding out of motivation. This can happen for two reasons. First, as with task shifting, pushing health workers to do more of one service can cause them to do less of another. Second, and more pressing, it can signal importance to the health worker. Thus, when the employer changes incentives, it suggests to health workers that income matters, not performance by itself. This can attract health workers who care more about income than performance, and it can teach health workers that their priorities are wrong.

Description of Health Worker Characteristics

Health workers respond by varying degrees to performance, satisfaction, income, and patient expenditures. Thus, each health worker's personality can be summarized by the weights they put on these attributes. These variables do not, however, explain why health workers are motivated to provide these characteristics.

Generally, health workers with intrinsic motivation do not need external incentives; they are motivated by performance, satisfaction, or expense.

Those with extrinsic sources of motivation care primarily about income. Of course, health workers can be motivated by both at the same time. Chapter 12 examines extrinsic motivation among health workers, and chapter 14 looks at intrinsic motivation.

In addition, the health worker's ability is an important characteristic. Here, ability measures the degree that health workers can learn or transform training into capacity, determined by the combination of training and ability.

Policy Levers

Policy can have an important impact in two ways. First, it can determine the characteristics of health workers, including their ability and intrinsic and extrinsic motivation. Second, it can interact with the characteristics of existing health workers, using their ability and motivation. This chapter cannot provide an extensive overview of policy, but can point out how policy interacts with our model.

First, policy levers can determine the underlying characteristics of those who choose to become health workers. This may be particularly important for intrinsic motivation and ability. As chapter 14 discusses, evidence shows that much of an individual's motivation is a stable characteristic, something he or she is either born with or learns early in life.

Second, policy levers can mold the intrinsic motivation triggered during the training experience through shared norms within the health profession. Thus, individuals are exposed to training that allows them to continue to enjoy acting as professionals for the remainder of their careers.

Third, through monitoring and incentives, or through changes in the workplace's structure, policy can boost the effort of health workers. These levers do not change the sources of motivation, but do change the opportunity to earn utility. The most straightforward example is offering additional payments (rewards, bonuses, pay for performance) for specific services when they are indicated. This incentive interacts with a health worker's extrinsic motivation to encourage further effort. Such examples can also be found for intrinsic motivation.

Changes in the workplace environment can alter how much effort a health worker is willing to exert to improve performance. For example, the Hawthorne effect shows that when the average health worker is observed by a peer, the health worker's effort greatly increases in the short run (box 5.2). This effect is unlikely to be caused by extrinsic motivation: if the health worker believed that the peer altered his or her

Box 5.2

The Hawthorne Effect as Evidence of Untapped Motivation

The effect of peer-based esteem-seeking is apparent in the Hawthorne effect, when peers observe health workers performing their normal activities. Leonard and Masatu (2006) examined the adherence to protocol of health workers in a sample of facilities in Tanzania. In each facility a clinician on the research team sat in and observed one of the clinicians working in the clinic. Box figure 5.2.1 shows average adherence before (t from −10 to 0) and after (t from 1 to 10) any clinicians knew the team had arrived. The team observed the activities of one clinician in each facility and the average is shown as the solid line; the dotted line shows the average for clinicians who were not observed.

Box Figure 5.2.1   Adherence Over the Course of One Day

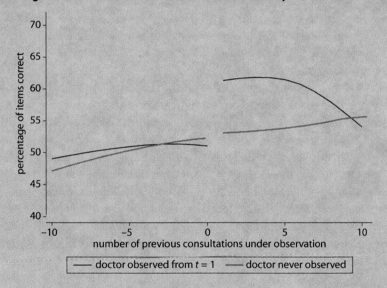

Both groups provide approximately the same quality care under normal circumstances. As soon as a peer entered the room, however, observed clinicians increased adherence by 20 percent (10 percentage points over a baseline of 50 percent). Typical of the Hawthorne effect, this change is only temporary. The clinicians returned to their normal adherence after approximately 10 patients. There was no change for other clinicians.

The large change in adherence to protocol shows that the average clinician can increase effort without any increase in competence or other resources.

income-earning possibilities, he or she would not return to normal effort in the peer's presence. Instead, it shows that health workers react to peers and expect peers to provide feedback. When the peer is passive, this changes the motivation of the health worker, and he or she returns to normal. The Hawthorne effect demonstrates the importance of the work environment for encouraging and rewarding intrinsic behavior.

Conclusion

A study in rural Tanzania found that a quarter of medically trained clinicians ask their patients only two questions, never touch the patient, and spend only three minutes from the moment the patient enters to the moment they leave with a prescription (Das, Hammer, and Leonard 2008). This is unacceptable health care. Almost all these clinicians can demonstrate that they know how to treat patients (Leonard and Masatu 2005), and in Tanzania, at least, the facilities have the medicines to treat most of the illnesses seen. More important, because the health workers are trained and have resources, this situation demonstrates a failure of effort and therefore motivation.

Thus, this book rightly discusses both the shortage of health workers and the low motivation of existing health workers. In developing a model of health worker performance, we set out to describe the interaction between health worker and patient in a way that allows for absenteeism, low effort, low training, and poor quality care. Moreover, we set out to show the link between these outcomes and motivation, and between these outcomes and policy levers. No health worker goes to work as a machine, seeking to accomplish all tasks they were trained to do. Health workers choose whether to go to work, how much effort to exert, and which circumstances to do so in. Their effort helps to determine whether they have patients, how many they will see, and which kinds they will see. The reasons they do this are many, and vary greatly from health worker to health worker. Two health workers with very different motivations may do the same thing, just as two similarly motivated health workers may do very different things in different work environments.

Notes

1. Research is documented in Leonard and Masatu (2005, 2006, 2007, 2008, 2010a, 2010b); Das, Hammer, and Leonard (2008); Klemick, Leonard, and Masatu (2009); and Leonard, Masatu, and Vialou (2007).

2. See Masatu, pers. comm.; Jack and others (2009); Lindelöw and Serneels (2006); Serneels and others (2004).

3. Masatu, pers. comm.

4. Adherence and competence are discussed in more detail below. The data for these graphs are discussed in Leonard and Masatu (2010b) and in more detail in chapter 14.

5. The model presented in this chapter is based on the more detailed presentation in Brock and others (2011).

6. Income for the health worker is not the same as expense to the patient, even in the private sector.

7. Raising fees only regulates patient flow. This type of health worker does not gain utility from increasing fees because either he or she cares nothing for money or he or she works in an institution that does not pass fees on to the health worker directly.

References

Boekeloo, B. O., L. Schiavo, D. L. Rabin, R. T. Conlon, C. S. Jordan, and D. J. Mundt. 1994. "Self-Reports of HIV Risk Factors by Patients at a Sexually Transmitted Disease Clinic: Audio vs. Written Questionnaires." *American Journal of Public Health* 84 (5): 754–60.

Brock, J. M., K. L. Leonard, and P. Serneels. 2011 "Health Worker Performance: A Model of Health Worker Motivation in Low Resource Settings." University of Maryland, College Park, MD.

Das J., and J. Hammer. 2005. "Money for Nothing: The Dire Straits of Medical Practice in Delhi, India." *Journal of Development Economics* 83 (1): 1–36.

Das, J., J. Hammer, and K. L. Leonard. 2008. "The Quality of Medical Advice in Low-Income Countries." *Journal of Economic Perspectives* 22 (2): 93–114.

Das J., and T. P. Sohnesen. 2007. "Variations in Doctor Effort: Evidence from Paraguay." *Health Affairs* 26 (3): w324–w337.

Fairbrother, G., K. L. Hanson, S. Friedman, and G. C. Butts. 1999. "The Impact of Physician Bonuses, Enhanced Fees, and Feedback on Childhood Immunization Coverage Rates." *American Journal of Public Health* 89 (2): 171–75.

Jack, W., J. de Laat, K. Hanson, and A. Soucat. 2009. *Incentives and Dynamics in the Ethiopian Health Worker Labor Market.* Washington, DC: World Bank.

Klemick, H., K. L. Leonard, and M. C. Masatu. 2009. "Defining Access to Health Care: Evidence on the Importance of Quality and Distance in Rural Tanzania." *American Journal of Agricultural Economics* 91 (2): 347–58.

Leonard, K. L., and M. C. Masatu. 2005. "The Use of Direct Clinician Observation and Vignettes for Health Services Quality Evaluation in Developing Countries." *Social Science and Medicine* 61 (9): 1944–51.

Leonard, K. L., and M. C. Masatu. 2006. "Outpatient Process Quality Evaluation and the Hawthorne Effect." *Social Science and Medicine* 63 (9): 2330–40.

———. 2007. "Variations in the Quality of Care Accessible to Rural Communities in Tanzania." *Health Affairs* 26 (3): w380–w392.

———. 2008. "Moving from the Lab to the Field: Exploring Scrutiny and Duration Effects in Lab Experiments." *Economic Letters* 100 (2): 284–87.

———. 2010a. "Professionalism and the Know-Do Gap: Exploring Intrinsic Motivation among Health Workers in Tanzania." *Health Economics* 19 (12): 1461–77.

———. 2010b. "Using the Hawthorne Effect to Examine the Gap between a Doctor's Best Possible Practice and Actual Performance." *Journal of Development Economics* 93 (2): 226–34.

Leonard, K. L., M. C. Masatu, and A. Vialou. 2007. "Getting Doctors to Do Their Best: The Roles of Ability and Motivation in Health Care." *Journal of Human Resources* 42 (3): 682–700.

Lindelöw, M., and P. Serneels. 2006. "The Performance of Health Workers in Ethiopia: Results from Qualitative Research." *Social Science and Medicine* 62 (9): 2225–35.

Rowe, A. K., D. de Sarigny, C. F. Lanata, and C. G. Victoria. 2005. "How can we achieve and maintain high quality performance of health workers in low-resource settings?" Lancet 2005 (Sep) 366 (9490): 1026–1035.

Santoso, B. 1996. "Small Group Intervention vs. Formal Seminar for Improving Appropriate Drug Use." *Social Science and Medicine* 42 (8): 1163–68.

Serneels, P., M. Lindelöw, J. G. Montalvo, and A. Barr. 2004. *An Honorable Calling? Results from a Survey with Final Year Nursing and Medical Students.* Washington, DC: World Bank.

Soumerai, S. B., and J. Avorn. 1990. "Principles of Educational Outreach ('Academic Detailing') to Improve Clinical Decision Making." *Journal of the American Medical Association* 263 (4): 549–56.

Tierney, W. M., S. L. Hui, and C. J. McDonald. 1986. "Delayed Feedback of Physician Performance Versus Immediate Reminders of Performance. Effects on Physician Compliance." *Medical Care* 24 (8): 659–66.

CHAPTER 6

Fiscal Issues in Scaling Up the Health Workforce

Agnes Soucat, Marko Vujicic, Aly Sy, and Claude Sekabaraga

Low public demand due to fiscal constraints is often considered a major impediment to the growth of the health workforce. Yet the effect of caps on expansion of the wage bill has been limited. Several African countries have developed innovative approaches to increase the number and remuneration of their health workers, some quite successfully. Most of Africa is now enjoying rapid economic growth, and fiscal constraints are likely to relax. The relevance of each policy depends on the country, and policy makers must weigh challenges against expected benefits.

Africa is the region with the lowest ratio of health workers to population. Restrictive wage bill policies in African countries are often invoked as a key factor restricting the growth of the health workforce. In most, a large number of health workers are employed in the public sector, their salaries often paid from the government's overall wage bill budget. When governments limit expansion of the overall wage bill—often for sound economic reasons—they may constrain health worker hiring. Much of the global debate on health worker deficiencies focuses on the limits that fiscal constraints place on the scaling up of the publicly employed health workforce (Vujicic, Ohiri, and Sparkes 2009). But are fiscal constraints really the most important obstacles to expanding the health workforce in Africa?

To date, policy experts have debated the health worker deficiency in a data void because of the lack of documented country experiences. This chapter aims to fill that void, at least in part, by reviewing how health wage bill budgets are determined and examining how fiscal policies affect the ability to expand health sector staffing. It draws on a review of literature and country case studies from Ghana (World Bank, forthcoming), Ethiopia, Kenya, Mali, Rwanda (World Bank 2010b), Uganda, and Zambia (Vujicic, Ohiri, and Sparkes 2009). It also looks at the strategies that countries pursue to expand public financing for health workers, and it concludes by outlining a way forward for policy analysis.

Although wage bill ceilings can be restrictive, they do not result from unsound fiscal policy. They generally are resorted to in systems where health workers are part of an integrated and centralized civil service system (box 6.1), rather than being a health sector issue per se. Several

---

Box 6.1

Wage Bill Ceilings

A wage bill ceiling is usually a short-term response to a fiscal crisis or to a wage bill that exceeds the budget. Governments may also enact a ceiling as part of an effort to reduce the size of the civil service. A ceiling usually provides only a short-term fix that must ultimately be supplanted by budget and civil service reforms.

Developing countries with International Monetary Fund (IMF) programs often focus on controlling the size of their overall wage bill. Half of all IMF Poverty Reduction and Growth Facilities have some form of wage bill conditionality, implemented in countries with high wage bills relative to gross domestic product or where government expenditures are growing rapidly. A wage bill ceiling should be accompanied by civil service reform and should be imposed only when other options have failed.

The IMF now recognizes that its programs overuse wage bill ceilings. Although a ceiling is a useful temporary device when out-of-control payrolls threaten macroeconomic stability, such situations are rare. In practice, the ceilings imposed often lack a clear rationale. Critics claim that they hinder low-income countries from expanding employment in areas that are key to reducing poverty, such as health and education, compromising the countries' ability to achieve the Millennium Development Goals.

(continued next page)

Box 6.1 *(continued)*

Recent evidence offers some support for that claim. In response to the criticism, the IMF reconsidered its position, issuing new guidelines that call for transparent and flexible ceilings that can accommodate higher spending in the social sectors, particularly spending of donor funds.

As countries' budgeting and payroll systems strengthen, the need for wage bill ceilings will diminish. Governments should impose ceilings only in exceptional cases and with clear justification, limited duration, sufficient flexibility, and periodic reassessment.

Source: Verhoeven and Segura 2007; Fedelino, Schwartz, and Verhoeven 2006; Vujicic, Ohiri, and Sparkes 2009.

African countries have addressed this problem successfully by improving management, decentralizing, giving facilities more autonomy, legal reform, and better alignment of donor funding to country systems.

The Links between Fiscal Policy and the Health Workforce

The gap estimated to exist between current public sector wage bills and the financing needed to support health workers in most African countries is large. Scheffler and others (2009) estimated that the annual wage cost for the number of health workers required to meet the health goals of 31 African countries would be about $3.6 billion (see chapter 2). Their study estimated that the current annual wage bill in those countries is about $1 billion. Even if enough additional health workers were available in the job market, bridging the $2.6 billion gap would require the countries to grow economically, as well as to mobilize both public and private financing.

The impact of fiscal policy on the health workforce depends on the workers' employment arrangements. In Africa three models predominate. The *integrated civil service model*, inherited from the postcolonial integration of public service delivery, remains common in many places. In it, the government employs health workers directly as civil servants, and their wages are part of the overall government wage bill, along with those of teachers, police, and other civil servants. Wage policies are often rigid, as they are constrained by cross-sectoral considerations. To gain flexibility, some countries experiment with contract workers. The legal framework often remains unchanged, however, and contractors are almost always hired as full civil servants as the result of political pressure (World Bank 2008). In Benin, for example, all short-term contract workers in the health sector were integrated in the general civil service in 2011.

The *decentralized model* is an increasingly common alternative. As more countries adopt fiscal decentralization, subnational units, such as districts or local governments, also employ health workers. In this model, health worker remuneration may still be part of the wage bill as an earmarked grant, as in Uganda. Or it may be part of a general needs-based block grant handled as a transfer, as in Ethiopia. Such decentralization can create more flexibility, but much depends on local political and economic conditions. Zambia famously decentralized the health wage bill to district health boards in the 1990s but later reverted to the integrated civil service model.

In the third, *health facility model*, health workers' wages are paid from the operating budgets of autonomous facilities, whether private or public. The government may subsidize wages through transfers, which do not count directly against its overall wage bill. Such transfers often occur via government subsidies to faith-based providers, as in Uganda and Zambia, or to community associations (CSCOMs), as in Mali. Health workers may also be self-employed and receive government subsidies to deliver important public services, as are general practitioners in rural Mali.

In the integrated civil service model, the ministry of health typically has little authority over its salary budget. That authority usually lies with treasury or ministry of finance. Because salaries are the largest share of government health spending (35 percent to 55 percent in Sub-Saharan countries), the ministry of health thus lacks effective control over a big part of its total budget (figure 6.1). Augmenting the health workforce thus requires either reallocating salary money from other sectors to health, or increasing the overall wage bill. Reallocating salary is politically difficult. Under the civil service model, the budgeting process for the health wage bill usually involves two steps. The central authority (often the ministry of finance) determines the overall resources available for the wage bill for the next one to three years. Line ministries and the central authority then negotiate which budgets to increase and which to cut. Reallocating salary budgets can also be difficult when governments do not implement their stated policies.

Wages are adjusted for all sectors at the same time. However, specific sector measures can also be implemented. Kenya, Rwanda, and Zambia

Figure 6.1   Example of Alternative Budgeting Systems

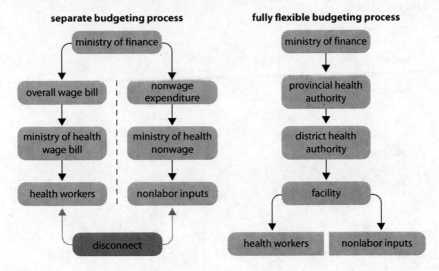

Source: Vujicic, Ohiri, and Sparkes 2009.

had explicit policies to protect the health sector during a period of overall government wage bill downsizing. In Kenya and Rwanda, the policies were effective: the health sectors benefited from steadily increasing shares of the overall wage bill. In Zambia, the health sector share of the overall wage bill decreased steadily, however. The government, contrary to its stated policy, cut the health wage budget more than those of other sectors and did not give priority to health spending. In another case, in the context of fiscal expansion, the health wage bill of Ghana increased over time as a share of the total wage bill. In Uganda, its share remained stable while the overall wage bill increased slightly over time (figure 6.2).

Reallocating salary budgets may also be of little help to scaling up the health workforce under the civil service model. In Kenya, despite the availability of a large number of health workers, and despite the priority given to the health sector in the budget, the number of staff hired each year remained flat. Reductions in the overall wage bill constrained any scaling-up of the health workforce, at least in the short term. If the over-all wage bill is shrinking, even a government that gives priority to the health sector may not be able to support large-scale hiring.

Increasing the overall wage bill also poses significant challenges. A strong economic rationale supports controlling the size of the public

Figure 6.2   Share of the Health Wage Bill in National Wage Bills in Selected African Countries

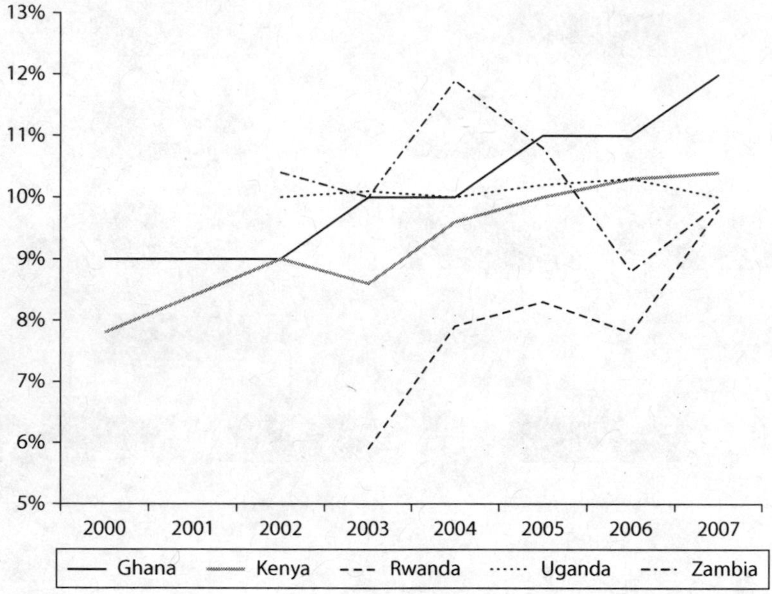

Source: Authors.

sector wage bill, measured in relation to gross domestic product (GDP). Excessive spending on wages can lead to macroeconomic volatility, crowding out other spending. The available evidence does not clearly define the level at which spending becomes too high, triggering those negative effects. Ministries of health may find it difficult to influence wage bill policy because they often are not party to the decision making.

Yet in most cases the direct fiscal impact of health sector hiring, even if it is greatly expanded, is small. In Sub-Saharan Africa, the health sector is a relatively small portion of the overall civil service at roughly 10 percent (figure 6.3). Simulations for Zambia and Kenya show that raising the number of doctors by 25 percent would only increase the overall wage bill by 0.24 percent in real terms. If the entire health work-force was expanded by 25 percent, the overall wage bill would increase by 2.6 percent. As long as GDP grows by at least that amount, which is well below forecast, such an increase in health hiring would not have much impact on the ratio of the wage bill to GDP.

In practice, however, it is difficult for governments to expand hiring or raise wages in one sector without doing so in other sectors. And when

Figure 6.3   Distribution of Civil Service Employees by Sector

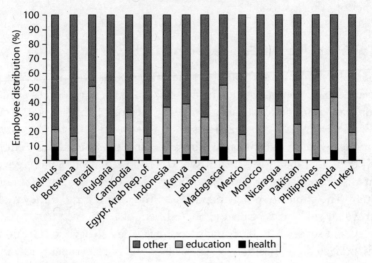

Source: Vujicic, Ohiri, and Sparkes 2009.
Note: For all levels of government.

increased hiring in the health sector spills over into education and other sectors, the fiscal implications become substantial. In Ghana, initially exceptional increases in pay for medical doctors were soon followed by increases for nurses, then teachers. The simulations for Kenya and Zambia show that if hiring in the education sector also increased, the overall wage bill would spike by a much larger amount.

The situation is different where local governments or facilities receive a block grant accounted as a transfer. Because health worker wages are not directly budgeted and accounted for within the overall wage bill, wage bill policies and the health workforce are not directly linked. Operating units (either facilities or local government entities) have significant autonomy over allocating their budgets across wage and nonwage items. They also have flexibility to channel funds from various sources, including facility revenues, to wages.

Expanding the health workforce in the facility model requires larger budgets for operating units. Additional funds may come from the government or other sources, including insurance, user fees, and donors. By mobilizing funds from nongovernment sources in autonomous units, health systems can raise expenditures without affecting the overall wage bill. In this case the health workforce is not part of the civil service, and changes in hiring and wage policies do not directly influence the wage bill policies of other sectors.

Policy Experiences in Sub-Saharan Africa

Africa's economic growth in the past 10 years, as well as increases in official development assistance for health, made more resources available to hire and remunerate health workers (Gottret, Schieber, and Waters 2008). Between 2001 and 2010, six of the world's 10 fastest-growing economies were in Sub-Saharan Africa. Countries adopted different policy options to expand the health workforce in situations where government fiscal policies remain restrictive. There is no one-size-fits-all solution. The choice of policy depends on the country, and policy makers must weigh challenges against expected benefits.

First, and somewhat surprisingly, countries may struggle to ensure that funds budgeted for health worker salaries are actually spent, as budget execution rates often fall well below 100 percent. Administrative inefficiencies in hiring processes, the timing of the budget cycle, and health worker shortages may be to blame. Low budget execution rates and persistently high vacancy rates clearly rule out fiscal constraints to hiring. In Zambia, the budget execution rate for health worker salaries was 50 percent in 2006 and 2007. The government offered jobs to fill vacancies of as much as 40 percent in rural health centers and hospitals (Picazo 2008). Kenya faced a similar ordeal: filling a nursing position advertised by the ministry of health took an average of 15 months. In Madagascar, budget execution rates were less than 70 percent between 2005 and 2008 (World Bank 2010a).

But sometimes resources may not be available. In those cases ministries of health can improve their negotiation strategies in wage bill budgeting processes. When the health workforce is part of the civil service, the health sector competes with other sectors for more money for wages. Ministries of health could ensure that human resources for health strategies are well designed and make a strong case for additional resources. Such efforts involve moving beyond the traditional focus on forecasting long-term staffing needs to a much more incremental, short-term, results-based approach. Ministries of health can identify priority, short-term actions and show how they can produce improvements in the delivery of health services, with corresponding benefits to national priorities.

Ethiopia illustrates this approach. Ethiopia's ministry of health analyzed elements in the system that were preventing increased use of high-impact interventions that support the Millennium Development

Goals, such as family planning and insecticide-treated nets. It prepared a strategy based on the evidence. As part of its strategy, the ministry designed a health extension package, creating a new cadre of health workers to deliver these high impact interventions (see chapter 16). Local governments identified, trained, and hired more than 30,000 young women in rural communities, deploying them over 2006–2009 (Bilal and others 2011). The program was fully financed by the government as part of Ethiopia's budget expansion.

Another way to expand the fiscal space for health wages is to partially disconnect the health workforce from the civil service. That involves enacting particular laws for health workers, who remain public workers but are exempt from general civil service rules. In 1998 Ghana (see Figure 6.4 for staffing and wage bill trend) introduced an Additional Duty Hours Allowance for highly qualified workers to prevent migration. In 2006 it enacted a law establishing an entirely new salary structure for health workers, under which their average wages grew by 20 percent (Appiah-Denkyira and others 2012).

In some countries, including Ethiopia and Nigeria, local government–run health systems are autonomous and receive government subsidies. Block grants to local governments provide flexibility if the national government wishes to raise health spending using domestic resources or donor aid. It can adjust the transferred funds to align with policy objectives and priorities, for example, by introducing a needs-based or poverty-based formula that gives poor rural regions more resources to attract health workers. Districts with the greatest need can expand staffing. Resources become more fungible as the budgeting processes for the health wage bill and for other expenditures are no longer separate.

Because the block grant is part of the transfers, it does not affect the size of the overall wage bill. In both countries, intergovernmental transfers from the federal government are formula-based, with no earmarks for wages. A challenge thus could arise if national objectives and local priorities and capacities are not aligned. Local governments may not give priority to health and may have low capacity to manage the health workforce.

Some countries fully separate the health workforce from the civil service, which brings them closer to the service delivery models of most Organisation for Economic Co-operation and Development (OECD) countries. Such a system requires autonomous facilities, which may be in place in some countries, as in Mali. In other countries, establishing such autonomy would require substantial public sector reforms.

Separating the health workforce and the civil service offers three important advantages: First, facilities that employ health workers have more

Figure 6.4 Public-Sector Health Care Staffing and Wage Bill of the Ministry of Health, Ghana, 1999–2009

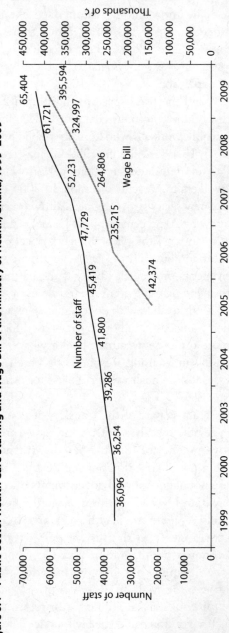

Source: World Bank (forthcoming); based on data from the Controller and Accountant General's Department, the Integrated Personnel and Payroll Database, and the Ministry of Health, Ghana (2005–2009).

control over how their budget is allocated across wage and nonwage items. That control gives them flexibility to combine inputs most effectively to deliver quality services. Second, expanding the autonomy of facilities allows more flexible combinations of finance sources. Government subsidies can be pooled with private sector contributions and donor contributions. Third, when the health workforce is separate from the civil service, health workers are accountable to the facility and no longer move with their budget allocation. If a health worker leaves a facility, the budget for his or her remuneration remains, allowing the facility to hire a replacement.

Rwanda's broad-based reforms show how some of the challenges associated with detaching the health workforce from the civil service can be addressed. In 2008 frontline health service providers moved out of the civil service, becoming employees of autonomous facilities. Of those facilities, 60 percent are public and autonomous, and 40 percent are private and not-for-profit. Rwandan health sector salaries include two components: a fixed component, paid out of a needs-based transfer to the facility, and a variable allowance component based on performance. Allowances, calculated with a well-defined formula, are a main source of remuneration, raising the basic salary by 50 percent to 120 percent (see chapter 13). Facilities can use block grants to hire additional staff and provide bonuses.

The Rwandan system gives districts and facilities much more control over the health wage bill. Facilities pay wages and social benefits, including contributions to the health insurance system and the social security fund. They can supplement the salary budget (which comes from earmarked central funds) and provide incentives to improve retention and health worker performance. The approach has led to greater overall health worker wages—on a performance basis—without any impact on the overall wage bill (box 6.2).

Box 6.2

Rwanda's Performance-Based Financing Reform

In 2008 Rwanda reformed its human resources for health, decentralizing the hiring, management, and payment of health workers to the individual facility.

Rwanda has four main sources of funding for human resources for health. The first is a transfer from the ministry of finance to the autonomous facilities in the form of population-based and poverty-based block grants. The second source is

(continued next page)

Box 6.2 *(continued)*

performance-based grants; some of the grants supplement salaries, but they are not necessarily earmarked for that purpose. The third source is local revenue generated by the facility, such as health insurance reimbursements and user copayments, which can be used to hire lower-cadre health workers. The fourth source is donor funding transferred directly to facilities, most often for HIV treatment and care. Donors fund salaries directly, in accord with Rwanda's policy.

The fixed compensation and the variable, performance-based financing provide substantial resources for paying salaries and allowances. Compensation in the form of fixed salaries grew from $6.4 million to $21.4 million, mostly as a result of a dramatic rise in the number of health workers.

Compensation from the performance-based, variable portion of earnings grew tenfold, from $0.8 million to $8.9 million in just three years (figure B6.2.1). Performance-based financing represented 11.9 percent of the funds paid as salaries in 2005 and 41.6 percent in 2008. As a share of overall public expenditures on human resources for health, this represents an increase from 10.7 percent to 29.4 percent.

Figure B6.2.1   Increases in Basic and Performance-Based Compensation

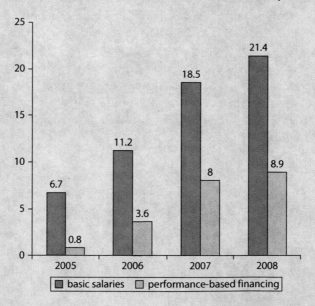

Source: World Bank 2010b.

Mali offers a variation on the full autonomy model. There the government supports community health centers that are run by community associations and private general practitioners in rural areas (see chapter 9). The community health associations and general practitioners operate on a fee-for-service basis but receive an installation grant to start their practices, as well as subsidies to deliver preventive and other public health services.

Donor assistance to developing countries for health has risen substantially in recent years, and donors increasingly identify health workforce capacity as a priority. But the duration of donor funding commitments and the current terms of work in the public sector often do not align. Health workers in the public sector are often hired under permanent contracts, but donor assistance for health is short-term, unpredictable, and volatile.

A recent analysis of wages in several countries suggests that government salaries often do not match those elsewhere in the economy (McCoy and others 2008). Donor funding can crowd out government funding by drawing health workers away from the public sector into donor-funded projects. In Rwanda, salaries in donor-funded projects were five to six times higher than public salaries (World Bank 2010b). If donors make long-term commitments and align their wage policies to the government's, that discrepancy could be corrected. Ghana, Mali, Mozambique, and Uganda receive donor support that helps pay their wage bills. In Malawi, donors provide budget support earmarked for raising health worker salaries (box 6.3). Projects also fund wages, as in Ethiopia, where the multidonor Protection of Basic Service (PBS) program provides block grants to local governments to help pay salaries.

Short-term contracting arrangements also help close the gap between public sector and donor-funded salaries by making it easier to finance salaries with donor aid. In Kenya, the Emergency Hiring Program hired health workers on three-year contracts to match donor commitments, paying their salaries with donor resources (box 6.4). In Rwanda, donor agencies, which cannot directly provide budget support, transfer funds to health facilities to support health workers, consistent with government policy.

Conclusion

Macroeconomic realities limit the expansion of fiscal space in all countries, rich or poor. Over the last decade the limitations have eased in most Sub-Saharan countries as a result of strong economic growth and increased development assistance for health. Although wage bill restrictions can

Box 6.3

Malawi Emergency Human Resources Programme, 2005–2009

To address an acute shortage of health workers in Malawi, the Department for International Development gave budget support to the government to enable it to offer incentives to aid in the recruitment and retention of Malawian staff in government and mission hospitals. The scheme includes a 52 percent taxed salary increment for 11 professional occupational categories, coupled with a major initiative to recruit, create new positions, and re-engage qualified Malawian staff. The Emergency Human Resources Programme—which also expanded health worker training—accomplished its primary goal of increasing the number of professional health workers in Ministry of Health and faith-based (Christian Health Association of Malawi) institutions. Across the 11 priority cadres, the total number of professional health workers funded by the civil service increased by 53 percent, from 5,453 in 2004 to 8,369 in 2009, for an additional cost of $0.70 per capita, representing 8 percent of total health expenditures. In addition, from 2009 salaries for civil servants increased uniformly by an average of 15 percent, compared to an inflation rate of around 8 percent, for a real increase of about 7 percent. Recently, however, the program has been jeopardized by macroeconomic mismanagement and interruption of donor support.

Box 6.4

Aligning Donors with Government Processes and Priorities in Kenya

Kenya shows how donor resources can help expand short-term hiring in the heath sector. Beginning in 2006, donors worked with the Kenya Ministry of Health to develop an Emergency Hiring Program to address staffing shortages in underserved areas. The U.S. President's Emergency Plan for AIDS Relief; the Global Fund to Fight AIDS, Tuberculosis, and Malaria; and the Clinton Foundation provided resources to support hiring health workers on three-year contracts, tied to specific geographic areas.

The program had a substantial impact on the fiscal space for hiring health workers in the public sector. In 2006 health worker hiring in the public sector was

(continued next page)

Box 6.4 *(continued)*

triple the level in previous years, with the majority (83 percent) funded by donors through the program.

Donors issue funds to the government, and the Ministry of Health employs the staff, offering the same salaries and allowances as for regular ministry employees. Because the staff are hired on short-term contracts, the government incurs no contingent wage bill liability. The government has indicated that after three years it will have the resources to absorb the additional staff, but it has not made a formal commitment. The donors have bought time for the government to raise resources.

Evidence suggests, however, that some staff were hired away from private sector clinical jobs and that the program had a limited additional effect in the availability of health service workers in Kenya.

Source: Vujicic, Ohiri, and Sparkes 2009.

limit spending for health worker wages, the constraints that such ceilings place on efforts to improve staffing have been overemphasized. Focusing the policy dialogue on wage bill restrictions is unlikely to make more money available for health workers in Africa.

As most of Africa is enjoying rapid economic growth, fiscal constraints are likely to relax. Many African countries have expanded financing for health workers in recent years. Several governments increased their subsidies for health worker wages dramatically, recruiting and training many workers and improving compensation. Successful strategies include fiscal decentralization, better management and greater efficiency in existing expenditure programs, and new laws to relax the constraints of a unified civil service. Strategies that allow providers autonomy—by separating the health workforce from the rest of the civil service and tapping other sources of financing—have freed up additional financing for health workers. Donors have also found ways to fund human resources through budget support and projects.

Strategies to improve financing for health workers must be country-specific, rooted in analysis of real constraints, and led by national policy makers. As seen in chapter 3, understanding the labor market is critical. When formulating health worker financing strategies, decision makers must consider factors, such as whether a labor shortage exists or unemployment is the problem, and whether reliable information is available on the wage equilibrium point and the market's public–private mix. Decision makers should systematically analyze the information against the fiscal space available for health, whether in the wage bill or as transfers to local governments or autonomous organizations.

References

Appiah-Denkyira, E., C. H. Herbst, A. Soucat, C. Lemiere, and K. Saleh. "Towards Interventions in Human Resources for Health in Ghana": Evidence for Health Workforce Planning and Results. Directions in Development, World Bank, Washington DC.

Bilal, K., C. Herbst, F. Zhao, A. Soucat, and C. Lemière. 2011. "Scaling Up HRH in Ethiopia: A Success Story." In *Yes Africa Can: Success Stories from a Dynamic Continent*, ed. P. Chuhan-Pole and M. Angwafo, 433–44. Washington, DC: World Bank.

Fedelino, A., M. Schwartz, and M. Verhoeven. 2006. "Aid Scaling Up: Do Wage Bill Ceilings Stand in the Way?" Working Paper WP06/106. International Monetary Fund, Washington, DC.

Gottret, P., G. J. Schieber, and H. R. Waters. 2008. *Good Practices in Health Financing: Lessons from Reforms in Low- and Middle-Income Countries.* Washington, DC: World Bank.

McCoy, D., S. Bennett, S. Witter, B. Pond, B. Baker, J. Gow, S. Chand, T. Ensor, and B. McPake. 2008. "Salaries and Incomes of Health Workers in Sub-Saharan Africa." *Lancet* 371 (9613): 675–81.

Picazo, O. 2008. " Struggling and Coping to Serve." The Zambian health workforce as depicted in the public expenditure tracking and quality of service delivery survey." HRH working paper, World Bank, Washington DC.

Scheffler, R. M., C. B. Mahoney, B. D. Fulton, M. R. Dal Poz, and A. S. Preker. 2009. "Estimates of Health Care Professional Shortages in Sub-Saharan Africa by 2015." *Health Affairs* 28: w849–w862.

Verhoeven, M., and P. Segura. 2007. "IMF Trims Use of Wage Bill Ceilings." *IMF Survey Magazine*, September 5.

Vujicic, M., K. Ohiri, and S. Sparkes. 2009. *Working in Health: Financing and Managing the Public Sector Health Workforce.* Washington, DC: World Bank.

World Bank. 2008. *Public Sector Reform: What Works and Why? An IEG Evaluation of World Bank Support.* Washington, DC: World Bank.

———. 2010a. "Madagascar: Sustainable Health System Development Project." Implementation Completion and Results Report ICR00001497. World Bank, Washington, DC.

———. 2010b. "Rwanda: Country Status Report on Health, Poverty and the MDGs." World Bank, Washington, DC.

———. Forthcoming in 2013. Ghana: Country Status Report on Health, Poverty and the MDGs. Directions in Development, World Bank. Washington DC.

CHAPTER 7

Politics and Governance in Human Resources for Health

Andrew Mitchell and Thomas J. Bossert

Governance structures and political processes shape the human resources for the health labor market, determining which reforms are implemented to improve labor market outcomes. This chapter reviews recent experience in Sub-Saharan Africa to suggest how types of political regimes, state capacities to make and enforce decisions, and governance arrangements between state and nonstate actors influence health labor market dynamics and reform policies. It also illustrates the role that stakeholders often play in reform, including the ministries of health, professional associations and unions, and international agencies or donors.

Government policy can profoundly affect health labor markets, influencing market balances (such as urban-rural, public-private, and centralized-decentralized), types of health services offered, and health worker performance (provider absenteeism and responsiveness to clients, for example), among other elements. Indeed, along with a well-performing workforce, one of the World Health Organization's six building blocks of a health system is leadership and governance, manifested through such actions as planning for a country's health needs, regulating health sector stakeholders, and establishing accountability mechanisms (WHO 2010).

Largely due to political legacies, some governments in Sub-Saharan Africa have created conditions that favor health workers in the public sector, while others have overseen policies that support greater sectoral pluralism or competition between public and private markets. In the public sector, and often as part of wider political reforms, some countries provide more local control over managing public health workers than others. As Sub-Saharan countries undertake reforms to respond to the human resource crisis, they will generally focus on changing government policies to alter the labor market.

This chapter reviews recent evidence from Sub-Saharan Africa to describe how different governance structures and political processes shape health labor markets, and how health system reforms affect the health workforce. There are many definitions of governance and politics, but most address the rules and practices of decision making—such as the roles of authority, legitimacy, and power, as well as the interests of civil society, the state, and political institutions and actors, rather than specific policies themselves (Brinkerhoff and Bossert 2008).

This chapter focuses on three elements of governance: contextual state characteristics (capacity and type of political regime), state policies and organizational forms that influence health labor markets (including private sector regulation and the locus of decision making for public labor markets), and the role of stakeholder political processes in adopting and implementing health workforce policies. Although we address these three elements separately, they are interrelated.

Many chapters in this book benefit from a combination of regularly collected, quantifiable data, but similar sources of data do not exist for governance. Such limitations preclude a systematic review of governance arrangements and health labor markets in Sub-Saharan Africa, though the chapter uses evidence from a range of countries and regions. Initial hypotheses relating governance to health labor markets were therefore based on our prior knowledge, with evidence sought from Sub-Saharan countries that could confirm or reject these hypotheses. While the chapter's country evidence supports the preliminary conclusions, more systematic evidence would strengthen the evidence base for those conclusions.

Regime Characteristics

Some state characteristics are apt to influence a country's ability to make and enforce rules for health labor markets. Regime "capacity"—running the gamut in Sub-Saharan Africa from long-unstable failed states riven by civil war to fairly stable governments generally able to enforce policy—is the first important characteristic. Regime type may play a role as well, with models of governance in Sub-Saharan Africa ranging from militaristic or authoritarian regimes (or both) to pluralistic democracies. How far regimes are entrenched in power over time, thus how able to promote or block health workforce reforms is a final characteristic that can improve work place reforms affect labor markets.

Regime Capacity

Sub-Saharan Africa offers many examples of failed or fragile states that have little power to impose rules and decisions on either their own administrative structures or the rest of civil society. In these contexts producing and retaining a skilled and motivated public-sector health workforce can exceed the government's financial and management capacities (Brinkerhoff 2007). Many health workers face stresses daily, including violence-ridden environments and health infrastructures that are inadequate due to chronic underinvestment. As a result, health workers may be particularly tempted to search for a better professional and economic environment, either within the country—such as urban areas or the private sector—or outside it (Doull and Campbell 2008). These contexts may also increase absenteeism, dual practice, and health workers' demands for informal payments to compensate for irregular or unpaid salaries.

International nonstate actors and raw free-market supply and demand may particularly affect labor markets for health workers in fragile and failed states. In some contexts, especially states in, or emerging from, conflict, a relatively free and unregulated market for health services can result. Unlicensed or unregulated providers may feature strongly, as could heavy reliance on out-of-pocket payment for services and major forms of corruption, especially in the drugs and medical equipment supply chains.

Most health workers in these situations seek the safest locations, often urban areas or even abroad. After the civil conflict that began in 2002 in Côte d'Ivoire, the health workforce changed greatly as the majority relocated, fled, or could not go to work. Further, the conflict accentuated a preexisting urban bias as most health workers relocated to the relative safety of the capital, Abidjan (Butera and others 2005). Skills distribution can also be adversely affected if the most highly educated (and therefore marketable) health workers emigrate to more secure countries. The exodus from both Angola and Sudan, for instance, led to greater use of lower skilled workers to meet demand once the conflict stopped (High Level Forum on Health Millennium Development Goals 2005). In short, a lack of central authority may shape or accentuate preexisting labor market imbalances, such as those between urban and rural workers or between worker skill levels.

International donor interventions and support may also profoundly affect health labor markets in these contexts. For weak or fragile states, donors often provide ministries of health substantial short-term budget support to enable continued provision of health services. Such support often targets personnel who remain in the public sector, providing salary incentives, for example; or to help nongovernmental organization (NGO) health providers to deliver services in the place of the public sector (Doull and Campbell 2008). Any such actions hold implications for the labor market.

In the Democratic Republic of Congo, for instance, donors supported long-standing involvement of faith-based organizations and NGOs, with the latter co-managing more than three-quarters of local health zones in the 1980s. The Democratic Republic of Congo subsequently built up public sector delivery capacity, but the violence that followed the fall of the Mobutu regime in the 1990s resulted in the near collapse of public services. Faith-based organizations and NGOs assumed responsibility for almost all the country's services—and today manage more than half the facilities (Waldman 2006).

In Mozambique internal distortions among public sector health workers were exacerbated during the civil war, from the mid-1970s until the early 1990s—both in skills (in the 1980s, unskilled staff made up about half the public health workforce, and fewer than 5 percent had a university education) and geography (such as a strong urban and hospital bias). With significant postwar technical and financial assistance from international agencies, the share of unskilled staff dropped to 36 percent 10 years later, and professionally trained staff grew to 64 percent. Geographic deployment also saw improvements (WHO 2009).

In short, donor choices in these cases—taken in the context of weak state capacity—affected the human resources labor markets. Their choices shifted the balance of provision to the private sector, making the market the arbiter of human resource distribution, even when supporting public services.

Regime Type

Most political regimes in Sub-Saharan Africa claim to be multiparty democracies, but in fact range from relatively liberal democracies to "thinly veiled personal dictatorships," with the majority somewhere in between (Collier and Levitsky 1997). The locus of power frequently lies with the executive branch (such as the president), which has historically used state resources to support networks of political clients (van de Walle 2002). Political scientists have attempted to demonstrate a relationship between basic types of regime—from authoritarian to democratic, and even more refined distinctions between—and government policies. But little evidence emerged that one type of regime is more conducive to major reform, such as for redistribution of land, and even less for specific health sector policies (Bienen and Herbst 1996).

Even so, recent reforms under two distinct types of regimes in Sub-Saharan Africa suggest that regime type may influence policies affecting health labor markets. A competitive political environment in some democracies can create conditions favoring health worker reforms. Ghana's relative success, including that in human resources, is one (rare) example. The country's ability to maintain its democratic regime while implementing different policy reforms, without generating major ethnic or class conflict, has created a good environment for reforms. Other countries will probably require major changes to establish such environments.

But some countries with authoritarian governments have also succeeded. Such regimes emerged from military insurgencies, and are led by progressive elites interested in mobilizing international resources toward new socioeconomic policies. Like authoritarian regimes elsewhere that do not rest on democratic legitimacy, such as China, Cuba, and Vietnam, these Sub-Saharan regimes aim to offer the population services or economic opportunities as a means of retaining power.

In Ethiopia, Rwanda, and Uganda, for example, regimes emerged that were committed to overcoming internal conflicts by providing better services to their populations—not only to establish legitimacy, but also to promote healing within society. Over time, relatively progressive governments have developed in these countries, growing the capacity to enforce decisions that implement reforms, including those affecting health workers. Certainly, not all authoritarian regimes are interested in this kind of legitimacy, preferring repression to services or economic opportunities: Zimbabwe is a striking example. It is also possible that these currently progressive requires may change their orientation over time. Still, such progressive authoritarian regimes are more capable of carrying out health workforce reforms than failed states or weaker democracies torn by ethnic conflicts, such as Kenya.

Political Entrenchment

Many innovations affecting health labor markets take a long time to realize their goals. Political entrenchment—the stability of a particular political elite—can thus affect not only whether reforms are attempted, but also whether they are seen through consistently, or repeatedly changed. Under authoritarian regimes or even democracies that lack true political contestation, for example, political commitment to a particular reform may be sustainable over a long period. Conversely, pluralist democracies with a highly contested balance of power may face difficulties in sustaining commitment to reforms.

Entrenched elites can also block reforms, particularly those in autocratic regimes. In addition, a lack of commitment can inhibit reforms. While governments in Uganda have generally been dedicated to fiscal decentralization, for instance, top-level leadership has not shown commitment to a planned public-private partnership in health strategy. This strategy remained dormant due to government inaction and lack of civil society pressure (Peters and others 2009). Zambia, Ethiopia, and Rwanda are three examples of countries where political entrenchment affects policies governing health labor markets (box 7.1).

Health Sector Governance

The combination of organization arrangement, political regime or legacy, and government regulatory policies can shape public-private balances in health labor markets. A sectoral balance heavily weighted toward publicly provided services, for instance, may be associated with *de facto* or *de jure* limits on private sector opportunities, dampening the free labor market. States' capacity to enforce regulations directed at private labor markets (such as dual-practice) may similarly affect the public-private labor market balance and outcomes.

State or Private

In some contexts historically left-leaning political orientations led to health care markets dominated by the public sector. In Ethiopia a long history of socialism significantly dampened private sector development until the mid-1990s, and even today the public sector is more dominant than in other Sub-Saharan countries (PSP-One 2007). Similarly, Tanzania banned private for-profit practice in 1977. Although the ban ended in 1991 (individual clinical practice was permitted), research in the early 2000s suggested that private for-profit facilities continued to struggle to survive, inhibited by institutional norms favoring religious-affiliated operations. Often these religious-affiliated operations not only charged higher prices than for-profit facilities for a common set of services, but

Box 7.1

Political Entrenchment and Health Sector Reforms

Under democratic or authoritarian regimes the degree of political entrenchment, power, or stability can determine policies and reforms in the health sector.

- *Zambia.* In the 1990s health workers were partly delinked from employment with the Ministry of Health, and granted contracts with newly created central or district boards of health. Delinking brought greater flexibility in staff financing, including user fees. After a few years, however, the government regarded the system as a policy failure, recentralizing it in 2006 and abolishing user fees. In both the delinking and relinking decisions, politics played a role. An intended full delinking to boards of health never took place because of labor union protests, and the subsequent relinking reflected political events, including the election of a new government "intent on bringing a 'new deal' for Zambia" in health, and the departure of a minister of health who had championed the previous reforms.

- *Ethiopia.* Since 1994 the Ethiopian government has conceptualized, initiated, and driven large-scale fiscal decentralization. Its statist approach was the most important factor in promoting adherence to policies. Accompanying the continuing fiscal decentralization, a recent important health sector reform pushed a large-scale expansion of community health extension workers. With more than 30,000 health extension workers deployed nationwide, this policy affects health labor markets into the future. Just as the fairly powerful position of the ruling party helped the earlier efforts to decentralize, its entrenchment may prove important in sustaining this expansion, despite limited financial resources.

- *Rwanda.* As part of a series of health reforms the government institutionalized performance-based financing, which pays facilities based on achieving outputs instead of providing inputs. Piloted in two districts in 2001–02, and scaled up nationwide only five years later, this approach has benefited from sustained political commitment from the president downward, as well as significant donor support. Both elements are central to the push to use performance-based financing. They have also contributed to the remarkable speed in going from pilot testing to nationwide implementation.

Sources: Peters and others (2009) for Ethiopia; CHESSORE and Wemos Amsterdam (2008) for Zambia; and Rusa and Fritsche (2007) and chapter 13 of this volume, for Rwanda.

also developed services specifically for patients with greater ability to pay (partly because of better access to outside investment such as donors) (Mackintosh and Tibandebage 2002).

In other contexts where underlying political leanings have not borne directly on public-private market distribution, the private sector may play a larger role in service delivery, even though regulations tilt the balance toward the public sector. In Zambia 80 percent of health workers work in government-owned health facilities, though the proportion of private health workers has grown. Fairly strict regulations help drive this public-private balance, such as bonding requirements for graduates of public medical schools (who must work for 18 months in public institutions after graduation), national guidelines that hinder the opening of private clinics, and policies that apparently discourage private sector expansion (Garcia-Prado and Gonzalez 2007; PSP-One 2007).

Similarly in Ghana only 65 percent of health workers are publicly employed. Part of the reason may be bonding requirements that affect cadres—nurses, for example, must either work up to five years for the Ministry of Health or repay schooling costs. While some workers obtain exemptions from these requirements, the system channels the large majority of health graduates into the public health sector after they graduate (Buchan and McPake 2007; Garbarino and others 2007).

Across all kinds of political contexts and in most countries in Sub-Saharan Africa, underdeveloped state capacity to regulate the private sector affects health labor markets. Although private health expansion is an explicit government policy in Ethiopia, poor regulatory capacity provides ample room for private moonlighting during public working hours, as well as self-referrals by public workers to private practice (Lindelöw and Serneels 2006). In these ways, the capacity to regulate and monitor the private sector affects opportunities to work there, as well as desire to do so, regardless of official regulatory policies.

Decentralization

Over the past 25 years governments in Sub-Saharan Africa and elsewhere have widely adopted decentralization in the health sector, and in the public sector more generally, shifting decision making from central to local officials. In health, fiscal decentralization aims to give local authorities greater discretion in using financial resources, while administrative decentralization confers greater local authority over a number of functions, such as managing human resources, organizing and delivering services, and targeting rules for coverage or exemption from fees. Although organizational reforms in Sub-Saharan Africa often focus on fiscal decentralization, some governments have also conferred greater authority over a range of human resource functions—from procedures for candidate selection to setting salary levels and bonus payments.

Governmental motivation to decentralize human resource functions frequently stems from a reaction to inefficiencies in central management of health personnel. In a typical central system, as in Kenya, a public sector commission (across civil service or across the health sector) is responsible for almost all human resource management, including determining local facility and area staffing requirements, allocating posts, selecting candidates, controlling staff movements and termination, and determining conditions of service, such as salary and allowances (Vujicic, Ohiri, and Sparkes 2009).

Decentralizing selected health workforce is a policy option to redress deficiencies in centralized administration and, as governments hope, to improve health labor market outcomes. In terms of efficiency, local recruitment could shorten the time it takes to fill a position, eliminating many steps in central approval. Local authority over hiring could also improve the chances that candidates willing to serve across the country are matched to positions, as local units can make the selection. When such units set salaries and allowances, they can consider local labor market conditions and attract and promote the best candidates if they have sufficient financing to offer appropriate incentives. Decentralized authority may eventually improve the quality of care as well. Health personnel drawn locally and willing to serve locally may be more motivated and productive in the workplace (Bossert 1998).

These arguments are often made to support decentralization. But some evidence suggests that local authorities may not have enough knowledge, funding, or management capacity to exercise these roles, or that local political conditions and corruption might reduce the ability of even skilled and motivated local administrators to make appropriate decisions.

Decentralization can take a variety of forms, involving a range of human resource powers. Relationships between particular decentralization arrangements that affect health labor markets are often mediated by oversight capacities of officials (both local and national) and mechanisms of accountability to both national and local authorities.

Deconcentration, delegation, and devolution. One aspect of decentralization policy is determining who receives greater decision-making power. Some forms of decentralization focus power on local health administrators: the deconcentration of authorities to line-ministry officials at lower levels of the system, for example, or delegation to semiautonomous institutions. Other forms are more political, such as devolving of authority to local governments (Rondinelli, Nellis, and Cheema 1984). In practice, systems of decentralization can be hybrids. Mozambique, for example, has devolved some responsibility to provincial governors—primarily decisions on health workers with preuniversity training—who may then delegate it to provincial directors of health. During the 1990s, these arrangements kept the management of physicians fairly centralized (Saide and Stewart 2001).

Human resource functions. A second aspect is how much authority is granted for various decisions. Subnational authorities may get power to decide on human resource functions, including hiring and firing, tenure (salaried or contracted), compensation, transfers, performance management, skill mix (such as establishing jurisdictional staffing and facility staffing patterns), and training. Many countries decentralize only some health workforce power, and corresponding human resource functions, such as those involved in primary health care or lower level cadres. Our review suggests the following five generalizations for Sub-Saharan Africa.

First, governments can decentralize fiscally without doing the same for human resources. Although Ethiopia, Kenya, and Mali devolve budgetary decisions on health to local governments, the centers keep control of most health workforce functions.

Second, consistent relationships between the official form of decentralization (deconcentration, delegation, or devolution) and decentralized health workforce authority are hard to discern. A deconcentrated context such as Namibia's may tend toward even greater local decision making than more extensive forms of decentralization, such as delegation in Ghana or devolution in Kenya.

Third, decentralization may affect only some (often lower) health cadres and institutions. Districts in Tanzania take the lead in recruiting and contracting lower staff positions, but only initiate these procedures for higher levels. In Uganda nearly all hospital workers are exempt from decentralized management (Ssengooba 2005; Steffensen and others 2004).

Fourth, the decentralization of human resource functions is often limited to basic administrative functions (such as transfers, training, and maternity leave) and not the myriad other functions previously cited. In Tanzania and Uganda base salaries largely follow civil service norms, but nonsalary remuneration comes under local government authority.

Fifth, health worker decentralization does not seem systematically related to regime type. The traditionally authoritarian regime in Rwanda covers a range of health workforce functions, while those in Ethiopia (another traditionally authoritarian regime) or Mali (heralded for its democratic institutions) are limited primarily to fiscal matters.

These trends show exceptions, but decentralization for human resource functions is limited. One reason for this limitation is that historical practices hinder local-authority innovation, relying on promotion by seniority, deferring to national civil service standards rather than performance or other locally relevant criteria (Das Gupta, Gauri, and Khemani 2003; Olowu and Wunsch 2004).

Evidence on Decentralization and Health Labor Markets

Designing studies that persuasively demonstrate decentralization's impact on health sector performance, including health labor markets, is difficult. Lacking such studies, we make the following three points, drawing on specific observations.

First, decentralization can improve some conditions that affect health labor market outcomes while worsening others, or leaving them unchanged. In Uganda most management functions are under district authority, while salary scales and payroll management remain centralized. Reflecting on that divide, interviews with 800 health workers in 2005 suggest that health personnel supply improved (interviewees felt that district employment processes were generally much faster than previously centralized ones), distribution may have improved (poorer districts usually had higher levels of workers in their home districts than in wealthier ones, which can help retention), and motivation may have improved (75 percent of interviewees expressed satisfaction at receiving salary more predictably and quickly under a decentralized process). Box 7.2 describes a stakeholder account of salary consolidation in Ghana.

Yet decentralized recruitment proved frustrating and costly for many job applicants, potentially affecting the future stock of workers. Many workers felt geographically isolated due to new administrative obstacles to cross-district transfers. And many felt that local selection was prone to nepotism and capture by local governments (Ssengooba 2005). Similar evidence has been documented in other Southern African countries (Tanzania) and worldwide (Indonesia, China), suggesting that such experiences may not be uncommon either in Sub-Saharan Africa or internationally.[1]

Box 7.2

A Stakeholder Account of Salary Consolidation in Ghana

Ghana's effort to consolidate salaries illustrates the impact of political influence on the shape of reforms that affect health labor markets. In 1999, lobbying by the Ghana Medical Association to address a lack of overtime compensation culminated in the Additional Duty Hour Allowance scheme for doctors. The scheme was administratively cumbersome, incurred ballooning costs, and was opposed by the Nurses Association for creating unequal pay. To address these problems, the public workforce's formal employer—the Ghana Health Services—hired an outside consultant (a Ghanaian national residing abroad) to work with a team of mid-level technocrats to reform the job evaluation process and recommend a new salary structure.

It became clear that the proposed reforms would lead to major changes in procedures for compensation and promotions, replacing the discretion granted to local managers with a more merit-oriented process. At that point, the Ministry of Health wrested control of the reform from the Ghana Health Services, delegating negotiations to higher level stakeholders from the Ministry of Health, Ghana Health Services, Ministry of Finance, staff of the Presidency, IMF advisors, and Chief Executives of the main Teaching Hospitals, along with the hired consultant. Pockets of opposition surfaced, including chief executives of the teaching hospitals (who reported directly to the Minister of Health and resisted being equated with heads of regional hospitals who reported to the Ghana Health Services) and the Ministry of Health's director of human resources (who reportedly objected to sharing responsibility for implementing the reform with other departmental directors). A personal rivalry among key officials further complicated agreement over the plan.

The Ministry of Health took ownership of the reform when the Minister of Health, upon recommendations of others, removed the consultant so that reform could be done "within Ghana." After hiring an in-country Ghanaian consultant to work with their officials, the Ministry of Health abandoned the scheme developed by the original consultant and the Ghana Health Services in favor of one developed using "their own intuition" about appropriate salaries. The new, consolidated salaries were offered to the professional associations as "take it or leave it" offers.

Much turmoil ensued when the government proceeded to pay the wage bill for health workers according to these new salaries. Nonphysician health workers banded together to protest what they viewed as an unfairly large gap between the salaries of doctors and other workers. Nurses in particular complained that the government had abandoned the objective process put in place by the consultant, and some initially went on strike (but eventually accepted the salaries reluctantly).

Source: Blanchet 2009.

Second, the capacity to exercise authority often mediates relationships between labor markets and the decentralization of human resource functions. Such decentralization can be administratively costly and require basic organizational changes, taxing national resource capacities.[2] Those charged with managing human (and other) resources rarely have the training (Uganda) or the staff (Rwanda, with only 35 people at the central Ministry of Health office). Rwanda's central office has responded by deconcentrating management functions—for example by giving district health facilities sole responsibility for district staff management—but it is unclear whether these staff possess the skills to manage all aspects of human resources at their level (Vujicic, Ohiri, and Sparkes 2009). In Kenya, even though districts are expected to manage performance of the public health workforce, they do not have the legal mandate to do so (Steffensen and others 2004). And in Tanzania a study of health workers in two districts found that poor recordkeeping and management undermined the employee appraisal system, and few appraisals were carried out (Manzi and others 2004). Capacity constraints in carrying out decentralized powers can therefore affect a variety of labor market outcomes, from the local active stock to individual motivation.

Third, accountability mechanisms matter—an aspect that is important from the perspective of political economy as well. Reports from countries where locally elected governments play a role in decentralized health workforce management suggest that employment procedures can be vulnerable to local capture. In Tanzania weak local institutions overseeing human resource management are reportedly "easily manipulated" by local elites (Munga and others 2009). Qualitative data suggest that some health workers there feel that political interference in recruitment by district officials—including threats against health managers if they do not select local politicians' candidates—resulted in selecting unqualified workers. Indeed, even though the government reduced the powers accorded to district politicians to address such concerns, there are indications of continuing politicization (Munga and others 2009). Such problems have also been reported in Uganda, where health workers have complained of favoritism in employment toward "sons and daughters of the soil" (Ssengooba 2005).

Stakeholder Influence

A common thread through the preceding discussion is that the interests of different stakeholders shape policy for the health workforce, from designing and adopting new policies to implementing them. Those with such a stake often have a strong interest in maintaining the system, while others see opportunities to benefit from reforms. Developing political strategies to work with stakeholders to address the power of various actors can be crucial for the success of reforms affecting health workers and their labor markets.

Because health policy reforms usually seek to either alter or entrench the balance of power between stakeholders, political challenges are common—particularly for workforce reforms. To push through reforms, decision makers must assess the political feasibility of a policy, manage policy design and acceptance, and create strategies that improve the prospects for implementation (Reich 1996). Such assessment involves evaluating the positions of different stakeholders on the proposed changes, the power they can exercise in deciding on those changes, and the opportunities and obstacles that the governance context offers. Health policy reform generally involves common sets of stakeholders, with often similar roles in, and positions toward, specific policy reforms (table 7.1).

The ministry of health leads many reforms, but civil service rules and other ministries affect the types of reform that it can initiate. In Swaziland it had to negotiate with the Ministry of Public Works to lift a ban on recruiting foreign nurses to address in-country shortages (Kober and Van Damme 2006). Similarly, reforms and policies for preservice education of professional health workers often fall under the purview of the ministry of education (see chapter 16).

Still, committed political leadership can overcome significant opposition, as the recent decision by Ethiopia's prime minister to increase substantially the production and deployment of physicians—against the resistance of medical schools and professional associations—demonstrates.[3]

Professional associations and unions also play an important role, often initiating salary-related reforms while blocking initiatives that affect labor market structures, such as changing a country's skill mix, task shifting, or introducing nonphysician health workers. Associations in Ethiopia strongly resisted junior physician health officers, managing to suspend the program for several years (Bossert and others 2007).

International donors are increasingly involved in making and supporting policies on human resources for health. Their influence in extremely weak states, where they are often the dominant source of public financing, can shape labor markets. In other contexts, they work in conjunction

Table 7.1   Stakeholders and Health Sector Reforms Affecting Human Resources for Health

Stakeholder	Position on reform	Power
Government		
Ministry of health (national)	Improved overall workforce production; increased workforce wages and training	High
Ministry of health (subnational): hospital and clinic managers	Increased local stock of human resources for health and local wage bill; increased flexibility in tenure; increased training	Medium
Ministry of education	Increased production; increased preservice training for some cadres (for example, physicians)	Medium
Ministries of finance and planning	Limited wage bill	High
Civil service agency	Limited wage bill; restricted workforce to public sector rules	High
Local governments	Increased stock; limited wage bill and/or employment (subnational)	Low
Nongovernment		
Professional associations and unions (physicians, nurses, pharmacists, etc.)	Limited production; increased wage bill; restricted labor market entry of nonprofessional cadres	Medium to high
Nongovernmental organizations (national and international)	Increased production, stock, wage bill, training; increased flexibility in tenure	Low
International institutions (donor, technical assistance agencies)	Increased production, wage bill, and training (often with special interest for specific disease programs)	Medium to high
Media	Report on conflict and poor performance; often ignore reform proposals	Low to medium

Source: World Bank data.

with each other and with the national government, to varying degrees of comfort.

In sum, although stakeholder positions may be similar across countries in Sub-Saharan Africa, as elsewhere, their powers and roles vary considerably depending on the regime characteristics, nature of reforms, and reformers' skills in building coalitions of support and reducing opposition. Since political processes are not easily determined by generally observed rules, each case requires careful analysis and testing of different strategies.

Conclusion

This chapter's analysis suggests the following in Sub-Saharan Africa:

- Experiences in fragile and failed states that are unable to enforce state policies can lead to an exodus of skilled health workers, unless donors intervene heavily.
- States with relatively stable political regimes can demonstrate capacity to spearhead policy reforms and marshal international financial assistance in ways consistent with improving labor market outcomes. These may include democratic states that have avoided political polarization or fracturing, as well as those founded on a history of authoritarianism or insurgent military coalitions, but dominated by an elite committed to reforms that improve service delivery.
- State-dominated health systems appear to be moving toward more market-oriented systems, and greater regulation is likely to depend on overall state capacity.
- The impact on labor markets of decentralizing heath workforce functions is generally limited because of continued centralized salary levels, which also create accountability issues affecting labor market outcomes.
- Stakeholder analysis highlights the political and governance issues that arise among key stakeholders in reforms affecting health labor markets.

This brief review suggests that more systematic study of the constraints and opportunities of different governance structures, processes, and stakeholder interactions would provide evidence-based guidance for recommendations on improving human resource policies in different country settings. In a field dominated by wish lists of technical recommendations for human resource policies, many never adopted or implemented, we need to pay attention to the political processes and the structural constraints that require careful strategies if we are to change policies in a positive direction.

Notes

1. See Dominick and Kurowski (2004); Kimaro and Sahay (2004); Munga and others (2009); Tang and Bloom (2000); Thabrany (2006); and Turner and others (2003).

2. Evidence from outside the region suggests that the financial implications of decentralization can be heavy: Mexico spent an estimated $450 million in administrative costs to transfer its federal health employees to the states (Homedes and Ugalde 2005).

3. Interviews of officials in Ministry of Health by second author 2008.

References

Bienen, H., and J. Herbst. 1996. "The Relationship between Political and Economic Reform in Africa." *Comparative Politics* 29: 23–42.

Blanchet, N. 2009. "Background Paper: A Stakeholder Analysis of Human Resources for Health Policy-Making in Ghana." Harvard School of Public Health, Boston, MA.

Bossert, T. 1998. "Analyzing the Decentralization of Health Systems in Developing Countries: Decision Space, Innovation and Performance." *Social Science and Medicine* 47 (10): 1513–27.

Bossert, T., T. Bärnighausen, D. Bowser, A. Mitchell, and G. Gedik. 2007. *Assessing Financing, Education, Management and Policy Context for Strategic Planning for Human Resources in Health*. Geneva: WHO.

Brinkerhoff, D.W. 2007. *Governance in Post-Conflict Societies: Rebuilding Fragile States*. London: Routledge.

Brinkerhoff, D. W., and T. J. Bossert. 2008. *Health Governance: Concepts, Experience, and Programming Options*. Bethesda, MD: Abt Associates, Health Systems 20/20.

Buchan, J., and B. McPake. 2007. "The Impact of the Department of Health, England, Code of Practice on International Recruitment." Queen Margaret University, Edinburgh, UK.

Butera, D., J. V. Fieno, S. D. Diarra, G. Kombe, C. Decker, and S. Oulai. 2005. *Comprehensive Assessment of Human Resources for Health in Côte d'Ivoire*. Bethesda, MD: The Partners for Health Reform Plus Project, Abt Associates.

CHESSORE (Centre for Health, Science, and Social Research), and Wemos Amsterdam. 2008. *Human Resources for the Delivery of Health Services in Zambia: External Influences and Domestic Policies and Practices*. Lusaka, Zambia: CHESSORE.

Collier, D., and S. Levitsky. 1997. "Democracy with Adjectives: Conceptual Innovation in Comparative Research." *World Politics* 49 (3): 430–51.

Das Gupta, M., V. Gauri, and S. Khemani. 2003. *Decentralized Delivery of Primary Health Services in Nigeria*. Africa Region Human Development Working Paper Series, World Bank, Washington, DC.

Dominick, A., and C. Kurowski. 2004. *Human Resources for Health—An Appraisal of the Status Quo in Tanzania Mainland.* Washington, DC: World Bank.

Doull, L., and F. Campbell. 2008. "Human Resources for Health in Fragile States." *Lancet* 371 (9613): 626–27.

Garbarino, S., T. Lievens, P. Quartey, and P. Serneels. 2007. Ghana Qualitative Health Worker Study: Draft Report of Preliminary Descriptive Findings. Oxford, U.K.: Oxford Policy Management.

Garcia-Prado, A., and P. Gonzalez. 2007. "Policy and Regulatory Responses to Dual Practice in the Health Sector." *Health Policy* 84 (2–3): 142–52.

High Level Forum on Health Millennium Development Goals. 2005. "Health Service Delivery in Post-Conflict States." Background Paper for the "High-Level Forum on the Health Millennium Development Goals (MDGs)," Paris, November 14–15.

Homedes, N., and A. Ugalde. 2005. "Human Resources: The Cinderella of Health Sector Reform in Latin America." *Human Resources for Health* 3 (1).

Kimaro, H. C., and S. Sahay. 2004. "An Institutional Perspective on the Process of Decentralization of Health Information Systems: A Case Study from Tanzania." *Information Technology for Development* 13 (4): 363–90.

Kober, K., and W. Van Damme. 2006. "Public Sector Nurses in Swaziland: Can the Downturn be Reversed?" *Human Resources for Health* 4 (13).

Lindelöw, M., and P. Serneels. 2006. "The Performance of Health Workers in Ethiopia: Results from Qualitative Research." *Social Science and Medicine* 62 (9): 2225–35.

Mackintosh, M., and P. Tibandebage. 2002. "Inclusion by Design? Rethinking Health Care Market Regulation in the Tanzanian Context." *Journal of Development Studies* 39 (1): 1–20.

Manzi, F., T. Kida, S. Mbuyita, N. Palmer, and L. Gilson. 2004. "Exploring the Influence of Workplace Trust over Health Worker Performance." London School of Hygiene and Tropical Medicine, London.

Munga, M. A., N. G. Songstad, A. Blystad, and O. Mæstad. 2009. "The Decentralisation-Centralisation Dilemma: Recruitment and Distribution of Health Workers in Remote Districts of Tanzania." *BMC International Health and Human Rights* 9 (1): 9.

Olowu, D., and J. S. Wunsch. 2004. "Nigeria: Local Governance and Primary Health Care." In *Local Governance in Africa: The Challenges of Democratic Decentralization*, ed. D. Olowu and J. S. Wunsch, 107–24. Boulder, CO: Lynne Rienner.

Peters, D. H., S. El-Saharty, B. Siadat, K. Janovsky, and M. Vujicic, eds. 2009. *Improving Health Service Delivery in Developing Countries: From Evidence to Action.* Washington, DC: World Bank.

PSP-One (Private Sector Partnerships One). 2007. *Why Policy Matters: Regulatory Barriers to Better Primary Care in Africa—Two Private Sector Examples*. Washington, DC: PSP-One.

Reich, M. R. 1996. "Applied Political Analysis for Health Policy Reform." *Current Issues in Public Health* 2: 186–91.

Rondinelli, D. A., J. R. Nellis, and G. S. Cheema. 1984. *Decentralization in Developing Countries: A Review of Recent Experience*. Washington, DC: World Bank.

Rusa, L., and G. Fritsche. 2007. "Rwanda: Performance-Based Financing in Health." In *Sourcebook on Emerging Good Practice in Managing for Development Results*, 2nd ed. Managing for Development Results.

Saide, M. A., and D. E. Stewart. 2001. "Decentralization and Human Resource Management in the Health Sector: A Case Study (1996–1998) from Nampula Province, Mozambique." *International Journal of Health Planning and Management* 16 (2): 155–68.

Ssengooba, F. 2005. "Human Resources for Health in Decentralized Uganda: Developments and Implications for Health Systems Research." Paper presented at Forum 9, Mumbai, India, September 12–16.

Steffensen, J., P. Tidemand, H. Naitore, E. Ssewankambo, and E. Mwaipopo. 2004. *A Comparative Analysis of Decentralisation in Kenya, Tanzania and Uganda*. Dar es Salaam, Tanzania: DEGE Consult.

Tang, S., and G. Bloom. 2000. "Decentralizing Rural Health Services: A Case Study in China." *International Journal of Health Planning and Management* 15 (3): 189–200.

Thabrany, H. 2006. "Human Resources in Decentralized Health Systems in Indonesia: Challenges for Equity." *Regional Health Forum* 10 (1): 75–88.

Turner, M. M., O. Podger, M. S. Sumardjono, and W. K. Tirthayasa. 2003. *Decentralisation in Indonesia: Redesigning the State*. Canberra: Asia Pacific Press.

van de Walle, N. 2002. "Elections without Democracy: Africa's Range of Regimes." *Journal of Democracy* 13 (2): 66–80.

Vujicic, M., K. Ohiri, and S. Sparkes. 2009. *Working in Health: Financing and Managing the Public Sector Health Workforce*. Washington, DC: World Bank.

Waldman, R. 2006. *Health in Fragile States, Country Case Study: Democratic Republic of the Congo*. Arlington, VA: Basic Support for Institutionalizing Child Survival.

WHO (World Health Organization). 2009. *Analysing Disrupted Health Sectors: A Modular Manual*. Geneva: WHO.

———. 2010. "The WHO Health Systems Framework." Geneva. http://www.wpro.who.int/sites/hsd/hsd_framework.htm.

PART 2

Distribution of Health Workforce

CHAPTER 8

How Many Health Workers?

Adam Ahmat, Nejmudin Bilal, Christopher H. Herbst, and Stephanie E. Weber

Sub-Saharan Africa has very few health workers in comparison to other regions of the world, with large variations between and within countries. Some of these variations are linked to economic status and others to colonial and institutional history. The density of health workers seems to be rising, however, albeit slowly. Nurses dominate the workforce. The size of the private and informal health workforce is underestimated and little is known about its nature and contribution to service delivery. Overall, the quality of available data is very poor, and making comparisons is difficult. There is an urgent need to understand human resources for health metrics better, rather than invest in projections and benchmarks made on unreliable data. Investments should focus on analyzing current trends and finding adequate solutions tailored to each national and sub-regional context.

Doctors, nurses, and midwives form the frontline of health care delivery and management. Several studies present evidence for the link between the availability of health workers and better health outcomes.[1] According to the 2006 World Health Organization's *World Health Report*, of the 57 countries deficient in health workers using this benchmark, 63 percent are in Sub-Saharan Africa. Since as far back as 2004, reports have argued that the region's scarcity of qualified health personnel is a major constraint to scaling up interventions for priority health programs and achieving the health-related Millennium Development Goals. So what is the status?

What Do Comparisons to International Benchmarks Tell Us?

The most widely cited health workforce benchmark was established by the World Health Organization (WHO) under the Joint Learning Initiative (WHO 2006). This benchmark proposes a density of 2.28 health workers (doctors, midwives, and nurses) per 1,000 people to achieve 80 percent coverage of skilled birth attendance (see chapter 2). It does not specify, however, the required skill mix, typically measured by the ratio of nurses and midwives to doctors.

In addition, many countries have their own benchmarks, usually based on a standard skill mix for each type of health facility. For example, in Benin a district hospital should have three doctors, while a primary health care center should have one. Given that these standards are rigid and do not take into account variations in disease burden (HIV/AIDS prevalence, for example), more sophisticated benchmarks have been designed in countries such as Tanzania and Chad, using clinical guidelines (Kurowski and others 2004).

Benchmarks, international or national, should be used with caution, as they often lack evidence to support broad implementation in health systems. They can be useful, however, for international comparisons.

Sub-Saharan Africa Has the World's Lowest Density of Health Workers

International comparisons reveal that Sub-Saharan Africa has the world's lowest density of physicians, nurses, and midwives—1.33 health workers per 1,000 population, well short of the WHO benchmark of 2.28 (table 8.1). Even South Asia, which is comparable to Africa in economic indicators, has a much higher density with 1.81, potentially contributing to better health outcomes.

Health Worker Availability Varies between African Countries

Health systems in Sub-Saharan Africa are diverse, and the health workforce density varies greatly across countries (annex 8A). Eight countries have a density above the WHO 2.28 benchmark (the Seychelles, Swaziland, Gabon, South Africa, Mauritius, Namibia, Botswana, and São Tomé and Príncipe). But most countries (30 countries) do not have even one physician, nurse, or midwife per 1,000 population. Such data must

Table 8.1   Health Worker Density per 1,000 Population by Cadre, 2009

WHO region	Physicians	Nurses and midwives	Total
Africa	0.24	1.09	1.33
Americas	2.29	5.49	7.78
Eastern Mediterranean	1.01	1.42	2.43
Europe	3.25	6.81	10.06
South Asia	0.58	1.24	1.81
East Asia	1.87	2.51	4.37
Western Pacific	1.40	2.08	3.48
Global	1.36	2.75	4.11

Source: Global Health Observatory, World Health Organization (http://apps.who.int/ghodata/#).

be interpreted with caution, however, because of the low quality of data (box 8.1).

Between 1960 and 1998, the density of physicians, nurses, and midwives increased in some countries, if slowly: the density of physicians climbed in Burkina Faso, Cameroon, and Kenya, but declined in Ghana, Tanzania, and Zambia; the ratio of nurses to physicians rose in Cameroon, Ghana, Kenya, Tanzania, and Zambia but declined in Burkina Faso, the Central African Republic, and Madagascar (Liese, Blanchet, and Dussault 2003). More recent data show that between 2004 and 2008, the overall number of health workers in Sub-Saharan Africa rose by 9 percent, and the increase in physicians (21.5 percent) was three times higher than that of nurses and midwives (6.5 percent).

The Availability of Health Workers Improves with Economic Status

Health workers generally consume much of the funding for health services, so differences in economic development help explain variations in distribution. When plotting the density of physicians, nurses, and midwives in Sub-Saharan countries against their per capita gross domestic product (GDP), one actually sees a positive association (figure 8.1).

In most cases, the density of health workers rises as GDP rises. Health worker density and economic development have, however, a complex relationship that cannot be accounted for solely by higher incomes. The Seychelles and Gabon, for instance, have higher than expected densities (9.44 and 5.45 health workers per 1,000 population) given their relatively low GDPs ($8,687 and $7,501, respectively), while Equatorial Guinea has a low density of health workers (0.83) but one of the highest GDPs ($15,397).

Box 8.1

Quality of Data Is a Major Issue

This chapter's data came from three main sources—WHO/Global Atlas, Africa Health Workforce Observatory, and national observatories. General observations can be highlighted from the review of existing data:

- *Data completeness varies by country and year* (estimates were used when data were missing).
- *There is limited to no data on some categories of health workers,* such as alternative mid-level cadres, even in countries with extensive data-reporting systems.
- *Many of the data refer to public health workers only.*
- *The quality of data varies greatly by country and source* (box table 8.1.1), and often depends on central and regional capacity to enter, update, and forward data to be analyzed. Therefore, although this chapter makes an effort to use the best data available—and to point out obvious quality constraints—variations in quality remain.

Box Table 8.1.1   Discrepancies in Nurse Data: An Example from Zambia

| | Source of data | | |
Title	Ministry of Health[a]	General nursing council[b]	Difference
Public health nurses	18	73	55
Registered midwives	347	2,542	2,195
Registered nurses	1,273	5,675	4,402
Registered psychiatry nurses	20	313	293
Registered theater nurses	57	411	354
Registered or enrolled ophthalmic nurses	2	12	10
Enrolled midwives	1,754	3,479	1,725
Enrolled nurses	5,205	9,442	4,237
Enrolled theater nurses	36	94	58

Source: Ferrinho and others 2008.
a. Public sector nurses, March 2008.
b. Nurses registered between January 2004 and April 30, 2008.

Data from different sources can diverge, and both cross-country and intra-country comparisons (when data come from different sources) need to be interpreted with caution. The major causes of poor quality data are generally the following:

(*continued next page*)

Box 8.1 *(continued)*

- Methodological differences in collecting and collating health worker data. Some of the total numbers may reflect workers registered at the facility level, while others may reflect those present in facilities, or show only workers registered nationally or on the government payroll.
- Data sources vary. Data either come from national censuses, facility surveys, national payroll records, or registration lists.
- Numbers of public versus private sector health workers are not well captured, and the differing methods can skew health worker numbers. Although most of the underlying health workforce data are for the public sector, payroll data in countries like Rwanda list publicly paid health workers who work in private health facilities. A census or count of health workers in public institutions would not capture this segment.
- Health worker has no universal definition. According to the countries, the term may include paid or unpaid, formal or informal, and clinical or nonclinical health workers. Health cadres also vary across countries: some use the word *nurse* as an umbrella term to cover both enrolled and registered nursing cadres, while others use it to refer to registered nursing cadres only. Similarly, some countries use the term "laboratory worker," for example, to include laboratory scientists and laboratory technicians, while others use it for laboratory scientists only, labeling the rest "laboratory technicians." As a result, the numbers of aggregated health workers may encompass different categories of workers, depending on the country and source.

The Coverage of Health Services Improves with the Availability of Health Workers

Using skilled birth attendance as an example—as it stands for an essential health service, often considered an indicator of health system functioning—we see a positive relationship between the coverage of health services and the availability of health workers: the higher the density of health workers, the higher the percentage of births attended (figure 8.2). Other factors (such as population distribution, geography, and culture) are also likely important determinants.

Health Worker Distribution within Countries Is Inefficient

Almost all countries in the region are experiencing imbalances in the geographic distribution of health workers. Most countries face major

Figure 8.1   Per Capita GDP and Health Worker Density, 2005–09

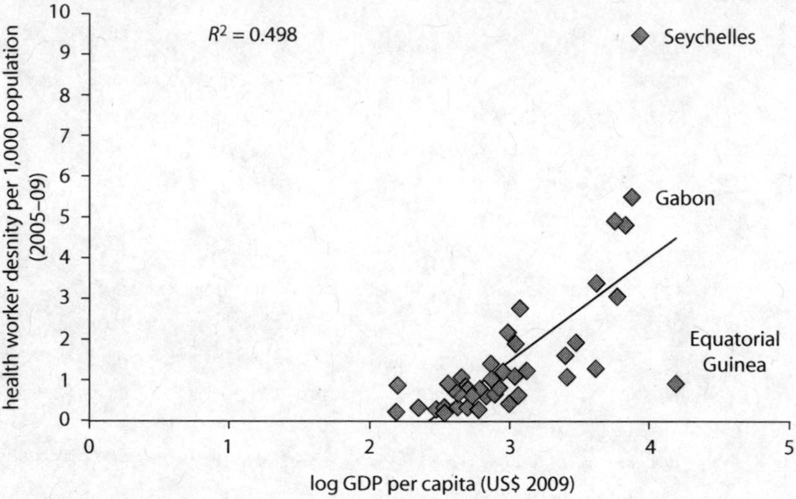

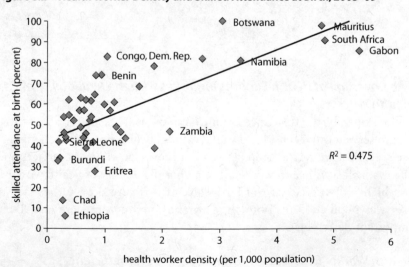

Sources: WHO/Global Atlas (2005–09) and World Bank (2010).
Note: Somalia is excluded as reliable GDP data are not available.

Figure 8.2   Health Worker Density and Skilled Attendance at Birth, 2005–09

Sources: WHO/Global Atlas (2005–09) and UNICEF (latest data available).
Note: Somalia and the Seychelles are excluded due to the absence of data.

shortages of health workers in rural areas, even those that do not have an overall national shortage. In addition, many health workers move between the public and private sectors in their careers. Chapter 9 provides further details on these issues.

Out-migration of health workers is a key reason for the diminished stock in many countries. African physicians' migration, estimated between 10 and 15 percent, is likely much higher than that of other African professionals and tertiary-educated workers (Docquier, Lohest, and Marfouk 2007). Indeed, African physicians' migration is the highest among all developing regions.

The Low Stock of Health Workers Is Detrimental to the Poor

In every Sub-Saharan country, the availability of health workers of all categories is generally higher in wealthy areas than in poor areas. Further, the difference across quintiles varies from one type of health worker to another, with differences among higher level workers greater than those among lower level ones. Even if workers are present in low-income areas, patients may not use their services for various reasons. Chapter 12 discusses in depth some of the equity implications related to health worker distribution.

Human Resources for Health Dynamics That We Need to Capture Better

What Are the Colonial and Cultural Impacts on Health Workers Availability?

State official languages often reflect colonial histories and cultures, and patterns of health workers can be drawn by language region (table 8.2). Multiple factors explain the differences in density and growth between subgroups: varying production capacities of nurses and physicians; varying workforce attrition due to retirement, resignation, and death; and health professionals' emigration. For instance, the negative growth for physicians in Francophone countries can be explained by the low production capacity of physicians in the region and the natural attrition not addressed with aggressive training of health personnel.

What Are the Demographics Underlying the Availability of Human Resources for Health?

Not all countries in Africa provide gender disaggregation of health workers. Although countries vary greatly, similar patterns emerge: there are

Table 8.2   Densities and Growth Rate of Health Workers by Language, 2005–09

Official language subgroup	Physicians		Nurses and midwives		Total	
	Density/1,000	Growth (percent)	Density/1,000	Growth (percent)	Density/1,000	Growth (percent)
Anglophone	0.2	6.3	1.31	1.1	1.51	1.9
Francophone	0.18	–3.9	1.21	2.2	1.33	1.3
Lusophone	0.23	2.3	0.84	6.5	0.11	6.1
Arabophone	0.16	n.a.	0.66	n.a.	0.82	n.a.
Sub-Saharan Africa	0.24	4.3	1.09	1.3	1.33	1.8

Sources: WHO/Global Atlas (2005–09); Africa Health Workforce Observatory Database (WHO African Region).
Note: For growth of health worker data, WHO (2004) was the baseline. The Africa Health Workforce Observatory provided data for late-2007–08. Estimates for countries without 2008 data were made on the basis of population size, leaving constant the ratio of physicians to nurses and midwives. n.a. = not applicable.

more male physicians than women, whereas midwives and nurses are predominantly women (figure 8.3). Other cadres of health workers (dentists, pharmacists, and radiographers) have a majority of male workers.

Overall, midwives (96 percent) and nurses (73 percent) make up the highest proportion of female health workers. Burkina Faso has a large male nurse population (83 percent), as do Côte d'Ivoire (82 percent), and Chad (78 percent). Cape Verde has a high proportion of female physicians (52 percent), followed by Guinea (51 percent), and Mozambique (48 percent). The lowest proportions of female physicians are in Comoros (8 percent), Mauritania (10 percent), and Ethiopia (11 percent).

What Is the Appropriate Skill Mix?

Skill mix (or staff mix) refers to either the composition or organization of health workers from different professional backgrounds that achieve the highest quality of care for the greatest number of people in the most cost-effective manner. In economic terms skill mix is "the combination of health workers that produce a given level of health care services at a particular quality for the lowest cost" (Fulton and others 2010). Policy makers and system managers in Sub-Saharan Africa have adjusted the skill mix through shifting tasks and expanding nonconventional cadres to alleviate workforce shortages, especially given increased demand for services (Fulton and others 2010).

The optimal skill mix depends on the local context and is influenced by inputs, processes, priorities, and funds (adapted from Fulton and others 2010). Inputs (such as health workers, facilities, and equipment)

Figure 8.3   Female Health Workers in Total Health Workers, 2005–09

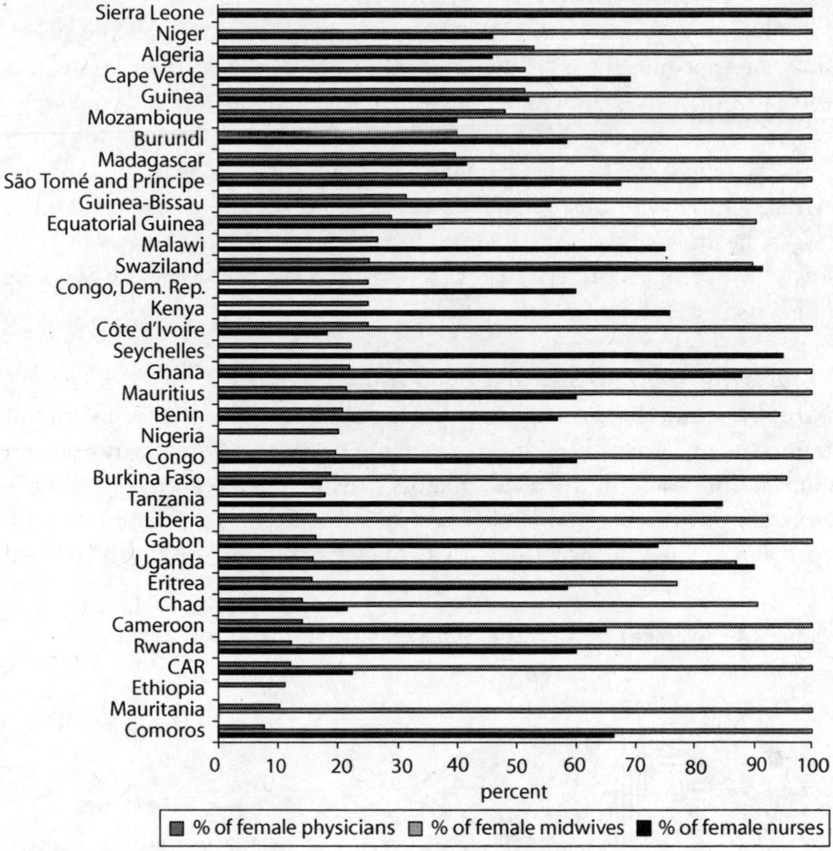

Source: WHO/Global Atlas (2005–09).

determine what enters the health system. Processes regulate how the inputs are organized and used. Priorities decide which type of service to produce (such as primary care, birth deliveries, and antiretroviral therapy), and funds—or the country's economic development—determine what the country can afford. As these four factors vary among and within countries, the optimal skill mix has no global benchmark.

There is no optimal nurse to physician ratio. Globally, this ratio is 1 physician for 2.04 nurses. High ratios of nurses and midwives to physicians likely indicate a physician deficit, while low ratios likely indicate a better supply of physicians. For every physician, Southeast Asia has 2.27

nurses and midwives, the European Region has 2.1, and the Americas have 2.4 (according to WHO regions).

Sub-Saharan Africa has 4.54 nurses and midwives for every physician, showing that nursing skills dominate the region's health workforce. But the ratio of nurses and midwives to physicians varies greatly between countries (see annex 8A) and according to language grouping: for every physician there are 6.72 nurses in Francophone Africa, 6.55 in Anglophone Africa, and 3.65 in Lusophone Africa. Still, nurses and midwives are the largest health worker category in Sub-Saharan Africa (50.8 percent), followed by administrative staff (12.5 percent) and public health workers (11.3 percent) (figure 8.4).

What Is the Role and Size of the Alternative Cadres?

Nonphysician clinicians. Nonphysician clinicians are "staff who are not trained as physicians but who are capable of many of the diagnostic and clinical functions of medical doctors" (Mullan and Frehywot 2007). Several nonexperimental studies demonstrated their positive impact on cost and quality of care in Africa. In Mozambique surgically trained

Figure 8.4   Average Skill Mix in the Sub-Saharan Region by Cadre, 2005

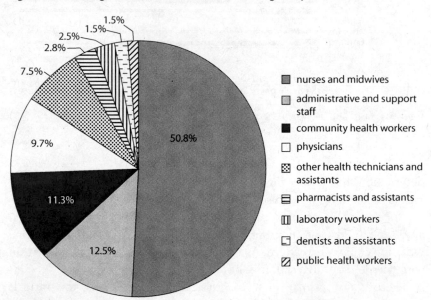

Legend:
- nurses and midwives
- administrative and support staff
- community health workers
- physicians
- other health technicians and assistants
- pharmacists and assistants
- laboratory workers
- dentists and assistants
- public health workers

Values: 50.8%, 12.5%, 11.3%, 9.7%, 7.5%, 2.8%, 2.5%, 1.5%, 1.5%

Source: WHO 2005.
Note: The table has data for only 46 countries, given problems of data availability. Cadres were aggregated into nine main categories, to allow for comparisons.

assistant medical officers produced patient outcomes similar to obstetricians and gynecologists at a quarter of the cost (Kruk and others 2007; Pereira and others 2007). In Malawi clinical officers and medical officers providing obstetric surgery produced similar patient outcomes (Chilopora and others 2007). And in Uganda nonphysician clinicians and physicians had considerable agreement on HIV/AIDS diagnosis and treatment as well as tuberculosis-status assessment (Vasan and others 2009). More rigorous studies are however required (Fulton and others 2010; see also chapter 16 of this book).

In 2005, 25 of 47 countries in Africa reported using nonphysician clinicians. In nine, including Kenya, Malawi, and Uganda, nonphysician clinicians even equaled or exceeded the number of physicians, and there is a tendency to raise the number of nonphysician clinicians. Ethiopia, for instance, produced 5,000 health officers between 2007 and 2010, putting them at the top of the country's production and use (see chapter 16). Ghana, Lesotho, Sierra Leone, South Africa, Sudan, and Zambia have also committed to expanding their number of nonphysician clinicians (Mullan and Frehywot 2007).

Community health workers. Estimates suggest that community health workers account for, on average, 11 percent of the health workforce in Sub-Saharan Africa, but this number is generally underestimated as community health workers are not always included in censuses. In addition, there are large disparities between countries: community health workers in Guinea-Bissau make up 73 percent of the health workforce, while more than 30,000 health extension workers in Ethiopia account for about half of its health workforce.

A high proportion of community health workers does not necessarily mean a low proportion of nurses and midwives. In Swaziland, nurses, midwives, and community health workers together make up 89 percent of all health workers (36 percent of the total health workers are community health workers).

Informal sector. The informal sector, though often overlooked, is a significant part of health care delivery in Sub-Saharan Africa, and so is its workforce. Informal workers—such as home-based care workers, self-employed health workers, nonregistered community health workers, and traditional medical practitioners—form the majority of the health workforce. The Joint Learning Initiative estimates that for each formal-sector health worker there are at least three informal workers.

These health workers are not reflected in conventional data on the health workforce stock. In Lesotho, for example, only 44 percent of those working in the health sector are employed by the formal health sector (Ministry of Health and Social Welfare of Lesotho 2004). In Sierra Leone, there are almost three times as many traditional birth attendants (trained and untrained) as the entire formal-sector health workforce (Ministry of Health and Sanitation of Sierra Leone 2006).

Conclusion

This chapter has shed some light on what we know, and still don't know, about human resources for health in Africa. We know that there are fewer health workers in Sub-Saharan Africa than in any other region of the world, even regions with comparable development. We also know that there is wide within- and between-country variation in the stock and distribution of health workers, with important equity implications. Finally, we know that national health worker density is correlated with income and delivery care coverage, if weakly.

But we still don't know many things, because data are missing or of poor quality. Further research is therefore needed to better understand the impact of culture and colonialism on countries' health workforce stock, the demographics of the health workforce, the determinants for an appropriate skill mix, and the role (existing and expected) of alternative cadres. Additional areas of poor knowledge include mobility patterns, the size of the informal sector, the size of the private sector, and the burden of absenteeism and ghost workers.

Therefore, there is a need to think outside the box and tackle the underlying causes of poor human resources for health. Major efforts should be put in every country to organize sound censuses of all health workers through workforce surveys. These could provide an evidence base to create more relevant benchmarks, adjustable to local needs and epidemiology, perhaps allowing for assessments of the quality of the health worker stock. A vast information gap on the number and profile of health workers in the private sector also needs to be filled. Finally, there is an urgent need to understand human resources for health met-rics better, rather than invest in projections and benchmarks made on unreliable data. Investments should focus on analyzing current trends and finding adequate solutions tailored to each country and sub-region context.

Annex 8A Density of Physicians, Nurses, and Midwives by Country and Ratio of Nurses and Midwives to Physicians, 2005–09

| Country | Density per 1,000 population | | | Ratio of nurses and midwives to physician |
	Physicians	Nurses and midwives	Total	
Angola (2005)	0.08	1.19	1.27	14.88
Benin (2008)	0.07	0.86	0.93	12.29
Botswana (2005)	0.4	2.65	3.05	6.63
Burkina Faso (2008)	0.06	0.71	0.77	11.83
Burundi (2005)	0.03	0.19	0.22	6.33
Cameroon (2009)	0.08	0.51	0.59	6.38
Cape Verde (2008)	0.73	1.13	1.86	1.55
Central African Republic (2009)	0.05	0.27	0.32	5.40
Chad (2009)	0.03	0.24	0.27	8.00
Comoros (2008)	0.16	0.6	0.76	3.75
Congo, Dem. Rep. (2009)	0.06	0.79	0.85	13.17
Congo, Rep. (2008)	0.11	0.94	1.05	8.55
Côte d'Ivoire (2008)	0.13	0.45	0.58	3.46
Equatorial Guinea (2005)	0.3	0.53	0.83	1.77
Eritrea (2008)	0.06	0.77	0.83	12.83
Ethiopia (2008)	0.03	0.28	0.31	9.33
Gabon (2005)	0.29	5.16	5.45	17.79
Gambia, The (2008)	0.03	0.6	0.63	20.00
Ghana (2008)	0.11	0.98	1.09	8.91
Guinea (2005)	0.11	0.56	0.67	5.09
Guinea-Bissau (2009)	0.05	0.62	0.67	12.4
Kenya (2007)	0.17	1.19	1.36	7.00
Lesotho (2005)	0.05	0.62	0.67	12.40
Liberia (2009)	0.01	0.28	0.29	28.00
Madagascar (2005)	0.29	0.32	0.61	1.10
Malawi (2008)	0.02	0.27	0.29	13.50
Mali (2008)	0.08	0.51	0.59	6.38
Mauritania (2009)	0.14	1.02	1.16	7.29
Mauritius(2005)	1.06	3.73	4.79	3.52
Mozambique (2007)	0.03	0.35	0.38	11.67
Namibia (2005)	0.3	3.06	3.36	10.20
Niger (2009)	0.03	0.16	0.19	5.33
Nigeria (2008)	0.37	1.49	1.86	4.03
Rwanda (2007)	0.09	0.65	0.74	7.22

(continued next page)

| Country | Density per 1,000 population | | | Ratio of nurses and midwives to physician |
	Physicians	Nurses and midwives	Total	
São Tomé and Príncipe (2008)	0.26	2.44	2.7	9.38
Senegal (2008)	0.06	0.41	0.47	6.83
Seychelles (2005)	1.51	7.93	9.44	5.25
Sierra Leone (2009)	0.02	0.18	0.2	9.00
Somalia (2006)	0.04	0.17	0.21	4.25
South Africa (2005)	0.77	4.08	4.85	5.30
Sudan (2007)	0.3	0.9	1.2	3.00
Swaziland (2009)	0.15	1.45	1.6	9.67
Tanzania (2007)	0.09	0.24	0.33	2.67
Togo (2008)	0.06	0.32	0.38	5.33
Uganda (2007)	0.08	0.72	0.8	9.00
Zambia (2005)	0.12	2.01	2.13	16.75
Zimbabwe (2008)	0.06	0.93	0.99	15.50

Source: WHO/Global Atlas (2005–09).

Note

1. See Dreesch and others (2005), Anand and Bärnighausen (2005), and Speybroeck and others (2006).

References

Africa Health Workforce Observatory. n.d. World Health Organization, Geneva. http://www.hrh-observatory.afro.who.int/en/home.html.

Anand, S., and T. Bärnighausen. 2005. *Human Resources for Health and Vaccination Coverage in Developing Countries.* Oxford: Oxford University Press.

Chilopora, G., C. Pereira, F. Kamwendo, A. Chimbiri, E. Malunga, and S. Bergstrom. 2007. "Postoperative Outcome of Caesarean Sections and Other Major Emergency Obstetric Surgery by Clinical Officers and Medical Officers in Malawi." *Human Resources for Health* 5 (17).

Docquier, F., O. Lohest, and A. Marfouk. 2007. "Brain Drain in Developing Countries." *World Bank Economic Review* 21: 193–218.

Dreesch, N., C. Dolea, M. R. Dal Poz, A. Goubarev, O. Adams, M. Aregawi, K. Bergstrom, H. Fogstad, D. Sheratt, J. Linkins, R. Scherpbier, and M. Youssef-Fox. 2005. "An Approach to Estimating Human Resource Requirements to Achieve the Millennium Development Goals." *Health Policy and Planning* 20 (5): 267–76.

Ferrinho, P., S. Siziya, F. Goma, and F. Ferrinho. 2008. "Alternative Health Workforce Skill Mix in Africa: Evidence and Lessons from Zambia." Human Resources for Health Working Paper, World Bank, Washington, DC.

Fulton, B. D., S. Sparkes, E. Auh, and R. Scheffler. 2010. "Structured Review of the Health Workforce Economics Literature, Part One: Skill Mix and Task Shifting." Global Health Workforce Economics Network.

Global Health Observatory. n.d. World Health Organization, Geneva. http://apps.who.int/ghodata/#.

Kruk, M. E., C. Pereira, F. Vaz, S. Bergstrom, and S. Galea. 2007. "Economic Evaluation of Surgically Trained Assistant Medical Officers in Performing Major Obstetric Surgery in Mozambique." BJOG–An International Journal of Obstetrics and Gynaecology 114 (10): 1253–60.

Kurowski, C., K. Wyss, S. Abdulla, and A. Mills. 2004. "Human Resources for Health: Requirements and Availability in the Context of Scaling-Up Priority Interventions in Low-Income Countries. Case Studies from Tanzania and Chad." Higher Education Foundation Programme, Working Paper 01/04, Health Economics and Financing Programme, Department of Public Health and Policy, London School of Hygiene and Tropical Medicine, London.

Liese, B., N. Blanchet, and G. Dussault. 2003. "Background Paper: The Human Resources for Health Services Crisis in Sub-Saharan Africa." World Bank, Washington, DC.

Ministry of Health and Sanitation of Sierra Leone. 2006. Sierra Leone Human Resource for Health Development Plan (2006–2010). Freetown, Sierra Leone: Ministry of Health and Sanitation.

Ministry of Health and Social Welfare of Lesotho. 2004. Human Resources Development and Strategic Plan (2005–2025). Maseru, Lesotho: Ministry of Health and Social Welfare.

Mullan, F., and S. Frehywot. 2007. "Non-Physician Clinicians in 47 Sub-Saharan African Countries." Lancet 370 (9605): 2158–63.

Pereira, C., A. Cumbi, R. Malalane, F. Vaz, C. McCord, A. Bacci, and S. Bergström. 2007. "Meeting the Need for Emergency Obstetric Care in Mozambique: Work Performance and Histories of Medical Doctors and Assistant Medical Officers Trained for Surgery." BJOG–An International Journal of Obstetrics and Gynaecology 114 (12): 1530–33.

Speybroeck, N., Y. Kinfu, M. R. Dal Poz, and D. B. Evans. 2006. "Reassessing the Relationship between Human Resources for Health, Intervention Coverage and Health Outcomes." Background Paper for The World Health Report 2006. World Health Organization, Geneva.

UNICEF (United Nations Children's Fund). 2011. The State of the World's Children 2011. New York: UNICEF.

Vasan, A., N. Kenya-Mugisha, K. J. Seung, M. Achieng, P. Banura, F. Lule, M. Beems, J. Todd, and E. Madraa. 2009. "Agreement between Physicians and Non-Physician Clinicians in Starting Antiretroviral Therapy in Rural Uganda." *Human Resources for Health* 7 (75).

WHO. 2006. *The World Health Report 2006: Working Together for Health.* Geneva: WHO.

WHO. 2005–2009. "Global Atlas of the Health Workforce." http://www.who.int/globalatlas/.

World Bank. 1993. *World Development Report 1993: Investing in Health.* Washington, DC: World Bank.

CHAPTER 9

Rural-Urban Imbalance of Health Workers in Sub-Saharan Africa

Christophe Lemière, Christopher H. Herbst, Carmen Dolea, Pascal Zurn, and Agnes Soucat

In most if not all countries in Sub-Saharan Africa, the geographical distribution of skilled health workers is imbalanced in favor of urban areas. Labor economics theory suggests reasons behind the uneven distribution of human resources for health. First, rural labor market demand (rural employers' funding ability to hire health workers) is usually low in Sub-Saharan countries, often because of a small private for profit sector in rural areas, limited decentralization of funding to rural areas, as well as the limited ability of rural populations to pay for services (or the limited ability of employers to charge for services). Second, health worker preferences often favor urban over rural areas due to differences in monetary and nonmonetary compensation (although this varies by cadre, gender, and socioeconomic and geographic background). Systematic analysis of in-country labor market conditions—including funding for human resources for health at all levels and health worker characteristics, preferences, and remuneration—will lay the foundation for better policy making to address the rural shortage.

Geographic Maldistribution of Health Workers within Countries

According to the World Health Organization (WHO), 36 of 47 Sub-Saharan countries have a critical deficiency of health workers (WHO 2006). But this focus on national numbers often masks the great deficiency of health workers in rural areas. Imbalances between urban and rural areas can be extreme (figure 9.1).[1]

Applying the Joint Learning Initiative (JLI)-WHO benchmark of 2.28 health workers (doctors, nurses, and midwives) per 1,000 population (or 22.8 per 10,000) to Benin, Côte d'Ivoire, Mali, and Senegal (four countries that produce many health worker graduates), we see that although none of the countries has a critical deficiency of doctors, all have a sizable shortage in rural areas. In these four countries—as in most other Sub-Saharan countries—the geographic distribution of health workers is highly skewed toward urban areas. In Côte d'Ivoire, for example, about 70 percent of doctors work in the southern urban regions, even though only 40 percent of the population lives there (Butera and others 2005).

Figure 9.1   Density of Doctors in Urban and Rural Areas, 13 Sub-Saharan Countries

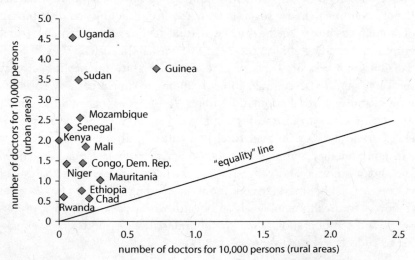

Note: If doctor densities in urban and rural areas were similar, the points (one point represents one country) would be close to the equality line. Densities are much higher in urban areas, so all points are above that line.

Almost all countries in Sub-Saharan Africa have health worker to population ratios that are significantly worse in rural areas, whilst surpluses are sometimes evident in urban areas. In Ghana, for example, the number of public sector doctors, nurses and midwives per 1,000 population is 1.43 in urban Greater Accra, and only 0.67 in the much more rural Northern Region. When you include private sector providers, the density in Greater Accra of these cadres is believed to exceed the 2.28 JLI/WHO benchmark (Appiah-Denkyira and others 2012). In Zambia, the total number of public and private sector clinical workers in the districts of Chililabombwe and Livingstone exceeds 2.5 per 1,000 population, whereas the rural and marginalized district of Chilubi is home to only 0.13 clinical health workers per 1,000 population (Herbst and others 2011). In Sudan, nearly 70 percent of health personnel work in urban settings, serving about 30 percent of the total country population (Sudan CSR—HRH Chapter, 2012).

Wide Variation in Geographic Distribution across Countries

A compact way to compare health workers' geographic distribution across countries is an aggregated index, such as a Concentration index. This index, alongside the Gini index and the Lorenz curve, has been extended from economics and applied to the health sector to measure health indicator imbalances (box 9.1).[2]

Box 9.1

Overview of Methods for Measuring Geographic Imbalances of Health Workers

Munga and Mæstad (2009) present a useful overview of Lorenz and concentration curves.

Lorenz Curves and the Gini Index

In Munga and Mæstad (2009) the Lorenz curve shows the cumulative share of health workers against the cumulative share of the population, with locations ranked from the least to the most health workers per capita (box figure 9.1.1).

(continued next page)

Box 9.1 *(continued)*

Box Figure 9.1.1   The Lorenze Curve and the Concentration Curves

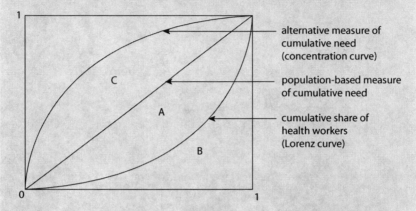

The Gini index measures the aggregate level of inequality, taking the values between 0 and 1, with higher values indicating higher levels of inequality. Graphically, the Gini index is the area A/(A + B) in box figure 9.1.1. For discrete distributions where the observations have been ranked from below, the Gini index can be calculated as

$$G = \frac{\sum_{i=1}^{n}(2i-n-1)X_i}{n^2\mu},$$

where G is the Gini index, n is the number of observations, X_i is the number of health workers in the ith location, and μ is the mean number of health workers.

Concentration Curves and the Concentration Index

Concentration curves, used extensively to characterize socioeconomic inequalities in health, here characterize health worker need. Thus, concentration curves plot cumulative expressions of need (that is, the cumulative number of inhabitants, under-five deaths, and HIV+ cases) against cumulative population. In contrast to the Lorenz curve, concentration curves are constructed by ranking observations by an external variable. By using the number of health workers per capita as the external variable, Munga and Mæstad (2009) superimpose the concentration curves in the same diagram as the Lorenz curve (see box figure 9.1.1). So, it becomes possible to make statements such as "50 percent of the population have

(continued next page)

Box 9.1 *(continued)*

access to x percent of the health workers, while their need would represent y percent of the aggregate need."

If need is expressed by the number of inhabitants, the concentration curve is simply the diagonal (see box figure 9.1.1). When need is expressed through other variables, the concentration curve may run both below and above the diagonal.

Concentration indices measure whether inequalities on average are increased or reduced by replacing the number of inhabitants with alternative measures of need. Technically, the concentration index is computed in the same way as the Gini index, and graphically, the concentration index is the area $C/(A + B)$. When the concentration curve lies above (below) the diagonal, the area 'C' is assigned a negative (positive) value.

The concentration index takes values between -1 and $+1$. When the index is 0, the alternative measure of need does not affect aggregate inequality, compared to when need is measured by the number of inhabitants. When the index is negative, which would occur if the concentration curve lies anywhere above the diagonal, health care needs per capita are on average larger in the districts with the fewest health workers per capita. So, the inequalities are larger when we use the alternative measure of need. The opposite is true when the concentration curve lies anywhere below the diagonal, which would imply a positive concentration index.

Source: Munga and Mæstad 2009.

When applied to nine Sub-Saharan African countries, the concentration index shows that most face a similar rural-urban distribution problem for doctors, whilst a more wide variation is evident for nurses (figure 9.2).

Variation in Geographic Distribution across Cadres, Education, and Gender

In all countries reviewed the distribution of doctors is more skewed toward urban areas than that of nurses. Highly trained or qualified health workers are more likely to remain in urban areas than those with low skills. Health workers with more formal education, such as doctors, are heavily concentrated in urban areas and especially sparse in rural areas, while cadres with less education, such as nurses or auxiliary nurses, are more concentrated in rural areas.

Figure 9.2   Concentration Indexes for Doctors and Nurses

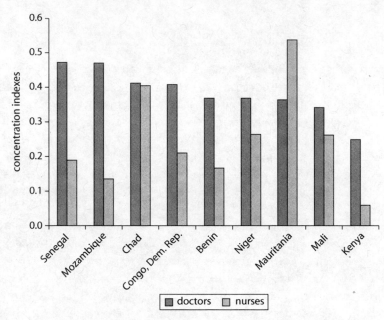

Note: The closer the index is to zero, the more equal the distribution; the closer the index is to 1, the less equal the distribution.

Tanzania provides an interesting example. Twenty percent of Tanzania's doctors (referred to as medical officers) serve about 80 percent of the population, which resides mostly in rural areas. Rural areas have more mid-level cadres, such as clinical officers, than urban areas.[3] As shown in figure 9.3, where all concentration curves[4] fall below the diagonal, no cadre has an equitable distribution.

Rural areas in Sub-Saharan Africa tend to have a higher proportion of health workers without formal training, including community health workers, health extension workers, and traditional healers. In Lesotho 8,600 health workers serve a population that is more than 75 percent rural, and only 44 percent have a formal education. The other 4,800 are community health workers, most working in rural areas. Sierra Leone is home to only 3,736 conventional workers but 10,723 traditional birth attendants, mainly in rural districts.

Urban and rural health workers generally have different gender profiles. Female workers are more concentrated in urban than rural areas.

Figure 9.3   Distribution of Health Workers per 1,000 Population by Cadre, All Districts in Tanzania

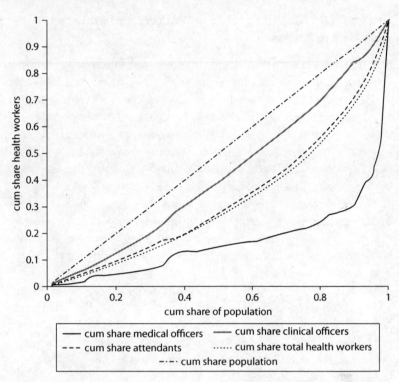

Source: Munga and Mæstad 2009.

In Zambia women account for the majority of health workers in both areas, but are significantly more represented in urban districts. This distribution also applies to cadres: in rural districts a smaller proportion of doctors, clinical officers, and nurses are female (Herbst and others 2011). Box 9.2 stresses the potentially negative impact the picture on distribution has on health care access.

Labor Market Dynamics of the Rural-Urban Imbalance

Labor economics offers two explanations for the rural-urban imbalance in health workers, related to the two key features of a labor market: supply and demand (see chapter 3). They are not mutually exclusive and a single country can experience both.

Box 9.2

Unequal Distribution of Health Workers and Reduced Health Care Access

Health indicators are often worse in rural and remote areas—the same areas with the fewest health workers. The paradox is often referred to as the inverse care law (Hart 1971). Since the Millennium Development Goals are closely related to expanded coverage of key interventions, such as assisted deliveries or antibiotic treatment of pneumonia, it is difficult for rural areas without adequate access to providers of these interventions to achieve them.[a] This is especially true for maternal mortality (Millennium Development Goal 5), because coverage of skilled birth attendants is a critical input for lowering maternal mortality (Anand and Bärnighausen 2004).

Some argue that fewer higher level cadres in rural areas is not always problematic, as the rural poor may be less interested in seeking care from higher level cadres than from informal health workers or lower level cadres. Community and traditional health providers are thought to be more trusted and respected than higher level cadres in some remote areas, and thus more appropriate (Stekelenburg and others 2005). While evidence shows that the rural poor seek fewer health services in general, this may pertain less to their preference for community or traditional health providers, and more to the lack of available or adequately performing higher level cadres, alongside financial constraints. Many surveys found that when the rural poor seek health services, they choose the same services and health cadres as the nonpoor (Ouendo 2005).

The uneven gender distribution may also disproportionately affect access to care for the rural poor. Rural areas have few midwives, and because women may be reluctant to receive care from a male health worker (such as in Niger and Mali [World Bank 2011]), and because many rural health workers are male, they may not seek care from a trained health worker.[b]

Notes:
a. Of course, an adequate density of health workers is not the only condition for guaranteeing access to care. Rural health facilities should have adequate drugs and equipment. They should also receive sufficient funding from the central level to cover recurrent costs (beside salaries and drugs). In addition, there can be bottlenecks related to the demand side, such as cultural obstacles or high user fees.
b. This preference at least applies to antenatal care and intrapartum care.

The first is reduced labor market demand for health workers in rural areas, as expressed by the employers' inability to hire them. Two kinds of employers predominate: public employers (government-owned and government-run health care facilities) and private employers (private health care facilities) (table 9.1). Governments may fund public-sector health

Table 9.1   Sources of Demand for Health Workers

	Public	Private
Institutions (facilities)	Government-run facilities employ health workers, using government and donor funding as well as fees collected by facilities.	Private facilities employ health workers. Donors support nongovernmental organization-run facilities.
Individuals (patients)	Government provides salaries. Patients pay user fees to public providers. Donors provide salary supplements.	Patients pay user fees to individual providers.

facilities and thus generate demand for labor. Patients may pay user fees to both the public and private sector and thus generate income, which can contribute to hiring health workers. Donors increase demand for health worker labor by subsidizing the public or private sector. Inadequately funded demand for health workers in rural areas contributes to the rural-urban imbalance.

The second explanation is limited supply of health workers, who are reluctant to work in rural areas, even when enough funding and demand exists. Labor market supply in rural areas is often worse than in urban areas due to inadequate monetary and nonmonetary compensation.

Labor market supply and demand help explain rural shortages of human resources for health (HRH), as well as the more varied situation in urban markets. Labor market supply and demand lead to the common rural shortage of high-level cadres (which is also occasionally present in urban areas), as well as urban underemployment (figure 9.4). But when observed in a rural labor market in Sub-Saharan Africa, the rural labor market finds itself in a market-clearing equilibrium. This equilibrium, which is sometimes observed in the urban labor market, reflects a perfect match of funding and willingness to work in the relevant labor market (see chapter 3).

Labor Demand for Health Workers Is Often Lower in Rural Areas

Funding to employ health workers is often disproportionately available in urban areas. This is linked to the fact that public sector funding is often disproportionately allocated towards urban areas (where most of the more expensive health workers are located), as well as towards secondary and tertiary level care provision (hospitals tend to be disproportionately located in urban over rural locations).

In addition, the private for profit sector is often more developed in urban than in rural areas within countries (Sudan and Uganda are good examples). In many countries the demand for labor from not for profit

Figure 9.4   Example of Labor Market Supply and Demand Leading to Urban Underemployment and Rural Shortages of Health Workers

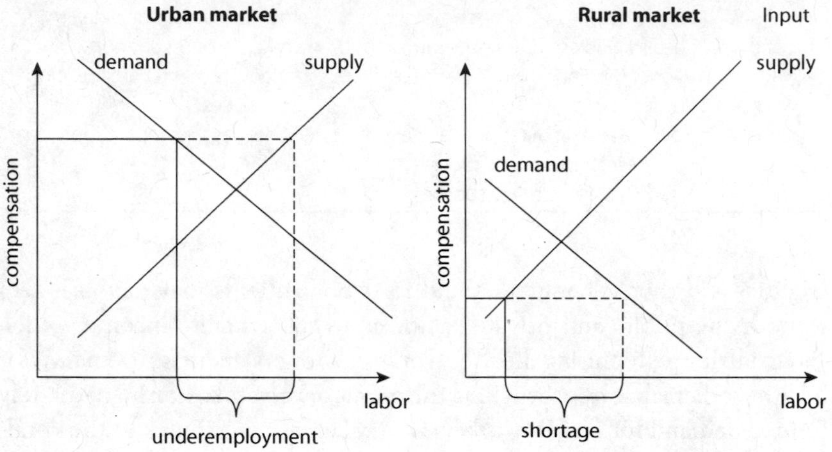

Source: World Bank data.

providers, which are often more evenly distributed, is relatively low, and often subsidized by public sector funds (see Rwanda, or Uganda for example).

Fiscal recentralization (including non functioning decentralization arrangements where most of the funding for HRH still ends up in urban centers), coupled with abolishing user fees in several countries (or the inability to generate them due to a limited number of patients willing to purchase services in rural areas), has curtailed local health facilities' income and ability to hire workers. In North Sudan for example, the more rural states such as North Kordofan, Kasala, or Red Sea receive much less revenue from federal transfers and own sources (user fees) than more urban or centrally located states (figure 9.5).

Limited revenues from rural populations constrain private demand for health workers. Assessments in Sub-Saharan Africa overwhelmingly show that rural populations are poorer than urban ones. Lack of health insurance for rural populations also prevents them from buying adequate health services and thus generating revenue and demand for HRH. Demand from households in rural areas is therefore lower than in urban areas, so revenue from private practice is lower in rural areas. This is an important reason why health workers (including civil servants with dual jobs) are reluctant to settle in rural areas, as in Mali.[5]

Figure 9.5   State's Revenue from Federal Transfers and Own Revenue in North Sudan

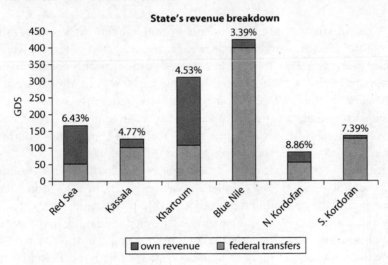

State's revenue breakdown

Sources: PER, World Bank 2011, as in Herbst and others 2011.

Finally, in countries where most health workers are recruited and paid centrally, rural health facilities face inadequate funding of demand because few health workers will work in rural areas. Health workers assigned to rural areas join in lesser numbers and turnover is high, as in Zambia (Picazo 2008).

The Supply of Health Workers for Rural Areas Is Limited by Job Preference

Even if rural demand for health workers were adequate, rural jobs are usually not attractive for health workers (in particular higher level cadres). These jobs have higher opportunity costs, including inadequate living and working conditions and lead to forgone income (such as revenues from private practice, which is usually less profitable in rural areas). Still, health workers have different preferences and do not face (or perceive) the same opportunity costs. Some may be more likely to work in rural areas than others.

Rural jobs and high opportunity costs. Health workers often view living and working conditions as substandard in rural areas. Various studies, including the World Health Report 2006, stress the lack of career-related incentives for health workers in rural settings, such as professional development and training. Most medical institutions and faculty are in urban areas.

A recent study of nursing students in Sub-Saharan Africa shows that these future health workers perceive rural areas negatively. Health worker students are reluctant to work in remote locations with poor infrastructure, poor health services, limited housing, and few recreational facilities (Mullei and others 2010). Compensation is frequently worse, too. In Ethiopia remuneration for doctors and nurses varied greatly between the capital city (Addis Ababa) and rural regions (Tigray and Southern Nations, Nationalities, and People's Region) (figure 9.6).

Although most rural areas offer a lower cost of living, such as housing rents, school fees, and food (Mullei and others 2010), health workers may incur indirect costs. Limited job opportunities for a spouse may lead to loss of income, and if the spouse stays in the city, the family may pay two sets of housing costs. Similarly, children often remain in the city to complete their education, implying housing costs for them, too. Fewer opportunities to moonlight are another opportunity cost. In Benin doctors can more than double their salary by accepting private clients after hours (World Bank 2010).

Health workers have different rural job preferences. Some groups of health workers, such as men, younger workers, lower level cadres, those with poorer or rural backgrounds, and even those who are intrinsically motivated—at times overlapping—seem willing to work in rural areas if they receive compensation to make up for the costs of living. Other groups, such as doctors, those with children, and those originally from urban areas (or trained in urban areas), are generally less willing to relocate, even with a comprehensive incentive package. The motivation for working in rural areas varies across cadres and groups.

Highly trained professionals' preference to work in urban areas in most Sub-Saharan countries contributes to the shortage of groups like doctors and surgeons in rural areas. In Niger young doctors cited "lack of opportunities for postgraduate training" as a key reason for not accepting rural positions (Souleymane 2005). The picture is often different with lower level cadres, although again varies greatly by country. In Ethiopia nurses tend to be more willing to work in rural areas than doctors (Jack 2008). A study in Ghana found that some lower level cadres appreciate the exposure to a wide range of pathologies that comes with rural service. Among the reasons the workers cited were that they were sometimes

Figure 9.6   Sources of Compensation for Doctors and Nurses Vary across Regions in Ethiopia

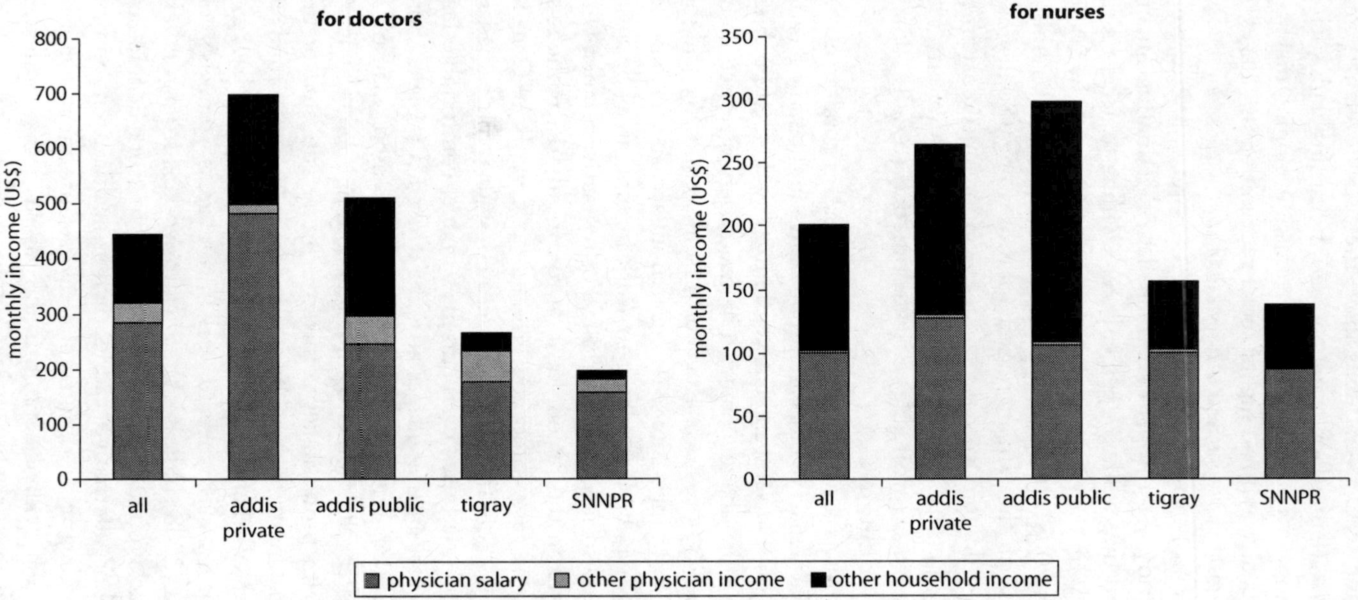

Source: Jack 2008.
Note: SNNPR = Southern Nations, Nationalities, and People's Region.

159

called doctor; were given duties above their skill level; had greater bonding among staff, thus facilitating on-the-job learning skills such as surgery; had more opportunities to manage teams, developing management and leadership skills; and had higher social recognition in villages, with more associated gifts (Lievens and others 2007).

Younger health workers may also be more willing to work in rural areas. A study in Ethiopia that tracked the graduating nursing class of 2004 found that while 34 percent were willing to accept a rural placement that year, the proportion declined to 18 percent by 2007 (Serneels and others 2008). In Niger older doctors cited "weak remuneration in rural areas" as their main reason for not going (Souleymane 2005). Many older doctors may face a steep opportunity cost in moving to rural areas, because the reputation they built in the city often allows them to have a (profitable) private practice (usually alongside their public sector duty).

Male workers are also more likely to work in rural areas. One review suggests that female doctors are prone to live in the same location as their husband's job (Dussault and Franceschini 2006). In the Republic of Congo, as in many Sub-Saharan countries, married couples are required by law to live together, "so providers assigned to rural areas marry and move to the cities to be with their spouse" (Crigler, Boniface, and Shannon 2008).

Women may be less willing to work in rural areas because of safety concerns and socioeconomic profile. For nonnative women without family or friends in the region, locating to a rural area without support or protection can carry safety concerns. In the Republic of Congo "rural settings are also considered too dangerous for unaccompanied women, as they cannot ride buses by themselves or feel comfortable leaving their homes to work in the villages at night if needed (Crigler, Boniface, and Shannon 2008). With women accounting for more than 61 percent of health workers, this further complicates staffing rural regions." Also, many female health professionals come from more educated or urban backgrounds, making them less likely to accept positions in rural areas.

A health worker's socioeconomic or geographic background may affect his or her willingness to work in rural areas. Serneels's cohort study in Ethiopia (2008) indicates that health workers from rural areas or less well-off backgrounds are more motivated to work in rural areas. Some lower level or "alternative" cadres, such as health extension workers, may be more willing to work in rural areas because they have a rural background. Much evidence supports the assertion that professionals from rural origins more readily settle in remote areas.[6]

Altruism may also motivate student health workers to work in rural areas. In Rwanda the main reason for final-year medical students to work long term in a rural area was the "opportunity to help the poor" (Lievens and others 2010). In Ethiopia the most common reason for rural place-ment among nursing and medical students was "to provide health care where it is needed most," although nursing students cited it more than medical students (Serneels and others 2005). That altruism diminished over time, once they began working (Serra and others 2008).

Policies Addressing Rural-Urban Imbalances in Sub-Saharan Africa

Various policies have addressed geographic imbalances of health workers in Sub-Saharan Africa.

The first approach to strengthening labor market demand for health workers in rural areas is to increase funding to rural districts and facilities. For the public sector, this may be achieved through the true decentraliza-tion of funding to hire health workers to the rural areas. Fiscal decentral-ization is already common in many countries in Sub-Saharan Africa. Depending on the model, funding for rural health worker wages is trans-ferred to local governments in block grants, as in Ethiopia and Nigeria, or earmarks, as in Benin, Mali, and Uganda. Elsewhere, funding for wages is directly transferred to facilities, as in Rwanda. Pending sufficient capacity to administer such decentralized arrangements (which is not always the case), the transferred funds are calculated as a function of needs and poverty—using, for example, the needs-based approach—adding to the demand for rural workers (chapter 5).

When households pay user fees to public or private practitioners, they also contribute directly to fund demand. Given that rural populations are usually poorer, this strategy is weaker than in urban areas. Another is to set up a health insurance mechanism, subsidizing poorer households' access to care.

Incentives to boost labor market supply for rural health workers, whether public or private sector, are also common. Most frequent is low-ering the opportunity cost of rural employment; almost all countries have tested at least one type. They vary widely, from very simple incentive schemes (as in Mauritania or Niger) to comprehensive packages (as in Zambia). Experience is mixed, with some success in Mali (box 9.3), South Africa, and Zambia.[7] Yet Niger's financial incentive program for doctors, where one of the few truly prospective evaluations was carried out, had no significant impact. Doctor distribution remained highly skewed to the capital city's benefit, with the proportion of all doctors working there staying virtually constant before the program's launch (34 percent) and after (35 percent) (Souleymane 2008).

Intervening in the health labor market and supply-side behavior of health workers, many countries have compulsory placement or bonding programs, which oblige graduates to work in rural areas after graduation. Although such policies may temporarily reduce shortages, they seem to have little or no impact on long-term rural retention. Anecdotal evidence suggests that they are also difficult to enforce.[8]

Rural pipeline policies have been implemented in some Sub-Saharan countries.[9] They place medical and nursing schools in rural areas to attract rural students, ensure that admission policies favor health workers with rural backgrounds, and adopt a curriculum that emphasizes rural health needs and rural work experience.

Benin created a regional medical school in 2001 to train general practitioners (Lemière 2008). Niger established two rural nursing schools in 2006, and Mali established 11 between 1997 and 2010. Senegal created a regional branch of the Dakar medical school in 2008. Ethiopia established nursing schools in not only the capital, but also the south and west.

Box 9.3

Incentives for Recruiting Private Rural Doctors in Mali

Mali supports young doctors in setting up rural private practices, working with a nongovernmental organization (Santé-Sud) and the Bamako medical faculty to identify young doctors who might be willing to work in rural areas before graduation (Coulibaly and others 2007). Those interested receive help in preparing a business plan that reflects the local population's incomes.

Once the doctors start their businesses, they get regular mentoring from older doctors. They receive a small fixed income ($200 a month) and sometimes housing from the community. Most of their income comes from user fees, half of which they keep. Active rural doctors can earn about $1,000 a month, not much less than they would in urban areas.

Since 2000 this strategy has encouraged more than 100 doctors to go to, and stay in, rural areas.

Source: Lemière and others 2010.

Between 2007 and 2009, it created nine new medical schools in regional capitals. South Africa has set up a successful program providing scholarships to medical students with a rural background that will return to their districts after graduating (Ross and Couper 2004).

Alternative skill mixes for rural areas also show promising results. Ethiopia has one of the better-known and more successful programs following the rural pipeline method: between 2003 and 2009, 31,831 health extension workers were trained and deployed to rural and hard-to-reach communities (Bilal and others 2010). Today, they provide outreach services in rural areas, diagnose and treat diarrhea, perform safe and clean deliveries, and diagnose and treat malaria and pneumonia.

In Zambia a clinical officer cadre (established in 1936) provides primary care, particularly in rural areas, to fill the gap of doctors. Clinical officers (with skills between a doctor's and nurse's) take on key responsibilities, particularly for antiretroviral therapy, including assessments of HIV/AIDS patients and follow-up. They refer complicated cases to physicians. In 2007 Zambia had close to 1,270 clinical officers, with about 70 percent in rural districts (Herbst and others 2010).

Malawi also has clinical officers for rural areas. Ghana has a community health program for rural areas. And Rwanda has cooperatives of community health workers, contracted by health facilities to provide Millennium Development Goal-related interventions.

Increasing the skill sets of lower level and mid-level professionals in addition to higher level professionals, like general practitioners, has also shown positive results when focused on a specific procedure, such as obstetrics or antiretroviral therapy. In Mozambique the lack of doctors—combined with the urgent need for emergency surgical care and maternal health skills—called for a reoriented health staff training. Comparing 1,000 consecutive cesarean sections conducted by medical assistants with the same number conducted by obstetricians and gynecologists showed no differences in quality (Pereira and others 1996). In Malawi, of more than 2,000 emergency obstetric operations performed by clinical officers, postoperative outcomes were comparable with those performed by medical officers (Philips, Zachariah, and Venis 2008).

Conclusion

Rural-urban imbalances of health workers are a bigger issue than national deficiencies, and are a problem in almost all Sub-Saharan countries.

Two sets of explanations can be identified. The first set stems from institutional arrangements that constrain rural demand for health workers: a lack of fiscal or management decentralization in government-run sectors, and a lack of health insurance for the rural population, preventing them from purchasing adequate health services. The second set stems from the high opportunity costs of rural jobs. Health workers are rational actors in labor markets and choose not to work in rural areas because of these opportunity costs. But, job preferences differ across health workers. Some, particularly young workers or those with rural backgrounds place less weight on these opportunity costs than other health workers.

These explanations could lay the ground for policies targeting these health workers and improving current policies. Sub-Saharan countries already experimented with various policies. The results are mixed, and these policies need to be better evaluated and refined by country analysis of the supply and demand constraints of the health labor market. What is needed? It is necessary to systematically assess health worker preferences and current remunerations, and evaluate new policies when implemented.

Notes

1. We do not claim that this issue is unique to Africa. Rural-urban imbalances of health workers occur anywhere, including developed countries (WHO 2010). We believe, however, that the impact on health outcomes is stronger in countries where densities of health workers are already very low, as in Africa.

2. Interested readers can look at Wagstaff and others (2007) and Lemière and others (2010) for details on calculations.

3. This cadre commonly has a skill set somewhere between that of doctors and nurses.

4. A concentration curve is simply the graphical equivalent of a concentration index: the closer the curve to the diagonal, the more equal the distribution of resources.

5. See Codjia, Jabot, and Dubois 2010. Health workers, here, are individuals working full-time in private practice ("private providers") and civil servants pursuing another activity (private practice) in addition to their normal duty ("civil servants with dual jobs or moonlighting activities").

6. Studies supporting this conclusion include Rolfe (1995), Dunbabin and Levitt (2003), and de Vries and Reid (2003).

7. In Mali more than 100 doctors agreed to start private practices in rural areas (Coulibaly and others 2007). Under the South African Rural Allowance and

Scarce Skills Allowance, 28–35 percent of rural health workers who received an 8–22 percent salary bonus believed it affected their career plans for the following year (Vujicic and Lindelow 2008). The Zambian Health Workers Retention Scheme attracted and retained more than 50 doctors in rural areas in less than two years (Koot and Martineau 2005).

8. Zambia's compulsory one-year placement of young doctors in rural areas was not strictly enforced, and when it was, many doctors resigned rather than work in rural areas (Koot and Martineau 2005). One exception to enforcement failure can be found outside Africa: Thailand enforced a comprehensive package of benefits and incentives for rural health workers as well as a rural pipeline program (Wibulpolprasert and Pengpaibon 2003).

9. There are no rigorous evaluations, and almost all empirical studies are from programs outside Africa. They show evidence of strong impact (see Murray and others (2006) and Rolfe and others (1995) for Australia, Rabinowitz (1999, 2001) for the United States, and Hsueh and others (2004) for Norway and Japan).

References

Anand, S., and T. Bärnighausen. 2004. "Human Resources and Health Outcomes: Cross-Country Econometric Study." *Lancet* 364 (9445): 1603–09.

Appiah-Denkyira, E., C. H. Herbst, A. Soucat, C. Lemiere and K. Saleh. 2012. *Towards Interventions on HRH in Ghana. Evidence for health workforce planning and results.* Ministry of Health, Ghana and The World Bank.

Bilal, N. K., C. H. Herbst, F. Zhao, A. Soucat, and C. Lemière. 2010. "Health Extension Workers in Ethiopia Improve Access and Coverage for the Rural Poor." Working Paper, World Bank, Washington, DC.

Butera, D., J. V. Fieno, S. Diarra, G. Kombe, C. Decker, and S. Oulai. 2005. *Comprehensive Assessment of Human Resource Requirements to Deliver the President's Emergency Plan for AIDS Relief and Other Basic Health Services in Côte d'Ivoire.* Bethesda, MD: The Partners for Health Reformplus Project, Abt Associates.

Codjia, L., F. Jabot, and H. Dubois. 2010. *Evaluation du programme d'appui a la medicalisation des aires de santé rurales au Mali.* Geneva: World Health Organization.

Coulibaly, S., D. Desplat, Y. Kone, K. Nimaga, S. Dugas, G. Farnarier, M. Sy, H. Balique, O. K. Doumbo, and M. Van Dormael. 2007. "Une médecine rurale de proximité: l'expérience des médecins de campagne au Mali." *Education for Health* 7 (online) 2007–67.

Crigler, L., S. Boniface, and S. Shannon. 2008. "Human Resource and Quality Rapid Assessment." Brazzaville, Republic of Congo.

de Vries, E., and S. Reid. 2003. "Do South African Rural Origin Medical Students Return to Rural Practice?" *South African Medical Journal* 93 (10): 789–93.

Dunbabin, J. S., and L. Levitt. 2003. "Rural Origin and Rural Medical Exposure: Their Impact on the Rural and Remote Medical Workforce in Australia." *Rural Remote Health* 3 (1): 212.

Dussault, G., and M. C. Franceschini. 2006. "Not Enough There, Too Many Here: Understanding Geographical Imbalances in the Distribution of the Health Workforce." *Human Resources for Health* 4 (12).

Hart, J. T., 1971. *The inverse care law,.* The Lancet, 27 February, 297 (7696): 405–412.

Herbst, C. H., M. Vledder, K. Campbell, M. Sjöblom, and A. Soucat. 2011. *"The Human Resources for Health Crisis in Zambia: An Outcome of Health Worker Entry, Exit, and Performance within the National Labor Health Market."* Working Paper 214, World Bank, Washington, DC.

Hsueh, Wayne. 2004. *What Evidence-Based Undergraduate Interventions Promote Rural Health?* New Zealand Medical Journal 117 (1204).

Jack, W. 2008. "Human Resources for Health in Ethiopia." Unpublished Report. World Bank, Washington, DC.

Koot, J., and T. Martineau. 2005. *Mid-Term Review of the Zambian Health Workers Retention Scheme 2003–2004.* Lusaka, Zambia: Government of Zambia.

Lemière, C. 2008. "The Benin Health Workforce: A Labor Market Analysis." World Bank, Washington, DC.

Lemière, C., C. Herbst, N. Jahanshahi, E. Smith, and A. Soucat. 2010. "Reducing Geographical Imbalances of the Distribution of Health Workers in Sub-Saharan Africa: A Labor Market Angle of What Works, What Does Not, and Why." Working Paper 209, World Bank, Washington, DC.

Lievens, T., P. Serneels, J. Butera, and A. Soucat. 2010. "Diversity in Career Preferences of Future Health Workers in Rwanda. Where, Why and for How Much." Working Paper 189, World Bank, Washington, DC.

Lievens, T., P. Serneels, S. Garbarino, and P. Quartey. 2007. *Ghana Health Worker Study.* Kigali: Ministry of Health of Rwanda.

Mullei, K., S. Mudhune, J. Wafula, E. Masamo, M. English, C. Goodman, M. Lagarde, and D. Blaauw. 2010. "Attracting and Retaining Health Workers in Rural Areas: Investigating Nurses' Views on Rural Posts and Policy Interventions." *BMC Health Services Research* 10 (S1).

Munga, M., and O. Mæstad. 2009. "Measuring Inequalities in the Distribution of Health Workers: The Case of Tanzania." *Human Resources for Health* 7 (4).

Murray, Richard, and Ian Wronski. 2006. *When the Tide Goes Out: Health Workforce in Rural, Remote and Indigenous Communities.* Medical Journal of Australia 185(1): 37–38.

Ouendo, E.-M. 2005. "Itinéraire thérapeutique des malades indigents au Bénin." *Tropical Medicine and International Health* 10 (2): 179–86.

Pereira, C., A. Bugalho, S. Bergström, F. Vaz, and M. Cotiro. 1996. "A Comparative Study of Caesarean Deliveries by Assistant Medical Officers and Obstetricians in Mozambique." *British Journal of Obstetrics and Gynecology* 103 (6): 508–12.

Philips, M., R. Zachariah, and S. Venis. 2008. *Task Shifting for Anti Retroviral Treatment Delivery in Sub-Saharan Africa: not a panacea,* The Lancet, Feb 23–29, 317.

Picazo, O. 2008. *Struggling and Coping to Serve: The Zambian Health Workforce as Depicted in the Public Expenditure Tracking and Quality of Service Delivery Survey, 2006.* World Bank, Africa Region, Human Development 1, Country Department 2, Washington, DC.

Rabinowitz, Howard. 2001. *Critical Factors for Designing Programs to Increase the Supply and the Retention of Rural Primary Care Physicians.* Journal of the American Medical Association 286 (9).

———. 1999. *A Program to Increase the Number of Family Physicians in Rural and Underserved Areas: Impact after 22 years.* Journal of the American Medical Association 281 (3): 255–60.

Rolfe, I. E., S. A. Pearson, D. L. O'Connell, and J. Dickinson. 1995. "Finding Solutions to the Rural Doctor Shortage: The Rules of Selective Versus Undergraduates Medical Education at Newcastle." *Australian and New Zealand Journal of Medicine* 25 (5): 512–17.

Ross, A. J., and I. D. Couper. 2004. "Rural Scholarship Schemes: A Solution to the Human Resource Crisis in Rural District Hospitals?" *South African Family Practice* 46 (1): 5–6.

Serneels, P. 2008. *Discovering the Real World: Health Workers' Early Work Experience and Career Choice.* The World Bank.

Serneels, P., M. Lindelow, J. G. Montalvo, and A. Barr. 2005. "For Public Service or Money: Understanding Geographical Imbalances in the Health Workforce." Policy Research Working Paper 3686, World Bank, Washington, DC.

Serra, D., P. Serneels, M. Lindelow, and J. G. Montalivo. 2008. *Discovering the Real World: How Health Workers' Early Work Experience Affects Their Career Choice.* Addis Ababa: Ministry of Health of Ethiopia.

Souleymane, S. 2005. *Etude sur la motivation des personnels de santé à servir en périphérie au Niger.* Niamey: Ministry of Health of Niger.

———. 2008. *Impact des mesures d'incitation financière accordées aux Médecins, Pharmaciens et Chirurgiens Dentistes.* Niamey: Ministry of Health of Niger.

Stekelenburg, J., B. E. Jagerb, P. R. Kolkc, E. H. M. N. Westenc, A. van der Kwaakd, and I. N. Wolffers. 2005. "Health Care Seeking Behavior and Utilization of Traditional Healers in Kalabo, Zambia." *Health Policy* 71 (1): 67–81.

Vujicic, M., and M. Lindelow. 2008. *Approaches to Reduce Health Worker Shortages in Remote Areas: A Global Review of Recruitment and Retention Policies.* Washington, DC: World Bank.

Wagstaff, A., O. O'Donnell, E. Van Doorslaer, and M. Lindelow. 2007. *Analyzing Health Equity Using Household Survey Data: A Guide to Techniques and their Implementation.* Washington, DC: World Bank.

WHO (World Health Organization). 2006. *The World Health Report 2006: Working Together for Health.* Geneva: WHO.

———. 2010. *Increasing Access to Health Workers in Remote and Rural Areas through Improved Retention: Global Policy Recommendations.* Geneva: WHO.

Wibulpolprasert, S., and P. Pengpaibon. 2003. "Integrated Strategies to Tackle the Inequitable Distribution of Doctors in Thailand: Four Decades of Experience." *Human Resources for Health* 1 (12).

World Bank. 2010. *République du Bénin: santé, nutrition et population—Rapport analytique santé pauvreté.* Report AAA51-BJ. Washington, DC: World Bank.

———. 2011. *République du Mali: Santé, Nutrition et Population—Rapport Analytique Santé Pauvreté.* Washington, DC: World Bank.

———. 2012. *Health Country Status Report (CSR) for Sudan,* Human Resources for Health chapter, The World Bank.

CHAPTER 10

Migration and Attrition

Çağlar Özden and Mirvat Sewadeh

With a quarter of its trained physicians living in Organisation for Economic Co-operation and Development countries (OECD), Sub-Saharan Africa has by far the highest health worker migration of any region, while at the same time facing some of the most severe public health challenges. This chapter presents an overview of African physicians' migration and reviews its implications. Using data from a survey of Ghanaian physicians who migrated abroad, the chapter explores determinants and causes of migration for one of the most important migrant-sending countries. The chapter concludes with a brief discussion of changes in policy and the health care environment that could reduce or reverse current migration patterns.

Health Worker Mobility

The mobility of highly skilled workers across international borders is a natural consequence of global integration. But developing countries are the net losers in the competition for talent. They compete with wealthier countries that offer better economic conditions and career prospects for highly skilled, and highly sought after, professionals.

Sub-Saharan countries occupy a special place in the analysis of global skilled migration. Over the past few decades, poor economic and professional opportunities and unstable political and social environments drove hundreds of thousands of the best qualified African professionals to the rest of the world (Docquier and Marfouk 2006). In 2000, tertiary-educated workers accounted for 43 percent of total migrants from the continent (Docquier, Lohest, and Marfouk 2007). The loss of so much skilled labor is worrisome for countries that already suffer from low human capital. As tertiary and professional education are financed with severely limited public education budgets, poor African countries implicitly subsidize rich countries through migration of highly skilled labor.

The emigration of health professionals from Africa triggers more controversy and emotion than the emigration of any other professional class. Public health experts argue that the medical brain drain contributes to a decline in health indicators in many African countries that already face some of the most difficult public health challenges in the world (Bundred and Levitt 2000). The number of doctors per 1,000 people is less than 0.05 in many Sub-Saharan countries—and 50 times higher in many of the OECD countries that are destinations for African doctors. Africa's low density of medical professionals is among the reasons many countries will not meet the Millennium Development Goals on child mortality, maternal mortality, and HIV/AIDS, malaria, and other diseases (United Nations 2008).

Links between the migration of medical professionals and public health outcomes in developing countries are only recently the subject of empirical analysis. Several new databases on health professional migration enable this analysis (Bhargava and Docquier 2008; Clemens 2007; OECD 2008). Numerous detailed studies, now complete, provide no clear consensus, and the debate will likely continue. Some studies suggest a clear link between medical professional migration and health outcomes. Bundred and Levitt (2000) and Beecham (2002) point to migration's direct negative effect on the provision of health care services. Bhargava and Docquier (2008) show that physician migration contributes significantly to the high adult mortality from HIV/AIDS-related complications.

Other analyses conclude that migration does not affect public health outcomes. Chauvet, Gubert, and Mesplé-Somps (2008) argue that low numbers of physicians do not affect human development indicators. Clemens (2007) argues that other constraints in health care services are more binding than the number of physicians and that migration is not responsible for low staffing and public health conditions. Bhargava,

Docquier, and Moullan (2011) analyze migration's effect on child mortality and vaccinations using a random effects model. Their nuanced results suggest that many health indicators improve with physician levels when adult literacy exceeds 55 percent. The Bhargava study demonstrates the complex links between migration, development, and the social and economic environment of the country in question. It finds that the number of physicians in a country is only one input in the provision of health services, and stopping physician migration would have a positive but small impact on human development indicators.

Insufficient health care is a great challenge for development experts and policy makers, especially in Sub-Saharan Africa. Proper training for health care professionals, adequate staffing in rural and high-demand areas, and appropriate facilities, equipment, and support staff all influence the provision and quality of health care services.

This chapter has three objectives. The first is to examine migration among African health professionals, primarily physicians. The second is to review the effects of international migration. The third is to present the main determinants of physician migration from Ghana.

Emigration Patterns of African Physicians

In 2004 there were about 25,000 African-trained physicians in OECD countries, almost a fourth of the total number of physicians in Africa that year (Bhargava and Docquier 2008). Migration of African physicians is much higher than for other African professionals and tertiary educated workers, estimated at between 10 and 15 percent (Docquier and Marfouk 2007). It is the highest among all developing regions (figure 10.1).

While high migration among African physicians is itself a cause for concern, the rise in migration since the early 1990s is even more worrisome. The number of African-trained doctors working in OECD countries rose by 91 percent between 1991 and 2005. The increase in the number of African-trained physicians working in Africa during the same timeframe was comparatively low, at 61 percent (figure 10.2).

African physicians leave their home countries for reasons similar to those that motivate the migration of other skilled workers to OECD countries. The shortage of qualified health care professionals in OECD countries due to rapidly aging populations is one pull. African physicians cite higher wages and better professional development prospects in destination countries, and social and political conditions at home, as their most important reasons for migration. Other reasons include insufficient postgraduate training opportunities and poor practice conditions in Africa,

Figure 10.1   Stock of Migrant Physicians in OECD Countries as a Percentage of Locally Trained Physicians in Source Region

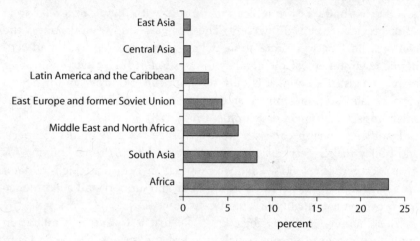

Source: Medical Brain Drain Database 1991–2004 in Bhargava, Docquier, and Moullan (2011).

Figure 10.2   Number of African-Trained Physicians in Africa and OECD Countries

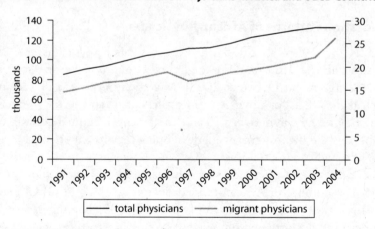

Source: Medical Brain Drain Database 1991–2004 in Bhargava, Docquier, and Moullan (2011).

especially facilities, equipment, medicine, and support staff. Culture also plays a key role in the emigration of physicians. In many African countries training and practicing abroad is a mark of success. Medical school faculty measure their success by whether their students are competent enough to practice in the competitive medical environments of the United States and Europe.

OECD Destinations for Migrant Physicians

The distribution of African physicians among OECD countries has not changed much since 1990. The United Kingdom, the United States, Canada, and Australia were the top four destinations in both 1991 and 2004, accounting for more than 85 percent of African physicians in OECD countries (figure 10.3). The United Kingdom dominated, with 55 percent of all Sub-Saharan doctors in OECD in both 1991 and 2004. The United States increased its share from a little below 9 percent in 1991 to more than 13 percent in 2004, surpassing Canada as the second-largest OECD destination. Ireland became the fifth-largest destination for African physicians among OECD countries, and the first among European Union members other than the United Kingdom.

Factors influencing physicians' destination countries are similar to those for other emigrant groups, skilled and unskilled. Colonial links, language, and economic and career prospects are some of the main factors determining the choice of destination. English-speaking countries dominate as the top destination for African physicians. Welcoming immigration policies and open professional environments contribute to their popularity.

Most physicians in developing countries are trained or fluent in English. Medical practice requires interacting with local populations who likely speak only their native languages. As a result, English-speaking

Figure 10.3   OECD Destinations for African Physicians

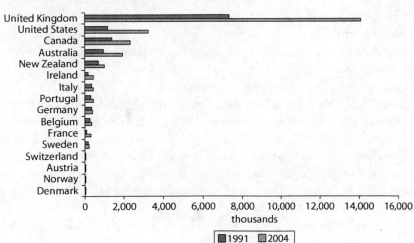

Source: Medical Brain Drain Database 1991–2004 in Bhargava, Docquier, and Moullan (2011).

countries are natural destinations for physicians from developing countries, because learning another language poses a hurdle to successful medical practice.

Selective immigration policies in destination countries, which often focus on attracting highly skilled labor, are an important factor influencing migrant destination choices. Laws and professional regulations for foreign-trained doctors are also important. For example, if a country's professional medical regulations impose criteria that discriminate against foreign-trained doctors, few foreign doctors will migrate to that country. Data from 2004 show that language and colonial links are the main determinants of destination choice among Sub-Saharan physicians. France and Belgium are the dominant destinations for physicians from Francophone countries, and the United Kingdom is the primary destination for physicians from English-speaking countries. The United States also receives a fair share of physicians from French-speaking countries, which suggests that economic prospects and selective immigration policies can supersede language and colonial links in determining destination.

Where Do the Migrant Physicians Come From?

A small group of countries—generally the most populous, with the largest physician pools—supply the vast majority of African physicians to OECD countries. Ethiopia, Ghana, Nigeria, South Africa, and Sudan (in that order) accounted for more than 87 percent of all African physicians in OECD countries in 2004. South Africa alone accounted for 60 percent.

Among the 46 countries with data for 2004, half had migration of 10 percent or higher (table 10.1). In seven countries more than 30 percent of locally trained doctors emigrated. Cape Verde and São Tomé and Príncipe, which have high general emigration, fall into this group. Ghana, Liberia, Malawi, South Africa, and Zimbabwe, all English speaking, also had more than 30 percent migration. Ethiopia, Somalia, Sudan, Uganda, and Zambia had migration in the 15–30 percent range. Different push factors help explain physician migration from these countries. In Ethiopia, Somalia, and Sudan, long-term political instability is the main reason for physicians to emigrate. In Uganda and Zambia proximity to South Africa and the prevalence of English push migration.

Between 1991 and 2004 the vast majority of countries with emigration rates over 10 percent experienced a rise in emigration (figure 10.4). Some countries, including Malawi, Tanzania, and Zimbabwe, saw especially

Table 10.1   African Countries Grouped According to Emigration Rates

Low (less than 10 percent)	Moderate (10–15 percent)	High (15–30 percent)	Very high (more than 30 percent)
Benin; Djibouti; Comoros; Chad; Madagascar; Namibia; Equatorial Guinea; Guinea-Bissau; Côte d'Ivoire; Gabon; Niger; Burkina Faso; Mauritania; Lesotho; Kenya; Rwanda; Mauritius; Botswana; Burundi; Congo, Dem. Rep.; Mozambique; Senegal; Seychelles; Suriname; Mali; Central African Republic; Swaziland	Gambia, The; Angola; Tanzania; Togo; Guinea, Cameroon; Sierra Leone; Eritrea; Nigeria; Congo Rep.	Somalia; Uganda; Ethiopia; Zambia; Sudan	Cape Verde; São Tomé and Príncipe; Liberia; Malawi; Zimbabwe; South Africa; Ghana

Source: Medical Brain Drain Database 1991–2004 in Bhargava, Docquier, and Moullan (2011).

Figure 10.4   Countries with the Highest Rates of Physician Emigration in 1991 and 2004

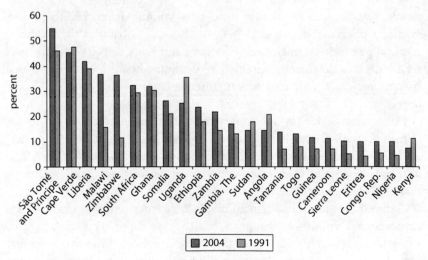

Source: Medical Brain Drain Database 1991–2004 in Bhargava, Docquier, and Moullan (2011).

large growth during that period. Small countries are most affected by brain drain: Cape Verde had the highest rate of migration at 55 percent, followed by São Tomé and Príncipe at 45 percent.

The data on nurse migration are more limited, but indicate that these rates are also high. In 2004, 17 Sub-Saharan countries had emigration of 20 percent or higher for locally trained nurses (figure 10.5). Many countries with high physician emigration also have high nurse emigration, suggesting that similar pull and push factors influence the migration decisions of health care professionals. For example, emigration of nurses from Cape Verde and São Tomé and Príncipe are around 40 percent. In Liberia the share of nurses who emigrate is double that of doctors.

What Drives the Migration of Physicians?

Migration decisions are complicated. It is almost impossible to identify all factors that persuade an individual to move from one country to another, and these factors interact in ways that make it even more difficult to disentangle their individual effects. In the aggregate, we can identify some factors in source and destination countries—the push and pull factors— that affect overall migration.

Low wages, poor working conditions, lack of professional development and career opportunities, and political and ethnic problems are among the main push factors. In addition, prevalent infectious diseases such as HIV and tuberculosis, together with the shortcomings of health care delivery systems, raises disease incidence among African health professionals. Concern about risks to personal health contributes to increasing medical professional migration (Bhargava and Docquier 2008). This pattern leads to a downward spiral where declining health outcomes induce migration, which in turn leads to further declines in health care outcomes.

Africa had by far the most prevalent HIV and tuberculosis in 2005, compared with East Asia, South Asia, the Middle East and North Africa. As HIV and tuberculosis fell in other regions, they rose in Africa. Africa also had the highest rates among developing regions for malaria, measles, diabetes, and cancer in 2004.

Limited health resources, including insufficient numbers of health care professionals, contribute to poor health conditions. For most health resource indicators, Africa has the second lowest among developing regions (table 10.2). It also compares poorly with other regions in public health expenditures (figure 10.6). Africa's heavy disease burden, coupled

Figure 10.5 Emigration among African Nurses

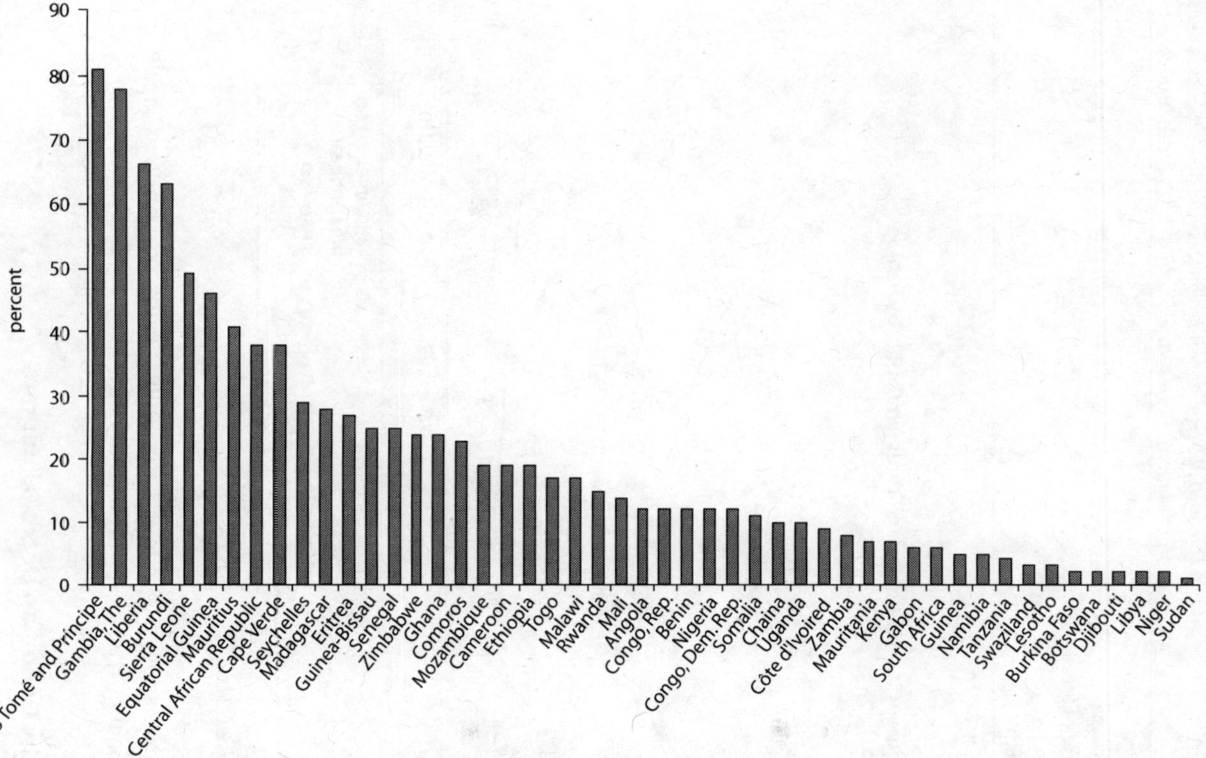

percent
0
10
20
30
40
50
60
70
80
90
São Tomé and Príncipe
Gambia, The
Liberia
Burundi
Sierra Leone
Equatorial Guinea
Mauritius
Central African Republic
Cape Verde
Seychelles
Madagascar
Eritrea
Guinea-Bissau
Senegal
Zimbabwe
Ghana
Comoros
Mozambique
Cameroon
Ethiopia
Togo
Malawi
Rwanda
Mali
Angola
Congo, Rep.
Benin
Nigeria
Congo, Dem. Rep.
Somalia
Chaina
Uganda
Côte d'Ivoired
Zambia
Mauritania
Kenya
Gabon
South Africa
Guinea
Namibia
Tanzania
Swaziland
Lesotho
Burkina Faso
Botswana
Djibouti
Libya
Niger
Sudan

Source: Clemens and Pettersson 2006.

Table 10.2   Health Resource Indicators, by Region

	Hospital beds (per 10,000 population)	Ratio of nurses and midwives to physicians	Physician density (per 10,000 population
Africa	16	9.5	3.6
East Asia	22	3.2	7.6
Middle East and North Africa	21	2	13.3
South Asia	12	2	5.1

Source: WHO n.d.

Figure 10.6   Health Expenditures per Capita, by Region

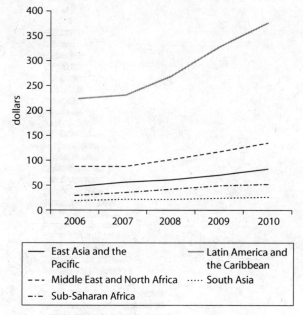

Source: WHO n.d.

with its low expenditures for public health, contribute to health professional migration from the continent.

Why Ghanaian Doctors Emigrate

The exodus of Ghanaian doctors is not new. In the 1930s a scholarship trained African physicians in the United Kingdom, planting the seeds for the first physician migrations from Ghana. For at least 20 years, medical schools in Ghana included a U.K. study component. By 2004 nearly one of every three Ghanaian doctors worked in an OECD country, mostly the United Kingdom and the United States. A 1999 study estimates that fewer than 40 percent of the 489 physicians who graduated from the University of Ghana between 1985 and 1994 remained in the country. More than half of these 489 graduates immigrated to the United Kingdom, and about a third to the United States (Dovlo and Nyonator 1999).

Between 1991 and 2004 the number of Ghanaian physicians in OECD countries grew steadily, though at a slower pace than that of domestic physicians (figure 10.7).

In 2004 the United States was the largest destination for Ghanaian physicians among OECD countries, absorbing 41 percent of all Ghanaian migrant doctors (figure 10.8). The United Kingdom followed close behind with 39 percent. These numbers are not surprising given the common language and colonial links. Large numbers of Ghanaian doctors also emigrated to Australia and South Africa. Data on those groups were not available and are not included in these figures.

A World Bank survey of Ghanaian physicians in the United Kingdom and the United States found that they do not come from a random sample of Ghanaian society. For example, 56 percent of the physicians' fathers and 27 percent of their mothers have bachelors or professional degrees, whereas only slightly above 3 percent of the Ghana workforce has a tertiary education (figure 10.9). Parents' education and social status

Figure 10.7   Number of Ghanaian Physicians at Home and Abroad, 1991–2004

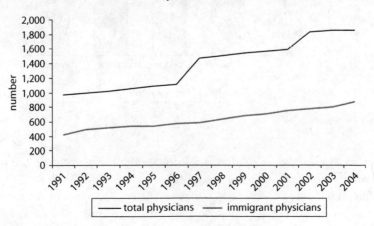

Source: Bhargava, Docquier, and Moullan 2011.

Figure 10.8   Distribution of Ghanaian Doctors in OECD Countries, 2004

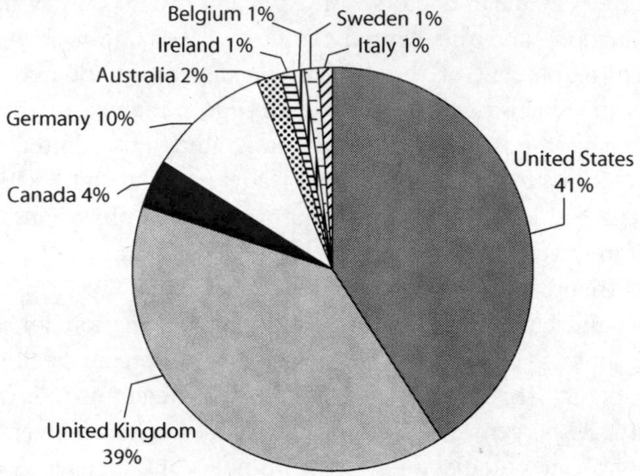

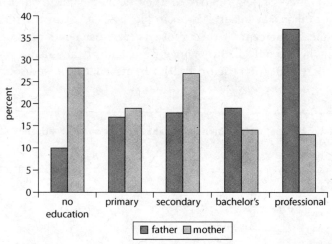

Source: Bhargava, Docquier, and Moullan 2011.

Figure 10.9   Education Levels of Migrant Physicians' Parents

Source: World Bank Ghanaian Physician Survey as cited in Ozden (2011).

influence their children's secondary education, which becomes the main determinant of entry into the highly selective medical schools.

The social and economic gap between the backgrounds of doctors and the rest of Ghanaian society seems to influence most physician career choices and preferences, including migration. The top three reasons why the interviewed doctors chose to study medicine include intellectual challenge (36 percent), opportunities to help others (20 percent), and family influence (18 percent) (figure 10.10).

The World Bank survey offers insights into not only the demographic attributes of migrant doctors but also the factors that affected their decision to migrate. More than 70 percent of Ghanaian migrant doctors cited better training opportunities as the top reason for leaving home (figure 10.11). Another 42 percent cited better medical practice opportunities as the top reason. Higher salaries (39 percent) and improved family life (45 percent) were also highly ranked. Political stability in Ghana and exposure to new cultures seem to have little effect on migration decisions. Of Ghanaian immigrant doctors 44 percent practice in university and teaching hospitals, which tend to be scientific and professional leaders. 28 percent are in private practice, and 16 percent are in smaller clinics.

The World Bank survey asked Ghanaian physicians practicing abroad what policy changes could keep physicians in Ghana. Better health care facilities was the top response, with 71 percent of respondents saying it strongly influences migration (figure 10.12). Higher salaries, improved pensions, free housing or automobiles, and better educational options for children follow close behind. Physicians strongly oppose the mandatory service requirements advocated by nonphysicians.

Figure 10.10   Reasons to Choose Medicine

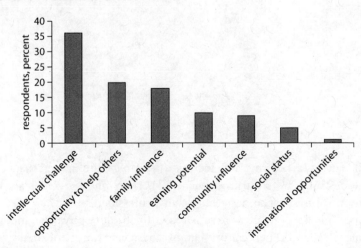

Source: World Bank Ghanaian Physician Survey as cited in Ozden (2011).

Figure 10.11   Top Reasons for Migration

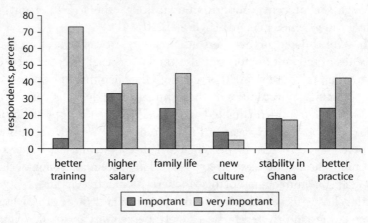

Source: World Bank Ghanaian Physician Survey as cited in Ozden (2011).

Figure 10.12   What Would Keep Physicians in Ghana?

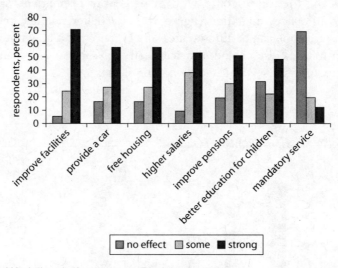

Source: World Bank Ghanaian Physician Survey as cited in Ozden (2011).

The survey asked migrant doctors to compare life in Ghana with life in the destination countries (table 10.3). Forty-one percent stated that incomes of physicians relative to other professionals in Ghana are satisfactory. Only 17 percent were satisfied with absolute physician income in Ghana. Close to 90 percent of migrant physicians think both relative and absolute incomes are satisfactory in their new country.

Table 10.3   What Are the Main Differences between Ghana and Abroad?

	Ghana			Abroad		
	Bad	Average	Good	Bad	Average	Good
Income relative to other professionals	29	31	41	3	10	86
Overall income	42	41	17	3	8	88
Opportunities for professional development	70	25	5	3	1	96
Incentives to work hard	78	18	4	3	8	89
Respect from community	4	11	85	7	34	58
Making a difference for others	4	13	83	3	24	74

Source: World Bank Ghanaian Physician Survey as cited in Ozden (2011).

More than 70 percent think professional opportunities and work incentives are weak in Ghana. By contrast, 96 percent appreciate the professional opportunities in their new countries, and 89 percent find that work incentives are strong.

Social issues tend to cut in favor of Ghana. More than 80 percent of respondents think doctors in Ghana receive great respect from the community and make a big difference in the lives of others. In destination countries, only 58 percent feel they receive respect and 74 percent think they make a difference. While most physisicans believe social respect and fulfillment are greater in Ghana, these factors do not outweigh the professional and financial benefits of practicing abroad.

Diaspora externalities—benefits that the diaspora generates for the home country—are analyzed in the migration literature. In addition to remittances, diasporas can create crucial links for trade, finance, and technology transfers. Sixty-seven percent of surveyed Ghanaian physicians sent remittances home in the 12 months preceding the survey. The average remittance was slightly more than $10,000, a relatively low share of the average annual physician income. Given that most doctors are from upper income families, their remittances are not likely to have a big impact. Families use remittances for general expenses (83 percent), weddings and funeral expenses (41 percent), housing (33 percent), school fees (30 percent), and health expenses (figure 10.13).

Remittances are not the only links between migrant doctors and Ghana (figure 10.14). Migrant physicians often return to Ghana for leisure and business travel. Many diaspora physicians provide advice to

Figure 10.13   Remittance Expense Categories

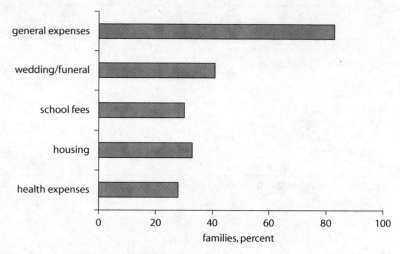

Source: World Bank Ghanaian Physician Survey as cited in Ozden (2011).

Figure 10.14   Main Links with Ghana

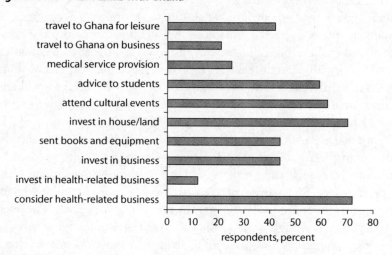

Source: World Bank Ghanaian Physician Survey as cited in Ozden (2011).

medical students considering emigration. Slightly more than 20 percent of respondents provided free medical service to Ghanaians abroad, and more than 40 percent send medical books and equipment to Ghana. While their investments in housing and land in Ghana are high (70 percent), other business links are minimal. More than 70 percent of respondents explored opportunities to invest in health-related business in Ghana, but only a small minority did so. This gap indicates problems in the overall business climate in Ghana.

The World Bank survey asked migrant physicians how many siblings they had, and how many were in the same country with them. A large portion of the siblings are also migrants, so physician migration appears to be part of larger decision making with consequences for all family members.

Ghanaian migrant physicians often remain emotionally tied to Ghana. More than 60 percent of respondents think they will return to Ghana within the next 10 years. Although a large portion of doctors stay in their destinations permanently, the majority would like to return to Ghana.

The Exodus of African Doctors—How Bad Is It?

Policy makers and some economists argue that physician emigration hurts the continent in three respects (Hagopian and others 2005). First, migrant physicians leave behind distressed health sectors that cannot care for a young and growing population. Second, their migration undermines the health sector's ability to organize and expand, ultimately leading to the contraction of health institutions. Third, their migration hollows out the middle class in Africa, with adverse impacts for economic and political development.

Several studies examine the impact of physician migration on health conditions in home countries.

- Anand and Bärninghausen (2004) find that the density of health workers is significant in accounting for maternal mortality, infant mortality, and under-five mortality.
- A later study by the same authors suggests that health worker density is significantly correlated with coverage of three vaccinations (Anand and Bärninghausen 2005). When the impact of doctors and nurses were assessed separately, only nurse density was positive and significant, while doctor density was not associated with coverage of the three vaccinations.
- Arah, Ogbu, and Okeke (2008) find in simple correlations that countries with better maternal health are likely to have higher physician migration and more human resources for health. For example, countries with higher migration to Australia have lower maternal mortality and more births attended by skilled staff.

- Bhargava and Docquier (2008) find that doubling the physician migration rate is associated with a 20 percent rise in adult deaths from AIDS.
- Clemens (2007) finds that Africa's low staffing and poor public health conditions are the result of factors entirely unrelated to migration of health professionals, such as segmented health workforce labor markets in the sending countries.

A benefit of physician migration is "brain circulation," where highly skilled immigrants return home after acquiring new skills that benefit the home economies. Return migration of African doctors could indeed benefit Africa's health sector. But the Ghana survey indicates that no evidence shows a large-scale return migration among African physicians.

Physician migration also has financial ramifications for African countries. African governments heavily subsidize medical education. In West Africa a medical education costs between $2,000 and $10,000 per student a year, excluding personal costs incurred by the student. Ghana spends $9 million a year on medical education, Nigeria $15–$20 million. Because most students come from upper income families and their later remittances flow back to their immediate relatives, publicly funded medical education of migrant doctors implies a transfer from lower income to higher income parts of society.

Conclusion

Policies for financing education are relevant to international migration. Most economists recommend that students should pay for part of their education, particularly if they migrate soon after graduation (Clemens 2008). But tuitions that reflect education's actual cost would limit eligibility to the rich because most African countries lack credit markets to finance education. And given the positive externalities that professionals generate, subsidizing professional education from public funds makes sense.

When Ghanaian migrant physicians were asked how much they would be willing to pay for their tuition (assuming they could borrow at low interest rates during their education), their answers varied widely. Many viewed education as a public good. But more than half indicated that they would be willing to pay $4,000–$10,000 in light of the financial opportunities they realized thanks to their education.

Ghanaian medical schools follow a tiered tuition system, with partial (or full) cost recovery for a portion of students—including those from foreign countries—and free tuition for others, mostly based on academic merit. Other African countries should consider this model. A tiered system might generate extra revenue which, in turn, could raise student supply and reduce reliance on government funding. Since a large part of the financial gains from migration accrue to the migrant and his or her social network, a partial recovery of education costs is economically efficient. The exact details of such policies will be critical to their success.

Different types of medical education could reduce emigration and increase health care workers in African countries. By training physicians' assistants rather than physicians, or health aides rather than nurses, a country may retain more of its qualified health workforce. Because training costs are lower for physician assistants than physicians, a country can afford to train more workers, which might improve overall health care outcomes. Less qualified professionals can provide many of the same critical services provided by physicians and nurses, such as immunizations. And migration may decline because the demand for less qualified professionals is likely to be lower in destination countries. These policy suggestions are controversial because they require a tradeoff between quantity and quality.

Policies that take effect after education is completed could also affect migration. Mandatory national service, especially in underserved rural and poor areas, is frequently suggested. Many countries, such as South Africa, implement national service requirements with varying coverage and success. The Ghanaian survey reveals that such policies can be unpopular among doctors. Such requirements should cover a reasonable time period. Otherwise, they could reduce the demand for education or lead to immediate emigration to escape the requirement.

Countries might also impose additional taxes or payments on migrants. Although such policies are efficient and fair, they may be difficult to implement because they require the cooperation of destination countries (Wilson 2008). Extra salaries are frequently granted to professionals (especially in health care) who stay in their home countries. No convincing evidence shows the cost effectiveness of such policies, given the vast wage gaps between the destination and origin countries. Restrictions on travel and refusal to issue passports or diplomas to students and recent graduates are also mentioned as options to control emigration.

Countries can encourage professionals to return home, offering return expenses, subsidized housing, and assistance in finding jobs. Again, no systematic evidence shows that these sorts of policies work. Policies that aim to attract the diaspora home are likely to create distortions, penalizing professionals who never migrated or subsidizing returnees who planned to return anyway. One simple policy that can provide significant benefits at low fiscal cost is removing inherent biases against returning professionals, such as recognizing qualifications or experience obtained abroad. African doctors living abroad frequently mention this in surveys and interviews.

Because wealthy western countries are the main beneficiaries of the migration of African health professionals, perhaps these countries should finance education expenses in the origin countries. But training directly financed by OECD governments might further encourage migration by focusing on OECD licensing requirements. African countries may be better served by OECD donations for health education. OECD scholarships or study abroad programs may be effective, but students use such programs as an entry into the labor markets of the destination countries. Due to public pressure, many OECD governments (such as the United Kingdom) follow "ethical" recruitment practices for medical professionals. Scant evidence shows that these policies work, despite significant political and diplomatic effort.

References

Anand, S., and T. Bärninghausen. 2004. "Human Resources and Health Outcomes: Cross-Country Econometric Study." *Lancet* 364 (9445): 1603–09.

———. 2005. *Human Resources for Health and Vaccination Coverage in Developing Countries*. Oxford, U.K.: Oxford University.

Arah, O. A., U. C. Ogbu, and C. E. Okeke. 2008. "Too Poor to Leave, Too Rich to Stay: Developmental and Global Health Correlates of Physician Migration to the United States, Canada, Australia, and the United Kingdom." *American Journal of Public Health* 98 (1): 148–54.

Beecham, L. 2002. "UK Government Should Stop Recruiting Doctors from Abroad." *British Medical Journal* 325 (7355): 66.

Bhargava, A., and F. Docquier. 2008. "HIV Pandemic, Medical Brain Drain, and Economic Development in Sub-Saharan Africa." *World Bank Economic Review* 22 (2): 345–66.

Bhargava, A., F. Docquier, and Y. Moullan. 2011. "Modeling the Effects of Physician Migration on Human Development." *Economics and Human Biology* 9 (2): 172–83.

Bundred, P. E., and C. Levitt. 2000. "Medical Migration: Who are the Real Losers?" *Lancet* 356 (9225): 245–46.

Clemens, M. 2007. "Do Visas Kill? Health Effects of African Health Professional Emigration." Working Paper 114, Center for Global Development, Washington, DC.

Clemens, M., and G. Pettersson. 2006. "Medical Leave: A New Database of Health Professional Emigration from Africa." Working Paper 95, Center for Global Development, Washington, DC.

Chauvet, L., F. Gubert, and S. Mesplé-Somps. 2008. "Are Remittances More Effective than Aid to Improve Child Health? An Empirical Assessment Using Inter and Intra-Country Data." Paper presented at the Annual Bank Conference on Development Economics, Cape Town, June 9–11.

Docquier, F., O. Lohest, and A. Marfouk. 2007. "Brain Drain in Developing Countries." World Bank Economic Review 21 (2): 193–218.

Docquier, F., and A. Marfouk. 2006. "International Migration by Educational Attainment (1990–2000)." In International Migration, Remittances and Development, ed. C. Ozden and M. Schiff, 151–200. New York: Palgrave Macmillan.

Dovlo, D., and F. Nyonator 1999. "Migration of Graduates of the University of Ghana Medical School: A Preliminary Rapid Appraisal." Human Resources for Health Development Journal 3 (1): 34–37.

Hagopian, A., A. Ofosu, A. Fatsui, R. Biritwum, A. Essel, L. G. Hart, and C. Watts. 2005. "The Flight of Physicians from West Africa: Views of American Physicians and Implications for Policy." Social Science and Medicine 61 (8): 1750–60.

OECD (Organisation for Economic Co-operation and Development). 2008. The Looming Crisis in the Health Workforce, How can OECD Countries Respond? Paris: OECD.

Ozden, C. 2011. "Ghanaian Physicians at Home and Abroad—The Pull and the Push Factors." World Bank, Washington, DC.

United Nations. 2008. Millennium Development Goals Report 2008. New York: United Nations.

WHO (World Health Organization). n.d. Global Atlas of the Health Workforce. http://www.who.int/globalatlas/.

Wilson, John, D. 2008. "Income Taxation and Skilled Migration: The Analytical Issues," in Skilled Immigration Today, ed. J. Bhagwati and G. Hanson, 285–314. Oxford University Press, Oxford.

CHAPTER 11

Public and Private Practice of Health Workers

Tim Ensor, Pieter Serneels, and Tomas Lievens

Until recently the public sector was nearly the only health care supplier in Sub-Saharan Africa. Although it remains the dominant supplier today, the private for-profit and not-for-profit sectors are gaining importance. Doctors and nurses have adjusted to this new reality, but health care policies are slow to catch up. In many countries policies are still based on a model with the public sector as the sole supplier. As a result, ineffective policies do not allocate health workers optimally across sectors. Parasitic forms of dual practice are prevalent.

Health Sector Options in Sub-Saharan Africa

In recent years, private sector health care options—both for-profit and not-for-profit—have expanded throughout Sub-Saharan Africa, with profound implications for the health sector. Health workers can choose from a wider set of jobs, each with its own benefits and drawbacks. A better understanding of how health workers perceive and choose between the public and private sectors is crucial for improved policy making.[1]

The public and private sectors are distinct in many ways. The public sector, often starved of cash, may struggle to retain and motivate workers.

The private for-profit sector is perceived as poaching staff to deliver sophisticated care mainly to urban elites. Private not-for-profit organizations, often viewed as a better-funded alternative to the public sector, attract individuals with similar, often altruistic, motivations.

Although there is some truth in these stereotypes, they mask important links between the sectors. Many workers move or work across sectors during the course of their careers. A considerable number begin their careers in the public sector and either move to the private for-profit sector, or combine public and private sector practice, routinely dividing their days. Although these links should be included in health care delivery assessments, human resource policies often overlook them.

Much of the data in this chapter comes from qualitative semistructured group discussions with different levels of health workers and users of health services. Group discussions in each country followed the same research design to allow cross-country comparison. These discussions sought a deeper understanding of performance and career choice among health workers to generate hypotheses for future quantitative research. A total of 48 doctors, 125 nurses, and 63 health care users participated in the group interviews over the three countries.[2] In Ethiopia and Rwanda the qualitative preresearch was followed by quantitative surveys. In Ethiopia the authors conducted a cohort study of 90 medical and 219 nursing students. The students were interviewed first during their final year of training and again three years later, after entering the labor market. In Rwanda a quantitative survey of 123 medical and 288 nursing students focused on expected career paths and occupational preferences.[3]

The data highlight four issues. First, jobs in the different sectors have distinct characteristics, and health workers often have a well-defined preference for a job in one sector over a job in another. Second, health workers may prefer to move from one sector to another over time. As in other sectors of the economy, private health is often reluctant to invest in training, preferring to employ workers with experience. Young health workers, aware of this preference, often start their career in the public sector to improve their chances of finding a private sector job in the future. Third, many work in two sectors simultaneously, particularly in the public and private for-profit sectors. Fourth, health workers' individual characteristics play a role in sector choice. For example, health workers with altruistic motivations are more likely to prefer a job in the not-for-profit sector.

Distribution of the Health Workforce across Sectors: Empirical Evidence

Few data measure manpower by sector for Sub-Sahara Africa. While international agencies such as the World Health Organization maintain information on numbers of public health workers, there is no similar information about workers outside the public sector. Even at the country level these figures are often difficult to obtain. Professional bodies are a potential source of information, but they often do not track employment sectors.[4] Workforce surveys are another potential source of information (Gupta and others 2003), but they often fail to gather information on the sector of employment and tend to rely on a small sample of health workers. In-depth health sector surveys are a more reliable source, but they are available for only a limited number of countries.

One way to obtain figures for cross-country comparison is to consider the total number of health workers registered with professional bodies and subtract public staff numbers. Although these estimates offer an idea of the orders of magnitude, they suffer from measurement errors. First, they overestimate the number of active health workers outside the public sector, because individuals who are inactive or working abroad are counted. Second, estimates underestimate the number of health workers outside the public sector because many combine jobs in the public and private sectors, and in some cases are permanently absent from health workers public sector job. The estimates thus include registered health workers who are not working in the public sector.

Among a selection of Sub-Saharan countries, an average of 42 percent of registered doctors work outside the public sector (figure 11.1). This number varies from 20 percent in Tanzania to 52 percent in South Africa. In a subset of these countries with available data, 32 percent of registered nurses work outside the public sector.

It is even more difficult to obtain reliable figures on whether the distribution of health workers between the public and private sectors has changed. Patient spending, formally called "private expenditure," provides some insight. Figure 11.2 reports the results for 39 countries in Sub-Sahara Africa over a five-year period using annual data. The solid line, and the corresponding vertical axis on the left, indicates that patient spending (formally "real per capita private health expenditures") rose from $17 to $30. The dotted line, using the vertical scale on the right, indicates that patient spending in the private sector as a proportion of total patient health expenditures fell from 62 percent in 2001 to 57 percent in 2005.

Figure 11.1   Nongovernment Sector as a Proportion of Total Health Sector Workers, Selected Countries

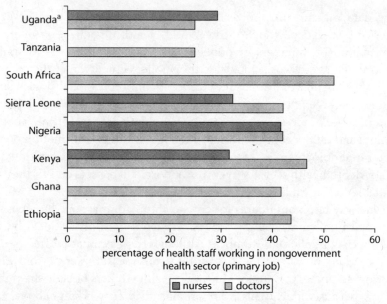

percentage of health staff working in nongovernment health sector (primary job)

■ nurses   ▢ doctors

Source: Authors' calculations from data obtained from the South Africa Medical & Nursing Council; Ministry of Health Sierra Leone; Macro International's Service Provision Assessment Ghana, Nigeria, Tanzania, and Uganda; World Bank, Ethiopia.
a. Excluding workers in the private for-profit sector.

Figure 11.2   Trends in per Capita Private Health Spending and Its Proportion of Total Health Spending in 39 Sub-Saharan Countries

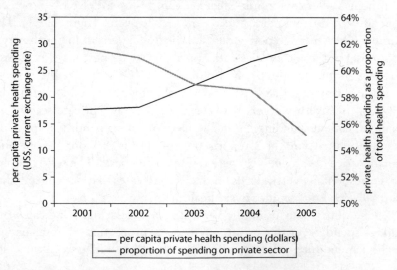

—— per capita private health spending (dollars)
······· proportion of spending on private sector

Source: Author's calculations from WHO's National Health Accounts database for 39 Sub-Saharan countries.

These numbers should be interpreted with care. For example, patient spending as reported in figure 11.2 reflects out-of-pocket expenditures. Patient expenditures in the public sector may be covered at least in part by the state. Even so, the data suggest that while private sector growth was strong over the studied period, the share of private spending as a proportion of total spending declined. This signals strong public sector growth.

Apart from health worker preferences, three factors influence the size and composition of the medical workforce: demand for health care in the private sector, budget constraints in the public sector, and the importance of the not-for-profit sector.

Rapid economic growth stimulated demand for private services by an increasingly wealthy middle class in Malaysia and Thailand (Hanson and Berman 1998) and other Asian countries. This growth may also occur in established or emerging middle-income African countries such as South Africa. For most Sub-Saharan countries, however, poor economic performances through the 1980s and 1990s constrained development of both the public and private medical sectors. As many countries adopted structural adjustment programs to instill fiscal discipline, public expenditures declined. This decline led to a persistent slide in the real salaries of civil servants—including health workers—and their reduced numbers (McCoy and others 2008).

At the same time, countries have encouraged private sector health initiatives. Policy makers may welcome dual practice as a way for doctors to secure decent salaries without pressuring public funds (Sewall 2000). In Tanzania real per capita public health spending fell substantially during the 1980s. This decline, together with economic liberalization policies allowing private practice, accelerated the private sector's development. As a result, the number of private dispensaries and hospitals increased rapidly (Kumaranayake and others 2000). In the mid-1990s the Ethiopian government cautiously allowed private initiative in the health sector after adopting a structural adjustment program (Lindelöw and Serneels 2006).

Faith-based not-for-profit providers play an important role in health services in many African countries. This role has changed over time and many networks now receive direct funding from the government or development partners. The most significant change, however, is the emergence of numerous new not-for-profit providers. High volumes of aid to Africa during the 1980s and 1990s and expanded HIV/AIDS funding funneled through nongovernmental organizations (NGOs) partly fed this trend. While in the past not-for-profit organizations were often associated with a church, the sector now includes large international and local organizations with sizable budgets to hire well-trained health professionals.

Choosing between Public and Private Sector Jobs

From a labor economics perspective, the choice between different types of employment is typically modeled on the happiness or utility derived from job attributes. Two types of attributes are central in these models: effort and earnings. Health workers choose their job or sector based on the labor effort they are required to supply and the payment they receive. Payment is typically interpreted broadly and includes benefits. Each health worker will evaluate options and choose the one with the highest utility. Although other job characteristics are explicitly considered in this model of decision making, they are indirectly included because the model assumes that unfavorable attributes require higher compensation.[5] The classic model assumes that labor markets function perfectly and that workers select the job or sector that offers them the highest utility. Applied to the health sector, this model implies that some workers will select the public sector, some will select the private for-profit sector, and some will select the private not-for-profit sector. This simplification clarifies some basic mechanics of sector choice.[6]

Intrinsic motivation falls outside the classic labor economic model but is worth examining. As argued elsewhere in this volume, intrinsic motivation plays a role in job choice, particularly in professions where a personal mission is important (Besley and Ghatak 2006). This role helps to explain why some health workers prefer to work in the not-for-profit sector: they are willing to accept lower pay in exchange for a better match between their own beliefs and the beliefs of their employer. Recent work finds empirical evidence that is consistent with this type of mission matching (Serra, Serneels, and Barr 2010).

The following labor economics framework for health worker choice takes these different components into account. An individual health worker (i) derives happiness or utility (U) from a wage (w), effort to deliver (e), and the difference between the organizational ethos and the personal mission ($mj - mi$). These factors are specific for each of the three sectors (j).

$$U_{ij} = u\left(w_{ij}, e_{ij}, m_{ij}\right) = \alpha_{1i} w_{ij} - \alpha_{2i} e_{ij} + \alpha_{3i}\left(m_i - m_j\right)$$

where α_{1i}, α_{2i}, α_{3i} reflect the importance health workers give to earnings, effort, and mission matching and wages may or may not be a function of effort.[7] A health worker will choose to work in the public sector when he or she derives more utility from a public sector job than from a job in either of the other sectors, that is $U_{i1} > U_{i2}$ and $U_{i1} > U_{i3}$.

To determine which attributes health workers value and which sectors they associate those attributes with, we carried out structured group discussions with doctors and nurses in Ethiopia, Ghana, and Rwanda. In each country we interviewed selected doctors and nurses[8] using the same study design, so we could compare the results across countries. Table 11.1 presents an overview of the job attributes mentioned most frequently and indicates whether the attribute was considered attractive (+) or unattractive (–) by the majority of respondents.

Overall, health workers associate the public sector with low and often-delayed salaries, low access to training, lower required effort, public welfare orientation, and a disconnect between effort and pay or promotion. This is consistent with findings from other studies. A study in Cameroon, for instance, indicated that government workers wished to stay in the public sector even in the face of wage cuts because of the job security (Israr and others 2000). But evidence also shows that despite the alleged security of a public sector job, receiving one's salary regularly is far from guaranteed. Evidence from Sierra Leone indicates that public health workers' salaries are often months in arrears (Ensor, Lievens, and Naylor 2008). Similar findings are reported in Ghana (Witter, Kusi, and Aikins 2007) and Zambia (Ministry of Health of Zambia 2007). In Zambia 10 percent of workers report making unofficial payments to administrators to speed up payment. This contributes to workers' decisions to engage in dual practice.

The public sector is also associated with corruption, confirming evidence from anthropological research in seven Francophone African countries showing that a culture of corruption and free riding is embedded in parts of the public health sector (Jaffré and Olivier de Sardan 2003). McCoy and others (2008) confirm low salaries for other countries, though they suggest that public sector wages are not lower everywhere.

By contrast, health workers typically associate the private for-profit sector with hard work, higher pay, performance-related pay, access to modern equipment, and a more dynamic work environment. On the down side, they associate the for-profit sector with profit-oriented behavior that may require overprescribing to cover costs of expensive equipment.

Health workers primarily associate the private not-for-profit sector with rural locale and a mission of patient care. Remuneration in the not-for-profit sector falls between for-profit and public sector wages and may be tied to performance. Health workers also associate access to training and exposure to an international environment with the not-for-profit sector.

Table 11.1 Health Worker Perspective on Work Sectors: Attributes Associated with the Different Sectors in Ethiopia, Ghana, and Rwanda

	Public sector	Private for-profit sector	Private not-for-profit sector
Incentive	− Lower salary − Delayed payment + Job security + Social recognition and status + Access to further training and specialization + Allows for clinical practice and facility management experience + Allows for absenteeism, embezzlement and dual practice	+ Higher salary + Urban location + Access to modern technology	− Salary usually less than in for-profit sector +/− Rural location + Access to training + Possible access to international labor market and training
Effort	+ Accepts lower effort +/− Lack of supervision − Lack of performance pay and promotion, independent of effort	− Expects hard work − Close supervision + Elements of performance pay	− Expects hard work − Usually close supervision + Elements of performance pay
Mission	+ Public welfare oriented − May be prone to corruption	− May require profit-driven health care (for example, encourage use of certain equipment) + Provide high-quality health care	+ Strongly altruistic + Often pro-poor

Source: Authors' analysis of qualitative data from group discussions with health workers in Ethiopia, Ghana, and Rwanda.

Health workers value the same job attributes differently. In the end, they choose the jobs that make them happiest. Because the public sector pays lower salaries but offers job security and accepts lower effort and supervision, it may attract less ambitious and risk-averse health workers or those keen to moonlight. But the public sector's access to training and specialization may also attract young and ambitious health workers. Private for-profit organizations usually offer higher but less secure pay and are more likely to draw health workers motivated by extrinsic incentives. Private not-for-profit organizations tend to attract health workers with high intrinsic motivations.

This framework underlines how health workers compare jobs across sectors. Given the public sector's historical dominance, policy makers tend to overlook the private sector. By failing to recognize that health workers compare public with private for-profit and not-for-profit jobs, they risk formulating ineffective health worker policies. Human resource policies should be based on a comparative analysis that explicitly accounts for how policy changes affect health worker tradeoffs between jobs in all sectors. For example, policy makers must know the income doctors derive from dual practice in urban centers to calculate the rural hardship allowance that will effectively increase the uptake of rural public jobs.

The more explicit the links between the sectors, the more important a comparative analysis of the effects of human resource policies across sectors becomes. In the next two sections we discuss two types of links between the sectors. The first considers why workers may prefer to change sectors over time; the second looks at how workers are active simultaneously in different sectors.

Moving from Public to the Private Sector Over Time

The labor economics framework presented above assumes that health workers stay in the same sector throughout their careers. But evidence from qualitative research indicates that health workers move between sectors. A common pattern is for workers to move from the public to the private sector, though some instances of reintegrating into the public sector, sometimes after return migration, are documented.

One reason for the move from the public to the private sector is a change in the health care supply. The gradual emergence of a private health sector over the last three decades in Sub-Saharan Africa grew private job openings. In Ethiopia physician employment in the private for-profit sector expanded from 1 percent in 1996 to 17 percent in 2006, and in the not-for-profit sector from 8 percent to 23 percent over the same period.[9]

Health workers may change sectors over time as part of their long-term career plan. Given the lower earnings in the public sector, many health workers prefer jobs in the private sector. Because private health care tends to be comparatively expensive to the patient, the private sector relies primarily on demand from a wealthy, often urban, but only slowly emerging middle class. This puts a natural ceiling on the sector's size. In addition, the scarcity of venture capital, the absence of well-functioning credit markets, and the regulatory hurdles to starting a private health business may limit the sector's growth. Together these factors limit the demand for labor in the private for-profit sector such that not all health workers who want a private sector job can get one. Because worker supply exceeds demand, private for-profit employers can be selective, choosing whom they consider the best or most skilled health workers. Health workers may therefore prefer to accumulate human capital in the early years of their career.

The labor economics framework presented above can be extended to take this perspective into account, using a more dynamic view of the employment decision. Taking a lifetime perspective, utility is now determined by the discounted sum of utilities across different periods, allowing for the health worker to have a job in a different sector in each period. Income in each period is now a function of the human capital accumulated in the previous periods (h_{t-1}).

$$U_{ij} = \sum_{t=0}^{n} \delta^t u_{ijt} \left(w_{jt} \left(h_{i(t-1)} \right), e_{ij}, m_{ij} \right)$$

$$= \sum_{t=0}^{n} \delta^t \left[\alpha_{1i} w_{jt} \left(h_{i(t-1)} \right) - \alpha_{2i} e_{ij} + \alpha_{3i} (m_j - m_i) \right]$$

In this modified framework, an individual may choose an employment route that delivers a relatively low income early on but offers opportunities for formal training and experience that will raise future earnings (Ben-Porath 1967). For the private employer, selecting the most skilled and experienced workers also helps to solve the classic inability to reap the benefits of investment in human capital of personnel. As in other sectors of the economy, private health firms are reluctant to provide training to health workers if they are uncertain that they will internalize the gain—for instance, if the worker leaves the firm for another organization that offers a higher salary.[10] Furthermore, the private sector serves a middle class that requests high-quality services and well-trained personnel. As a consequence, health workers are more likely to start in the public sector where they build human capital, improving their prospects for private sector employment later on.

More factors may contribute to health workers' decisions to work for the public sector early in their careers. As in other labor markets where the public sector is dominant, the limited demand for labor in the private sector causes health workers to wait in the public sector for a private sector job to become available.[11] Younger workers tend to be more mobile and more likely to switch jobs, so private employers avoid hiring them, as they impose transaction costs. A worker early in his or her career is also less likely to secure the capital or client base required to establish a private practice. Low average incomes limit demand for private sector services. In these circumstances private practice becomes a speculative venture, and chances of feasibility and success increase as a health worker's career matures.

As workers age and assume family responsibilities their valuation of job attributes may change. For example, their target income may go up, making private income more attractive. The likelihood of this scenario increases when salaries fail to rise substantially over time, as is common in public health sectors, where civil service wages rise marginally with years of service.

Empirical evidence shows that workers seek employment in different sectors at different stages of their careers. Health workers in Ethiopia, Ghana, and Rwanda emphasize the distinct qualities of jobs in each sector. Workers often suggest that there is an "ideal career path," which starts in the public sector, possibly in a rural area. According to this ideal path, health workers gain clinical and facility management experience in public sector positions before completing further training or specialization. Later, the health worker moves to the private sector, possibly by establishing a private practice.

> I would advise to start in the rural areas and in the long run, after having done clinical work, when one needs money, one can look out for other opportunities, the private sector, NGOs that pay more.
>
> Doctor, rural district, Rwanda

> I think the private sector is often for people who are nearing the tail end of their service. Such people become consultants after having served the public for years.
>
> Doctor, rural district, Ghana

Concerning requirements, the public sector is least demanding; it's the diploma only; the faith-based sector, it's the diploma and the recommendation; the private sector is more demanding, they require both experience and recommendation.

Doctor, rural district, Rwanda

Quantitative evidence from Rwanda indicates that almost all students graduating from training first work in the public sector. About half the students expect to work outside the public sector after five years, and more than 60 percent expect employment outside the public sector in the long term.[12] Evidence for Ethiopia shows that two years after graduation 82 percent of doctors retain a public sector position,[13] substantially above the labor market average of 60 percent. That suggests a similar gradual shift from public to private sector over the course of the doctor's career.

Qualitative research for Rwanda confirms the importance of the public sector in providing access to further training and in offering a secure salary, albeit lower than outside the public sector (Lievens and Serneels 2006). In Ghana respondents felt that the public sector offers more opportunities for training and specialization, though larger private facilities may have on-the-job opportunities to update skills. Group discussions in Ethiopia also highlighted the high workload and lack of training opportunities in the private sector (Lindelöw and Serneels 2006).

I served five years in the private sector and have not attended any form of training. If it were not for the higher earnings, I would not stay in the private sector.

Doctor, rural district, Ethiopia

In the private hospitals personal development does not come in at all.

Doctor, Accra, Ghana

A specialization is generally obtained in the public sector; it's far more difficult to specialize in the private sector.

Doctor, Kigali, Rwanda

The group discussions also revealed the sophistication of health workers' view of training. Nurses in Ghana, for example, acknowledged training as a draw to the public sector but only if it is of sufficient quality. Training posts in Accra hospitals are perceived as being more valuable because they take place in a well-resourced environment with good equipment (Garbarino and others 2007).

A career path approach may also explain the choice of job location. Health workers in Ghana, for example, suggest that rural areas provide learning-by-doing training because the absence of senior staff, lack of equipment, and large variety of diseases forces them to develop their own skills quickly and broadly (Garbarino and others 2007).

Mobility between sectors can vary substantially across countries. Health workers in Ghana can easily move from the public to private sector, but reintegrating is more complex. Health workers hoping to move back into public service face long wait times and adverse regulations: years of experience outside the public sector are not counted, for example, when calculating position and salary. These obstacles discourage doctors and nurses who want to move back to the public sector after long spells of employment in the private sector. Although they have gained considerable experience, they must pick up where they left off a long time ago (Garbarino and others 2007). In Rwanda, however, movement between the public and private sector seems fairly straightforward.

> I started working in the public sector and then left for the private sector. I can't see any obstacle to introduce my file for a place in the public sector, like any other interested party. (…) So I know that if I postulate like the others my chances are equal to the others.
>
> Nurse, Kigali, Rwanda

The interviews in Ethiopia underline the barriers doctors face in establishing their own clinics. Limited access to capital and slow and burdensome regulations are significant hurdles (Lindelöw, Serneels, and Dessalegn 2005). Health workers in Ghana point out that opening a private clinic is capital intensive and requires a good client base, clinical experience, and familiarity with sophisticated equipment. The administrative barriers to setting up a business are onerous, but the biggest challenge is accumulating sufficient startup capital (Garbarino and others 2007).

Simultaneous Links between Sectors: Dual Practice

A health worker may not need to choose to work exclusively in the public or private sector. Dual work in both sectors is a feature of medical labor markets around the world. A seminal survey of 138 medical doctors working in the public sector in low- and middle-income African, Asian, and Latin American countries found that 87 percent maintained a second job (Macq and others 2001). Accurate and detailed information on the prevalence of dual practice remains limited.

Dual practice comes in a variety of forms. At one end are private doctor clinics, group practices, and even private hospitals run by out-of-hours public sector staff. At the other end is the unofficial payment provided to medical staff in public facilities for providing what should be free service, also a form of dual practice. Unofficial payments may buy extras such as improved room service. Private clinics and hospitals run by out-of-hours public employees tend to be predominant in systems where dual practice is tolerated or permitted. Unofficial payments to public health workers can be present in any system but particularly where dual practice is officially illegal.

We can extend the original static model presented earlier to reflect dual practice. In the spirit of shirking models, dual practice can be modeled as the use of public office for private gain (Rijckeghem and Weber 1997; Shapiro and Stiglitz 1984; Yellen 1984). In this framework the public sector offers an additional benefit: an individual can remain in the public sector but undertake private practice by embezzling publicly contracted resources such as time, services, or practice space. Abstracting from the utility derived from mission matching, which we expect to be less important for those who engage in embezzlement of resources from the public sector, we extend the model presented earlier as follows:

$$U_{ij} = u_i\left(w_{ij}, e_{ij}, w_{ij}, p, f\right) = \alpha_{1i} w_{ij} - \alpha_{2i} e_{ij} + \beta_i \left[(1-p)\left(w_{ij'} * t\right) - pf \right]$$

where p is the probability of detection, $w_{ij'}*t$ the earnings in the second sector, and f the fine or sanction if caught. β then reflects the importance (or otherwise) given to the possibility of taking up a second job.

In the dual practice framework the possibility of a second job is an additional factor driving sector choice. The value of this benefit depends on the expected income from the secondary activity, which in turn depends on the wage in the second sector, the probability of being caught, and the penalty if caught. In Sub-Saharan Africa a worker typically does not run the risk of losing his or her job for engaging in dual practice. If the additional terms are positive, jobs that permit dual work will be more attractive to workers. Within this framework a higher wage in the main activity does not automatically end dual practice.[14] Efforts to end dual practice are likely to succeed only if the probability of being detected and the sanction if caught are substantial.

Empirical studies across Latin America offer some support for the dual practice framework. They suggest that raising real wages has relatively little impact on unofficial payments and other illicit practices when the probability of detection is low (Di Tella and Savedoff 2001). The qualitative research for Ethiopia and Rwanda also suggests that the chances of being caught in the act and fined are low in the public sector (Serneels and Lievens 2008).

An alternative approach is to regard shirking and absenteeism in developing countries as a survival strategy. In economic terms an individual requires a target subsistence income, and below it he or she is willing to indulge in unofficial behavior. In these circumstances simply increasing monitoring and punishment for unofficial activity is counterproductive. Attempting to curtail prohibited behavior by, for example, clamping down on required work hours may induce workers to leave the public sector entirely (Ensor 2004).

Empirical evidence points to various motivations for dual practice. Nonfinancial motivations include more decision-making powers, greater flexibility in work schedules, and the ability to offer better service by spending more time with patients or offering more treatment options (Humphrey and Russel 2004; Svab, Progar, and Vegnuti 2001). Available studies appear, however, to be primarily confined to richer countries. The overwhelming reason for a second or dual job in low-income countries is financial. Employees engaged in dual practice seek either to raise household income to a subsistence level or provide an improved lifestyle for family through, for example, the ability to attend better schools or acquire better health care (Van Lerberghe and others 2002). A discrete choice experiment in Ethiopia found that the ability to work in private practice was the most highly prized job attribute (valued at 48 percent of the base public sector salary) and one of the main reasons why health workers are reluctant to work in rural areas (Hanson and Jack 2010). Qualitative findings from Ghana and Rwanda also emphasize the central role of additional income from dual practice in the popularity of urban jobs.

A number of studies support the notion that dual practice and unofficial activity may be coping strategies that begin early in a worker's career (box 11.1). Public sector salaries are often not sufficient to support a worker and family. A study of doctors in Portuguese-speaking African countries found that an average public wage provides sufficient income for seven days a month (Ferrinho and others 1998). One respondent in a study in Tanzania suggested that the main reason for private payments to public staff was that salary itself can "never sustain even food for the whole month" (Stringhini and others 2009).

In Rwanda dual practice tends to be unofficial and, at least for doctors, mainly confined to urban areas. Motivation is largely financial. Medical

Box 11.1

Dual Practice in Ethiopia

The Ethiopia cohort study shows that even at an early stage in their career medical professionals adopt dual practice. It found that three years out of college, close to 20 percent of doctors worked exclusively in the private sector and a further 18 percent had a secondary job in a private clinic (box figure 11.1.1). Usually a secondary job in the private sector is work as a clinician in a private facility although there were a few cases of public doctors working in a private (medical) college. For nurses, secondary practice opportunities are rarer but still possible. The number of medical professionals engaged in dual practice tends to grow as the health workers develop career experience. The main motivation for dual practice in Ethiopia is to increase earnings (Serra, Serneels, and Lindelöw 2008).

Box figure 11.1.1   Proportion of Ethiopia Cohort, by Sector, 2007

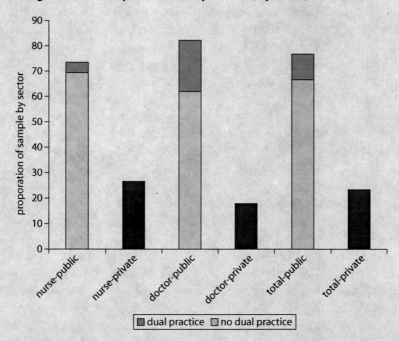

The survey results underline the weakness of the current regulations. While workers whose studies were funded by the government require an official "release" to work in the private sector, the vast majority of doctors active in the private sector (70 percent) did not obtain this release. Complementary qualitative discussions indicated that absenteeism and nonapproved private employment are rarely punished.

officers work in private facilities, and nurses often provide clinical services through pharmacies. The Rwanda focus group discussions drew attention to the parasitic nature of much dual practice. One user described doctors using public clinic hours "to 'embezzle' patients to their private sector practice." Another user suggested that doctors may even make public hospital experiences less pleasant for patients or extend the lead time for lab results to encourage patients to come to their private clinic (Lievens and Serneels 2006). Dual practice is almost structurally embedded in the health system. According to one survey, half the medical students who expect to be working in the public sector five years after graduation anticipate an additional income of 47 percent of their base public salary from dual practice (Lievens and others 2010).

Health workers and users in Ghana point to frequent dual employment for financial reasons. Higher educated health workers such as doctors and professional nurses who pursue second jobs tend to do so in the health sector. Lower educated health workers are more likely to have nonhealth-related second jobs. Doctors say that income from moonlighting complements their salary; auxiliary nurses suggest that their base salary is not sufficient to cover basic needs (Garbarino and others 2007).

> In Accra, depending on your rotation, you could close around 2 pm to do a four-hour locum in a private clinic and then come home by 6 or 7pm. There is also the tacit arrangement with colleagues to stay in for us so that when we come back we will make up the time lost.
>
> Doctor, rural district, Ghana

Opinions on whether dual practice interferes with the public delivery of services are split. Some analysts believe that the practice is largely parasitic, with private practice eating into the hours and quality of care a public worker can provide to patients. Others believe the relationship is symbiotic, and that dual practice ensures that staff can afford to work in the public sector and provides them with credibility to develop a successful secondary private practice.

There is little doubt that unregulated dual practice can severely inhibit public sector functioning. In some parts of rural Bangladesh worker absenteeism is largely attributed to doctors who are treating private patients in the cities (Chaudhury and Hammer 2003). In Ghana health workers suggest that combining two jobs is exhausting, leading to decreased efficiency and negative attitudes toward patients. Invariably workers give priority, in hours and effort, to their private sector jobs (Garbarino and others 2007).

Regulated dual practice, by contrast, may improve the quality of public services. The best public practitioners are likely to be the most sought after during their private hours. Gonzales proposes circumstances where the incentive to develop out-of-hours private practice leads to enhanced efforts to diagnosis and treat public sector patients (González 2004).

A study of Portuguese-speaking African doctors found that most doctors engaging in private practice acknowledged its negative impact on the quality of public provision (Ferrinho and others 1998). But it also recognized that the practice may have "a stabilizing effect on qualified personnel" by allowing them to achieve a better level of income from within the sector. Indeed, without the additional income the quality of public services may also suffer. As one respondent in a survey in Cameroon remarked, "low salaries do not allow one to practice medicine ethically, our morale is down and this encourages malpractice" (Israr and others 2000).

Individual Characteristics and Intrinsic Motivation

Though the public and private sectors are clearly linked, and health workers may move between sectors or work in both at the same time, each sector may attract distinct profiles of workers, with distinct preferences and characteristics.

We currently have little insight into demographic differences among workers in different sectors. Existing studies do not find differences in gender, ethnicity, or marital status. A number of studies find that health workers who grew up in a rural area are more likely to work in a rural area, where the private for-profit sector is often less prevalent. Some evidence shows that the private sector tends to attract older workers (Serra, Serneels, and Barr 2010) and that religious workers may be more likely to work for religious organizations. The private for-profit sector seems to attract the most technically competent workers (measured by medical knowledge tests), while not-for-profits may attract less technically competent workers (Leonard, Masatu, and Vialou 2007; Serra, Serneels, and Barr 2010).

Intrinsic motivation in job choice is receiving increased attention. In a simplified framework, one can distinguish extrinsic and intrinsic motivations. Extrinsic motivations include financial reimbursement and other rewards, such as professional advancement and training opportunities. Intrinsic motivations include a desire to help others or fulfill professional norms. This is clearest in the not-for-profit sector, which often has a mission to provide health care to the poor. But intrinsic motivation may also play a role in the public sector (Deci 1975).

Le Grand talks about "Knights" and "Knaves," suggesting that because Europe's public sector salaries are traditionally modest and stable, and the sector emphasizes service, trust and motivation, it attracts more altruistic individuals (Knights) (Le Grand 2003). NGOs can be better placed to fulfill intrinsic motivation by providing a "better match between the ends of the organization and its workers" (Besley and Ghatak 2007). Government services are often influenced by electoral vicissitudes, but NGOs can maintain a stable focus on organizational goals and ethos (see chapter 14 for an overview of intrinsic motivation in job choice).

Group discussions provide both direct and indirect evidence that different sectors employ different profiles of health workers. Discussions confirm that health workers choose a job and sector based on their preferences and self-select in particular sectors. The discussions also indicate that it may be overly simplistic to characterize health workers in the private for-profit sector only by a preference for financial advancement. The Ghana focus group discussions suggest that health workers are attracted to the private sector for its clear rules and accountability, apart from the higher salary (Garbarino and others 2007a). In Rwanda and Ethiopia workers often feel that higher quality care is possible in the private sector because of the better standards of equipment, while there is little supervision or discipline in the public sector (Lindelöw and Serneels 2006). This suggests that those who wish to work in a well-regulated environment offering high standards are attracted to private providers if the public sector cannot offer these attributes.

Increasing evidence shows the importance of intrinsic motivation. In Rwanda more altruistic students were more likely to prefer a public sector job in the long term and require a lower salary to work in less popular areas such as rural or high-HIV prevalence areas (Lievens and others 2010). In Ethiopia results from contingent valuations suggest that chances for promotion and other income opportunities increased the preference of final-year medical and nursing students to join the private for-profit sector (Serra, Serneels, and Lindelöw 2008). In contrast, health workers with more philanthropic preferences, measured both by a survey and an experimental measure of pro-social motivations, are more likely to work in the not-for-profit sector and earn lower wages than their colleagues (Serra, Serneels, and Barr 2010). In Tanzania the potential for clinical excellence measured by a vignette technique is lower for workers in the not-for-profit sector, but the gap between actual and potential performance is smaller, indicating both lower competence and higher commitment in not-for-profit sector workers (Leonard 2002).

In Ghana health workers report that faith-based organizations offer salaries comparable to the public sector but are characterized by a higher commitment, suggesting that these organizations attract more committed workers (Garbarino and others 2007a).

> The mission hospitals are better than the public hospitals. They have stronger ethics and make sure everything goes accordingly. The doctors are there at the right time to take care of the people. When you go to a public hospital you will find that most of the doctors working there own a private clinic and give that priority.
>
> User, Accra, Ghana

Drawing a conclusive picture about health worker profiles in different sectors remains difficult, if only because not everyone gets their preferred job, and some may end up in a job that does not match their preferences. In the many countries with smaller private sectors, the public sector is more likely to harbor health workers frustrated by the gap between their preferred and actual job. This highlights the importance of how health workers are allocated to posts. A mismatch between health worker and post may lead to frustration, poor motivation, and efforts to change jobs. A number of countries regulate allocation, which may lead to more mismatches. In Ethiopia public health workers were allocated to rural and urban posts through a lottery. In this system workers may be placed in jobs they do not want. This makes it difficult for good physicians to signal their quality and may compromise the allocative efficiency of the labor market, possibly encouraging brain drain (De Laat and Jack 2008).

Conclusion

In many Sub-Saharan countries, policies continue to emphasize the dominant—if not exclusive—role of the public sector in health service delivery. While this was appropriate in the past, it is unlikely to be the best solution for the future. The private for-profit health market has gradually expanded in many countries, supplying higher quality services to a wealthier and often urban middle-class. And many new not-for-profit health suppliers have been established over the years, with more donor funding. In many countries the private sector now provides a sizable and growing share of the health services and health-related jobs.

Public policies should acknowledge the links between the public and private health sectors—or risk having health workers end up in jobs that do not correspond with their preferences. This mismatch leads to frustration, efforts to change jobs, and nonproductive forms of dual practice. It may also result in high concentrations of workers in urban centers. Regulations that impose high entry and exit barriers to prevent movement between sectors, or that try to force workers into rural service without compensating for the income lost from urban dual practice, are counterproductive.

Policy makers have attempted to recapture hours from the private sector by banning private practice or providing incentives to health workers to not engage in it. These policies raise major regulatory problems. It is difficult to enforce such bans (García-Prado and González 2007), primarily because professional practice remains largely unobserved to the regulator. Ample evidence shows that medical professionals find multiple ways to develop their own informal medical practice with unofficial payments, kickbacks, and absenteeism from their public sector job. The Ethiopia cohort study reveals how quickly new professionals develop secondary practices, even without official permission to practice (Serra, Serneels, and Lindelöw 2008).

A ban on private practice may have other unintended consequences. Doctors and professional nurses are highly marketable internationally, and the drain of workers to richer countries is a well-established development issue (Connell and others 2007). Preventing professionals from undertaking private practice may induce them either to leave the sector entirely or migrate overseas. It is beyond the scope of this review to examine policies to tackle the "brain drain" issue.

In some countries the public sector "buys out" practitioners to refrain from private practice. Used in several countries, these "nonpractice" allowances can be too expensive for many low-income countries (Jan and Bian 2005), as the value of private dual practice to individuals is considerable. In Ethiopia contingent valuation experiments found that the ability to work privately is worth almost half the public sector wage (Hanson and Jack 2010). In Burkina Faso private practice is not officially permitted, and reported earnings from secondary sources are modest (around 17 percent of income). Yet a study found that workers are unwilling to accept contracts prohibiting private employment (Ensor, Chapman, and Barro 2006). On average, workers (mostly nurses and assistant nurses) required a salary increase of around 100 percent before committing (on pain of losing their jobs) to refrain from private work. The same workers require a salary increase of at least 50 percent before accepting an alternative contract for a job 50 kilometers from their current workplace. These results suggest that buyout may not be the best way forward.

Another approach is to allow dual practice while requiring guaranteed hours in the public sector. It recognizes the benefits of private practice but also acknowledges that it can lead to a decline in the quality of public service. Young practitioners often value their public position, while more experienced health workers want the freedom to practice privately. If dual practice can be regulated in the context of a better-remunerated but realistic public contract, this may provide a more effective and cheaper alternative to outright bans on practice. And if public sector salaries increase enough, they may result in an actual foregoing of private practice.

In Ghana private practice is not prohibited but a substantial rise in public sector income seems to have sizably reduced the financial incentive to undertake additional private work. According to one study private midwives earn more than 40 percent less than their public sector counterparts, while public sector doctors' proportion of earnings from dual practice is relatively small, below 10 percent (Witter, Kusi, and Aikins 2007). Public salaries for doctors are now sometimes higher than private salaries (Ministry of Health of Ghana and World Bank 2009).

An additional approach is for public agencies to purchase private health services—a form of public-private partnership. Purchasing priority services from the nongovernment sector can widen the range of services available to publicly financed or priority populations. The premise of public-private purchasing is based on the idea that nongovernment services can, in certain circumstances, offer at least as good value for money as public alternatives. There is some support for this. Evidence from Tanzania suggests that not-for-profit providers are able to deliver higher service quality than the public sector without paying more or recruiting significantly better qualified personnel, perhaps attributable to the motivation from a decentralized management model (Leonard, Masatu, and Vialou 2007). This approach typically requires both a mature nongovernment sector able to deliver quality basic services and public service's capacity to specify and monitor contracts.

To improve policies, we need to collect more evidence. We see four main areas for future research and data collection. First, we need better basic data on the numbers of health workers in each sector, including overlaps through secondary and dual practice. Second, we need to better understand what impedes growth of the private sector. Limited purchasing power and lack of business capital are undoubtedly important, but there are also bureaucratic regulations that deter formalized private business arrangements in favor of unofficial practice. Third, we need to better understand the distinct characteristics of health workers who prefer to work in one sector over another, including performance differences, commitment, and so on. Fourth, we need to extend work on how health workers choose or end up in different sectors, and how this might be exploited to enhance service delivery. While addressing these issues may seem challenging, this chapter presents insights from a small and emerging body of work that offers a starting point for further analysis. It also shows that a systematic approach can generate useful insights and inform policy making about fruitful ways forward.

Notes

1. In many countries there has been a boom in underqualified or unqualified health workers providing health care, including selling drugs. This segment of the private health market is not considered in this chapter.

2. For more details see Lindelöw and Serneels (2006), Lievens and Serneels (2006), Garbarino and others (2007a, 2007b), and Lievens and others (2010).

3. See Serneels and others (2010) and Lievens and others (2010), respectively.

4. Although private sector health workers may be required to register with the government, registration records are often unreliable and poorly managed. Even when registration records are reliable, they may be collected at the local level.

5. This relies on the theory of compensating differentials or hedonic pricing, which argues that wage (or price) differences reflect differences in attractiveness of the attributes.

6. In reality we typically do not observe labor supply only, but rather the meeting of labor demand and supply. The more recent literature emphasizes the matching process between types of workers and types of jobs, rather than the selection of types of workers into types of jobs (Blundell 1999; Cahuc and Zylberberg 2004).

7. Where wages are not a function of effort, we substitute: $w_{ij} = w_{ij} (e_{ij})$.

8. We selected the participants to create maximum variation in dimensions of interests like gender, having children, current sector of work, and combining public and private work or not.

9. Authors' calculation based on PHRD data.

10. Some large private organizations, including not-for-profits, may provide training if they are confident that they offer attractive career prospects and can retain their staff. In the largest organizations, specialist postgraduate qualifications may be available that are comparable to those in the public sector.

11. This is common in labor markets with a large public and small private sector. See, for instance, Mengistae (1999).

12. Lievens and others 2008. While requirements that students with government funding work for the state for a period following graduation may play a role, the data indicate that these rules are often poorly understood and enforced. For instance, a third of students in Rwanda who receive state support suggest they have no obligation after graduation.

13. Evidence indicates that rules requiring graduates to seek permission to work in the private sector are poorly enforced in Ethiopia as well.

14. A more general presentation allows for the embezzlement and use for private purpose of resources other than time: $U_{ij} = u_i\left(w_{ij}, e_{ij}, w_{ij'}, p, f\right)$ $= \alpha_{1i}w_{ij} - \alpha_{2i}e_{ij} + \beta_i\left[(1-p)\sum_k I(r_k) - pf\right]$, where $I(rk)$ is the income derived from embezzling resource, k.

References

Ben-Porath, Y. 1967. "The Production of Human Capital and the Life Cycle of Earnings." *Journal of Political Economy* 75 (4): 352–65.

Besley, T., and M. Ghatak. 2007. "Reforming Public Service Delivery." *Journal of African Economics* 16 (Suppl. no. 1): 127–56.

Blundell, R. 1999. "Labor Supply: A Review of Alternative Approaches." In *Handbook of Labor Economics*, ed. O. Ashenfelter and D. Card, 1559–695. Amsterdam: Elsevier Science.

Cahuc, P., and A. Zylberberg. 2004. "Compensating Wage Differentials and Discrimination." In *Labor Economics*, ed. P. Cahuc and A. Zylberberg, 245–305. Cambridge, MA: MIT Press.

Chaudhury, N., and J. S. Hammer. 2003. "Ghost Doctors: Absenteeism in Bangladeshi Health Facilities." Policy Research Working Paper 3065, World Bank, Washington, DC.

Connell, J., P. Zurn, B. Stilwell, M. Awases, and J.-M. Braichet. 2007. "Sub-Saharan Africa: Beyond the Health Worker Migration Crisis?" *Social Science and Medicine* 64 (9): 1876–91.

De Laat, J., and W. Jack 2008. "Adverse Selection and Career Outcomes in the Ethiopian Physician Labor Market." Cahiers de recherche 0828, Centre inter-universitaire sur le risque, les politiques économiques et l'emploi, Montreal, Canada.

Deci, E. L. 1975. *Intrinsic Motivation*. New York: Plenum.

Di Tella, R., and W. D. Savedoff, eds. 2001. *Diagnosis Corruption: Fraud in Latin America's Public Hospitals*. Washington, DC: Inter-American Development Bank, Latin American Research Network.

Ensor, T. 2004. "Informal Payments for Health Care in Transition Economies." *Social Science and Medicine* 58 (2): 237–46.

Ensor, T., G. Chapman, and M. Barro. 2006. "Paying and Motivating CSPS Staff in Burkina Faso: Evidence from Two Districts." Initiative for Maternal Mortality Programme Assessment, University of Aberdeen, Aberdeen, Scotland.

Ensor, T., T. Lievens, and M. Naylor. 2008. "Public Expenditure Review of the Health Sector in Sierra Leone." Oxford Policy Management, Oxford.

Ferrinho, P., W. Van Lerberghe, M. R. Julien, E. Fresta, A. Gomes, F. Dias, A. Goncalves, and B. Backstrom. 1998. "How and Why Public Sector Doctors Engage in Private Practice in Portuguese-Speaking African Countries." *Health Policy and Planning* 13 (3): 332–38.

Garbarino, S., T. Lievens, P. Quartey, and P. Serneels. 2007. *Ghana Qualitative Health Worker Study: Draft Report of Preliminary Descriptive Findings*. Oxford: Oxford Policy Management.

García-Prado, A., and P. González. 2007. "Policy and Regulatory Responses to Dual Practice in the Health Sector." *Health Policy* 84 (2–3): 142–52.

González, P. 2004. "Should Physicians' Dual Practice be Limited? An Incentive Approach." *Health Economics* 13 (6): 505–24.

Gupta and others 2003.

Hanson, K., and W. Jack. 2010. "Health Worker Preferences for Job Attributes in Ethiopia: Results from a Discrete Choice Experiment." *Health Affairs* 29 (8): 1452–60.

Humphrey, C., and J. Russell. 2004. "Motivation and Values of Hospital Consultants in South-East England Who Work in the National Health Service and Do Private Practice." *Social Science and Medicine* 59 (6): 1241–50.

Israr, S. M., O. Razum, V. Ndiforchu, and P. Martiny. 2000. "Coping Strategies of Health Personnel during Economic Crisis: A Case Study from Cameroon." *Tropical Medicine and International Health* 5 (4): 288–92.

Jaffré, Y., and J. P. Olivier de Sardan. 2003. *Une médecine inhospitalière: les difficiles relations entre soignants et soignés dans cinq capitales d'Afrique de l'Ouest*. Paris: Karlhala.

Jan, S., and Y. Bian. 2005. "Dual Job Holding by Public Sector Health Professionals in Highly Resource-Constrained Settings: Problem or Solution?" *Bulletin of the World Health Organization* 15 (4): 357–67.

Kumaranayake, I., S. Lake, P. Mujinja, C. Hongoro, and R. Mpembeni. 2000. "How Do Countries Regulate the Health Sector? Evidence from Tanzania and Zimbabwe." *Health Policy and Planning* 15 (4): 357–67.

Le Grand, J. 2003. *Motivation, Agency and the Public Sector: Of Knights and Knaves, Pawns and Queens*. New York: Oxford University Press.

Leonard, K. L. 2002. "When Both States and Markets Fail: Asymmetric Information and the Role of NGOs in African Health Care." *International Review of Law and Economics* 22 (1): 61–80.

Leonard, K. L., M. C. Masatu, and A. Vialou. 2007. "Getting Doctors to Do Their Best: The Roles of Ability and Motivation in Health Care Quality." *Journal of Human Resources* 42 (3): 682–700.

Lievens, T., and P. Serneels. 2006. *Synthesis of Focus Group Discussions with Health Workers in Rwanda*. Washington, DC: World Bank.

Lievens and others 2008.

Lievens, T., P. Serneels, J. D. Butera, and A. Soucat. 2010. "Diversity in Career Preferences of Future Health Workers in Rwanda. Where, Why and for How Much?" Working Paper 189, World Bank, Washington, DC.

Lindelöw, M., and P. Serneels. 2006. "The Performance of Health Workers in Ethiopia: Results from Qualitative Research." *Social Science and Medicine* 62 (9): 2225–35.

Lindelöw, Serneels, and Dessalegn 2005.

Macq, J., P. Ferrinho, V. De Brouwere, and W. Van Lerberghe. 2001. "Managing Health Services in Developing Countries: Between Ethics of the Civil Servant and the Need for Moonlighting: Managing and Moonlighting." *Human Resources Health Development* 5 (1–3): 17–24.

McCoy, D., S. Bennett, S. Witter, B. Pond, B. Baker, J. Gow, S. Chand, T. Ensor, and B. McPake. 2008. "Salaries and Incomes of Health Workers in Sub-Saharan Africa." *Lancet* 371 (9613): 675–81.

Mengistae, T. 1999. "Wage Rates and Job Queues: Does the Public Sector Overpay in Ethiopia?" Policy Research Working Paper 2105, World Bank, Washington, DC.

Ministry of Health of Ghana and World Bank. 2009. *Analysing Health Labour Market Outcomes and Determinants in Ghana: A Status Report on HRH*. Accra: Ministry of Health of Ghana; Washington, DC: World Bank.

Ministry of Health of Zambia. 2007. *The Zambia Public Expenditure Tracking and Quality of Service Delivery Survey in the Health Sector*. Lusaka: Ministry of Health of Zambia.

Rijckeghem, C. V., and B. Weber. 1997. "Corruption and the Rate of Temptation: Do Low Wages in the Civil Service Cause Corruption?" Working Paper 97/73, International Monetary Fund, Washington, DC.

Sewall, M. 2000. "From Cooperation to Competition in National Health Systems—And Back? Impact on Professional Ethics and Quality of Care." *International Journal of Health Planning and Management* 15 (1): 61–79.

Serneels, P., and T. Lievens. 2008. "Institutions for Health Care Delivery: a Formal Exploration of what Matters to Health Workers, Evidence from Rwanda." Working Paper Series 2008-29, Centre for the Studies of African Economies, Department of Economics, Oxford University, Oxford.

Serneels, P., M. Lindelöw, J. G. Montalvo, and A. Barr. 2007. "For Public Service or Money: Understanding Geographical Imbalances in the Health Workforce." *Health Policy and Planning* 22 (3): 128–38.

Serra, D., P. Serneels, and M. Lindelöw. 2008. *Discovering the Real World: How Health Workers' Early Work Experience Affects Their Career Preferences.* Addis Ababa: Ministry of Health of Ethiopia.

Serra, Serneels, and Barr 2010.

Shapiro, C., and J. E. Stiglitz. 1984. "Equilibrium Unemployment as a Worker Discipline Device." *American Economic Review* 74 (3): 433–44.

Stringhini, S., S. Thomas, P. Bidwell, T. Mtui, and A. Mwisongo. 2009. "Understanding Informal Payments in Health Care: Motivation of Health Workers in Tanzania." *Human Resources for Health* 7 (53).

Svab, I., I. V. Progar, and M. Vegnuti. 2001. "Private Practice in Slovenia after the Health Care Reform." *European Journal of Public Health* 11 (4): 407–12.

Van Lerberghe, W., C. Conceicao, W. Van Damme, and P. Ferrinho. 2002. "When Staff is Underpaid: Dealing with the Individual Coping Strategies of Health Personnel." *Bulletin of the World Health Organization* 80 (7): 581–84.

WHO (World Health Organization). 2006. *The World Health Report 2006: Working Together for Health.* Geneva: WHO.

Witter, S., A. Kusi, and M. Aikins. 2007. "Working Practices and Incomes of Health Workers: Evidence from an Evaluation of a Delivery Fee Exemption Scheme in Ghana." *Human Resources for Health* 5 (2).

World Bank. 2007. *Ethiopia Health Sector Development Program. Implementation, Completion and Results Report.* Report ICR383. Washington, DC: World Bank.

Yellen, J. 1984. "Efficiency Wage Models of Unemployment." *American Economic Review* 74 (2): 200–05.

CHAPTER 12

The Equity Perspective

Davidson R. Gwatkin and Alex Ergo

Equity approaches to human resources for health typically focus on geographic inequalities. This chapter extends those approaches by assessing human resource inequalities from an economic perspective. The data on economic poverty confirm that poor groups are less well served than better-off groups. They also suggest a tenuous relationship between geographic and economic approaches to poverty, since many better-off people live in poor geographic areas, while many poor people live in even the best-off areas. Much more than a geographic focus will be needed to reach poor people.

This chapter offers an initial look at Africa's human resources for health from an equity perspective, covering the five countries where the World Bank is conducting comprehensive studies: Ethiopia, Ghana, Mozambique, Rwanda, and Zambia. These countries are in different parts of Sub-Saharan Africa and have different historical traditions. Economic conditions vary widely between them: overall incomes range from $220 per capita a year in Ethiopia to $770 in Zambia; economic inequalities, measured by the Gini coefficient, vary to an unusually low .30 in Ethiopia to a far higher .50 in Zambia (World Bank 2009).

Concepts and Definitions

"Health equity" is a normative concept that refers to the absence of "health inequity," which in turn is typically defined as "health inequality" that is unfair and avoidable.[1] According to this definition, health inequity is one type of health inequality—an empirical concept that refers to any intergroup or interindividual difference in health, regardless of whether it is unavoidable, unfair, or both.

Health inequalities often qualify for consideration as health inequities—but not always, since some inequalities are widely viewed as unavoidable or fair. (Examples include higher death rates among elderly people than young adults, which seem unavoidable; and special wages for hazardous occupations, often seen as fair in light of the extra health risks.)

Some types of health inequality might even be necessary to achieve health equity, as with human resources for health. Disadvantaged groups usually suffer from poorer health than better-off ones, and thus have a greater need for the services of health personnel. For the many who argue that health equity requires service availability to be proportionate to need, such equity would call for more available workers per capita to disadvantaged group members.

Applying these definitions across groups raises the question of how to delineate groups. Traditionally, the most common approach for studying developing countries has been to divide people by economic status, especially income. Since such status is usually difficult to assess, proxy measures like occupation, education, or place of residence are often used instead.

More recently, changing concepts of development and poverty have led to additional measures, such as gender, race, religion, and health status, and to measures like education and place of residence as dimensions of inequality and inequity in their own right, rather than simply proxies for some other measure like income. Thus one prominent recent formulation, expressed as the acronym PROGRESS, puts forward eight dimensions of inequality worthy of concern: place of residence, race, occupation, gender, religion, education, socioeconomic status, and social capital (WHO 2004).

Implications

Concepts and definitions like these are fairly clear in principle, but leave ample room for uncertainty and disagreement in practice. Opinions vary widely about what is remediable and fair, for example, and thus whether a particular inequality constitutes an inequity. (Is affirmative action to lessen disparities fair?) Similarly, different schools of thought pay far more attention to different dimensions of inequality. (Development economists tend to focus on economic inequalities; human rights practitioners on gender, ethnic, and religious disparities.)

There is no intellectually satisfying way to select from these different outlooks. Nor can any coherent presentation accommodate nearly all of them, so we must choose guiding concepts and definitions that are at least partly—and sometimes largely—arbitrary. Here are our choices, which will guide what follows.

First, all the inequalities that appear most prominently in discussions of health status, service availability, and service use constitute inequities. This statement implies that all people have the same right to healthy lives and adequate health services, regardless of their gender, ethnicity, religion, or economic status.[2] It also implies that differences in health status, service availability, and service use are avoidable, and can be greatly reduced at a cost that lies within the range of what an enlightened society can reasonably bear.

Second, the economic dimension of inequality is intrinsically significant, and important enough to merit explicit attention. It is especially so for those concerned with progress toward the Millennium Development Goals, because these are expressed primarily in economic terms: the first goal, for example, calls for a 50 percent reduction in the proportion of people living on less than $1 a day—the classic definition of severe economic poverty.[3]

(This is not to argue that other dimensions of poverty like gender, race, and religion are unimportant. The argument is simply that the economic dimension of health inequity is important enough for a focus on it to be legitimate, particularly in cases like the present, where practical considerations impose a need to limit the discussion.)

Third, place of residence is a proxy for some other measure of poverty like economic status, rather than something that is of interest in itself. This implies a greater concern for the well-being of a poor person, whether in a rural or urban area, than that of a rural resident, whether poor or rich. It also implies that people living in rural areas or remote provinces are of interest not because of where they live, but because they are more likely to be poor than urban residents.

The Economic and Geographic Dimensions of Health Equity

The third of the foregoing points is especially relevant because discussions of human resources for health give far greater prominence to the geographic than to the economic dimension of poverty. Whole papers—including a chapter in this volume—have been written on the geographic maldistribution of the health workforce, which is skewed toward urban and better-off areas. Although many envisage geographic differences as proxies for differentials in economic status, the extensive reading undertaken for this paper found no explicit references to economic inequalities in access to or use of health human resources.

Whether this distinction between geographic and economic differences has practical consequence depends on two things: the geographic distribution of poverty within a country, and the economic status of the people served by health workers in the parts of the country where they live.

Consider first the geographic distribution of poverty, measured by the percent of people living below a poverty line. Suppose that, to redress a current geographic imbalance in available health workforce, a country decides (and is able) to assign all new health workers to areas with the highest prevalence of poverty. How many of these new workers would be available to the country's poor?

Two extreme situations illustrate the range of possible answers to this question. First, imagine that all the economically poor people in a country are in one province, and all the people in that province are economically poor. Increasing health workers in that province alone will benefit all of the country's poor, without any "leakage" to its better-off. Second, suppose that economic poverty is evenly distributed throughout the country, with the same proportion of people in each province living below the poverty line. In that case, focusing on only a few parts of the country would produce no greater accuracy than randomly distributing the new health workers across all its provinces.

It is safe to expect that the situation in most countries, perhaps all, lies somewhere between these two extremes. But the extremes are so far apart that differences among countries can still be quite large.

For four of the countries of interest here—Ethiopia, Ghana, Mozambique, and Zambia—it is possible to determine the size of those differences from the estimated proportion of the population in each district living below the poverty line.[4] These estimated proportions permit us to assess who would benefit (the economically poor or better-off), and how much, from stationing all additional health workers in, for example, the poorest 50 percent or 25 percent of the country's districts—that is, in districts with the highest percent of the population living below the poverty line.

The data can be addressed from two perspectives. The first examines how many better-off people live in economically poor areas, and thus could benefit from additional health workers posted there (a figure often referred·to as leakage, or error of inclusion) (figure 12.1). The second concerns the number of economically poor people who live outside poor areas, and would be missed by any services delivered outside those areas (undercoverage, or error of exclusion) (figure 12.2).

On average, 48 percent of people in one of these countries—or in a randomly selected district in one of them—lives above the poverty line (see figure 12.1). When chosen from the poorest half of all districts only about 35 percent live above the poverty line, and 28 percent when chosen from a district in the poorest quarter.

So, focus on the poorest half of districts can reduce the potential leakage of benefits to the nonpoor by about a quarter (48 percent to 35 percent), while focus on the poorest quarter of districts can lower leakage from 48 percent to 28 percent (see figure 12.1). This reduction indicates a significant drop in beneficiaries that do not belong to the highest priority population—the nonpoor. But, it still falls well short of perfection, since more than a quarter of people in the service areas is above the poverty line.

Such precision comes at a cost, however, as the second perspective shows (see figure 12.2). The data indicate that, in each country, a large

Figure 12.1   Geographic Distribution of the Non-Poor in Ethiopia, Ghana, Mozambique, and Zambia

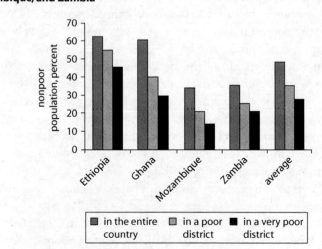

Source: World Bank data.
Note: A poor district is one of the country's poorest 50 percent of districts; a very poor district is one of the country's poorest 25 percent of districts. Ethiopian data are available for only around 90 percent of zones (referred to as "districts" here for the sake of comparability). Averages are unweighted.

Figure 12.2   Geographic Distribution of Poverty in Ethiopia, Ghana, Mozambique, and Zambia

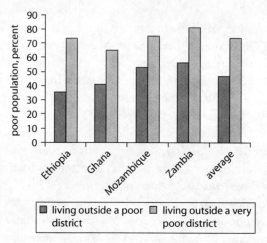

Source: World Bank data.
Note: A poor district is one of the country's poorest 50 percent of districts; a very poor district is one of the country's poorest 25 percent of districts. Ethiopian data are available for only around 90 percent of zones (referred to as "districts" here for the sake of comparability). Averages are unweighted.

portion of the population below the poverty line lives outside the poorest districts. On average, almost half (46 percent) of the poor live outside the economically poorest half of districts; nearly three-quarters (74 percent) live outside the poorest quarter of districts. These people would be missed by a program taking only a geographic approach to identifying the poor.

At this point, the second of the two considerations mentioned at the start of this section comes into play: the economic status of the people served by the additional health workers within the parts of the country where they are assigned. This consideration is important because, as just seen, some nonpoor people live in even the poorest districts, while some poor people live in the districts where poverty rates are lowest overall.

Such a pattern presents two possibilities. First, additional health personnel assigned to the poorest district might serve many people who are not economically poor. To be sure, it would be hard to go too far astray when working in an area where, for example, more than 80 percent of the population is below the poverty line. Still, in even the poorest parts of the poorest countries, there is likely a significant minority of people who are considerably less poor than others; and some types of health personnel (for example, specialized surgeons in district hospitals that charge for surgical procedures) would benefit primarily the better-off within the areas covered.

Second, health professionals in better-off districts might serve mostly poor people if they work in programs designed with those people in mind—for example, clinics where field workers regularly visit poor people to ensure that they come for health services.

Focus on the geographic dimension of poverty can take us much of the way toward reaching the economically poor, but by no means all the way. The relationship between the geographic and economic dimensions of poverty is far from exact. If the objective of a human resources for health policy is to serve economically poor people, it will need to look beyond its current emphasis on disadvantaged areas.

Availability of Health Workers to the Poor

What can be said about health workforce equity from an economic rather than geographic perspective? Given the scarce attention paid to the economic perspective, limited empirical information is available. Still, enough exists to justify summarizing it, if only as a starting point for the further explorations that are required.

There are two types of information: the availability of health workers to economically disadvantaged people, and the use of health workers by those people.

The information on health worker availability presents an indirect estimate of health workers per 1,000 people, for each economically defined 20 percent (quintile) of the population. Analysts construct these estimates by combining data from two sources. One comprises the same data on poverty prevalence (and number of people) in each district that formed the basis of the calculations represented in figures 12.1 and 12.2. The second source is information about the number of health workers drawn from national censuses of health personnel. Since data from such censuses are available only for Ghana and Zambia, the discussion will be limited to these countries.

Tabulating these data consists of three steps: first, to sort districts in order of the proportion of the population below the country's poverty line, from high to low; second, to divide the districts into five groups, each containing 20 percent of the country's population; and third, to calculate the health worker-to-population ratio for each of the five population groups, by calculating the average number of workers (weighted by district population).

Limited confidence can be placed in the results of this exercise, however, due to the large variation in health worker availability among districts within each population quintile. Still, the pattern of differences shown from those results is regular and in line with reasonable expectations. If one interprets them with this statistical limitation taken into account, they cautiously suggest two findings—and an instructive exception.

The first finding is that the availability of all categories of health worker is higher in areas inhabited by better-off people than in areas inhabited by the poor (figure 12.3). Worker density is far higher in the highest quintile than in the lowest two quintiles for each type of health worker in each country. Also noteworthy is the shape of the curve across the quintiles: worker density is more or less equal across the two or three bottom quintiles, then rises rapidly as one moves up the economic scale—mirroring the pattern for infant and child mortality in Africa.[5]

The second finding, also in line with expectations, is that the difference across quintiles varies from one type of health worker to another, with greater differences among higher level workers than among lower level personnel. Ghana has about five times as many high-level workers serving

Figure 12.3   Density of Health Workers by Economic Quintile, Ghana and Zambia

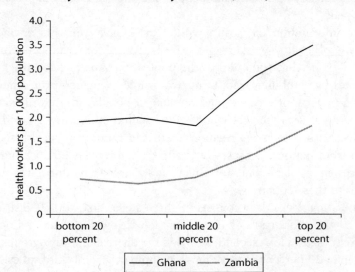

Source: World Bank data.
Note: Data for Ghana refer to the total of high-, mid-, and low-level workers. Data for Zambia refer to the total of doctors, nurses, and midwives.

the highest quintile of the population than the lowest, compared with 1.5–2 times as many mid-level or lower level workers. Zambia is similar, though less extreme. There, the doctor-to-population ratio for the top quintile is just under five times that for the bottom quintile, compared with around 3.5 times for nurses and midwives. As with density shown in figure 12.3, the largest differences are between the top 20–40 percent of the population and the bottom 60 percent. Across the bottom quintiles, differences are relatively small.

The instructive exception concerns community health nurses in Ghana. There are around 3,200 such nurses, salaried mid-level employees of the government's Ghana Health Service who are recruited from and trained near where they are subsequently posted.[6] Such providers are a pillar of Ghana's current 2007–11 health human resources strategy, which calls for their number to increase by 20 percent annually.[7]

These community health nurses are more prevalent in areas where poor people live than in those inhabited primarily by the better-off. Certainly, the interquintile range is not large: the bottom two quintiles have about 23.5 community health nurses per 100,000 people, compared with about 19.5 in the top two. But even this orientation toward the poor, modest as it may be, is enough to make the community health nurse program stand out against the distribution of the other, higher-level workers, who are much more common in areas where the best-off people live.

Use of Health Workers by the Poor

There is a sharp distinction between availability of health workers and use of their services. Even when workers are in areas inhabited primarily by the poor, many people might not use them. Expense is an obvious reason for this, especially where user fees apply. Another reason is knowledge: poor and uneducated people might know less about the potential benefits from available services than their better-off peers. Or poor people might fear contemptuous treatment by service providers belonging to a higher social stratum.

These factors make it important to go beyond availability and look at use. The most relevant data on use come from household surveys that cover the type of health providers visited by different economic groups for different problems. The most widely available, and those used here, were performed under the auspices of the Demographic and Health Survey (DHS) program, which has sponsored surveys typically covering

5,000–30,000 households, sometimes many more, in more than 75 low-
and middle-income countries.[8]

Data from a recent DHS survey are available for each of the five countries here: 2005 in Ethiopia, 2003 in Ghana, 2003 in Mozambique, 2005
in Rwanda, and 2001–02 in Zambia. Each survey contains information on
25–30 or more household possessions and characteristics, enough to construct a viable wealth index for measuring economic status.[9] Two factors
limit the survey information on visits to health workers. First, the basic
DHS survey is oriented toward maternal and child health, so survey data
have nothing to say about health service use by adults and the elderly,
which constitute a large portion of total use. Second, maternal and child
health information tends to report the type of facility visited rather than
type of provider seen.

Despite these drawbacks, it is possible to present a rather clear picture of two related types of service provided by professionals in the
formal health sector: antenatal care and attended deliveries (figures 12.4
and 12.5).[10]

**Figure 12.4   Receipt of Antenatal Care by Economic Quintile, Ghana, Mozambique,
Rwanda, and Zambia**

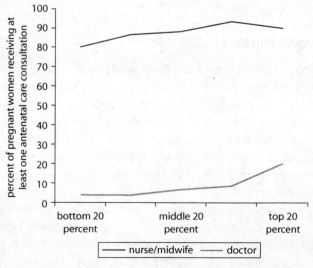

Source: World Bank data.
Note: Figures are unweighted averages for the four countries. Figures for nurses/midwives include auxiliary
nurses and midwives in Ghana and Mozambique, which list them separately.

Figure 12.5   Attended Delivery by Economic Quintile, Ghana, Mozambique, Rwanda, and Zambia

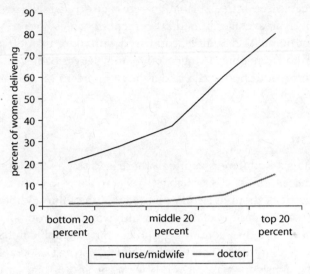

Source: World Bank data.
Note: Figures are unweighted averages for the four countries. Figures for nurses and midwives include auxiliary nurses and midwives in Ghana and Mozambique, which list them separately.

Two summary points on antenatal care can be made on the basis of the data in figure 12.4. First, in all four countries, nurses or midwives provide at least some antenatal care to almost all pregnant women, in the poorest as well as the best-off economic groups. Coverage is almost always close to 80 percent, and usually more, regardless of economic quintile. In Ghana and Rwanda coverage is actually higher in the lower and middle groups than in the topmost. In only one—Mozambique—is there a notable difference in coverage between the lowest and highest quintiles.

Second, doctors provide much less antenatal care overall, and what they provide is concentrated among higher quintiles. In only one group (Ghana's highest quintile) do doctors deliver antenatal care to more than a quarter of pregnant women. On average, doctors provide such care for only around 4 percent of women in the lowest quintile, compared with about 20 percent of women in the highest.

For delivery attendance the picture changes, especially with respect to nurses and midwives. As with antenatal care, nurses and midwives provide many more services than doctors. But unlike antenatal care, where nurses and midwives saw most poor as well as most better-off women, deliveries by doctors and nurses and midwives are primarily of children born to women in higher economic groups.

These data need little explanation (see figure 12.5). Nurses and midwives deliver, on average, around 20 percent of babies born to women in the poorest population quintile, compared with more than 80 percent of those born to women in the highest. Doctors deliver babies of almost no women in the bottom quintile, and about 15 percent of those in the top quintile.

Conclusion

What has been said here is about all there is to say on the topic at hand until further information is available.[11] What remains, in closing, is to offer three suggestions about its significance—about the value addition of looking at the maldistribution of Africa's health workforce from an economic perspective, rather than continuing to focus on geographic imbalances.

First, a solid argument exists for retaining a strong geographic focus, even if one considers place of residence as no more than an imperfect proxy for economic status: poor areas are far easier to identify than poor people, which can be an important point in African countries with weak administrative structures. Correcting geographic inequalities in health worker distribution is an obvious way to start correcting other types of inequality in access, including the economic.

Second, from an analytical perspective, an economic-inequality approach to health worker issues can identify patterns missed by a more conventional geographic outlook. Much of this approach confirms what is already known from geographic studies: for example, that access to health workers, especially higher level workers, is much easier for better-off than for disadvantaged groups. At the same time, some potentially significant, less intuitively obvious findings have emerged—particularly which health personnel strategies seem to work better than others in reaching the poor.

The most significant of these findings touches on antenatal care by nurses and midwives. They appear to serve 80 percent or more of even the poorest women, offering services that, while far from ideal, seem complete enough to provide some health benefit (box 12.1). Might these workers constitute a platform for delivering additional services, simple but potentially valuable to disadvantaged groups?

A second example is the Ghana program of community health nurses, who seem considerably more likely than other personnel to be available

Box 12.1

How Good Is Antenatal Care for Poor Women?

It is encouraging that so many poor women receive at least some antenatal care. But how good is it?

Hints about the quality of care, as defined in terms of its comprehensiveness, are available from the same DHS surveys that provided the data on antenatal care in figure 12.4. Surveys asked women obtaining antenatal care which of the following services they had received: recording weight, height, and/or blood pressure; taking a blood or urine sample; and providing an iron supplement, tetanus injection, and/or information about where to go in case of complications.[a]

The findings, expressed in unweighted averages for Ethiopia, Ghana, Mozambique, Rwanda, and Zambia, show that:

- Women in the poorest quintile of the population received an average of 4.2 of seven services.
- Ninety percent received the one service that professionals could provide without additional supplies or equipment: information about where to go in case of complications.[b] Eighty-four percent were also weighed, and 56 percent received a tetanus injection. Urinalyses were less frequent, received by 28 percent of poor women.
- The number of services rose steadily by economic status, with the top quintile of women receiving around 5.3 of the services.

Source: World Bank data.
a. The survey counts the absence of response as a failure to receive the service in question.
b. This is an unweighted average for Ethiopia, Ghana, Mozambique, and Rwanda; data for Zambia are unavailable.

to the poor. Are there lessons to be drawn from this experience for other countries?

A third finding concerns the concentrated use of traditional practitioners among the poor (box 12.2). Does this constitute a reason to renew efforts to upgrade their skills as a more central part of human resources for health?

The third contribution of an economic perspective is the most fundamental: geographic inequalities form only part of the overall economic inequality story. Yes, they are an important part, and as noted above, addressing them is often an obvious place to start. But as argued in the

Box 12.2

Traditional Practitioners and the Poor

While the patients of most African health providers are concentrated among the better off, one group of medical personnel appears to serve primarily the poor, at least for basic maternal and child care, for which data are available: traditional practitioners.

The best-known type of such practitioner is the traditional birth attendant. According to the DHS surveys, such attendants helped with 34 percent of births among the poorest quintile of women in the countries covered. This figure declined to 30 percent in the middle quintile, and 13 percent in the top quintile.[a]

The same general pattern applies to treatment of childhood cough, diarrhea, and fever. Traditional practitioners' involvement in such conditions is lower than for deliveries in the countries with available information. But services that traditional providers deliver in this area are concentrated primarily among the poor. On average, such practitioners deal with approximately 12 percent of cases in the lowest population quintile, compared with 4 percent of cases in the highest.[b]

a. All figures are unweighted averages for trained and untrained traditional attendants in Ethiopia, Ghana, Mozambique, Rwanda, and Ethiopia.
b. Unweighted averages for Mozambique, Rwanda, and Zambia.

section *Availability of health workers to the poor*, better-off areas almost always have many poor people, just as poor areas have many relatively well-off people.

Thus to focus on poor areas alone is to miss what health personnel in high-income areas can do to reach disadvantaged groups, and to overlook the possibility that health workers in low-income areas might not be serving many of the poor people there. It is necessary to look beyond geographic maldistribution if the economically poor are to benefit fully from health workforce strategies.

Notes

1. This definition is a paraphrase of the classic definition of health equity presented in Whitehead and Dahlgren (2006).
2. The statement also implies that all people have an equally strong desire to use health services once the services are available, so there is no volitional element in any observed disparities in health service use.

3. More on the Millennium Development Goals is at: http://www.un.org/millenniumgoals/poverty.shtml.

4. For Ethiopia, poverty line data have been calculated from Central Statistical Agency of Ethiopia, Ministry of Finance and Economic Development (2004); population figures come from Central Statistical Agency of Ethiopia (2007). Poverty data for Ghana, for 2000, are taken from Coulombe (2005). 1997 data for *Mozambique* are drawn from Simler and Nhate (2005). 2000/02–03 data for *Zambia* appear in Simler (2007). (Mozambique and Zambia figures refer to the international poverty line of $1 per day in 1986. In Ethiopia and Ghana, the reference is to the country's national poverty line.)

5. Africa mortality figures are from Gwatkin and others (2007).

6. Information on characteristics of community health nurses is from Nana Twum-Danso, pers. comm., March 2010.

7. Figures for annual intake of certified community health nurse training programs appears in Ministry of Health of Ghana (2007).

8. For more of the DHS, see http://www.measuredhs.com.

9. Further detail can be found in Rutstein and Johnson (2004).

10. The data in both figures exclude Ethiopia because the survey there did not differentiate among the different types of health professionals providing the services. Overall, the Ethiopia data for all types of health professionals produce a picture similar to that for comparable data from the other countries: for both antenatal care and delivery, coverage by a professional is far higher for women in the upper than the lower economic quintiles (12.7 percent in the lowest quintile, compared with 58.1 percent in the highest for antenatal care, and 0.8 percent versus 30.9 percent for attended deliveries).

11. Such additional information need not be difficult to develop, at least in principle, since its production would require relatively modest supplements to the information currently collected through routine household surveys. For basic maternal and child health, it would mean expanding the services DHS surveys, disaggregated by qualifications of service provider. Information about the use of medical personnel for other services could be gathered by modifying the health modules of the questionnaires in household expenditure studies to include questions about the type of provider for individual services.

References

Central Statistical Agency of Ethiopia, Ministry of Finance and Economic Development. 2004. *2004–05 Household Income, Consumption Expenditure Survey*. Addis Ababa: Central Statistical Agency of Ethiopia.

Central Statistical Agency of Ethiopia. 2007. *2007 Population and Housing Census*. Addis Ababa: Central Statistical Agency of Ethiopia.

Coulombe, H. 2005. *Ghana Census-Based Poverty Map: District and Sub-District-Level Results*. Accra: Ghana Statistical Service.

Gwatkin, D. R., S. Rutstein, K. Johnson, E. Suliman, A. Wagstaff, and A. Amozou. 2007. *Socio-Economic Difference in Health, Nutrition, and Population within Developing Countries: An Overview*. Washington, DC: World Bank.

Ministry of Health of Ghana. 2007. *Human Resource Policies and Strategies for the Health Sector, 2007–2011*. Accra: Ministry of Health.

Rutstein, S. O., and K. Johnson. 2004. *The DHS Wealth Index*. DHS Comparative Reports 6. Calverton, MD: ORC Macro.

Simler, K. R. 2007. *Micro-Level Estimates of Poverty in Zambia*. Lusaka: Central Statistical Office of Zambia.

Simler, K. R., and V. Nhate. 2005. "Poverty, Inequality, and Geographic Targeting: Evidence from Small-Area Estimates in Mozambique," Food Consumption and Nutrition Division Discussion Paper 192, International Food Policy Research Institute, Washington, DC.

Whitehead, M., and G. Dahlgren. 2006. *Concepts and Principles for Tackling Social Inequities in Health: Leveling Up (Part 1)*. Studies on Social and Economic Determinants of Population Health, No. 2. Copenhagen: World Health Organization Regional Office for Europe.

WHO (World Health Organization). 2004. *World Report on Knowledge for Better Health: Strengthening Health Systems*. Geneva: WHO.

World Bank. 2009. *World Development Indicators 2009*. Washington, DC: World Bank.

PART 3

Performance of the Health Workforce

CHAPTER 13

Incentives for Provider Performance

Agnes Soucat, Paul Gertler, Paulin Basinga, Jennifer Sturdy, Christel Vermeersch, and Claude Sekabaraga

Pay for performance (P4P) is generating interest in Africa. This chapter is an early look at Sub-Saharan Africa's experience with this approach. To date more than 20 African countries have pilots or programs providing some elements of P4P to their health workers. The chapter proposes a framework to analyze how P4P affects the number, distribution and performance of health workers, and examines the evidence from the literature to date. The experience of Rwanda is an example of how P4P can be an essential component of a reform program to strengthen the availability and performance of health workers in Africa. The number of health workers in rural areas increased and performance improved. But the design of P4P related reforms matters. Looking forward, the experience from other African countries will need to be carefully documented.

Why Pay for Performance in Sub-Saharan Africa?

Many policy makers in Sub-Saharan countries believe that pay for performance (P4P) can address deeply entrenched problems, fostering better results and efficiency in the health sector. To date more than 20 countries have pilots or programs providing some elements of P4P to their health workers (World Bank 2010). Rwanda and Burundi have P4P as part of their national health systems. Sierra Leone and Burkina Faso are preparing to follow suit. Are these policy makers right?

How Pay for Performance Improves Health Worker Outcomes

P4P can be defined as the "transfer of money or material goods conditional on taking a measurable health related action or achieving a predetermined performance target" (Eichler and Levine 2009). It is payment for attaining well-defined results and can affect workforce outcomes in three main ways (following the framework in chapter 1): number, distribution, and performance of health workers.

P4P can potentially affect the number of health workers by providing additional resources to salary supplements and wages. Giving higher wages to health workers (according to the labor market framework in chapter 3) leads to more health workers available to work and potentially less migration.

P4P can also affect the distribution of health workers if it encourages different payments for specific areas or populations with specific needs. Chapters 9 and 15 suggest that including equity or geographic distribution as part of performance-based indicators could lead to better pay for health workers serving in poor areas, growing their number (Zurn and others 2004).

Finally, as discussed in recent policy debates, policy makers introduced P4P to improve the performance of health workers, which can have several dimensions (in the framework of chapter 5). P4P can affect productivity by providing direct incentives linked to the quantity and quality of services supplied (box 13.1).

Global Experience of Pay for Performance

The literature strongly suggests that P4P mainly influences the quantity of services produced. Its impact on quality is promising but less well studied. In fact, pay-for-quality is still at an early stage, with governments and insurers—particularly in Organisation for Economic Co-operation and Development (OECD) countries—searching for the best ways to maximize its impact and reduce its adverse effects.

Globally, P4P offers four main insights.

First, the impact of fee-for-service (or pay-for-quantity) on producing and consuming health services is clear. When governments or insurers pay for each unit of output, and as long as the fee is greater than the marginal cost, providers increase output, and consumers consume more of it

Box 13.1

Health Worker Performance

To examine the impact of P4P we propose a simple health workers' performance model with two dimensions: what health workers know (x-axis)—the ability to do, including technical knowledge—and what health workers do (y-axis)—actual services in both quantity and quality (box figure 13.1.1). Ideally health workers would always operate at their full potential and do what they are capable of doing. At this point, they work at what we call their production possibility frontier. But in reality many workers do less than what they know (the "know-do" gap of chapter 5), creating a performance gap. Traditional supply-side interventions lead to higher ability to do, but have limited impact as they only shift the—rather low—performance curve. P4P is expected to shift the performance curve and bring it closer to the production possibility frontier, leading to much higher performance with comparable intensity of traditional supply side intervention.

Box Figure 13.1.1   A Simple Two-Dimensional Model of Health Worker Performance

Ideally, health workers would always do what they are able to do—that is, work at the production possibility frontier.

But in most contexts there is a performance gap, between potential and actual performance.

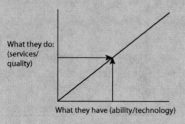

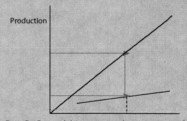

This lessens the impact of traditional supply-side interventions (T1 to T2).

But P4P could increase the impact of traditional interventions.

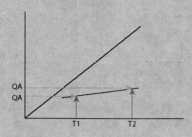

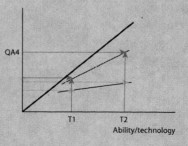

(Barnum, Kutzin, and Saxenian 1995; Christianson, Leatherman, and Sutherland 2007). Fee-for-service is thus expected to lead health workers to produce more, improving the intake of essential health interventions, particularly if targeted toward the poorest areas and underserved groups. In Haiti a before-and-after study showed that payments for immunization and assisted deliveries led to an increase of outputs and coverage with these indicators (Eichler and others 2006).

Increasing quantity may, however, come at the expense of access and quality. P4P may induce adverse incentives that exacerbate inequalities in access to health care (Greene and Nash 2009), involve "gaming" strategies (Khanduja and others 2009), or encourage adverse selection by health providers to avoid more sick patients (Karve and others 2008).

Second, the impact of P4P on quality of care is less clear cut (Eldridge and Palmer 2009). Most global evaluations reveal positive results for quality (as well as efficiency and patient outcomes) (Dudley and others 2004; Greene and Nash 2009). A review of experience in OECD countries concludes that many P4P schemes show promise for improving quality (Scheffler, Fulton, and Borowitz 2010). A before-and-after study of the United Kingdom's Quality and Outcome Framework P4P program found that quality increased for some ailments (asthma and diabetes) but not for others (heart diseases) (Roland and others 2009). In California a study of 230 physician groups showed a rise in quality metrics of 3 percent annually (Robinson and others 2009). Studies in Brazil, by contrast, have not shown a clear effect of P4P on quality or efficiency (Borem and others 2010; La Forgia and Couttolenc 2008). A major weakness of all studies is, however, that they do not include control groups, because most P4P programs are implemented without a rigorous evaluation component (Khanduja, Scales, and Adhikari 2009).

Third, the positive effect of P4P is observed in these studies in a context where payments go to providers' organizations, including single practices, raising the firm's incentives to be more productive. When used to provide bonuses to individual public servants in integrated civil services, however, P4P generally has little effect (OECD 2005). Some qualitative research even suggests that P4P may compete negatively with other incentives, public ethos, or health workers' self-motivation.[2] To be effective, P4P likely requires some provider autonomy and purchaser-provider separation, allowing the firm to determine individual incentives.

Fourth, most authors recognize that how P4P is used and designed determines its success or failure. The U.K. experience suggests that its P4P program may have chosen targets that were too easy, because most providers reached the maximum points (Doran and others 2006). The thresholds there were subsequently adjusted. Prices set too low can also lead to P4P being ineffective.

The objectives of P4P schemes in developed and developing countries are different (Eichler and Levine 2009). Those in developed countries aim to improve the quality of care, reducing less desirable services in favor of more desirable ones, and lowering costs (Bell and Levinson 2007; Greene and Nash 2009). In Sub-Saharan Africa, the main issues are still related to insufficient access and low use of services, particularly for high-impact interventions and for the poor. For the next decade, the four main objectives of P4P in Africa are therefore likely to be:

- Increase the intake of proven high-impact Millennium Development Goal-related health services that require universal coverage, such as immunization, insecticide-treated nets, assisted birth delivery, and emergency obstetrical care.
- Improve the quality of these interventions to maximize impact.
- Provide flexible remuneration increases to health workers to improve retention and reduce migration.
- Increase health services for the poor through higher payments for health workers in rural or poor urban areas, thus improving demand for human resources for health in urban areas.

A Country Example: Rwanda's Performance-Based Financing

Rwanda scaled up its national P4P program since 2005 on the basis of a positive evaluation of a three-year pilot phase in two provinces (box 13.2). The program channels funds directly from the treasury to the bank accounts of the country's 400 health centers—40 percent faith-based and 60 percent public—on the basis of a contract, with the payment based on 13 quantitative indicators and 13 qualitative measurements (tables 13.1 and 13.2).

The PBF payment schedule uses a three-part price model for facilities and a two-part model for health workers. PBF payments to health facilities are based on the formula:

$$Payment_{it} = \left(\sum_j P_j U_{ijt} \right) \times \left(\sum_k w_k S_{ikt} \right)$$
$$\text{where } 0 \leq \sum_k w_k S_{ikt} \leq 1$$

Box 13.2

Rwanda, a Story of Successful Reforms

With about 10 million people in Central Africa, Rwanda is one of the world's poorest countries. During 2000–07 the Demographic and Health Survey showed a rise in facility-based deliveries from 39 percent to 52 percent, and family planning from 10 percent to 27 percent, alongside a 30 percent decrease in infant mortality.

These results can largely be attributed to a paradigm shift in public finance and service delivery subsidized by the public purse, based on five pillars.

The first is *decentralization* of health services, with a strong emphasis on government structures that are community-based. The fiscal decentralization was rapid, immediately translated into large sums of cash to local governments. Block grants gave flexibility to local governments—some were earmarked (to achieve national goals) and some were not (to foster local initiatives).

The second is the *Imihigo,* a performance contract between the country's president and district mayors. It has multisectoral indicators for all key sectors, including agriculture, health, and infrastructure. Health has few indicators, but they are focused on high impact interventions: family planning, assisted birth delivery, insecticide-treated nets, and enrollment in microinsurance, all priorities the central government established as essential to the Millennium Development Goals. The earmarked grants were aligned with the Imihigo, whose indicators were used to monitor the grants' impact.

The third is *community-based health insurance,* which supports locally owned and managed risk-funding pools from user premiums collected in sub-districts. The treasury and donors (mainly the Global Fund to Fight Tuberculosis, AIDS, and Malaria) subsidize the micro-insurance pools, called *mutuelles,* for about 20 percent of the population. In 2002–09, enrollment in health insurance rose from about 4 percent to 91 percent, expanding service use.

The fourth is the *autonomy of health facilities.* In 2008 Rwanda granted full autonomy to facilities, including the right to hire and fire health workers. This was the most dramatic reform (few governments have moved in that direction in Sub-Saharan Africa).

The fifth is *P4P,* called performance-based financing (PBF).

Table 13.1   Indicators and Fees for Performance-Based Financing, Rwanda

Performance-based financing output indicator (Uj)	(Pj) Amount paid per case
Curative case	0.18
Prenatal care, first visit	0.09
Pregnant women who completed four prenatal care visits	0.37
Pregnant women given tetanus vaccine	0.46
Pregnant women given preventive treatment for malaria	0.46
At-risk pregnancy referred to hospital for delivery	1.83
Growth-monitoring visit for child ages 12–59 months	0.18
Fully vaccinated child	0.92
Malnourished children referred	1.83
Deliveries at the health center	4.59
Family planning, new users (DIU, pills, injections, implants)	1.83
Family planning (DIU, pills, injections, implants resupply)	0.18
Emergency referrals	1.83

Source: World Bank data.

Table 13.2   Quality Indicators for Performance-Based Financing, Rwanda

Service	Weight	Share of weight allocated to structural components	Share of weight allocated to process components	Means of assessment
General administration	0.052	1.00	0.00	Direct observation
Cleanliness	0.028	1.00	0.00	Direct observation
Curative care	0.170	0.23	0.77	Medical record review
Delivery	0.130	0.40	0.60	Medical record review
Prenatal care	0.126	0.12	0.88	Direct observation
Family planning	0.114	0.22	0.78	Medical record review
Immunization	0.070	0.40	0.60	Direct observation
Growth monitoring	0.052	0.15	0.85	Direct observation
HIV services	0.090	1.00	0.00	Direct observation
Tuberculosis service	0.028	0.28	0.72	Direct observation
Laboratory	0.030	1.00	0.00	Direct observation
Pharmacy management	0.060	1.00	0.00	Direct observation
Financial management	0.050	1.00	0.00	Direct observation
Total	1.000			

Source: World Bank data.

and where P_j = payment per unit of each PBF service j (13 *output indicators*); U_{ijt} = number of patients using service j in facility i in period t; S_{ikt} = 1 if facility i has quality characteristic k in period t (13 *quality characteristics*); ω_k = weight for characteristic k, weights sum to one (500 *points total*).

PBF is one of five mechanisms of health facility payments (figure 13.1). Eighty percent of PBF payments are for health worker incentives. An individual's additional income is not, however, directly linked to the services he or she provides, but is calculated as a salary bonus based on skills, years of service, and attendance weighted for the overall PBF of the facility. The remaining 20 percent is used for operating costs, equipment, and other nonlabor costs.

PBF payments are made every quarter. A district-level steering committee approves the payment with reference to a quantity audit, a quality assessment, and a supervision report prepared by the district supervision team. One focal point in the administrative district conducts the quantity audit, and the district supervisors conduct the quality assessment (based in the district hospital). Supervisors randomly sample patients to identify phantom patients, and conduct random visits to verify the quality score. A study found less than 5 percent of patients to be phantom (Management Sciences for Health, Boston).

Figure 13.1   Fund Flows to Rwandan Health Centers

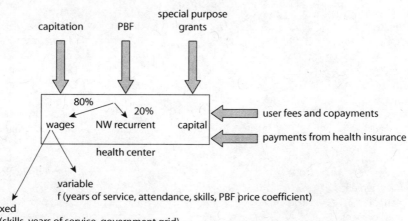

Source: World Bank data.
Note: PBF = performance-based financing.

Impact Evaluation in Rwanda

An impact evaluation of PBF was nested into the P4P program. Its objective was to look at the incentives' effect on both the quantity of services (measured as use of essential services) and their quality. It also examined the impact on child health and the availability and financing of human resources for health.

Design

During the scaling-up and rollout of the program, 7 districts of the 30 in the country were allocated to a control group. Health facilities in this group received equal funding to the facilities under the PBF program through a general input contract, but no results-based payments. The control group helped distinguish the effect of the results contract from the effect of increased payments and resources.

The evaluation sampled 166 primary care clinics (of 401 in the country) chosen from "naïve" districts that had no previous experience with P4P. The clinics were grouped into similar pairs based on population density, rainfall, and predominant livelihood (figure 13.2).[3]

These clinics were then randomized into a phase 1 (treatment) group, which implemented the P4P program 2006, and a phase 2 (control) group, which implemented the program two years later. District allocation was subsequently modified, however, because the decentralization process redesigned district boundaries on the basis of administrative criteria. Some clinics were then reallocated to different groups to ensure that the districts would be homogenous and have all their clinics as either treatment or control. This affected two of eight pairs in the experimental design where the treatment and control districts switched, as P4P had to be expanded to all clinics in partially covered districts.

To isolate the incentive's effect (provider payment) from that of additional resources (increased supply), control facilities received financial compensation that was not linked to performance, calculated as the average compensation provided to the treatment facilities. Both groups were granted the same flexibility in spending the funds, which could be used for paying salary bonuses or purchasing other nonlabor inputs.

Both facility-based and population-based data were collected. These included administrative use and outcome data, information on staffing, budget, equipment and drugs, and exit interviews of pregnant women. Household surveys were also conducted in all 166 clinic areas, collecting socioeconomic characteristics, service use, and child anthropometric information for a random sample of 13 households in each area.

Figure 13.2   Design and Sampling of the Rwandan P4P Impact Evaluation

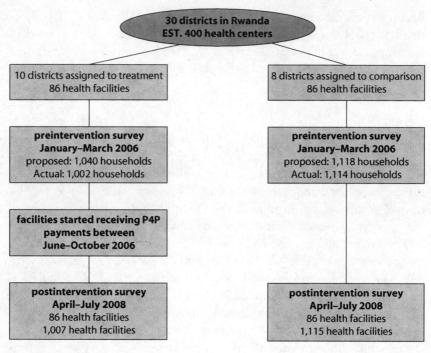

Source: Baginga and others 2011.

Quality of care (both competency and quality rendered) was measured through health worker observations and patient exit interviews. Knowledge and competency were assessed through interviews of health workers using standardized vignettes, based on the Rwandan Clinical Guidelines (Minisante Rwanda) (23 items). Quality rendered was estimated through exit interviews assessing the actual clinical content of care. The "know-do" gap (or provider effort, see chapter 5) was then estimated by comparing provider knowledge and actual behavior.

The baseline data showed no difference between the intervention and control clinics for expenditure and use of services, confirming that the samples were comparable.

Impact on Health Worker Funding, Numbers, and Distribution

From 2003 to 2007 the transfers to provinces and districts rose from about 37 percent to 85 percent of the recurrent budget. Financing to human resources tripled from $6.7 million to $21.4 million. PBF grew more than 10-fold from $.8 million to $8.9 million, reaching $1–$2 per capita in 2007. Wages increased by 60–100 percent depending on the clinic. This relative bonus is a much larger than generally implemented in OECD countries, where the bonus payment was 5 percent or less of the physician and hospital earnings, except in the United Kingdom where it is estimated to be 15 percent.

As Rwanda carried out decentralization and reform, personnel in publicly funded facilities almost doubled in four years (2005–08) (figure 13.3). A large share of these workers was hired for rural facilities, improving the distribution of the health workforce.

It is not clear however whether the performance contract played a role as compared to the size of the bonus. Whether or not the clinics were receiving funds on the basis of performance did not affect the number of health workers hired by the clinics. This is probably due to health workers's bonus not being directly related to performance. Clinics receiving non performance related lumpsums provided comparable salary bonuses to their health workers. Yet the P4P approach allowed the flexibility for clinics to hire the health workers they needed and increase their remuneration.

Figure 13.3   Increase in Number of Health Workers, Rwanda

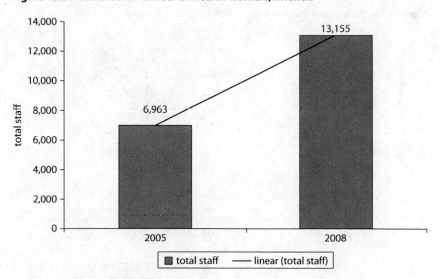

Source: Minisante-Country Status Report on Health and Poverty (2009).
Note: Total health personnel in publically funded facilities has almost doubled in 3 years.

Impact on Performance: The Quantity and Quality Effects

Over the period of analysis, all health interventions went up. Most health indicators improved in 2005–07 (Sekabaraga and others 2001). Use of most services increased in both the treatment and the control groups, as the Demographic and Health Surveys (DHS 2000–05 and 2007) show. Assisted deliveries were low (about 10–15 percent) before the reform; they started to climb in 2005 for both groups (figure 13.4), but grew 7 percentage points more in PBF facilities.

Using the productivity framework presented in section 1, we can see that PBF had an independent effect on the quantity of services in the treatment group (see figure 13.4) (Basinga and others 2011). After 2006 the use curves of the treatment and control facilities start diverging, with better performance in the treatment group. We can see a similarly significant effect for preventive child visits (growth monitoring). More growth monitoring and early identification of malnourished children led to an increase in weight for age 0–12 months and increase in height for weight at 24–48 months. No effect was found on immunizations, antenatal care, or curative care (Gertler and Vermeersch 2012).

Figure 13.4   Increased Deliveries at Health Facilities, Rwanda

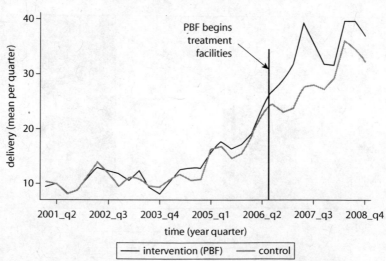

Note: Performance-based financing

PBF also had a positive effect on quality of care. It was similar at base-line in both treatment and control clinics, but after two years the quality of antenatal services improved in the treatment group (figure 13.5) (Gertler and Vermeersch 2012).

Most important, the quality of antenatal care improved even more for providers who had a higher competency, showing a synergistic effect of basic knowledge and incentives (figure 13.6). It has been desmonstrated that PBF reduces the efficiency gap by 3.5 percentage points, or about 20 percent of the gap, on average (Gertler and Vermeersch 2012).

A Question—And Some Possible Answers

To date, the impact evaluation in Rwanda is the only rigorous analysis of incentives' effect in a low-income country. Availability and distribution of health workers improved, their remuneration increased. Improvements in service use and quality over time were observed in both P4P and control

Figure 13.5   Impact of Pay for Performance on Antenatal Care

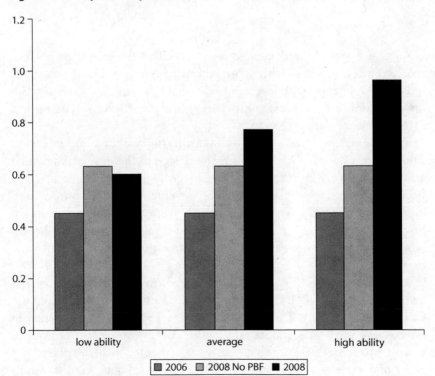

Source: World Bank data.

Figure 13.6   PBF Improves the Performance of Better Trained Health Workers

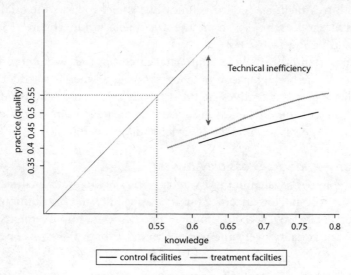

Source: World Bank data.

groups, as both received greater resources. The treatment group that received more resources with a P4P contract performed better on several indicators. P4P appears to leverage traditional interventions, such as training and monitoring, as more competent providers performed better when incentives were introduced.

A key question: Why could we measure impact for some interventions but not others? One answer is the design of the evaluation, which aimed to measure the impact of the incentives independent of additional resources. P4P's potential to leverage more resources and increase remuneration—and thus health worker motivation—cannot, however, be neglected. It certainly played a role in Rwanda as health workers in both the treatment and control group saw their income rise.

Another answer is the role of the other reform pillars. Fiscal decentralization, autonomy, and health insurance also contributed to increased use and quality of services. The role of Imihigo was particularly important in establishing political accountability and a culture of results. As Imihigo and other reforms were simultaneously implemented in all districts, P4P's effect may have been underestimated and could be higher in other countries if its entire size could be captured in the design.

A third answer is that relative prices are important, and the incentive system needs to get the interrelationship right. The observed effect on assisted delivery is likely related to the fact that the bonus was highest for this intervention, and the return on effort was high and in the provider's control.

Conclusion

P4P, taking off in Sub-Saharan Africa, appears to improve the availability distribution and performance of health workers, increasing quantity and to some extent quality of services. The Rwanda impact evaluation confirms that P4P can improve both health worker productivity and service quality. It shows that incentives play a role and that the health system probably "gets what it pays for." Several countries are implementing the strategy, and some of them—including Burundi and Burkina Faso—are institutionalizing the approach and practicing it nationally.

Rwanda also shows, however, that P4P is no panacea. It did not have an effect on all interventions. Many questions remain about how to maximize the effect on all important health interventions. The long-term political economy effects are also unknown. As several countries are now implementing the strategies and conducting impact evaluations (Benin, Democratic Republic of Congo, Zambia), we may learn more on the conditions that make P4P valuable in improving the performance of health workers in Sub-Saharan Africa.

Yet the approach seems promising to address some of the health sector's problems. The flexibility of the P4P approach within the Rwanda reform package lead to health workers working in larger numbers in rural areas and being better paid. Bonus payments better link salary increases to improved performance—an outcome attractive to policy makers. Performance-based transfers for facilities help separate purchasing and provision, and reduce the conflict of interest of local governments. They also provide an avenue for civil service reform and flexibility in wage policies. Wages can be brought more in line with the labor market and are no longer constrained by rigid civil service rules and wage bills constraints (chapter 6).

As more and more African countries implement P4P approaches it will be essential to evaluate those experience rigorously. This will require using a broad set of metrics that include number distribution remuneration of health workers as well as performance in terms of quantity and quality of services delivered.

Notes

1. The Millennium Development Goals call for a two-thirds decrease in child mortality by 2015 relative to the 1990 baseline (UNICEF 2008).

2. This is likely explained by the complexity of assessing and attributing performance in multitask and team activities, such as those in the health sector (Holmström and Milgrom 1991).

3. The details of the design and analysis can be found in Basinga and others (2010).

References

Barnum, H., J. Kutzin, and H. Saxenian. 1995. "Incentives and Provider Payment Methods." *International Journal of Health Planning and Management* 10 (1): 23–45.

Basinga, P., P. Gertler, A. Binagwaho, A. Soucat, J. Sturdy, and C. Vermeersch. 2010. *Paying Primary Health Care Centers for Performance in Rwanda.* Washington, DC: World Bank.

Basinga, P., P. Gertler, A. Binagwaho, A. Soucat, J. Sturdy, and C. Vermeersch. 2011. "Effect on Maternal and Child Health Services in Rwanda of Payment to Primary Health-Care Providers for Performance: An Impact Evaluation." *The Lancet* 377 (9775): 1421–28.

Bell, C., and W. Levinson. 2007. "Pay for Performance: Learning About Quality." *Canadian Medical Association Journal* 176 (12): 1717–19.

Borem, P., E. Alves Valle, M. Silva Monteiro De Castro, R. Kenzou Fujii, A. Luiza de Oliveira Farias, F. Leite Gastal, and C. Connor. 2010. *Project Brazilian Pay-For-Performance Case Study.* UNIMED-Belo Horizonte Physician Cooperative. Bethesda, MD: Health System 20/20 Project, Abt Associates.

Chaudhury, N., J. Hammer, M. Kremer, K. Muralidharan, and H. Rogers. 2006. "Missing in Action: Teacher and Health Worker Absence in Developing Countries." *Journal of Economic Perspectives* 20 (1): 91–116.

Christianson, J., S. Leatherman, and K. Sutherland. 2007. *Paying for Quality: Understanding and Assessing Physician Pay-for-Performance Initiatives.* Princeton, NJ: Robert Wood Johnson Foundation.

Doran, T., C. Fullwood, H. Gravelle, D. Reeves, E. Kontopantelis, U. Hiroeh, and M. Roland. 2006. "Pay-for-Performance Programs in Family Practices in the United Kingdom." *The New England Journal of Medicine* 355: 375–84.

Dudley and others 2004.

Eichler, R., P. Auxila, U. Antoine, and B. Desmangles. 2006. "Haiti: Going to Scale with a Performance Incentive Model." Working Group on Performance-Based Incentives, Center for Global Development, Washington, DC.

Eichler, R., and R. Levine. 2009. *Performance Incentives for Global Health: Potential and Pitfalls*. Washington, DC: Center for Global Development.

Eldridge, C., and N. Palmer. 2009. "Performance-Based Payment: Some Reflections on the Discourse, Evidence and Unanswered Questions." *Health Policy and Planning* 24: 160–66.

Filmer, D., J. Hammer, and L. Pritchett. 2000. "Weak Links in the Chain: A Diagnosis of Health Policy in Poor Countries." *World Bank Research Observer* 15 (2): 199–224.

Gauthier, B., and W. Wane. 2009. "Leakage of Public Resources in the Health Sector: An Empirical Investigation of Chad Dagger." *Journal of African Economies* 18 (1): 52–83.

Gertler, P., and C. Vermeersch. 2012. Using Performance Incentives to improve Health Outcomes. Policy Research Working Paper, Nr 6100. Washington, DC: World Bank.

Greene, S., and D. Nash. 2009. "Pay for Performance: An Overview of the Literature." *American Journal of Medical Quality* 24 (2): 140–63.

Holmström, B, and P. Milgrom. 1991. "Multitask Principal Agent Analysis: Incentive Contracts, Asset Ownership, and Job Design." *Journal of Law, Economics and Organization* 7: 25–52.

Karve, A. M., F. S. Ou, B. L. Lytle, and E. D. Peterson. 2008. "Potential Unintended Financial Consequences of Pay-For-Performance on the Quality of Care for Minority Patients." *American Heart Journal* 155 (3): 571–76.

Khanduja, K, D. C. Scales, and N. K. Adhikari. 2009. *Pay for Performance in the Intensive Care Unit—Opportunity or Threat?* Toronto: Sunnybrook Health Sciences Centre.

La Forgia, G. M., and B. Couttolenc. 2008. *Hospital Performance in Brazil: The Search of Excellence*. Washington, DC: World Bank.

OECD (Organisation for Economic Co-operation and Development). 2005. *Performance-Related Pay Policies for Government Employees*. Paris: OECD.

Robinson, J. C., T. Williams, and D. Yanagihara. 2009. "Measurement of and Reward for Efficiency in California's Pay-For-Performance Program." *Health Affairs* 28 (5):1438–47.

Roland, M., M. Elliott, G. Lyratzopoulos, J. Barbiere, R. Parker, P. Smith, P. Bower, and J. Campbell. 2009. "Reliability of Patient Responses in Pay for Performance Schemes: Analysis of National General Practitioner Patient Survey Data in England." *British Medical Journal* 339: b3851.

Scheffler, R. M., B. D. Fulton, and M. Borowitz. 2010. "Pay for Performance Programs in Health: Evidence from the OECD." Working Paper, Global Center for Health Economics and Policy Research, School of Public Health, University of California, Berkeley, CA.

Sekabaraga, C., B. Meessen, and A. Soucat. 2011. "Performance-Based Financing: Just a Donor Fad or a Catalyst towards Comprehensive Health-Care Reform?" *Bulletin of the World Health Organization* 89: 153–56.

UNICEF (United Nations Children's Fund). 2008. *State of the World's Children.* New York: UNICEF.

World Bank. 2010.

Zurn, P., M. Dal Poz, B. Stilwell, and O. Adams. 2004. "Imbalance in the Health Workforce." *Human Resources for Health 2* (13).

CHAPTER 14

Intrinsic Motivation

Kenneth L. Leonard, Pieter Serneels, and J. Michelle Brock

This chapter starts with the model of health worker performance presented in chapter 5, examining the role of intrinsic motivation in more detail. Much evidence on intrinsic motivation comes from outside the health service literature, but a growing body of evidence indicates that intrinsic motivation is consequential in health care, for at least two reasons. First, the motivation of health care workers is one of the more important elements of the health care system, and we will show empirical evidence that intrinsic motivation is a central part of total motivation. Second, although evidence increasingly shows that extrinsic incentives can change the performance of health workers, little evidence shows how this type of motivation interacts with health workers' intrinsic motivation.

Intrinsic motivation and its role in service delivery have received considerable attention. Earlier writings suggested that it was especially relevant for social and public services,[1] such as teaching and health care, which are often described as "vocations." Intrinsic motivation may therefore be as important as—if not more than—motivation derived from extrinsic incentives, even though the latter receives more attention in policy debates.

Recent literature recognizes this, revitalizing the debate on the relative roles of intrinsic and extrinsic motivation (box 14.1). Delfgaauw and Dur

Box 14.1

Intrinsic Motivation in the Words of Health Workers

Serneels and Lievens (2008) discuss the results from focus group discussions with health professionals and users of health services, focusing on motivation, norms related to professional and workplace culture in Rwanda.

Self-Regarding Motivation and Job Choice

Health workers in Rwanda make generous use of religious vocabulary when describing their motivation to work in the health sector, using words like "vocation," "devotion," and "apostolate." Since health workers can choose where they work in Rwanda, and social relations are perceived as less important to get a job than in the past, those with high intrinsic motivation self-select into positions they like—such as posts in the faith-based sector or in rural areas. The for-profit sector, which often puts more demands on health workers and provides higher payment, may draw a different profile of health workers. The public sector seems to attract health workers who plan to continue for further specialization, or those who do not find a job in the for-profit or not-for-profit private sector.

Some say being a health worker is an apostolate.

Doctor in a rural district

Whether you want it or not: when you study medicine, you have a vocation. If you do not have this vocation, you will fail. A doctor needs to be permanently devoted; a doctor without devotion is not a doctor.

Doctor in Kigali

When you have a vocation, it is impossible to do something else.

Auxiliary worker in a rural district

There is always this vocation, which pushes you to continue even if conditions are not met: the salary, the equipment, the other colleagues, the professional environment; but since lives are threatened, you are pushed to continue, the situation is more or less comparable in the public, private, or faith-based sector.

Doctor in a rural district

We always work longer than planned in the timetable, it's a vocation; you cannot leave a patient because it's time to go.

Nurse in Kigali

(continued next page)

Box 14.1 *(continued)*

Professional Norms

With the foundation of the Ordre des Médecins in 2001, professional norms are receiving considerable attention, and health workers place high hopes in this self-regulatory body to enforce internal rules and provide credible punishment where needed. Nurses have expressed their desire to have an Order soon.

The regulations are clear, if you are working for the government, you are expected to have a proper attitude.

Doctor in a rural district

The bylaws consist of a number of rules to follow. If a person does not respect a rule, he is told so and informed about the sanction, the first time orally, the second time in writing. If it happens another time, the sanction is applied.

Nurse in a rural district

If you compare the public and the faith-based sector, you'll find that there are more problems in the public sector because the health workers know they cannot be sacked easily.

User in a rural district

I have the impression that there is a system in place that guarantees when it really goes very badly, when it is absolutely clear that there is a problem, then, something is done.

Doctor in Kigali

Since the order of doctors has been created, there have been investigations, and some doctors have been suspended.

Doctor in a rural district

People love to go to the private sector because health personnel there speak kindly. They treat few patients and take time to speak at length with them; consequently, when the patients leave the health centre, they are happy.

Auxiliary worker in Kigali

Extrinsic Motivation, Intrinsic Motivation, and Workplace Norms

In 2001 the Government of Rwanda started the Initiative for Performance in a number of public and faith-based facilities. The Initiative for Performance specified

(continued next page)

Box 14.1 *(continued)*

that a portion of the government funding a facility receives would depend on its performance. The Initiatives for Performance in Rwanda measure the facility's performance, and not the individual's, so the facility receives the reward if it performs well. The facility determines how to distribute the premium among the health workers, and there is scope to pay higher wages to better-performing health workers; it can also use the funding to hire extra personnel. Thus, extrinsic motivation interacts with intrinsic motivation through workplace norms.

A health worker knows that if he does not perform well, if he is absent, if he is too late, if his service is not appreciated, this will decrease the premium the health centre receives. It makes personnel control each other. Everybody knows that the one who works badly can be sacked and risks being accused by his colleague; this leads to a higher degree of accountability and increases productivity.

User in Kigali

Usually one is the only doctor to consult. But with the Initiative for Performance (IP), one recruits, and instead of one doctor, you're, for example, five. So there's an improvement in the work conditions and one is no longer stretched.

Doctor in a rural area

(2008), Prendergast (2007), and Francois (2000) show that intrinsically motivated public service providers exert more effort and require fewer extrinsic incentives than self-interested providers. Evidence from quantitative and experimental analysis confirms this. Since most health workers are driven by both intrinsic and extrinsic motivation, however, it is important to understand how these two sources of motivation interact.

Insights from Economic Theory

The study of intrinsic motivation in economics is grounded in the literature on "social preferences." This section reviews the terminology and insights commonly used in this field, focusing on what is relevant for health service delivery, to build a model that examines the role of intrinsic motivation for health service delivery in developing countries.

Economists evoke the term social preference to explain decision making that goes beyond self-interest. Charness and Rabin (2002) characterize a person with social preferences as "not maximizing own monetary pay-offs when those actions affect others' payoffs" and consider people to be both self-interested and concerned with the payoff of others. Behavior is pro-social when individuals voluntarily engage in activities that are costly to themselves but benefit others (Bénabou and Tirole 2006).

Becker (1974) explains individuals' willingness to contribute to public goods by suggesting that they gain from consuming the public good and are willing to provide it when others do not. Sugden (1982) suggests that individuals may feel a moral obligation to contribute to the public good, even if they do not consume it. Andreoni (1989, 1990) builds on Sugden's insight, suggesting that individuals contribute to the material gain of others because it makes them feel good. According to Andreoni, individuals contribute to a public good for two reasons: first, they demand more of the public good, as in the Becker model; second, they get private benefit from their gift, which Andreoni refers to as a "warm glow."

Rabin (1993) argues that individuals' interest for other's welfare is conditional, viewing reciprocal kindness as the driving force of pro-social behavior. Feeling good about doing something nice for another may also depend on who the recipient is or how they react to the gift. Bénabou and Tirole (2006) bring in concerns for social reputation and self-respect, con-centrating on happiness derived from others' perceptions. Ellingsen and Johannesson (2008) go one step further and include the "feeling of being esteemed" by others, or pride. This is equal to the other's actual esteem for you, weighted by how much you care about the other's esteem.

This analysis assumes the existence of a public good or a setting where individuals can make gifts to others. Thus, health care workers may appre-ciate that there is health care, they may experience a warm glow from helping people, or they may earn esteem from being seen to have helped people. It is important to think about pro-social behavior in a work envi-ronment, where the organization as a whole, the employer, and coworkers are potential beneficiaries of actions. To the extent that workers exert more effort than is minimally required to retain their job, they may be acting out of interest for the welfare of any or all of these groups. At the same time, employers attempt to shape their employees' behaviors using extrinsic and intrinsic tools.

The literature on social preferences also examines workplace behavior, focusing on "crowding out," organizational goals, and norms. Kreps (1997), following the insights of others,[2] shows how extrinsic motivation such as rewards and punishments may dissuade individuals from working as hard as they otherwise would. This is referred to as crowding out of intrinsic motivation, because extrinsic motivation replaces rather than supplements it.

Kreps identifies two reasons why this may happen: task ambiguity and a change in preferences due to external cues. The first arises when the compensation metric is not well connected to the underlying task, encouraging workers to refocus effort on the metric rather than the task. This improves effort as it is measured, but can cause people to contribute less to the public good. A change in preference occurs when the effort previously defined as "something I do that benefits others," changes to "something I do that I need to be compensated for doing." Loosely, the employer teaches employees not to enjoy something by insisting that they need to be directly compensated for it.

A number of papers discuss how crowding out may be addressed, including trust (Sliwka 2007) and rewarding employees with status (Fershtman and Weiss 1993). Other work in this vein includes Canton (2005), Seabright (2004), Francois (2007), and Acemoglu, Kremer, and Mian (2008). The literature provides a well-vetted economic argument for the possibility that extrinsic incentives may crowd out intrinsic incentives.

Some authors have argued that the way employers respond to employees depends on the organization's goals. Francois (2003) concludes that a not-for-profit organization is better than a for-profit alternative for obtaining "care-motivated effort," in the form of labor donations, even when effort earns pecuniary rewards.[3] Besley and Ghatak (2005) extend this reasoning and emphasize mission matching between employers and workers. They argue that health care providers with stronger pro-social missions find a better match with a not-for-profit employer and, as a consequence, will deliver the same effort for a lower wage.

Many authors take a different approach, examining norms, suggesting that individuals follow rules of behavior and earn utility from conforming to (or deviating from) these rules. According to Ramalingam and Rauh (2009), the principal, or the employer, determines the work ethic for the firm and the employee chooses whether or not to internalize that work ethic. Basu's (2006) theory of teacher truancy in India supports the idea that norms are important for determining behavior in the workplace. In Basu's work, however, norms are not set by the employer but preexist in society. Akerlof and Kranton (2008) explore these ideas more thoroughly to focus on how effort is monitored, arguing that "what matters is . . . how employees think of themselves in relation to the firm."

Intrinsic Motivation and Health Care: A Framework for Analysis

We now integrate these concepts from the general economics literature into a framework to better understand motivation's role in health care. The delivery of such care combines dimensions discussed above. First, health care has components of a social good, because it tries to improve the health of patients and the population as a whole.[4] Second, it occurs in a workplace. And third, it is subject to professional norms. Individual health workers draw motivation from different sources depending on time, place, and context. We develop a typology, focusing on the sources of motivation and social preferences, leading to eight types of intrinsically motivated physicians (table 14.1).

A first distinction is between social preferences that are other-regarding and self-regarding. Other-regarding orientation involves a reciprocal gift-exchange in which effort earns the esteem of others, whereas self-regarding orientation corresponds to the warm glow from doing something good for another.

A second distinction is whether health workers see their activities as helping patients or peers. Other-regarding behavior can be motivated by desire for the esteem of patients or peers, and self-regarding behavior by the warm glow of doing something good for patients or for peers (the organization or profession, for example).

Since other-regarding patient-oriented health workers seek the esteem of patients, they focus on patient satisfaction, whereas self-regarding patient-oriented health workers focus on performance and therefore the patient health. Peer-oriented health workers, by contrast, focus on shared norms, which may not be the same as performance. Although peers are, by definition, better able than patients to evaluate the value of services, they are not always present or able to notice that value. Thus, other-regarding behaviors—motivated by peer esteem—are more likely than

Table 14.1   Sources of Intrinsic Motivation, Social Preferences, and Physician Types

| | Patient oriented | | Peer oriented (norm-based) | |
	Neutral	Identity-based	Neutral	Identity-based
Other-regarding	Status seeking	Discriminating status seeking	Scrutiny responsive	Approval seeking
Self-regarding	Altruistic	Discriminating altruistic	Norm conforming (professional)	Subgroup norm conforming

Source: World Bank data.

self-regarding behaviors to focus on services that are observed or noticed by peers.[5]

A third distinction is whether the health worker is differentially motivated by the identity of the patient or peer. A self-regarding health worker may care more about the well-being of some patients than others (the poor, for example), and an esteem-seeking health worker may care more about the esteem of some patients than others (for example, the poor or the educated). Similarly, a peer-oriented health worker may care more about the esteem of some health workers than others.

The Eight Physician Types

From these social orientations and sources of intrinsic motivation, we construct eight physician types.[6] *Status seeking* is a form of patient-based esteem, when health workers enjoy the esteem of all patients and seek it by providing services that increase patient satisfaction. Some health workers may value the esteem of particular types of patients (or devalue the esteem of others), so the source of motivation varies by patient characteristics. These health workers exhibit *discriminating status seeking*, and seek the esteem of some patients more than others, providing more satisfaction-enhancing services for the preferred group.

We choose the term *altruistic* to describe a health worker who gains utility from knowing that his or her patients are better off—even when those same patients may not know that they are better off, or even appreciate the health worker's efforts. This self-regarding patient-oriented behavior can be discriminating or nondiscriminating based on the characteristics of the patients. Thus, *discriminating altruistic* health workers may feel even better when they help the poor or underserved.

A health worker with a *scrutiny-responsive* personality is one motivated by the esteem he or she earns from peers. *Approval seeking* is a form of scrutiny responsiveness; this health worker responds to some peers more than to others.[7] Both personality types focus on services that conform to peer-based norms and are in some sense observable to their peers. Ideally, peer-based norms are also performance-enhancing services (though they may not achieve this). Self-regarding peer-oriented health care workers are not motivated by esteem from their peers, but gain utility from contributing to their workplace, organization, or profession. *Norm-conforming* personalities measure themselves against the expectations (norms) of the entire profession, while *subgroup norm–conforming* personalities measure themselves against norms that apply to a smaller group of peers. Unlike other-regarding peer-oriented personalities, norm-conforming personalities are not exclusively focused on observable services: they gain utility from knowing that they have contributed, not from being recognized as having contributed. When norms are general and tied to performance, norm-conforming personalities are professionals. *Professional* health workers provide services that conform to (and improve the image of) the profession by improving the health, not the satisfaction, of all patients. Professionals resist direct control over their activities precisely because they believe professionalism is necessary where such control is not useful. In the words of Freidson (2001):

> The two most general ideas underlying professionalism are the belief that certain work is so specialized as to be inaccessible to those lacking the required training and experience, and the belief that it cannot be standardized, rationalized, or (as Abbott put it)[8] "commodified."

Intrinsic Motivation in the Health Performance Model

The model of health performance in chapter 5 suggests that health workers exert effort, which means that patients experience four attributes of a visit to a particular health care worker: presence, performance, satisfaction, and expense. Effort is costly for health workers, but they get utility from income as well as performance, satisfaction, or expense. Extrinsically motivated health workers gain utility from income, and the employer of the health worker can choose to tie income to performance (or satisfaction); intrinsically motivated workers get utility not only from income but also from providing the other three attributes.

A health worker can also care about performance in general, as well as performance in a particular environment or for a particular service. He or she can care about satisfaction in general, or about satisfaction for particular types of patients. And he or she can care about the expenditure of patients in general, or about the expenditure of particular types of patients.

Table 14.2 shows the weights that particular personalities place on each of these three attributes, as well as on income. Each column assumes that the health worker fits one personality exactly; in reality, many health workers have features of multiple personalities. The table also assumes that behavior norms are based on the same understanding of medical activities as performance—where norms exist, they improve behavior with respect to performance.[9] Note that, to the degree that health workers care about expenses, they prefer low expenses for their patients.

The following two examples illustrate how to read this table. Status-seeking personalities weigh general satisfaction highly, and are different

Table 14.2 Health Worker Personalities and Utility, Weights Assigned to Service Attributes in a Physician's Utility Function

Service attributes	Physician types							
	Status seeking	Discriminating status seeking	Altruistic	Discriminating altruistic	Scrutiny responsive	Approval seeking	Norm conforming	Subgroup norm conforming
Performance								
General	Low	Low	High	High	Low	Low	High	Low
Service and environment based	Low	Low	Low	Low	High	High	Low	High
Satisfaction								
General	High	Low	Low	Low	Low	Low	Low	Low
Identity based	Low	High	Low	Low	Low	Low	Low	Low
Income	Low	Low	Low	Low	Low	Low	Low	Low
Expenditure								
General	Low	Low	High	Low	Low	Low	Low	Low
Identity based	Low	High	Low	High	Low	Low	Low	Low

Source: World Bank data.

from discriminating status seekers who put a high weight on the satisfaction of some patients and potentially the expenses of some patients. Norm-conforming personalities weigh performance highly, as opposed to sub-group norm-conforming personalities who put different weights on performance depending on the environment. (All personalities put a low weight on income.)

Intrinsic Motivation, Job Choice, and Occupational Choice

What can this framework teach us about the type of job or sector that certain types of health workers choose, or even about the kind of individual who would choose to be a health worker? A career in health care provides the opportunity to earn money, esteem, and self-satisfaction. Different jobs and subsectors may differ in income, kinds of patients served, and esteem from peers or patients. How much more likely are certain types of health workers to choose certain types of jobs, or certain subsectors of work, such as a rural or urban area, public health or clinical care, hospital or clinic, and high-infected, high-risk areas or low-infected, low-risk areas?

No matter what their motivation, all health workers are concerned about income. Though some ignore monetary compensation when choosing to work hard, they still care how much they are paid. Consider, for example, a purely extrinsically motivated health worker and a professional health worker, each choosing between a low-incentive, low-effort public sector job and high-incentive, high-effort private work. The extrinsically motivated worker compares the two sectors and chooses the one that works out best. But because he or she is only motivated to provide effort by extrinsic motivation, the worker finds it hard to decide: the income is preferred in the high-incentive job, but the required effort is higher as well. The professional health worker, however, provides high effort in either sector, but in the high-incentive sector is well paid to do what he or she likes, and will be surrounded by other workers delivering high effort. This self-sorting may cause the high-incentive sector to deliver high quality and the low-incentive sector to deliver low quality.

Or it may not. If the high-incentive sector compensates health workers for some services but not others, the extrinsically motivated health worker will do only those things that are compensated. The professional continues to provide high quality but the extrinsically motivated health worker does not. Moreover, the very fact that the high-incentive sector is attractive to the extrinsically motivated may cause other health workers to hold everyone in that sector in low esteem. Recall that the peer esteem-seeking health worker gets utility from the esteem of peers, and this esteem drives his or her willingness to exert effort. So if health workers perceive the high-incentive sector as less worthy, they will not esteem people who work in that sector. This will lower the utility of many intrinsically motivated health workers but will not influence the extrinsically motivated provider. The difference in pay and effort across sectors may thus have adverse consequences on the choices of professional health workers.

The same reasoning applies to the job choice of status-seeking health workers who care about patient esteem. If patients no longer esteem health workers who are paid for their every action, patient-oriented status-seeking health workers may prefer to work elsewhere.

Altruistic health workers have similar complications. They feel a warm glow when providing health care to others. Like professional health workers, they provide high effort and are therefore attracted to the high-incentive sector. Because they do not draw motivation from peers or patients, they are not concerned with how these two groups perceive them. They are concerned, however, with the fees that their patients have to pay and with the types of patients they are likely to see. So if the high-incentive sector charges higher fees than the low-incentive sector, or is in a place that isolates them from poorer patients, their utility declines (but not the utility of extrinsically motivated health workers).

In short, facing choices between multiple jobs that differ in incentives, professional and altruistic health workers may choose work environments that compensate them well for their efforts, even when compensation is not their main concern. But a perverse and opposite result is also possible. A high-incentive job could attract health workers motivated only by money and who do not provide any effort that is not compensated, leaving professional and altruistic health workers in the low-incentive sector.

The same reasoning can be applied to career choice, or the choice of whether to work in health. Individuals who enjoy warm glow may choose a job outside the health sector, as may individuals who care about esteem. For example, if health care professionals perceive the health sector as transformed into a lucrative, profit-oriented, pay-for-service industry, then those who look to help the poor, feel good about helping the poor, or derive utility from high esteem may be driven from the health sector. Such a result would not come from the increase in pay for health workers but from its direct link to effort, and illustrates the occupational choice variant of crowding out of intrinsic motivation.

Empirical Evidence

This section discusses direct and indirect empirical evidence on motivation. We rely on evidence from three sources: qualitative research (interviews), laboratory experiments (asking subjects to make decisions in controlled situations), and quantitative survey evidence of actual behavior. The qualitative research is especially interesting when combined with quantitative evidence, and we use it in this way. But we cannot observe motivation directly—we can only measure its manifestation. We summarize existing evidence on motivation's impact on behavior, and then discuss evidence on the possible sources of motivation.

The Impact of Motivation on Behavior

Experimental evidence. Most recent evidence on motivation, drawn from the experimental literature, comes from developed-country settings. That literature shows a common focus on comparing intrinsic and extrinsic (usually monetary) motivations. The advantage of laboratory experiments comes from controlling payoffs and the ways that individuals can earn them. While motivation remains unobservable, the experiment can be designed to test the source of variation in behavior—for example, revealing whether people make decisions solely for their own benefit or for that of others.

Pro-social behavior has been documented in countless laboratory experiments. In public-good games, where individuals are asked to contribute to the general good, Goeree, Holt, and Laury (2002) and Andreoni (1995) show self-regarding and other-regarding motivations, respectively. Results from a range of experimental settings show that individual behavior cannot be explained by self-interest alone (Andreoni and Miller 2002; Forsythe and others 1994; Palfrey and Prisbrey 1996, 1997). Many studies document gift exchange in the workplace to explain how workers decide on effort (Akerlof 1982; Gneezy and List 2006; Gneezy and Rustichini 2000; Rigdon 2002). This evidence from relatively simple games forms the foundation for a more detailed look into pro-social attitudes among workers. While the evidence for pro-social behavior is overwhelming, how to interpret the sources of this social behavior remains a crucial challenge.

Some studies examine how individuals react to combinations of intrinsic and extrinsic motivation. Gneezy and Rustichini (2000) conducted experiments that paid some subjects to do a task but not others. Higher compensation induced higher effort if offered at the outset, but when subjects were moved from no compensation to compensation, performance was lower. In an investigation of taxi drivers in New York (using actual data, not laboratory experiments), Farber (2008) found that many set a target income, taking leisure after reaching their goal for the day, and forgoing income if the goal was reached before normal quitting hours. This is counterintuitive because it means that when their effective wage increased (earning more in less time) they stopped working earlier, not later as economic theory would predict.

Dohmen and Falk (2011) also illustrate the consequences of motivation for selection. They find that different experimental payment schemes systematically attract people with different abilities, preferences, self-assessments, personalities, and gender. In other words, health worker performance may differ by sector because each sector attracts health workers with varying levels of motivation.

Other quantitative evidence. Encouraged by increasing awareness among economists that behavioral traits can *influence* labor market outcomes,[10] nonexperimental evidence is emerging, though less voluminous, on *motivation's* role. The quantitative evidence of intrinsic motivation focuses on observed differences in *worker* behavior that can be explained either by qualitatively described sources of motivation or by theoretical models of intrinsic motivation. Green, Machin, and Wilkenson (1998), are a good example of the first, reporting that U.K. employers cite deficits in candidates' motivation and attitudes as the primary reason for recruitment problems. Rotolo and Wilson (2004) find evidence of "higher civic mindedness" (measured by people's likelihood to volunteer outside the workplace) of nonprofit employees. They find a positive correlation between that and job type.

Similarly, Gregg and others (2008) compare donated labor, measured as unpaid overtime, in "caring industries," between public (not-for-profit) and private (for-profit) organizations. Those with more unpaid overtime have "high public service motivation." They find that people working in caring industries are more likely to choose a job in the public sector. But they also generate evidence that people who switch between the private and public sectors do not change their propensity to put in extra hours after switching.

Jaffré and Olivier de Sardan (2003) conclude that health worker motivation is important, after carrying out anthropological research on health care delivery in seven capital cities in Francophone Africa. In Ethiopia the primary motivation students identify for becoming a health worker is "to help people" (Serneels, Lindelöw, and Montalivo 2004).

Using data on final-year medical and nursing students, Serneels and others (2007) concentrate on social preferences as their proxy for motivation and find that those who are more motivated to help the poor are more likely to choose a job in rural areas. Using a similar approach, they confirm these results for a joint analysis of Ethiopia and Rwanda (Serneels and others 2010) and for Ghana (Akleh 2009), suggesting that the results from studies by Rotolo and Wilson and by Gregg and others are relevant for health workers.

Interviews with health workers in Ethiopia, Rwanda, and Ghana suggest that certain positions attract more motivated health workers than others (Lievens, Lindelöw, and Serneels 2009; Lindelöw and Serneels 2006; Serneels and Lievens 2008). In all three countries, health workers who choose to work in rural areas are perceived as having a stronger vocation and more motivation. Those working at for-profit private facilities are perceived to be more money oriented and less intrinsically motivated, while those working in not-for-profit facilities are perceived to be more motivated.

The evidence is also important for the sector that health workers enter. Serra, Serneels, and Barr (2010) find evidence in Ethiopia that philanthropically motivated health professionals, as measured by experimental and survey measures, self-select the not-for-profit sector (rather than the public and for-profit sectors) and find confirming evidence for Besley and Ghatak's (2005) prediction that mission matching increases organization efficiency.[11] Serneels and others (2010), using panel data for Ethiopia, show that unobserved individual willingness to work in rural areas, after controlling for monetary incentives, are also highly correlated with proxies of intrinsic motivation, and predict sector choice.

Leonard and Masatu (2008) show how the Hawthorne effect (chapter 5) demonstrates intrinsic motivation in the average clinician in outpatient settings in Tanzania. When a peer arrives to observe a clinician, that clinician initially increases effort greatly to earn the esteem of the peer. When the peer does not provide feedback, however, the clinician no longer experiences pride from earning esteem of the peer, causing him or her to return to previous effort, even while the peer is still observing. When clinicians are motivated only by extrinsic concerns, they will ignore the peer if they believe the peer cannot help or hurt their position, or they will strive to impress the peer independent of feedback if they believe the peer can help or hurt them. The analysis shows that only intrinsic motivation, here as peer esteem, can explain the pattern observed by the Hawthorne effect.

Leonard, Masatu, and Vialou (2007) and Leonard and Masatu (2010b) compare the performance of public, private, and nongovernmental organization (NGO) employees in Tanzania, showing that competence does not fully explain their effort. Clinicians in NGOs and private facilities provide better care even without higher training. Although this result does not distinguish between extrinsic and intrinsic sources of motivation, it does demonstrate the importance of work environment in motivating health worker effort.

Leonard and Masatu (2010a) attempt to measure whether clinicians are professional in their job, as defined above. They find that clinicians demonstrate three types of behavior: high levels of rewarded and unrewarded effort, high levels of rewarded effort and low levels of unrewarded effort, and low levels of both types of effort. Professionally motivated clinicians and altruistic clinicians should exert high rewarded and unrewarded effort because they highly value the profession and patients' health, respectively. Peer esteem-seeking clinicians only provide high effort for services and activities that are observed by their peers. Health workers who are not motivated by professionalism or esteem will provide low levels of observed and unobserved effort.

Using this typology to classify clinicians in their study area (Arusha region, Tanzania), Leonard and Masatu find that approximately 20 percent of clinicians show behavior consistent with professional or altruistic behavior, providing high rewarded and unrewarded effort. These clinicians are almost evenly distributed across the public, not-for-profit, and private for-profit sectors. Combined with the findings from Leonard and Masatu (2007), which considers the same study area, this suggests that professional or altruistic health workers are a key source of high-quality care—and that while "nonprofessional" clinicians in the public sector provide low levels of observed effort, those in the not-for-profit and private for-profit sectors provide high effort. In short, these institutions motivate people who are not self-motivated.

Explaining and Changing Health Worker Motivation

The natural way to look at intrinsic motivation is to consider it an individual "preference" or "taste," with some health workers having higher motivation than others for unexplained reasons. Economic analysis usually takes this approach. But, as for other personality traits, this raises the question of whether intrinsic motivation is constant over time, and the deeper question of whether it is innate—predetermined by genetics or early childhood experiences—or the result of socialization.

Although we know very little about the latter, evidence shed light on the former. Serneels and others (2004) find that pro-social preferences among health workers have a part that is stable over time. They also observe changes over time, however, suggesting that intrinsic motivation consists of time-variant and time-invariant parts, fitting with the notion that intrinsic motivation is internalized norms over time (Deci, Cascio, and Krusell 1975)—and since norms may change, motivation may also change.

We now examine the evidence and theory that support changes in motivation based first on norms and then esteem.

Norms. Most evidence on norms comes from experiments and, referring to a range of social preferences, shows how group culture can alter behavior. Experiments show that subjects in teams may punish socially inefficient behavior of group members and so elicit greater cooperation.[12] Carpenter (2002) finds that familiarity between subjects seems to improve the efficacy of punishment in public-good games, suggesting that group stability may be important. When both reward and punishment are allowed, efficiency may be even further improved (Dickinson 2001; Sefton, Shupp, and Walker 2007).

A number of studies analyze the interplay of workplace norms and financial incentives. Playing the role of workers in a laboratory experiment, subjects delivered more effort when wages were set higher, explained as behaving according to norms—to share fairly and reciprocate acts of generosity (box 14.2; Charness 2004; Fehr, Kirchsteiger, and

---

Box 14.2

Generosity, Workplace Norms, and Protocol Adherence

A recently completed study in Arusha Region of Tanzania, financed in part by the World Bank, examined pro-social tendencies in a laboratory setting. After giving health workers money, the researchers measured how much the health workers were willing to share with strangers in another room whom they would never meet (known in the economics literature as the "dictator game"). About 37 percent of the health workers in this study gave at least half of the money they received to the stranger, even though they knew they would receive nothing in return and the recipient would never know who gave them the money. The researchers (Brock, Lange and Leonard) explore the implication of the assumption

(continued next page)

Box 14.2 *(continued)*

that these clinicians are more generous than those who did not share at least half of the money. Comparing the sample of generous and not generous doctors, the researchers examine clinicians' adherence to medical protocol in the outpatient setting. They find that generous doctors provide almost 10 percent higher quality than those who are not generous. This suggests a strong association between a simple form of intrinsic motivation and health care quality.

In addition, they look at how the health workers in the sample react to peer scrutiny (the Hawthorne effect) and an encouragement intervention in which health workers were asked by a peer to work harder and then visited about six weeks later (box table 14.2.1). (See Brock 2011 for details of the study and the interventions.)

Box Table 14.2.1   Protocol Adherence and Changes in Protocol Adherence for Generous Doctors

Public		Voluntary sector		Private	
All	*Generous*	*All*	*Generous*	*All*	*Generous*
Proportion of doctors who are generous in each sector					
32		35		48	
Baseline protocol adherence for the reference patient					
77	84 (+7)	87 (+10)	87 (+10)	95 (+18)	82 (+5)
Percentage point change in protocol adherence when faced with peer scrutiny					
+7	+4	−3 (N.S.)	−3 (N.S.)	−10	−1 (N.S.)
Percentage point change in protocol adherence six weeks after encouragement visit					
+17	+17	−2 (N.S.)	+3 (N.S.)	−2 (N.S.)	+12

Source: Brock, Lange, and Leonard.
Note: A linear regression model and the use of a reference patient allows adherence to exceed 100 percent in a few cases. N.S. = not significant at the 10 percent level.

Box table 14.2.1 shows four comparisons: the percent of doctors in each sector who are labeled as generous; the protocol adherence of doctors in each of three sectors (public, voluntary sector, and private) by whether they are labeled as generous; the change in protocol adherence for each of these doctors when faced with peer scrutiny; and the change in protocol adherence for the same doctors six weeks after the encouragement visit.

Generous doctors are found in all three sectors, particularly the public. Counter to prevailing assumptions, the only sector more likely to have generous doctors is the private.

Confirming most studies in Africa, the baseline quality of care is lowest in the public sector and highest in the private sector. In the public sector,

(continued next page)

Box 14.2 *(continued)*

generous doctors provide higher quality care than other doctors do (7 percentage points higher than their public sector peers). In the private sector, both types provide higher quality care than the public sector, but generous doctors provide lower quality care than others in the private sector (5 percentage points higher than the average public sector doctor compared to 18 percentage points higher). There is no difference between generous and nongenerous doctors in the NGO sector.

In the public sector, both generous and nongenerous doctors change their behavior when faced with peer scrutiny, but NGO doctors do not change their behavior. In the private sector, nongenerous doctors do less when faced with peer scrutiny but generous doctors do not change their behavior.

In the public sector, both generous and nongenerous doctors exhibit a large change in behavior after the encouragement (17 percentage point increase in quality, over a 20 percent increase in quality). NGO doctors, on the other hand, do not change their behavior. In the private sector, generous doctors raise their quality by 12 percentage points over their baseline, but nongenerous doctors have no change in behavior.

These results suggest that generosity is important when there is weak supervision and few extrinsic reasons to care for patients; generosity improves public sector doctors' performance but not NGO or private sector doctors, who have other reasons to provide high quality care. Being observed by a peer changes the setting for a public sector doctor and encourages him or her to do more; it does not change the setting much for an NGO sector doctor, who interacts more frequently with his peers. The presence of a peer can cause a private sector doctor to do less, suggesting that private sector doctors may be over-providing care under normal circumstances.

It would be surprising if NGO sector doctors improved care when told that their work is important; they should already know this. Public sector doctors are clearly missing this encouragement, information, and attention in their normal settings. Some private sector doctors also respond positively to encouragement, suggesting it is absent from their normal practices.

If we think of peer scrutiny and encouragement as alterations to incentives that health workers usually face, we see changes in behavior resulting from these alterations as evidence of workplace norms that are not optimally exploited for improving quality of care. These findings support this chapter's view that there are multiple sources of motivation and that existing workplace norms are one of the more important sources of intrinsic motivation.

Riedl 1993). Some work shows how extrinsic incentives may crowd out efficiency-enhancing social norms (Huck, Kubler, and Weibull 2003).

Other illustrations on the role of workplace norms in motivation come from nonexperimental evidence. Bartel and others (2004), studying different branches of the same U.S. bank, found that employee attitudes differ between workplaces, affecting workplace productivity. Bandiera, Barankay, and Rasul (2005), identifying group characteristics like size, homogeneity of nationality, skills that affect behavior, argued that collusion, not altruism, drives cooperation between workers. Finally, Hamilton and others (2003) show how a shift from individual pay to group performance pay can greatly change (in their case raise) productivity. Here, too, is evidence on the interplay between workplace culture and incentives.

Applied to the health sector, the evidence suggests substantial differences in workplace norms across facilities. A specific example is between sectors. With differences in effort norms, remuneration schemes, and the types of health workers they attract, facilities in the private for-profit sector may develop an entirely different workplace culture than public or non-profit operations. This difference may translate to client services. Interviews in Rwanda indicate that private for-profit facilities are more client oriented, but also more money oriented, and have a heavier work load, while health workers in not-for-profit facilities have a reputation for being dedicated. Public sector facilities are perceived as having weak work ethics.

Professional norms also affect motivation. Workers typically acquire norms in professional training, and survey evidence suggests that norms' strength can vary across schools (Serneels and others 2007). Professional organizations enforce such norms. Norms' importance in motivation is perhaps best reflected in the Hippocratic Oath, where doctors take a vow to "treat the sick to the best of one's ability."

Additional group or society-wide norms influence motivation. Growing evidence shows how religious norms may play a role, with religious workers described as "more committed" (Lievens and others 2011) and found to be less absent in Uganda (Reinikka and Svensson 2003). Health workers in Rwanda frequently use religious terms to describe the importance of intrinsic motivation, with words like vocation and apostolate to describe their own motivation. Serneels and others (2007) find that students from a Catholic NGO school in Ethiopia are more philanthropic than students from other schools. Religious norms may also lead to separate institutions. Serneels and others (2010) discuss how the funding of Adventists in Rwanda is organized as a local bonding scheme, encouraging health students to take up a job in a rural area.

As discussed, recent evidence from experimental and survey work indicates that group and workplace norms and culture can strongly affect individual motivation and behavior. Barr, Lindelöw, and Serneels (2009) provide some specific evidence for health workers. Conducting a laboratory game with health workers in Ethiopia to test for embezzlement, they find that when the game is framed as health care delivery, the standard deviation in embezzlement increases, and more experienced workers embezzling more. They interpret this as evidence that health workers have socialized into corrupt behavior: they have revised their preference or reference point and adapted their behavior.

Esteem. Earning esteem is a crucial source of motivation for health workers with other-regarding preferences. Low motivation among health workers who derive esteem from peers thus indicates that they do not believe their effort will earn esteem. The Hawthorne effect demonstrates what happens when a health worker has the opportunity to earn esteem: effort *rises* significantly. *So*, if effort is *normally* low, it means that these health workers are not presented with an opportunity to earn esteem. The lack of such opportunity is apparent in the *isolated* rural practitioners described in chapter 5: they are required to travel to town to meet with their peers or supervisors and have no chance to earn esteem from their daily activities.

Those who seek esteem from patients are presented with opportunities for esteem with every service they provide. Esteem is earned, however, from patient satisfaction, not performance. These health workers may, in fact, be satisfied with the esteem they earn from patients, but this does not translate into high-quality care because patients may value the wrong services. This is what health workers themselves argue: if they do the right thing, patients are not satisfied.

There is more to this. It has been well documented (perhaps most convincingly by Jaffré and Olivier 2003) that clinicians in Francophone Africa are often rude to their patients, appearing unconcerned with patient esteem. This can be explained in two ways: either these health workers gain no utility from esteem, or the interaction is not "salient." Ellingsen and Johannesson (2008) argue that esteem is earned only from salient interactions—that is, you must value the other person in the interaction before you care whether they esteem you. This view fits the typical health situation more accurately: health workers do not respect their patients and so do not care about their opinions. It is not difficult to see how this can lead to a bad equilibrium outcome, where health workers provide no effort because they do not care about the esteem of patients, and patients do not esteem health workers because the health workers provide low effort. How can we break this vicious circle?

Still, when health workers try to exert more effort than normal, patients notice and appreciate the change (Leonard 2008). So, although the doctors might earn esteem from doing the wrong thing, they also earn esteem from doing the right thing. What remains to be seen is whether there is a way to get health workers to value their patients' esteem and to get patients to deliver esteem noticeably to health workers.

If esteem is to become a type of currency in the health care system, its value will come from its scarcity. If every patient esteems every health worker, no health worker will value esteem. The advantage of esteem as currency is that, whereas income is held by the wealthy and not by the poor, esteem is held more evenly across the economic spectrum. There is a stock of potential esteem in rural and poor Africa, whereas the financial resources necessary for a functioning health system are held in the capital or economic strongholds. Esteem can never pay for medicine or feed the family of a health worker, but it can be currency that encourages the health worker to provide more effort.

Conclusion

Intrinsic motivation plays an important role in the decision to become a health worker, what sector to work in, whether to exert effort, and what services to provide. But it is not as simple as an internal drive to do the right thing. This chapter shows that various types of motivation, and the resultant personalities of health workers, are driven by different environmental factors, and that these types and personalities can lead to differences in quality of care, by sector and patient.

The literature on intrinsic motivation in health care in Africa shows that such motivation is inadequate to ensure high-quality care across the system, but that, nonetheless, many health workers provide services mainly because they care about their patients. This suggests that many health workers might be motivated by extrinsic motivation, but it also suggests that extrinsic motivation may adversely influence those who are intrinsically motivated.

The chapter raises the possibility of crowding out, where increases in extrinsic incentives change who decides to be a health worker, who enters what sector, and (potentially) how health workers feel about their patients. Whereas extrinsic motivation must become a greater concern in improving health worker performance, care should be taken to understand intrinsic motivation and the impact of extrinsic incentives on intrinsically motivated health workers.

Experimental evidence suggests that norms change and that this can lead to changes in behavior. Many health workers in Africa have long worked in an environment that discourages effort and tolerates activities that fail to improve the population's health. At the same time, organizations (public and private, for example) have different norms, raising the possibility that all health workers can gain utility from collectively following different sets of norms. On less evidence, the same could be said for esteem: health workers who ignore their patients' esteem may gain utility from esteem in different sets of circumstances.

Notes

1. See, for instance, Deci, Cascio, and Krusell (1975).

2. Deci 1971, 1972; Deci, Cascio, and Krusell 1975.

3. The theory relies on a residual claimant story, where the individual worker prefers not to donate extra effort in the event that their boss is the one to gain from the work. If, instead, a worthy cause reaps the rewards from extra work, the pro-social worker is more likely to donate additional labor. Since the result holds even when effort earns extrinsic rewards, there is no crowding out; organizations with a culture of profits elicit fewer "labor donations" than organizations with a nonprofit culture.

4. Whether health is a public good (as defined in economics) is not important to an individual's pro-social preferences. What matters is whether health is seen as contributing to the welfare of society and whether there is a social construct that individuals deserve good health.

5. Peers can evaluate the services of a health worker even when they are not physically present. Referral systems, for example, facilitate peer evaluation and feedback, although generally proximity improves the chances of seeking and earning peer esteem.

6. Note that these types describe physicians with respect to intrinsic motivation and do not exhaustively classify physicians with respect to other types of motivation.

7. We do not consider the desire to impress one's employer as part of these as it is typically driven by extrinsic motivation, namely to obtain promotion or a pay raise. Of course, this may lead to some peers being held in high regard, and other health workers more anxious to seek their approval.

8. See Abbott (1991).

9. Thus, we do not consider norms that make behavior worse such a "norm" to mistreat patients; this would be the absence of a positive norm in the view we have here. In addition, we are not allowing for norms over other aspects of care such as patient satisfaction.

10. For instance, Bowles, Gintis, and Osborne (2001) and Heckman, Stixrud, and Urzua (2006).

11. It may seem odd to single out the nonprofit sector. In principle, we would expect the public sector and public servants to be motivated by the notion of public service, a mission that, especially in a poor country, seems closer to philanthropy than profit maximization. In many low-income countries, however, including Ethiopia, the original mission of the public sector—to provide adequate health services to all segments of the population—has been eroded by decades of central planning, weak monetary incentives, and poor accountability, leading to widespread opportunism on the part of public health care providers (Lindelöw and Serneels 2006).

12. For instance, Ostrom, Walker, and Gardner (1992) and Fehr and Gächter (2000).

References

Abbott, A. 1991. "The Future of Professions: Occupation and Organization in the Age of Expertise." *Research in the Sociology of Organizations* 8: 17–42.

Acemoglu, D., M. Kremer, and A. Mian. 2008. "Incentives in Markets, Firms, and Governments." *Journal of Law, Economics, and Organization* 24 (2): 273–306.

Akerlof, G. A. 1982. "Labor Contracts as Partial Gift Exchange." *Quarterly Journal of Economics* 97 (4): 543–69.

Akerlof, G. A., and R. E. Kranton. 2008. "Identity, Supervision, and Work Groups." *American Economic Review* 98 (2): 212–17.

Akleh, A. N. 2009. "What Would it Take for Medical Doctors to Work in Rural Ghana?" M.Sc. Diss., Department of Economics, University of Sussex.

Andreoni, J. 1989. "Giving with Impure Altruism: Applications to Charity and Ricardian Equivalence." *Journal of Political Economy* 97 (6): 1447–58.

———. 1990. "Impure Altruism and Donations to Public Goods: A Theory of Warm-Glow Giving?" *Economic Journal* 100 (401): 464–77.

Andreoni, J. 1995. "Warm-Glow versus Cold-Prickle: The Effects of Positive and Negative Framing on Cooperation in Experiments." *Quarterly Journal of Economics* 110 (1): 1–21.

Andreoni, J., and J. Miller. 2002. "Giving According to GARP: An Experimental Test of the Consistency of Preferences for Altruism." *Econometrica* 70 (20): 737–53.

Bandiera, O., I. Barankay, and I. Rasul. 2005. "Cooperation in Collective Action." *Economics of Transition* 13 (3): 473–98.

Barr A., M. Lindelöw, and P. Serneels. 2009. "Corruption in Public Service Delivery: An Experimental Analysis." *Journal of Economic Behavior and Organization* 72 (1): 225–39.

Bartel, A., R. Freeman, C. Ichniowski, and M. Kleiner. 2004. "Can a Work Organization Have an Attitude Problem? The Impact of Workplaces on Employee Attitude and Economic Outcomes." Discussion Paper 0636, Centre for Economic Performance, London School of Economics, London.

Basu, K. 2006. "Teacher Truancy in India: The Role of Culture, Norms and Economic Incentives." SSRN eLibrary. http://papers.ssrn.com/sol3/papers .cfm?abstract_id=956057#.

Becker, G. S. 1974. "A Theory of Social Interactions." *Journal of Political Economy* 82 (6): 1063–93.

Bénabou, R., and J. Tirole. 2006. "Incentives and Prosocial Behavior." *The American Economic Review* 96 (5): 1652–78.

Besley, T., and M. Ghatak. 2005. "Competition and Incentives with Motivated Agents." *American Economic Review* 95 (3): 616–36.

Bowles, S., H. Gintis, and M. Osborne. 2001. "The Determinants of Earnings: A Behavioral Approach." *Journal of Economic Literature* 39 (4): 1137–76.

Brock, J. M., A. Lange, and K. L. Leonard. 2012. "Generosily Norms and Intrinsic Motivation in Health Care Provisions, Evidence from the Laboratory and the Field". Working Paper European Bank for Reconstruction and Development.

Canton, E. 2005. "Power of Incentives in Public Organizations When Employees Are Intrinsically Motivated." *Journal of Institutional and Theoretical Economics* 161 (4): 664–80.

Carpenter, J. P. 2002. "Information, Fairness, and Reciprocity in the Best Shot Game." *Economics Letters* 75 (2): 243–248.

Charness, G. 2004. "Attribution and Reciprocity in an Experimental Labor Market." *Journal of Labor Economics* 22 (3): 665–88.

Charness, G., and M. Rabin. 2002. "Understanding Social Preferences with Simple Tests." *Quarterly Journal of Economics* 117 (3): 817–69.

Deci, E. L. 1971. "Effects of Externally Mediated Rewards on Intrinsic Motivation." *Journal of Personality and Social Psychology* 18 (1): 105–15.

———. 1972. "Intrinsic Motivation, Extrinsic Reinforcement, and Inequity." *Journal of Personality and Social Psychology* 22 (1): 113–20.

Deci, E. L., W. F. Cascio, and J. Krusell. 1975. "Cognitive Evaluation Theory and Some Comments on the Calder and Staw Critique." *Journal of Personality and Social Psychology* 31 (1): 81–85.

Delfgaauw, J., and R. Dur. 2008. "Incentives and Workers' Motivation in the Public Sector." *Economic Journal* 118 (525): 171–91.

Dickinson, D. 2001. "The Carrot vs. the Stick in Work Team Motivation." *Experimental Economics* 4 (1): 107–24.

Dohmen, T., and A. Falk. 2011. "Performance Pay and Multidimensional Sorting: Productivity, Preferences and Gender." *American Economic Review* 101 (2): 556–90.

Ellingsen, T., and M. Johannesson. 2008. "Pride and Prejudice: The Human Side of Incentive Theory." *American Economic Review* 98 (3): 990–1008.

Farber, H. S. 2008. "Reference-Dependent Preferences and Labor Supply: The Case of New York City Taxi Drivers." *American Economic Review* 98 (3): 1069–82.

Fehr, E., and S. Gächter. 2000. "Cooperation and Punishment in Public Goods Experiments." *The American Economic Review* 90 (4): 980–94.

Fehr, E., G. Kirchsteiger, and A. Riedl. 1993. "Does Fairness Prevent Market Clearing? An Experimental Investigation." *Quarterly Journal of Economics* 108 (2): 437–59.

Fershtman, C., and Y. Weiss. 1993. "Social Status, Culture and Economic Performance." *Economic Journal* 103 (419): 946–59.

Forsythe, R., J. L. Horowitz, N. E. Savin, and M. Sefton. 1994. "Fairness in Simple Bargaining Experiments." *Games and Economic Behavior* 6 (3): 347–69.

Francois, P. 2000. "'Public Service Motivation' As an Argument for Government Provision." *Journal of Public Economics* 78 (3): 275–99.

———. 2003. "Not-for-Profit Provision of Public Services." *Economic Journal* 113 (486): C53–61.

———. 2007. "Making a Difference." *RAND Journal of Economics* 38 (3): 714–32.

Freidson, E. 2001. *Professionalism: The Third Logic.* Chicago, IL: University of Chicago Press.

Gneezy, U., and J. A. List. 2006. "Putting Behavioral Economics to Work: Testing for Gift Exchange in Labor Markets Using Field Experiments." *Econometrica* 74 (5): 1365–84.

Gneezy, U., and A. Rustichini. 2000. "Pay Enough or Don't Pay at All." *Quarterly Journal of Economics* 115 (3): 791–810.

Goeree, J. K., C. A. Holt, and S. K. Laury. 2002. "Private Costs and Public Benefits: Unraveling the Effects of Altruism and Noisy Behavior." *Journal of Public Economics* 83 (2): 255–76.

Green, F., S. Machin, and D. Wilkinson. 1998. "The Meaning and Determinants of Skills Shortages." *Oxford Bulletin of Economics and Statistics* 60 (2): 165–87.

Gregg, P., P. A. Grout, A. Ratcliffe, S. Smith, and F. Windmeijer. 2008. "How Important is Pro-Social Behaviour in the Delivery of Public Services?" *Journal of Public Economics* 95 (7–8): 758–66.

Hamilton, B., J. Nickerson and H. Owan. 2003. "Team Incentives and Worker Heterogeneity: An Empirical Analysis of the Impact of Teams on Productions and Participation." *Journal of Political Economy* June 111(3): 465–97.

Heckman, J. J., J. Stixrud, and S. Urzua. 2006. "The Effects of Cognitive and Noncognitive Abilities on Labor Market Outcomes and Social Behavior." *Journal of Labor Economics* 24 (3): 411–82.

Huck, S., D. Kubler, and J. Weibull. 2003. "Social Norms and Economic Incentives in Firms." Discussion Paper 5264, Institute for the Study of Labor, Bonn, Germany.

Jaffré, Y., and J. P. Olivier de Sardan, eds. 2003. *Un medecine inhospitaliere. Leas difficiles relations entre soigants et soignes dans cinq capitales d'Afrique de l'ouest.* Paris: Karthala.

Kreps, D. M. 1997. "Intrinsic Motivation and Extrinsic Incentives." *American Economic Review* 87 (2): 359–64.

Leonard, K. L. 2008. "Is Patient Satisfaction Sensitive to Changes in the Quality of Care? An Exploitation of the Hawthorne Effect." *Journal of Health Economics* 27 (2): 444–59.

Leonard, K. L., and M. C. Masatu. 2007. "Variations in the Quality of Care Accessible to Rural Communities in Tanzania." *Health Affairs* 26 (3): w380–92.

Leonard, K. L., and M. C. Masatu. 2008. "Moving from the Lab to the Field: Exploring Scrutiny and Duration Effects in Lab Experiments." *Economic Letters* 100 (2): 284–87.

———. 2010a. "Professionalism and the Know-Do Gap: Exploring Intrinsic Motivation among Health Workers in Tanzania." *Health Economics* 19 (12): 1461–77.

———. 2010b. "Using the Hawthorne Effect to Examine the Gap between a Doctor's Best Possible Practice and Actual Performance." *Journal of Development Economics* 93 (2): 226–34.

Leonard, K. L., M. C. Masatu, and A. Vialou. 2007. "Getting Doctors to Do Their Best: The Roles of Ability and Motivation in Health Care." *Journal of Human Resources* 42 (3): 682–700.

Lievens, T., M. Lindelöw, and P. Serneels. 2009. "Qualitative Data to Prepare Quantitative Analysis on Health Service Delivery." In *Handbook on Monitoring and Evaluating Health Workforce*, ed. M. R. Dal Poz and A. Soucat, Geneva: WHO.

Lievens, T., P. Serneels, S. Garbarino, and P. Quartey. 2011. *Incentives to Work. Ghana Health Worker Study.* Washington, DC: World Bank.

Lindelöw, M., and P. Serneels. 2006. "The Performance of Health Workers in Ethiopia: Results from Qualitative Research." *Social Science and Medicine* 62 (9): 2225–35.

Ostrom, E., J. M. Walker, and R. Gardner. 1992. "Covenants with and without a Sword: Self-Governance Is Possible." *American Political Science Review* 86: 404–17.

Palfrey, T. R., and J. E. Prisbrey. 1996. "Altruism, Reputation and Noise in Linear Public Goods Experiments." *Journal of Public Economics* 61 (3): 409–27.

———. 1997. "Anomalous Behavior in Public Goods Experiments: How Much and Why?" *American Economic Review* 87 (5): 829–46.

Prendergast, C. 2007. "The Motivation and Bias of Bureaucrats." *American Economic Review* 97 (1): 180–96.

Rabin, M. 1993. "Incorporating Fairness into Game Theory and Economics." *American Economic Review* 83 (5): 1281–302.

Ramalingam, A., and M. T. Rauh. 2009. "The Firm as an Intrinsic Motivation Device." SSRN eLibrary. http://papers.ssrn.com/sol3/papers.cfm?abstract_id=1198362.

Reinikka, R., and J. Svensson. 2003. "Working for God? Evaluating Service Delivery of Religious Not-For-Profit Health Care Providers in Uganda." Policy Research Working Paper 3058, World Bank, Washington, DC.

Rigdon, M. L. 2002. "Efficiency Wages in an Experimental Labor Market." *Proceedings of the National Academy of Sciences of the United States of America* 99 (20): 13348–51.

Rotolo, T., and J. Wilson. 2004. "Employment Sector and Volunteering: The Contribution of Nonprofit and Public Sector Workers to the Volunteer Labor Force." *Sociological Quarterly* 47 (1): 21–40.

Seabright, P. 2004. "Continuous Preferences Can Cause Discontinuous Choices: An Application to the Impact of Incentives on Altruism." SSRN eLibrary. http://papers.ssrn.com/sol3/papers.cfm?abstract_id=536185.

Sefton, M., R. Shupp, and J. Walker. 2007. "The Effects of Rewards and Sanctions in Provision of Public Goods." *Economic Inquiry* 45 (4): 671–90.

Serneels, P., and T. Lievens. 2008. "Institutions for Health Care Delivery: A Formal Exploration of What Matters to Health Workers: Evidence from Rwanda." Working Paper 309, Centre for the Study of African Economies, Oxford University, Oxford. http://www.bepress.com/csae/paper309.

Serneels, P., M. Lindelöw, J. G. Montalivo, and A. Barr. 2004. *An Honorable Calling? Results from a Survey with Final Year Nursing and Medical Students.* Washington, DC: World Bank.

Serneels P., J. G. Montalvo, M. Lindelöw, and A. Barr. 2007. "For Public Service or for Money: Understanding Geographical Imbalances in the Health Workforce." *Health Policy and Planning* 22 (3): 128–38.

Serneels, P., J. G. Montalvo, G. Pettersson, T. Lievens, J. D. Butera, and A. Kidanu. 2010. "Who Wants to Work in a Rural Health Post? The Role of Intrinsic Motivation, Rural Background and Faith Based Institutions in Rwanda and Ethiopia." *Bulletin of the World Health Organization* 88: 342–49.

Serra, D., P. Serneels, and A. Barr. 2010. "Intrinsic Motivations and the Non-Profit Health Sector: Evidence from Ethiopia." *Personality and Individual Differences* 51 (3): 309–14.

Sliwka, D. 2007. "Trust as a Signal of a Social Norm and the Hidden Costs of Incentive Schemes." *American Economic Review* 97 (3): 999–1012.

Sugden, R. 1982. "On the Economics of Philanthropy." *Economic Journal* 92 (366): 341–50.

CHAPTER 15

Facility-Level Human Resource Management

Christophe Lemière, Christine Mahoney, and Jennifer Nyoni

Researchers have widely explored human resource management (HRM) at the central level. This chapter focuses on management at the facility level and its impact on health worker motivation. HRM is an important factor in health workers' performance, but researchers have paid little attention to it in Africa. Several features of health systems—including management training and accountability—can make decentralization of human resource decision making and supportive management styles more prevalent, two "success factors" that are rare in African public health systems.

What Is Effective Human Resource Management?

HRM can be defined simply as the institutional and behavioral ways the following decisions are made: recruitment, selection, allocation, performance appraisal, compensation, promotion, ongoing training, career development, retention, safety, employee discipline, termination, and transfers.[1] An effective human resource manager motivates workers to perform by aligning workers' goals with those of the organization and narrowing the gap between an employee's ability and performance.

A review of the extensive theoretical literature on effective HRM is far beyond the scope of this chapter,[2] and its usefulness would be limited because no evidence on African health sectors is available to confirm (or deny) its theoretical propositions. So, we focus on two HRM "best practices."[3]

- *Decentralization of HRM decision making to the local level, or increasing line managers' autonomy.* This can be effective because line managers have the most accurate and current information on health workers' ability, effort, and performance.[4]
- *Supportive management styles.* This practice can have a positive impact on employee performance.[5] A supportive manager treats employees fairly, grants them appropriate autonomy in completing tasks,[6] and provides feedback that motivates the employee to develop skills. For feedback to motivate in this way, it must focus on specific behaviors that the employee can control, use subjective behavioral terms, and be given at the appropriate time and place.

We hypothesize that, to observe these best practices, managers need to:

- Be adequately *trained in management skills*, particularly in a supportive management style.
- Have adequate *autonomy in their decision making* to manage effectively.
- Have consistent *incentives* and be *accountable* to manage effectively. These incentives can come from numerous motivational sources; some examples are managers' pay structure, their access to adequate resources, and how they are monitored. Conversely, managers should not have incentives that compete with effective management of their subordinates (such as getting paid more to do off-site training than to manage on-site).

Our simple analytical framework is summarized in figure 15.1.

Improving Health Worker Performance through Human Resource Management

Data are scarce on health worker performance in Africa. Because of this scarcity, and because some studies exist on African health workers' motivation, we use motivation as a proxy for performance (Dieleman and

Figure 15.1   A Simple Framework for Analyzing Relationships between Management and Health Workers' Performance

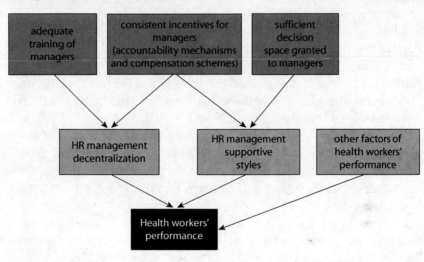

Source: World Bank data.

others 2006). This section explores evidence on how the above-mentioned best practices in HRM—decentralization and supportive management styles—improve motivation.

Giving Line Managers Autonomy in Decision Making (HRM Decentralization)

HRM decentralization grants line managers the autonomy to recruit, appraise performance, and reward or sanction their staff, rather than defer these decisions to higher level off-site managers. This autonomy can be effective because line managers have daily interaction with employees, giving them the most accurate information on how employees perform, leading to better-informed performance appraisals.

Few African countries have this kind of decentralization, at least in the government sector, and its implementation has usually been partial, inconsistent, or both. Ghana and Tanzania offer relevant examples. In these countries, substantial efforts have been made to decentralize HRM, but line managers still cannot hire or fire workers, except casual staff (WHO 2009).

An important success factor for health sector decentralization is "to ensure that the newly empowered organization is required to deliver clearly identifiable and measurable objectives. At the same time, the organization is given the necessary resources and discretion over their use, to permit these objectives to be met" (Ensor and Ronoh 2005). That has rarely happened in Africa, especially in health.

Previous studies have assessed the impact of such decentralization on African health sectors, and all conclude that there is either no impact or that it is negative (Kolehmainen-Aitken 2004; Wang and others 2002). But, these studies explored only the government sector. Because most countries have not fully decentralized government HRM, these studies do not paint the full picture.

Thus one must look at the private sector to assess the impact of HRM decentralization in Africa.[7] For full decentralization—where facility managers are granted resources and decision rights in line with their objectives—the best evidence comes from Tanzania (Leonard and Masatu 2008; Mliga 2003).

In 1996 Mliga studied performance of clinicians in government-run facilities and private not-for-profit (faith-based) facilities, along one dimension: the quality of care. He collected information through direct clinical observations. Mliga ranked facilities by degree of decentralization,[8] defining a facility as fully decentralized if the manager had the power to recruit and fire workers, set salaries, and pay these salaries. This HRM structure was found only in the not-for-profit private sector; the government-run facilities were constrained by highly centralized HRM.

Mliga found a significant association between the degree of decentralization and the quality of care provided by clinicians. This association was even stronger for one component of quality: attentiveness, which has been shown in other studies to be more strongly related to clinicians' motivation than to their experience or technical skills (Leonard and Masatu 2008). Mliga concluded that "local control of personnel, along with staff salaries linked to facility revenues, gives health care providers the incentive to provide quality service and to attract clients" (Mliga 2003, 220).

Leonard and Masatu (2008) performed a similar analysis from 2001 to 2003 in Tanzania, measuring various confounding factors in each facility: staffing and training levels, availability of drugs and equipment, and possible Hawthorne effects. They found that even after controlling for these factors the association between degree of decentralization and quality of care provided by clinicians remained strong and positive.

They conclude: "the success of these [private] organizations is not due to the greater capacity of their employees nor to the presence of large numbers of professional clinicians, but rather to their ability to get each clinician to work at levels closer to their ability. As such, this finding adds empirical weight to the argument that management, not simply training or medicines, must be addressed in order to improve health care in developing countries" (Leonard and Masatu 2008, 21).

Adopting Supportive Management Styles with Health Workers

Decentralizing HRM will result in more autonomy for health managers' decision making, but this may not be enough to improve effectiveness of health workers' management. Managers must also be trained in HRM. This training should help managers relate to their employees and master technical tools, such as HRM strategic planning, in order to improve performance. Indeed, supportive monitoring (as opposed to "controlling" monitoring) is widely acknowledged as a major source of motivation and job satisfaction. Frustration from a lack of "supportive monitoring" was noted by a Tanzanian health worker: "The supervision is not friendly and lovingly done. (...) You can see two people having papers and pen in their hands coming asking questions like a policeman; it is not a friendly one but faults-finding supervision" (Manongi, Marchant, and Bygbjerg 2006).

We focus on two aspects of supportive monitoring, both with available evidence on African health sectors: fairness and respect displayed by line managers to their employees, and autonomy granted by line managers to employees in completing their tasks.

Being fair and respectful with workers. An important body of literature shows that fairness and respect by managers contribute greatly to workers' motivation and job satisfaction.[9] For instance, in behavioral economics, Ellingsen and Johannesson (2007) argue that

> Economic theory generally, and the principal-agent model specifically, emphasize the role of material incentives. The standard assumption is that people work hard only if they receive monetary compensation for doing so. However, a substantial body of evidence contradicts the standard economic model. Many salaried academics, for example, work diligently year after year, continuing to exert themselves as they approach retirement, although financial incentives are then usually absent. (...) While workers appreciate monetary rewards, they also get utility from what (they believe) others think about them. Thus, employers can pay their workers with a combination of monetary rewards and respect.
>
> (Ellingsen and Johannesson 2007, p. 135).

Evidence on African health sectors shows that health workers highly value fairness and respect by managers. A survey of health workers in Uganda found that an important cause of motivation was how respectful a supervisor was to them.[10] Gilson, Palmer, and Schneider (2005) observed similar responses in South Africa. In Malawi, McAuliffe (2009a) explored the relationship between job satisfaction and interaction with managers, finding that managers' honesty and fairness could explain 45 percent of variance in job satisfaction. In this study health workers appeared to be motivated more by "procedural justice" (the HRM decision-making process used by managers) than by "distributive justice" (how equitable the results of the HRM decisions are).

Conversely, health workers' motivation can be strongly effected when they are abused by managers. Punitive, subjective feedback can be verbally abusive. This behavior does not seem rare, at least in Uganda, where 24 percent of health workers reported having been recently abused (physically, emotionally, or verbally) by their managers (Hagopian and others 2009).

While showing respect is probably a question of adequate training for managers, fair decision making seems much more difficult to implement. Managers may learn to show employees respect through management training. But fairness in HRM decisions is not just a matter of a manager's attitude—it is also influenced by the legal and organizational constraints managers face every day.

With the rampaging clientelism in African public sectors,[11] management decisions (local or central) are rarely based on an accurate appraisal of health workers' performance. To restore some neutrality in health workers' appraisal, a promising solution lies in pay-for-performance (P4P) schemes, currently rolled out in Rwanda and Burundi. A key feature of these schemes is external appraisal of health facility performance—and indirectly of health workers' performance (chapter 13). This external and therefore neutral evaluation can reduce clientelism and nepotism in rewarding health workers.

Granting autonomy to health workers in completing their tasks. Another aspect of a supportive management style is giving workers autonomy in their tasks. Many management specialists have shown that task autonomy can increase a sense of empowerment, and therefore performance, of workers. Tendler (1994) found that health community workers in Brazil performed more effectively when they had wide autonomy in their duties, even when carrying out tasks beyond their job descriptions.

Similar evidence has not been found in Africa, where many health workers seem to value precise job descriptions and detailed operating procedures. In Mali, for example, a study reported that "lack of a clear job description" is a major demotivating factor for health workers.[12] Similarly in Malawi, McAuliffe (2009b) found that "control over practice" (the ability to carry out tasks not explicitly mentioned in one's job description) contributed much less than "management support" in explaining health worker motivation.

These disturbing results could be related to other African non-health case studies showing that worker performance increases when standard operating procedures are introduced (D'Iribarne and Henry 2007). This suggests that more "red tape" may lead to better performance, a result that contradicts management theories. Additional research is needed.

Why Is Good Human Resource Management so Rare in Africa?

As argued earlier, to be effective, managers need to be trained, be allowed to manage (through decentralization), and have incentives to do so. But these ingredients seem rare in African public health sectors. We now explore why.

Managers' Training

Evidence abounds that very few health facility managers have received any systematic health management training. Being a doctor is usually considered sufficient to manage a health facility. That explains why in Uganda, 55 of 56 directors of district health services are physicians (Dwyer and others 2006). In some other countries, such as Ghana and Tanzania, doctors are required to have a degree in public health or management to be managers. But even with these minimal requirements, few health care managers are qualified. In Ghana only 36 percent of hospital directors have such a degree. Purpose-trained managers are very rare and usually serve as administrative staff (WHO 2009).

Two reasons could explain the lack of management training. The limited capacity of governments to invest in training programs is one. Another is lobbying by doctors' bodies. Many argue that only physicians can manage health facilities. One suspects that these lobbies continue to frame the debate as "who should manage a health facility?" rather than "what skills are needed to do this?" Moving the debate to the second question would probably allow for progress in health management training programs. The strong reluctance of doctors' lobbies to give up these jobs may be related to the fact that health management positions can be more lucrative than clinical ones, encouraging doctors to become managers rather than provide patient care.[13]

Decentralizing Human Resource Management

African government health sectors show many forms of HRM decentralization. One is common in countries that have adopted community involvement in health management (usually in relation to the Bamako Initiative),[14] as in Mali (World Bank 2004) and Benin (World Bank 2010). Communities in these countries have been granted some control over local health facilities, notably to recruit and pay health workers out of revenues from user fees. These health workers are not civil servants. They have "precarious" contracts and are usually underpaid. Rigorous evidence is lacking, but their productivity and quality of services seem low.

A handful of countries have pursued more ambitious strategies targeting civil servants, not just community-funded health workers. Uganda, for instance, sets civil service salaries nationally but allows benefits and allowances to be defined locally (Kolehmainen-Aitken 2004). Similarly, Tanzania implemented some decentralization in recruiting civil servant health workers (Munga and others 2009).

Ghana went further and set up a "board" system, where civil servants in the health sector are managed differently than other civil servants. Little evidence shows, however, that these changes have affected HRM because this "board" system (such as the Ghana Health Service) still centralizes the main decisions, including hiring, promoting, and firing.

Even fewer countries have started to "delink." In this radical policy, all civil servants become contract-based employees of local government health entities. Zambia experimented with this approach in the 1990s, but returned to its traditional system in 2006.[15] Rwanda launched a similar experiment in 2007. Results seem more promising, though they have not yet been rigorously analyzed.

Most African governments have been reluctant to decentralize HRM for civil servants, including health workers. A main reason may be clientelism. Political leaders may use civil servant recruitment to build political and social support, such that civil servants become an important clientele. Clientelism may then become a major part of the national social contract, enforced daily by unions, rendering decentralization more political than technical. Decentralization can breach this social contract.[16]

Managers' Incentives and Accountability

Base salaries of health facility managers are usually little higher than those of other health workers.[17] But their positions are coveted as they allow the employee to earn additional (sometimes illegal or informal) income in several ways. Managers decide, for example, which staff can go on training, including themselves, and therefore who receives daily allowances for training.[18] This motivation inevitably keeps managers away on training for a large portion of their time,[19] and they may take some of their employees' daily allowances. Managers also have access to more informal payments (extracted from patients) than other wealth workers. And, they can determine their own work schedule, allowing them to work more hours privately.[20] In short, managers have little incentive, if any, to make their facility perform well and attract more patients.

Similarly, accountability mechanisms are rare. Managers are usually appointed in a discretionary manner, not on the basis of past performance. They are seldom appraised (World Bank 2009, 2010).[21]

Conclusion

This review points to two conclusions. The first is the dearth of evidence on this topic for Africa. We found rigorous studies for few aspects of the relationship between HRM and health workers, perhaps because public health policy makers and development researchers still view HRM as a new field in Africa. They are more familiar with the concept of central-level HRM planning, and may not be aware that facility-level HRM can contribute greatly to health workers' motivation—or more often demotivation. As behavioral economists enter the field, more analytical efforts may be devoted to HRM in health.

The second is that there may be too much emphasis on HRM training (GHWA 2008). It is important of course, but institutional arrangements also greatly effect HRM, including decentralization of HRM decision making and implementation of consistent and effective incentives and accountability. These are major areas to be explored in future research to understand how HRM of health workers can improve performance.

Notes

1. This chapter is not a comprehensive review of management of health workers in Africa. For that, see, for example, Fritzen (2007) and Egger and others (2005). Our perspective is more focused.

2. Buchan (2004) provides a useful overview.

3. Best practices in HRM result in effective performance. They are generally adapted from similar organizations in the same field where they have proven successful.

4. Grindle (1997), analyzing performance of government workers in 29 organizations in Bolivia, the Central African Republic, Ghana, Morocco, Sri Lanka, and Tanzania, found that organizations where local managers have autonomy overwhelmingly have better-performing employees.

5. For instance, Drach-Zahavy (2004) found that when nurses have supportive management, their performance is more effective.

6. Oldham and Cummings (1996) offer a more precise definition of a supportive style of supervision: "When supervisors are *supportive*, they show concern for employees' feelings and needs, encourage them to voice their own concerns, provide positive, chiefly informational feedback, and facilitate employee skill development" (p. 611). Conversely, "when supervisors are *controlling*, they closely monitor employee behavior, make decisions without employee involvement, provide feedback in a controlling manner, and generally pressure employees to think, feel, or behave in certain ways" (p. 611).

7. Here, we refer to the not-for-profit private sector, given the lack of evidence on the for-profit (commercial) private sector (in Africa).

8. In this paper, the degree of HRM decentralization was a composite index reflecting the ability (or not) of managers to fire their employees, the hierarchical level at which salaries were set, and the hierarchical level making decisions on staff deployment.

9. See, for instance, Falk and Kosfeld (2004) or Ichino and Mauhlheusser (2004).

10. Hagopian and others 2009. One health worker reported, "My immediate supervisor cares about me as a person" (p. 869).

11. Clientelism refers to a social organization characterized by patron-client relationships. Relatively powerful and rich patrons promise to provide relatively powerless and poor clients jobs, protection, infrastructure, and other benefits in exchange for votes and other forms of loyalty, including labor. In developing countries many civil servants act as agents of these patrons. Consequently, decisions by these civil servants are driven more by the need to please their patron than to provide neutral and high-quality services (see, for instance, Rauch and Evans 2000).

12. Dieleman and others 2006, p. 4. This piece of evidence has to be interpreted with caution. One could rightly argue that the absence of (precise) job description does not equate with task autonomy (and reciprocally). Ultimately, task autonomy depends on the management style, with or without a job description.

13. Studies in Africa on official and unofficial revenues of health workers are extremely rare. But one in Benin found that although hospital managers and clinicians have similar base salaries (about $400 a month), hospital managers could earn 50 percent more, simply through collecting more of the daily allowances given for attending training sessions (Kanakin, Kessou, and Koutchikap 2008).

14. The Bamako Initiative—sponsored by UNICEF and WHO, and adopted by African ministers of health in 1987—was based on the realization that by the late 1980s many countries, especially in Sub-Saharan Africa, were burdened by a lack of resources and practical implementation strategies. Many patients had lost confidence in the inefficient and underresourced public health facilities. The Bamako Initiative was based on the concept that communities should participate directly in the management and funding of health facilities. One of the features of the Bamako Initiative was to allow health facilities to hire health workers to be paid with user fees.

15. One reason for this reversal is the following. Civil servants' unions required that all pension benefits be paid in full and in advance to the civil servants agreeing to become contract-based workers; the government could not face this tremendous financial burden.

16. Note that HRM decentralization does not—by itself—prevent clientelism. When recruitment is decentralized, it may simply change who is the patron (that is, local politicians instead of national politicians). In other words, opposition to decentralize HRM can be explained by an understandable reluctance of national politicians to lose control on their clientele.

17. A generalist doctor in the government-run sector in many West African countries earns about $400 a month, and a regional health officer less than $500.

18. A study in Malawi found that a nurse can earn the equivalent of 35–40 percent of monthly salary by attending a five-day training session (MSF 2007). Kanakin, Kessou, and Koutchikap (2008) record similar figures for Benin.

19. Kanakin, Kessou, and Koutchikap (2008) found that in Benin facility managers in a health district could spend about 20 percent of their time on training, generating daily allowances equivalent to six months of salary. This district was not supported by donors (usually heavy funders of training), strongly suggesting that these findings grossly underestimated the real situation. See also Ridde (2010).

20. As said, the overwhelming majority of health managers are doctors. They usually combine their role of manager with clinical work. That leads to high absenteeism among managers, naturally detrimental to good management.

21. P4P schemes may help change this situation (chapter 13).

References

Buchan, J. 2004. "What Differences Does ('Good') HRM Make?" *Human Resources for Health* 2 (6): 1–7.

D'Iribarne, P., and A. Henry. 2007. *Successful Companies in the Developing World: Managing in Synergy with Cultures.* Research Department, Notes and Documents 36. Paris: Agence Française de Développement.

Dieleman, M., J. Toonen, H. Touré, and T. Martineau. 2006. "The Match between Motivation and Performance Management of Health Sector Workers in Mali." *Human Resources for Health* 4 (2): 1–7.

Drach-Zahavy, A. 2004. "Primary Nurses' Performance: Role of Supportive Management." *Journal of Advanced Nursing* 45 (1): 7–16.

Dwyer, J., M. Paskavitz, S. Vriesendorp, and S. Johnson. 2006. "An Urgent Call to Professionalize Leadership and Management in Health Care Worldwide." Occasional Paper 4, Management Sciences for Health, Cambridge, MA.

Egger, D., P. Travis, D. Dolvo, and L. Hawken. 2005. "Strengthening Management in Low-Income Countries." Making Health Systems Work: Working Paper 1, World Health Organization, Geneva.

Ellingsen, T., and M. Johannesson. 2007. "Paying Respect." *Journal of Economic Perspectives* 21 (4): 135–49.

Ensor, T., and J. Ronoh. 2005. "Impact of Organizational Change on the Delivery of Reproductive Services: A Review of the Literature." *International Journal of Health Planning and Management* 20 (3): 209–25.

Falk, A., and M. Kosfeld. 2004. "Distrust—The Hidden Cost of Control." Discussion Paper 1203, Institute for the Study of Labor, Bonn, Germany.

Fritzen, S. 2007. "Strategic Management of the Health Workforce in Developing Countries: What Have We Learned?" *Human Resources for Health* 5 (4): 1–9.

GHWA (Global Health Workforce Alliance). 2008. *Financing and Economic Aspects of Health Workforce Scaling-Up and Improvement: Framework: Alliance Financing Task Force.* Geneva: World Health Organization.

Gilson, L., N. Palmer, and H. Schneider. 2005. "Trust and Health Worker Performance: Exploring A Conceptual Framework Using South African Evidence." *Social Science and Medicine* 61: 1418–29.

Grindle, M. 1997. "Divergent Cultures? When Public Organizations Perform Well in Developing Countries." *World Development* 25 (4): 481–95.

Hagopian, A., A. Zuyderduin, N. Kyobutungi, and F. Yumkella. 2009. "Job Satisfaction and Morale in the Ugandan Health Workforce." *Health Affairs* 28 (5): w863–75.

Ichino, A., and G. Mauhlheusser. 2004. "How Often Should You Open the Door? Optimal Monitoring to Screen Heterogeneous Agents." Discussion Paper 987, Institute for the Study of Labor, Bonn, Germany.

Kanakin, J., L. Kessou, and O. Koutchikap. 2008. *Etude sur la gouvernance dans le secteur de la santé: cas de la zone sanitaire d'Abomey-Calavi So-Ava au Benin.* Washington, DC: World Bank.

Kolehmainen-Aitken, R.-L. 2004. "Decentralization's Impact on the Health Workforce: Perspectives of Managers, Workers and National Leaders." *Human Resources for Health* 2 (5): 1 11.

Leonard, K. L., and M. C. Masatu. 2008. "Professionalism, Latent Professionalism and Organizational Demands for Health Care Quality in a Developing Country." Working Paper 42883, Department of Agricultural and Resource Economics, University of Maryland, College Park, MD.

Manongi, R., T. C. Marchant, and I. C. Bygbjerg. 2006. "Improving Motivation among Primary Health Care Workers in Tanzania: A Health Worker Perspective." *Human Resources for Health* 4 (6): 1–7.

McAuliffe, E., O. Manafa, F. Maseko, C. Bowie, and E. White. 2009a. "Understanding Job Satisfaction amongst Mid-Level Cadres in Malawi: The Contribution of Organizational Justice." *Reproductive Health Matters* 17 (33): 80–90.

McAuliffe, E., C. Bowie, O. Manafa, F. Maseko, M. MacLachlan, D. Hevey, C. Normand, and M. Chirwa. 2009b. "Measuring and Managing the Work Environment of the Mid-Level Provider—The Neglected Human Resource." *Human Resources for Health* 7 (13): 1–9.

Mliga, G. 2003. *Decentralization and the Quality of Health Care in Tanzania.* Berkeley, CA: University of California Press.

MSF (Medecins Sans Frontieres). 2007. *Help Wanted: Confronting the Health Care Worker Crisis to Expand Access to HIV/AIDS Treatment: MSF Experience in Southern Africa.* Johannesburg: MSF.

Munga, M., N. G. Songstad, A., Blystad, and O. Maestad. 2009. "The Decentralization-Centralisation Dilemma: Recruitement and Distribution of Health Workers in Remote Districts of Tanzania." *BMC International Health and Human Rights* 9 (9): 607 63.

Oldham, G., and A. Cummings. 1996. "Employee Creativity: Personal and Contextual Factors at Work." *Academy of Management Journal* 39 (3): 607–34.

Rauch, J., and P. B. Evans. 2000. "Bureaucratic Structure and Bureaucratic Performance in Less Developed Countries." *Journal of Public Economics* 75 (1) 49–71.

Ridde, V. 2010. "Per Diems Undermine Health Interventions, Systems and Research in Africa: Burying Our Heads in the Sand." *Tropical Medicine and International Health.* http://onlinelibrary.wiley.com/doi/10.1111/i.1365 -3156.2010.02607.x/abstract

Tendler, J. 1994. "Trust in a Rent-Seeking World: Health and Government Transformed in Northeast Brazil." *World Development* 22 (12): 1771–91.

Wang, Y., C. Collins, S. Tang, and T. Martineau. 2002. "Health Systems Decentralization and HR Management in Low and Middle Income Countries." *Public Administration and Development* 22 (5): 439–53.

WHO (World Health Organization). 2009. *Who Are Health Managers? Case Studies from Three African Countries.* Geneva: WHO.

World Bank. 2004. *Mali: Analytical Report on Health and Poverty.* Washington, DC: World Bank.

———. 2009. *Ghana HRH Report.* Washington, DC: World Bank.

———. 2010. *Benin: Analytical Report on Health and Poverty.* Washington, DC: World Bank.

PART 4

Education and Training of Health Workers

CHAPTER 16

Health Worker Education and Training

Kate Tulenko, Emmanuel Gasakure, and Andre-Jacques Neusy

Preservice training defines how and, often, where health workers practice. It determines the cadre, skill, motivation, and expectations of health workers, influencing all aspects of the labor market. This chapter explores how preservice education affects stock shortfalls, performance, and distribution of health workers in Sub-Saharan Africa. It analyzes the latest data on African health training schools from a labor market viewpoint. The chapter first explores the factors in preservice education that contribute to the low stock of health workers, particularly among certain cadres. It then examines the dynamics within preservice training institutions that may lead to inadequate health worker performance. Finally, the chapter reviews how existing preservice training approaches lead to distribution imbalances among health workers and suggests alternate approaches to correct this imbalance. The chapter closes with a call to policy makers and stakeholders to renew attention to training adequate numbers of highly qualified health workers, willing and able to serve Sub-Saharan Africa's underserved populations.

Preservice education largely determines the supply and quality of health workers. In Sub-Saharan Africa the supply of health workers is too low to meet demand, and the quality of health services does not meet local needs. The situation in rural and underserved areas is dire, as the majority of health workers seek employment in urban areas.

How do education and training affect the stock, performance, and distribution of health workers in Africa? These three elements are often interconnected: the same conditions that contribute to the low stock may contribute to poor performance and inequitable distribution. But it helps to explore each element separately, noting that some overlap is inevitable.

How Preservice Education Leads to the Low Stock

Sub-Saharan Africa does not train enough health workers to meet its basic health needs. The Joint Learning Initiative and World Health Organization's (WHO) 2006 *World Health Report* estimate that Africa requires a million additional health workers just to meet primary health care needs. WHO cites the scarcity of training opportunities for health workers as a major cause of this shortage (Anyangwe and Mtonga 2007).

The shortage of training spots may be even greater than previously thought. A recent WHO analysis revealed that in 10 of the 12 African countries surveyed, preservice education is insufficient to maintain current health worker density. Even if attrition was limited to mortality and retirement (excluding migration and career changes), it would take the combined countries 36 years to meet the Millennium Development Goal targets for physicians, and 29 years to meet the targets for nurses and midwives. Some countries have such low graduation numbers that under current conditions they will never reach the WHO's minimum target of 2.28 health professionals per 1,000 population.

Shortfalls of Specific Cadres

The low health worker stock in Sub-Saharan Africa occurs both in the aggregate and in particular occupations. Some countries that appear to have adequate numbers of health workers do not have the appropriate skill mix to meet basic needs. Large numbers of one cadre may mask shortages in others. Both the absolute low stock and the stock imbalance (often referred to as "skill mix imbalance") damage health systems (Naiker and others 2009). A country may have plenty of nurses but a dire shortage of pharmacists and lab technicians, severely constraining the nurses' ability to delivery care (Dussault and others 2009). This analysis focuses on physicians, because they are the most studied and documented cadre. Additional research is needed on the training of nonphysician health workers.

In her global analysis of medical schools, Eckhert (2002) found that Africa had the highest ratio of population to medical schools, with 9.09 million people per medical school, compared with 1.67 million people per medical school in Europe. The shortfall's size is compounded by the fact that many African medical schools graduate fewer than 20 students per year. The positive news is that the number of African medical schools increased tenfold from 1955 to 2001, with most of the growth in the last two decades, as countries began to permit private medical schools. As a result, countries must establish or strengthen school accreditation and professional licensure programs to maintain the quality of graduates.

Africa has a great gap to close. There are only 87 medical schools in the 46 Sub-Saharan countries, with a total population of 417 million (Hagopian 2004). The distribution of schools is uneven and tends to be highest in countries that have permitted or encouraged private medical schools. Nigeria, home to 27 percent of Sub-Saharan medical schools, welcomes private education. Eckhert notes that 16 Sub-Saharan countries with populations between 5.4 million and 17.8 million have only a single medical school—clearly not enough to meet their needs. Eleven countries have no medical school (Anyangwe and Mtonga 2007). Countries with more medical schools per capita tend to have better health indicators, but they also tend to be wealthier.

The number of physicians produced in Africa is also limited by small class sizes. The average number of students per class year is 300 in Western Europe and 500 in China, Eastern Europe, and the former Soviet Union. In most African medical schools there are fewer than 100 students per class year, and many have fewer than 50. It is unclear why African medical schools do not make adequate use of their resources to produce more medical students per class. With only 5,100 new graduates a year, Africa has the lowest number of annual medical school graduates per capita of any region.

Training shortfalls are large throughout Africa. Ethiopia's population is 75 million but until recently it trained only 200 doctors a year. The United Kingdom has a population of 60 million and trains 6,000 doctors a year. The paucity of graduates is particularly troubling given Africa's rapid growth in population, set to increase 150 percent from 1998 to 2050. It is unreasonable to expect that Africa's existing medical schools will both make up the current physician deficit and compensate for the rise in population. With population growth and the likely increased demand as African economies improve, the shortage of physicians and other health workers will worsen unless annual graduation numbers improve (Kinfu and others 2009).

In additional to graduating too few doctors, African preservice education institutions underemphasize prevention and public health, leading to shortages of public health cadres. In their analysis of public health preservice education in Africa, Beaglehole, Sanders, and Dal Poz (2003) conclude that Africa is training significantly fewer public health workers than it needs. This undertraining extends from frontline workers (such as sanitarians) to mid-level workers (such as public health nurses) and to high-level workers (such as biostatisticians).

Disconnect between Training Institutions and Country Conditions

Low stock, poor performance, and uneven distribution can all be traced in part to the disconnect between training institutions and local conditions. Schools, rarely connected with local employers, are unaware of employer needs for numbers, cadres, skills, and other attributes (Okwero 2009, pers. comm. with K. Tulenko). This divide tends to be greatest in countries where the ministry of education rather than the ministry of health is responsible for health science training institutions (Beaglehole, Sanders, and Dal Poz 2003).

For many countries the lack of qualified local students limits the number of health workers they can train (High Level Forum for the Health MDGs 2004), as does the lack of qualified faculty (Dolvo 2003). Countries can establish special health high schools in rural district capitals and offer bridging courses to help less qualified students catch up. The Walter Sisulu Medical School in South Africa and the medical school in Malawi both discovered that bridging programs augment their output of highly qualified graduates. Malawi, with a bridging program, tripled its medical school enrollment from 20 to 60 (Broadhead 1998).

Much of the health worker shortage is attributable to training institutions' focus on clinical and specialty training to the exclusion of public health training (Anyangwe and Mtonga 2007). The AfriHealth Project's mapping of advanced public health training in Africa revealed that more than half of countries (55 percent) do not have a postgraduate public health program (Ijsselmuiden and others 2007). Francophone and Lusophone countries are less likely to have public health programs than Anglophone countries. Such programs tend to focus on training physicians in public health skills rather than other clinical or nonclinical cadres, such as engineers, veterinarians, or primary public health specialists. With fewer than 500 full-time staff, the "total academic public health workforce in Africa could fit into the department of epidemiology at Johns Hopkins" (Ijsselmuiden and others 2007, p. 918). Some countries such as

Ethiopia, however, are developing large programs of indigeneously developed training (box 16.1).

Box 16.1

Ethiopia's Health Extension Workers

Impressive success stories are emerging from Africa's efforts to produce adequate numbers of appropriately trained health workers. Perhaps the brightest example is Ethiopia, and its scale-up of health extension workers and health officers.

There are three reasons for Ethiopia's success. The first is leadership. The Minister of Health, Dr. Tedros Ghebreyesus, provides strong, consistent leadership and gives priority to training more health workers to meet basic needs.

The second reason is that Ethiopia flooded the markets with qualified workers. The Ministry of Health acknowledged that in the face of growing health worker demand from wealthy countries, Ethiopia could not compete for salaries, and that its health workers would continue to emigrate. In response, Ethiopia adopted a "flooding" strategy, producing large numbers of health workers. Some workers will leave the country, but many will stay and deliver services to their home communities. The unleashed power of private health science schools contribute to the flooding. Extended families and the diaspora are also frequently tapped to pay for preservice education—this is viable in the health sector, where graduates are practically guaranteed jobs that pay better than average in the country.

The third reason for Ethiopia's success is the Ministry of Health's choice of which health worker cadres to scale up. After analyzing the disease burden and access to care, the ministry concluded that the greatest health needs were preventive and primary care in communities. Looking at health worker retention in communities, the ministry decided to focus on health extension workers and health officers. Health extension workers deliver a basic package of preventive services including sanitation, immunizations, contraception, and basic malaria, diarrhea, and pneumonia diagnosis and treatment. Health officers are roughly equivalent to nurse practitioners and are able to perform curative care for the most common health conditions that contribute to excess morbidity and mortality in Ethiopia.

A total of 31,831 health extension workers were trained and deployed through 2009, exceeding the Ministry of Health's target of 30,786. Because health officers require more training and more sophisticated training sites, their numbers have not grown as quickly, but the numbers are still impressive compared with other countries. The ministry expects more than 5,000 health officers to graduate in the next five years.

High Student Attrition Rates

Another reason for the shortfall in health workers is high student attrition, in some countries 40 percent or higher (Lugina 2006). Medical schools in the Democratic Republic of Congo report attrition as high as 95 percent (Longombe 2009). Attrition wastes resources, time, and money, resulting not only in personal disappointment for students but also in long-term economic losses—both direct, such as the potential loss of trained health workers, and indirect, such as the loss of future earnings. Nurses and physicians can earn tens to hundreds times more than the average gross domestic product per capita in their countries and often serve as the economic heads of their extended family. The attrition of a single student can thus have permanent ripple effects on dozens of people. Other indirect effects and long-term costs of attrition include the loss of tax revenue from that individual and the loss of income by those who would have been treated for the worker but died or lost days of work due to illness.

High attrition is attributed to various factors including family obligations, student or family member illness (especially HIV/AIDS), lack of funding for school fees or living expenses, lack of adequate academic preparation, lack of appropriate study skills, lack of dorms and other infrastructure, and lack of student mentoring and support (especially to identify and support students at risk of dropping out). Policy makers need additional information on attrition to design and implement initiatives to identify and support students at higher risk of dropping out.

Lack of Adequate Financing

In many countries the government is the sole source of financing for health worker education, which limits the number of health workers who can be trained. There are many reports that qualified students cannot enter training or drop out due to the lack of student loans or scholarships (Kemp and Tindiweegi 2001). Some countries ban private health training schools. If governments lift these bans, they can tap private funding for capital investments in schools, increasing the overall investment in health worker education. African countries must create financing systems that take advantage of varied financing sources, including public and private grants and loans, private investors, nongovernmental organizations, faith-based organizations, future employers, international recruiters, the diaspora, and donors.

Inadequate financing may also affect the health worker distribution. High fees select wealthier urban students and are a barrier for students from underserved communities, who are more likely to work in these communities after training. And high student debt may drive health workers to the private sector or abroad, where they can earn more money to pay off student loans. This phenomenon is widely seen in the United States, where higher educational loans drive medical students away from lower paid primary care.

The rigid schedules of many training programs present another financial constraint for students. Most training programs in Africa are full-time, leaving little room for students with jobs or family obligations. Programs that are inflexible in their schedule shut out a potential pool of qualified students. Some institutions are becoming more flexible with evening and weekend training or modular training (sometimes called "sandwich" training), which alternates periods of training with periods when the student is free to work, tend a farm, or care for his or her family. A flexible program at the University of the Western Cape in South Africa improved equity in access to training.

Links between Training and Migration

Almost all health worker retention and immigration studies show that lower level workers are more likely than their higher level counterparts to stay in rural areas and service underserved populations (see chapters 9 and 10). These frontline workers provide valuable preventive care, such as education on nutrition and sanitation, as well as support to clinical care, such as bathing and feeding patients. Unfortunately many countries are eliminating training programs for frontline workers and focusing on higher level workers. Rwanda recently eliminated training of lower level nurses (Capacity Project 2007). Not only do higher level workers take longer and cost more to train, they are also more likely to emigrate or to serve in urban areas, which already have the highest densities.

Several factors motivate health science graduates to emigrate rather than practice at home, including curricula more aligned to developed country than developing country needs (Eastwood and others 2001; Oman and others 2007). Students usually practice in tertiary or quaternary hospitals that are completely different from the community clinics and district primary hospitals that need health workers most (Parry and Parry 1998). As a result, doctors trained at many African universities are better prepared to work in western health systems than in an African setting (Tulenko and Preker 2012).

Three factors are strongly associated with retention and rural practice: a rural background, targeted training for rural practice at the postgraduate level, and positive clinical and education experiences in rural settings as part of undergraduate medical education. In their study of migrant Ghanaian nurses and physicians, Ozden and Winter (2009) found that health workers have strong ideas about which schools' graduates are most likely to find work abroad—a recruiting point for these schools.

In the past many African countries sent students abroad for all or part of their training. Programs such as the U.K. Overseas Doctors Training Scheme institutionalized this practice (Sridhar 2000; Welsh 2001). These programs are now widely seen as ineffective, because graduates rarely return, and if they do, their skills do not match the disease burden and available technology in their home country (Macdonagh, Jiddawit, and Parry 2002). The loss of Malawian medical students to practices in the United Kingdom and South Africa is one of the reasons Malawi founded its medical school.

Even today, many African medical schools send graduates to a more developed neighbor, such as South Africa, or to a former colonial ruler. Many students never return. Of African physicians 10 percent practice in just two wealthy countries: the United States and Canada. Thirty percent of Ghanaian physicians and 43 percent of Liberian physicians practice abroad (see chapter 10).

Malawi has improved its stock of physicians through preservice education. Until the 1990s Malawi sent health science students abroad for training, either in Africa or elsewhere. The costs were extraordinary and few graduates returned to Malawi to practice. Manchester, England has more Malawian doctors than all of Malawi. To address the issue, the government founded its first medical school, tailored to the country's needs. The Malawi College of Medicine follows an integrated curriculum focusing on local health needs. In the first two years of study it introduces basic sciences in relation to clinically relevant health problems. About 25 percent of the curriculum's contact hours are dedicated to community health. The aim is to produce doctors rooted in Malawi, with the right competencies and attitude to serve where they are most needed. Students spend more time learning to prevent, diagnose, and treat diseases that affect poor Malawian communities—like diarrhea, malnutrition, pneumonia, malaria, and HIV/AIDS—than diseases more prevalent in developed countries, like cancer, diabetes, and dementia.

Malawi's strategy has borne fruit. Graduates of the Blantyre-based medical school are far more likely to stay: of the first 168 graduates, 112 still work in Malawi. Malawi's recent retention is better than most other African medical schools, which do not make a point of training to meet community needs. Improving the health worker stock by tailoring education to community needs has been so successful that Malawi is now starting schools of dentistry, pharmacy, and physical therapy.

Public Sector Monopolies on Preservice Education

Many African countries do not permit private health science schools, severely limiting resources for preservice education and therefore the number of graduates. Yet, many Sub-Saharan countries that increased the health worker supply rely on faith-based, not-for-profit, or for-profit private institutions. In the 1990s Ethiopia allowed private nursing schools to open, eliminating the shortage of nurses without cost to the government. In Uganda faith-based hospitals are the primary preservice trainer of nurses.

Private health science schools are more likely to be located in rural or underserved areas than public schools (Longombe 2009). Situated in such areas, they can fill a critical gap in services. Ministries of health and education should improve coordination to maximize health system resources for education and training. They should also integrate public and private clinical training and ensure adequate supervision. Accreditation bodies are needed to ensure the quality of both public and private schools.

A study by the Gates Foundation found that 35 percent of all African medical schools are private and private schools are the fastest school ownership model in Africa (Gates 2010). It is estimated that a higher percent of nursing schools are private, for example in Tanzania 55 percent of nursing schools were faith based, and their graduates are more likely to work in underserved communities (Capacity Project 2009). Faith-based schools increasingly require postgraduation contracts as a condition on acceptance, requiring that graduates work for them for a year or two to repay training costs.

School Governance

In many countries the ministry of education rather than the ministry of health governs health science schools, leading to budgetary problems and opening a rift between the trainers and future health sector employers. When the budget for preservice education is separate from the ministry of health budget, the ministry of health cannot set preservice education as a priority over other investments. Many ministries of health build clinics they cannot staff and buy drugs they cannot dispense because they do not have the budgetary flexibility to shift funding to preservice education.

Ministries of health should be responsible for health science schools, increasing budgetary flexibility and enabling schools to take advantage of the technical knowledge, clinical access, and employer status of the ministry of health. Oversight from the ministry of health could better align training, research, health system, and population needs. Training institutions should, however, maintain a relationship with the ministry of education to take advantage of its pedagogical knowledge.

How Preservice Education Does Not Lead to Good Performance

In addition to failing to produce enough health workers, preservice training institutions often fail to produce high-performing health workers. Several factors—knowledge, skills, motivation, and the enabling environment—affect health worker performance, and preservice training influences all of them.

Misaligned Curricula

In their analysis of public health preservice education in Africa, Beaglehole and others (2003) determined that the majority of graduates do not have the skills or experience to perform their jobs adequately. They cite outdated teaching methodologies, a lack of field experience, and the shortage of appropriate mentors for public health students. Health workers carry the knowledge and skills they learn in preservice training throughout their careers. In-service education rarely affects the long-term practice of health workers. Health workers may practice differently immediately following an in-service training course, but over the long run they revert to previous practices.

Even when the quality of education is high, there may be a mismatch between curricula and local conditions. Schools do not align their curricula with local disease realities, particularly the disease burden of the poor. In Mozambique nonphysician surgeons receive no training in HIV/AIDS, even though it is the most common disease they treat. Research should identify the competencies needed to meet prevalent health needs and guide curriculum development accordingly.

Rwanda, recognizing that its previous curricula and student evaluation emphasized knowing more than doing, updated its curriculum with the help of the United States Agency for International Development's Capacity Project, establishing a competency-based curriculum that emphasized actual practice. It followed the Malawian model of tailoring content to meet the community's most pressing needs (Capacity Project

2007). Other medical schools are moving to a need-driven and outcome-driven education program, following a social accountability model of health worker production. Examples include South Africa's Walter Sisulu University and community-based programs at Jimma University in Ethiopia and University of Gezira in Sudan. Makere University in Uganda and the National University of Rwanda are making epidemiology-based curriculum revisions.

Curricula should also reflect local practice conditions. Health workers trained almost exclusively in hospitals may learn to diagnose illness with laboratory tests and imaging unavailable in community facilities.

Low Motivation

Poor health worker performance is often attributed to inadequate knowledge. A growing body of evidence shows that this is not so. Recent studies by Leenard and others (2010) and Mæstad, Torsvik, and Aakvik (2010) in Tanzania found a significant gap between health workers' knowledge and action in diagnosing and treating patients (see chapters 4, 5, 11, and 14). When asked how to examine a child with fever, for example, a physician may list all the proper elements (take temperature, determine heart rate, auscultate lungs, and so on) but when actually examining a child, the same physician may not even touch the child, even when high patient load is not an issue. The gap between what a health worker knows and what a health worker does, the "know-do gap," is thought to result from lack of motivation to do a good job. By recruiting students who are more motivated to help others and integrating motivation into curricula, schools can produce more motivated graduates who make better use of their skills. Student selection criteria should be based not only on academic performance but also on predictors of a future practice in rural and underserved areas, such as rural upbringing and a demonstrated interest in serving others.

Poor Educational Infrastructure

World Bank studies in Ghana, Liberia, and Sierra Leone indicate that the libraries, equipment, and physical plant of many schools are deteriorated or out of date. Many institutions need to upgrade their facilities and equipment. Investments in technology should, however, reflect the reality of student needs. Similarly, cosmetic improvements are often overemphasized. Motivated students can learn just as well in a classroom with peeling paint as they can in one that is freshly painted.

Skill Mix Imbalances

Most African countries use an outdated health team model that is overly reliant on physicians and specialists. This model results in unnecessarily high costs in training and paying health workers. It also creates inefficiencies in providing care and neglects disease prevention and population health (Chen and others 2004). The Global Health Workforce Alliance's Task Force on Scaling Up Education estimates that the annual cost of training a doctor in Africa is twice as much as the annual cost of training a nurse, and five times the annual cost of training a community health worker (Crisp, Gawanas, and Sharp 2008). Countries that pursue a health team strategy biased toward nurses and doctors will spend more money and retain fewer health workers than those that pursue an evidence-based strategy of training frontline workers to meet local needs. WHO's Commission on Macroeconomics and Health recommends that the skill mix of various priority cadres and their practices should be aligned with the diseases that must be addressed to reach the Millennium Development Goals by 2015 (Commission on Macroeconomics and Health 2001). Education systems must develop workforces able to meet the actual needs of local health systems, rather than workforces built around traditional professional roles.

Poor Quality Teaching

Even when curricula are up-to-date and aligned with country needs, teaching remains poor in many schools. Courses are taught by formal lecture, with little opportunity to interact. Students learn by rote memorization rather than practice or case studies. Teacher quality usually is not assessed, and there is no mechanism for students to provide feedback on teacher performance. Faculty receives little support to improve their teaching. Many faculty advance through seniority or research rather than the effectiveness of their teaching, the primary goal of any health science school.

The International Training and Education Center for Health works in Mozambique to improve the pedagogy of professors in the medical officer training program. It focuses on building skills to assess teaching techniques, lesson planning, the schedule and flow of courses, and the relevance of course material to the realities of practice (Jacob and others 2009). When the program began, only 36 percent of professors had any knowledge of adult learning theory and participation methods. The Center has continued mentoring professors to improve their effectiveness

(Kawooya and others 2010). Jhpiego has a similar program to support teaching staff in Côte d'Ivoire.

How Preservice Education Leads to Distributional Imbalances

Africa is predominantly rural, and the majority of preventable deaths and disabilities occur in rural areas. Yet only 23 percent of doctors and 38 percent of nurses practice in rural areas in Africa (Anyangwe and Mtonga 2007). In South Africa rural-born physicians are three times more likely to work in rural areas than urban-born physicians (de Vries and Reid 2003). They are also more likely to be primary care physicians (83 percent) than the urban-born (55 percent), and therefore to better serve South Africa's health needs. When reporting reasons for choosing their practice location, one of the main factors differentiating rural-born physicians was their desire "to feel needed."

Given that most African countries are predominantly rural and that the disease burden is greatest in rural areas, this evidence has profound implications for the future of recruiting health worker students.

School Factors and the Maldistribution of Health Workers

Various elements of preservice education can increase the likelihood of graduates to work in underserved areas. A study in the Democratic Republic of Congo, which is 70 percent rural, examined the effect that a medical school's rural location (rather than rural origin of the students) has on graduates' practice sites (Longombe 2009). The study showed that 81 percent of the graduates from rural medical schools served in rural areas, compared with 24 percent of the graduates from urban medical schools. Of graduates of both rural and urban schools, 55 percent work within 78 kilometers of their school, supporting a widely held belief that health workers prefer to practice near where they trained. In addition, graduates of urban schools are more likely not only to work in urban areas, but also to leave the province where they were educated and practice elsewhere in the country.

Hanson and Jack (2010) show that graduates of Catholic schools express a greater willingness to work in rural areas than graduates of public schools. It is unclear whether this is due to traits in the students before recruitment or whether these attitudes developed in response to the social missions of Catholic schools. Graduates of faith-based schools, which tend to be in underserved rural communities, are more likely to work in underserved areas than other graduates. Again, it is unclear whether this is due to the selection of students with higher levels of altruism or whether factors related to the education experience increased altruism.

In many countries the shortage of professors is a hurdle in expanding preservice education to rural sites. One solution is to expand rural-based preservice education through information and communication technology, particularly Internet-based learning. As broadband Internet and cell phone coverage grow in Africa, distance education becomes more viable. Lectures could be broadcast on the Internet or prerecorded on DVDs. Health science schools, in the same country or even several countries, can pool and share faculty. Students training in rural district capitals could take advantage of teaching by specialists in centers of excellence in the capital. Even basic technologies, such as cell phones, can support the supervision of students doing clinical rotations in rural clinics.

Collaboration among training institutions can also help expand preservice training to rural and underserved areas. The Training for Health Equity network is a collaborative of need-driven and outcome-driven medical schools in neglected, rural, and remote regions of Africa, Asia, Australia, North America, and Latin America. Its core mission is to raise the number, quality, retention, and performance of health professionals in underserved communities. Member schools direct their education, research, and service activities toward the priority health concerns of the community they serve. The network is developing and testing joint evaluation tools to assess programs' impacts on health system and community needs, including retaining graduates where they are needed the most.

Student Profile and Maldistribution of Health Workers

Students from urban areas, particularly capital cities, are greatly overrepresented in medical and nursing schools. This is the case even in countries that consider origin from an underserved population as an admissions criterion. In the only public medical school in Mozambique, 44 percent of the students are from Maputo or Maputo province, jurisdictions with only 6 percent of the country's population (Sousa and others 2007). This imbalance means fewer physicians are willing work in rural areas. Throughout Africa a career in health, especially as a physician, is seen as a means to move to the capital or to a wealthy country. The Mozambican data reveal that most medical students, even those from outside Maputo, expect to practice in an urban area. In addition, the majority of the Mozambican medical students surveyed indicated that they planned either to work exclusively in the private sector or to combine private and public practice, even if educated in public schools.

The data also show that health careers are a family business. Ninety percent of Mozambican medical students surveyed had at least one parent working in health care. This has significant implications for student recruitment. Not only do schools need to recruit more students from rural areas, but also should recruit students with a stated desire to serve underserved communities. In addition, students must shift their idea of a health care career from one of urban elitism to one of service to the underserved. Curricula should reflect this shift by integrating social justice and ethics discussions and experiences.

Conclusion

Over the next five years many resources will be invested in scaling up health worker training. These investments must be evidence-based and follow best practices (box 16.1 examines a successful program in Ethiopia). More research is needed on health worker education in Africa—high-quality research that goes beyond program descriptions to ask critically important questions about what type of health workers programs should teach, what to teach them, how to teach them, and how many of them to enroll.

WHO estimates that Sub-Saharan Africa needs to grow its number of health workers by 140 percent (around 1 million) to attain the basic coverage needed to meet the Millennium Development Goals (Anyangwe and Mtonga 2007). A concerted political effort and major investments from stakeholders—including governments, professional councils, unions, and donors—is essential to train this high number of workers to deliver quality health services in all areas of their countries.

References

Anyangwe, S., and C. Mtonga. 2007. "Inequities in the Global Health Workforce: The Greatest Impediment to Health in Sub-Saharan Africa." *International Journal of Environmental Research and Public Health* 4 (2): 93–100.

Beaglehole, R., D. Sanders, and M. Dal Poz. 2003. "The Public Health Workforce in Sub-Saharan Africa: Challenges and Opportunities." *Ethnicity and Disease* 13 (S2): S24–30.

Broadhead, R. L. 1998. "Community-Based Pediatric Curriculum: The Malawi Experience." *Annals of Tropical Paediatrics* 18: 527–32.

Capacity Project. 2007. *Developing the Health Workforce: Training Future Nurses and Midwives in Rwanda*. Voices from the Capacity Project 10. Chapel Hill, NC: Capacity Project.

————. 2009. Training Health Workers in Africa: Documenting Faith-Based Organizations contributions. Technical Brief 17. Chapel Hill, NC: Capacity Project.

Chen, L., T. Evans, S. Anand, J. I. Boufford, H. Brown, M. Chowdhury, M. Cueto, L. Dare, G. Dussault, G. Elzinga, E. Fee, D. Habte, P. Hanvoravongchai, M. Jacobs, C. Kurowski, S. Michael, A. Pablos-Mendez, N. Sewankambo, G. Solimano, B. Stilwell, A. de Waal, and S. Wibulpolprasert. 2004. "Human Resources for Health: Overcoming the Crisis." *Lancet* 364 (9449): 1984–90.

Commission on Macroeconomics and Health. 2001. *Macroeconomics and Health: Investing in Health for Economic Development*. Geneva: World Health Organization.

Crisp, N., B. Gawanas, and I. Sharp. 2008. "Training the Health Workforce: Scaling Up, Saving Lives." *Lancet* 371 (9613): 689–91.

de Vries, E., and S. Reid. 2003. "Do South African Medical Students of Rural Origin Return to Rural Practice?" *South African Medical Journal* 93 (10): 789–93.

Dovlo, D. 2003. "The Brain Drain and Retention of Health Professionals in Africa." Prepared for a Regional Training Conference, "Improving Tertiary Education in Sub-Saharan Africa: Things That Work." Accra, September 23–25.

Dussault, G., I. Fronteira, H. Prytherch, M. R. Dal Poz, D.Ngoma, J. Lunguzi, and K. Wyss. 2009. *Scaling Up the Stock of Health Workers: A Review*. Geneva: International Centre for Human Resources in Nursing.

Eastwood, J. B., J. Plange-Rhule, V. Parry, and S. Tomlinson. 2001. "Medical Collaborations between Developed and Developing Countries." *QJM: An International Journal of Medicine* 94 (11): 637–41.

Eckhert, N. 2002. "The Global Pipeline: Too Narrow, Too Wide or Just Right?" *Medical Education* 36: 606–13.

Gates Foundation, 2010. The Sub-Saharan African Medical School Study: Data, Observation, and Opportunity, seattle, WA: Gates Foundation.

Hagopian, A., M. J. Thompson, M. Fordyee, K. C. Johnson, and L.A. Hart. 2004. The Migration of Physicians from Sub-Saharan Africa to the United States of America: Measures of the African Brain Drain. Human Resources for Health, Dec 14, 2(1): 17.

Hagopian, A., A. Ofosu A. Fatusi, R. Biritwum, A. Essel, L. Gary Hart, and C. Watts. 2005. "The Flight of Physicians from West Africa: Views of African Physicians and Implications for Policy." *Social Science & Medicine* 61 (8): 1750–60.

Hanson, K., and Jack, W. 2010"Incentives Could Induce Ethiopian Doctors and Nurses to Work in Rural Settings." *Health Affairs* 29 (8):1452–60.

High Level Forum on the Health MDGs. 2004. "Addressing Africa's Health Workforce Crisis: An Avenue for Action." Abuja, December.

Ijsselmuiden, C. B., T. C. Nchinda, S. Duale, N. M. Tumwesigye, and D. Serwadda. 2007. "Mapping Africa's Advanced Public Health Education Capacity: The AfriHealth Project." *Bulletin of the World Health Organization* 85: 914–22.

Jacob, S., C. J. Portillo, D. Goldman, D. Winters, M. Vitiello, and Y. Konjore. 2009. "Strengthening Support for HIV Pre-Service Nursing Education in Resource-Limited Settings." Paper presented at the International Council of Nurses Conference, Durban, South Africa, June 27–July 4.

Leonard, K. L., and M. C. Masatu. 2010. "Professionalism and the know-do gap: exploring intrinsic mottivation among health workers in Tanzania." Health Econ. Dec, 19(2): 1461–77.

Kawooya, M. G., B. B. Goldberg, W. De Groot, P. D. Matovu, E. K. Malwadde, and O. H. Baltarowich. 2010. "Evaluation of US training for the Past 6 Years at ECUREI, the World Federation for Ultrasound in Medicine and Biology Centre of Excellence, Kampala, Uganda." *Academic Radiology* 17 (3): 392–98.

Kemp, J., and J. Tindiweegi. 2001. "Nurse Education in Mbarara, Uganda." *Journal of Advanced Nursing* 33 (1): 8–12.

Kinfu, Y., M. R. Dal Poz, H. Mercer, and D. B. Evans. 2009. "The Health Worker Shortage in Africa: Are Enough Physicians and Nurses Being Trained?" *Bulletin of the World Health Organization* 87: 225–230.

Longombe, A. O. 2009. "Medical Schools in Rural Areas—Necessity or Aberration?" *Rural and Remote Health* 9 (3): 1131.

Lugina, H. 2006. *Human Resources for Health: Situation Analysis in Seven ECSA Countries*. Arusha, Tanzania: Health Community Human Resources Development and Capacity Building.

Macdonagh, R., M. Jiddawit, and V. Parry. 2002. "Twinning the Future of Sustainable Collaboration." *BJU International* 89 (S1): 13–17.

Mæstad, O., G. Torsvik, and A. Aakvik. 2010. "Overworked? On the Relationship between Workload and Health Worker Performance." *Journal of Health Economics* 29 (5): 686–98.

Naiker, S., J. Plange-Rhule, R. C. Tutt, and J. B. Eastwood. 2009. "Shortage of Healthcare Workers in Developing Countries—Africa." *Ethnicity & Disease* 19 (S1): 60–64.

Oman K., B. Khwa-Otsyula, G. Majoor, R. Einterz, and A. Wasteson. 2007. "Working Collaboratively to Support Medical Education in Developing

Countries: The Case of the Friends of Moi University Faculty of Health Sciences." *Education for Health* 20 (1): 12.

Ozden, C. 2010. "Ghanaian Physicians Abroad and at Home." Development Economics Research Group. World Bank, Washington, DC.

Parry, E., and V. Parry. 1998. "Training for Tropical Health in Developing Countries: The Work of the Tropical Health and Education Trust." *Medical Education* 32: 630–635.

Sousa, F., J. Schwalbach, A. Yussuf, L. Gonçalves, and P. Ferrinho 2007. "The Training and Expectations of Medical Students in Mozambique." *Human Resources for Health* 5 (11).

Sridhar, M. 2000. "What is the Future of Training Overseas Graduates?" *British Medical Journal* 321: 307.

Welsh, C. 2001. "Training Overseas Doctors in the United Kingdom." *British Medical Journal* 321: 253–54.

WHO (World Health Organization). 2006. *The World Health Report 2006: Working Together for Health*. Geneva: WHO.

CHAPTER 17

Becoming a Health Worker Student

Petra Righetti, Roger Strasser, Peter Materu, and Christopher H. Herbst

Successful recruitment into health science education programs depends on high-quality secondary education and future career options to attract motivated applicants. Beyond an adequate supply of well-prepared students, successful health science training programs require capable institutions. In most cases the number of applicants to health programs exceeds the admission rate by 70 percent, demonstrating that limited institutional capacity is a barrier to greater access to medical and health science education. This capacity deficit is reflected in a lack of equipment, infrastructure, and teachers throughout Sub-Saharan Africa. Government and other institutions can increase the accessibility and quality of tertiary health education programs in three main ways. They can improve science education in secondary schools. They can provide better remuneration to health workers. And they can boost institutional capacity by lowering the costs of health training programs through modular courses, distance learning, and localized training in rural areas.

Health Science Education in Context

The path to employment as a health worker starts with enrolling in a health education program. Most Sub-Saharan countries face lower enrollments in health science fields than in other tertiary programs, contributing to the overall shortage of health workers. This chapter addresses three components of health science education enrollment. First, it examines constraints on enrollment from the student perspective, considering students' academic preparation, their perceptions of the private returns to tertiary health science education, and the financial and time barriers to health science education. Second, it examines constraints on enrollment from an institutional perspective, highlighting the capacity and resource gaps that hinder institutions' ability to absorb students. Third, it reviews the government's role in supporting broader access for students and greater institutional capacity through targeted policies.

To understand the causes of health worker shortages, it is important to look at the wider health service and education contexts. In most African countries the majority of people live in rural areas. Frontline health care providers in these areas are not registered nurses or doctors but practical nurses and medical assistants. To the extent possible, this chapter addresses admissions into education programs for these mid-level health workers, as well as doctors and nurses. The training of frontline and mid-level health workers often takes place informally, however, and documentation is scarce. So, this chapter draws conclusions primarily from official health systems and formal tertiary training, which have available documentation.[1]

African countries inherited hierarchical education systems designed for the elite. Most education systems have changed little since the colonial era, despite capacity and quality issues caused by more recent socioeconomic and political developments. Sub-Saharan Africa's youth population, growing rapidly, is now more than four times its 1950 level. In response to the changing demographics, the international community has shifted funding from tertiary education to lower education. As more students complete secondary education, demand for tertiary education increases (table 17.1). The growth of enrollments in tertiary education in Africa is now the highest in the world—16.3 percent average annual growth for 1999–2004 compared with 6.6 percent in the rest of the world (World Bank 2010).

From 1980 to 2000, as tertiary education rates grew, Sub-Saharan Africa experienced economic decline and austerity. University budgets shrank or stagnated amid rising enrollments and inflation. From 1991 to 2006 the mean ratio between the average increase in enrollments and the increase in resources was 1.45. In the rest of the world public financing has generally kept pace with growth in higher education students. Sub-Saharan Africa is the only region with a decline in the volume of public expenditure per student at the tertiary level (30 percent over the last 15 years). Unit costs fluctuated from $6,800 in 1980 to $1,200 in 2002 and to $2,000 in 2006 (World Bank 2010).

Table 17.1   Enrollments in Tertiary Education in Sub-Saharan Africa, 1991–2004

Country	Average annual growth of tertiary enrollment (%)			Total growth
	1991–96	1996–99	1999–2004	1991–2004
Sub-Saharan Africa (regional total)	7.5	10.1	8.7	189.5
Central Africa	4.7	2.4	9	108
East Africa	6.2	10.2	8.4	170.9
Southern Africa	8	−2.5	2.8	56.7
West Africa	9	26.4	12.1	448.3

Source: World Bank 2010.

The shortages in financial and human capacity hit schools of medicine and nursing, which are comparatively expensive, particularly hard (World Bank 2008f). Clinical specialties—which require adequate facilities, close supervision during training, and other expensive inputs—were also affected by cost constraints in the education system.

The private provision of higher education is expanding in response to limited public financing. Even so, private providers remain on the periphery. Tertiary institutions that are not universities are the fastest-growing private providers and generally emphasize law, social sciences, and economics and business, because of their lower start-up costs (World Bank 2008a). Usually located in urban areas, private institutions undertake little research and tend to respond to student interest rather than labor market demand (World Bank 2008a). For these reasons, their role is limited in the provision of health science programs.

Enrollment Patterns in Health Science

Despite the large increase in demand for higher education, tertiary enrollment ratios in the region are low, ranging from 1 percent in several countries to 17 percent in Mauritius, with the majority somewhere between 2 and 4 percent.[2] These numbers are attributable to socioeconomic inequality, gender inequality, low secondary enrollment, increased cost-sharing, poor institutional capacity, and high graduate unemployment.

In this already constrained context, health science faculties register particularly low student intakes compared with other fields (figure 17.1). Among the countries analyzed, South Africa currently enrolls the most health science students (51,720), followed by the Democratic Republic of Congo (13,019), Tanzania (3,991), Zimbabwe (3,086), and Madagascar (2,671). Swaziland enrolls the least at 386 (Kotecha 2008).

Figure 17.1   Number of Students (All Levels of Study) per Major Field of Study in Selected African Countries

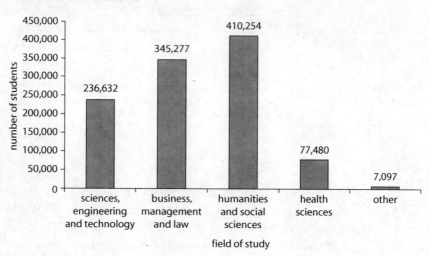

Source: Kotecha 2008.
Note: Figures represent the sum of totals for Angola, Botswana, Democratic Republic of Congo, Lesotho, Madagascar, Malawi, Mauritius, Mozambique, Namibia, South Africa, Swaziland, Tanzania, Zambia, and Zimbabwe.

Tertiary enrollments are especially low relative to country populations (table 17.2). Among 20–24 year olds an average of 95 percent of eligible individuals do not have access to tertiary education. Of the 4 percent enrolled in tertiary programs, only 5.6 percent study health sciences. The Democratic Republic of Congo (18.9 percent), Malawi (11.1 percent), and Tanzania (11.4 percent) have the largest intake of students in health sciences among the countries analyzed.

Constraints on the Supply of Health Worker Students

Enrollment in health science programs in Africa is affected by the student applicant pool in three ways. First, secondary schools do not adequately prepare students in math and science, fields central to health science programs. Second, the financial and time costs of health worker education are often prohibitively high, presenting a barrier to otherwise qualified applicants. Third, students perceive the benefits and drawbacks of health education differently. In some countries employment in the health sector is considered prestigious, but in others the sector struggles with wage and workload issues that make health education less desirable.

Table 17.2   Enrollment in Tertiary Education and Health Sciences, by Relevant Age Group

Country	Population aged 20–24 (2010) (thousands)	Numbers in tertiary education	Numbers in health science (undergraduate)	Percent of relevant age group in tertiary education	Percent of tertiary education group in health science (undergraduate)
Angola	1,723	47,373	1,394	2.75	2.94
Botswana	215	15,710	346	7.31	2.20
Congo, Dem. Rep.	6,071	57,664	10,880	0.95	18.87
Lesotho	230	8,508	no data	3.70	no data
Madagascar	1,937	41,691	2,077	2.15	4.98
Malawi	1,325	7,869	873	0.59	11.09
Mauritius	95	9,720	427	10.23	4.39
Mozambique	2,100	46,865	1,201	2.23	2.56
Namibia	233	8,378	63	3.60	0.75
South Africa	4,720	746,538	36,389	15.82	4.87
Swaziland	153	5,785	386	3.78	6.67
Tanzania	4,322	33,420	3,823	0.77	11.44
Zambia	1,339	14,395	755	1.08	5.24
Zimbabwe	1,674	52,453	2,587	3.13	4.93
Total	26,137	1,096,369	61,201	4.19	5.58

Source: Data from SARUA and Edstats.

Secondary Education's Impact on Tertiary Health Studies

To understand the low intake of health science students, it is important to examine the outcomes of the secondary education systems that produce potential tertiary students. The portion of students who complete secondary education in most African countries does not exceed 20 percent and in many cases is close to 5 percent or lower.[3] Students who complete secondary education are generally from the highest income quintile, so the pool of graduates is small and inequitable. Despite the exponential increase in enrollments at all levels, access to secondary and tertiary education in Sub-Saharan Africa remains more highly restricted than in other regions.

Students in Sub-Saharan Africa perform poorly in secondary leaving exams, especially in disciplines requiring higher cognitive skills, such as math and sciences. Based on documented exams, the majority of students in the region pass in the lowest category (World Bank 2008d). Three Sub-Saharan countries participated in the 2003 Trends in International Mathematics and Sciences Study, which measured student ability in math and science. These three countries—Botswana, Ghana, and South Africa—came in last with the overall lowest scores (World Bank 2008d). Low performance in math and science may orient students, either by choice or by default, away from medicine to less scientific faculties, such as humanities and social science.

Although science and math scores are low, secondary schools emphasize math and science in their curricula. Science and math are compulsory at junior secondary and senior secondary levels in all countries, which means that every secondary-school student takes three to four years of science and math (World Bank 2007). Senior secondary schools offer elective science courses, including biology, physics, chemistry, physical science, and science and technology (World Bank 2007).

The Financial and Time Costs of Medical Education

The higher fees and longer duration of health science studies compared with other faculties can deter enrollment in health science programs. Health science schools are costly because the required technology, laboratories, and practical training limit enrollment capacity (World Bank 2008c). A study of Chad, Madagascar, Mauritania, Niger, and Rwanda shows that unit costs of scientific programs in public institutions are on average 1.8 times higher than those of other programs (humanities, social science, other) (World Bank 2008c). At Uganda's Makerere University School of Public Health, local students pay $2,500 per year in tuition plus an additional $5,000 in registration fees, examination fees, travel, accommodation, stationery, books, and computers.[4] These costs are an impossible burden for many potential students given Uganda's average per capita income of around $1,200. Even training programs for mid-level cadres have high fees relative to income per capita (table 17.3). Because financing mechanisms such as scholarships and loans are limited,

Table 17.3   Training Costs per Year for Nonphysician Clinicians in Selected Sub-Saharan Countries

	Training costs per year in US$ (tuition plus room and board)/year	Length of training (years)
Ethiopia	1,200–1,500	3
Ghana	4,000	1
Malawi	2,000	3
Tanzania	1,300–2,000	3
Zambia	1,000–1,500	3

Source: Mullan and Frehywot 2007.

there are few opportunities for lower socioeconomic groups to finance their studies.

In addition to their high costs, medical programs require significant investments in time. Senegal's two public universities offer medical programs that last four to eight years. In Kenya medical education for doctors lasts five to six years. The long duration and traditional pedagogy in medical schools partly explains why these programs are unappealing to students. Students may find the opportunity cost of a six-year investment in an expensive education too high.

The Role of Student Perceptions in Health Science Education Enrollment

Student perception of health science professions are mixed and vary according to the specific profession. Medical degrees are traditionally considered prestigious. For countries like the Democratic Republic of Congo, Tanzania, and Malawi (see table 17.2), the higher number of students choosing the medical track correlates with the prestige and security of a medical position. At the University of Ghana, for example, students' consistent first choice is the medicine program.[5]

Students generally perceive the labor market for health workers as a source of guaranteed employment. Job assurance is a valued component in a student's choice of faculty, especially given the struggles in many African economies to absorb graduates. Moreover, the medical track is associated with high future incomes, especially if the student ends up in private practice. Finally, the possibility of working overseas motivates many future doctors and nurses.

But in some countries the labor market for health professionals is perceived as struggling—with relative wage rigidity, heavy workloads, and a lack of facilities, promotion opportunities, and supervisory support (WHO 2006). Nursing and mid-level health professions are considered especially dangerous, isolated, and low paid (WHO 2006). As wages in the public sector remain low, many health workers must supplement their government salary to repay student loans by taking on second jobs in private practice or nonmedical fields.

Students' exposure to health care systems and medical role models when growing up also affects their perceptions of health sciences. Students apply for medical and nursing programs because they are familiar with doctors and nurses. They may have little information about or experience with the wider range of available health professions, a knowledge deficit that can contribute to the lower intake of health professionals in some countries. Classroom case studies also affect student perceptions. Recent studies show that education experiences can shape personal values and choices. Examples of health workers in rural areas or different professions in the medical field influence students' career choices (Kaye, Mwanika, and Sewankambo 2010).

Applicants to tertiary studies in Sub-Saharan Africa can now choose from a greater variety of institutions than ever. In response to growing demand, private education has exploded in the region, including specialized institutions that focus on distance (World Bank 2008a). In Ghana alone, private universities' share of enrollment shot up from 4 percent to almost 20 percent in the last four years. In the last five years nine private universities opened in Ghana (Ministry of Education of Ghana 2008). The private sector can offer short professional training programs at low cost. Moreover, private institutions can provide learning opportunities through distance learning or open-source programs, which in theory have lower operating costs than face-to-face learning (World Bank 2008c). The overall growth in education choices influences health science enrollment: when applicants are spread over many options, those applying to any single program decline.

The "feminization" of some health professions also affects health science enrollment rates and patterns. Women may be less attracted to physician training in regions where it is viewed by society as incompatible with traditional values and family assignments (box 17.1). They may be drawn instead to nursing, often perceived as more in line with traditional gender roles. Women may also gravitate to nurse training rather than physician training because of gender-related disparities in investments throughout the education system. The regional average gender parity index at the junior secondary level is 0.84. At the senior secondary level it is 0.89, meaning that fewer women finish secondary education and thus are eligible for tertiary (World Bank 2008b). Those who access tertiary education tend to enroll in nursing and midwifery schools, which require less qualification, funding, and time. When access to education increases, including access to math and science at the secondary level, women choose medical and nursing schools in greater numbers. In Canada, Australia, and the United States the number of female doctors exceeds males. In South Africa women outnumber men in nursing, obstetrics, and physiotherapy.[6]

Box 17.1

Physician Education in South Africa, with an Emphasis on Women

Since 1994 higher education policy in South Africa has been committed to equity of access, irrespective of race and gender. Researchers investigated progress toward these goals for physician education, with an emphasis on gender. They used databases from the Department of Education, the Health Professions Council of South Africa, and the University of Cape Town Faculty of Health Sciences to explore undergraduate trends at all eight medical schools, and postgraduate trends at University of Cape Town.

Women have outnumbered men in medical undergraduate enrollments since 2000, with figures ranging from 52–63 percent at seven of the eight medical schools in 2005. The rate of change in the medical profession lags behind, however, and it will take more than two decades for female doctors to outnumber male doctors. A study of University of Cape Town postgraduate enrollments shows that women increased to 42 percent of postgraduate medical enrollments in 2005. Female postgraduate students concentrated in disciplines such as pediatrics and psychiatry, making up 11 percent of enrollments in the surgical disciplines between 1999 and 2005. Overall, reforms support the changing profile of medical enrollments and highlight questions about women's career choices and the social factors influencing these choices.

Source: Brier and Wildschut 2008

Capacity and Financial Constraints on Enrollment

Health science institutions in Sub-Saharan Africa are limited in their capacity to enroll students. As student numbers grew in recent years, infrastructure and staff numbers remained the same or even dropped. In 2007 there were only 493 full-time faculty in public health in Africa (854 when part-time staff are counted). In 2005 there were only 42 doctoral students and 55 master's students in public health in Sub-Saharan Africa (Ijsselmuiden and others 2007). These numbers do not reflect doctoral and postdoctoral students who either train outside Sub-Saharan Africa or train informally through doctoral-level programs that are not accredited or institutionalized. South Africa trains specialists from other countries, and has agreements with other governments for improved student mobility and international accreditation.[7]

The lack of adequate funding affects the teaching and research capacity of health science institutions by limiting their ability to offer faculty adequate remuneration and to invest in new infrastructure, research facilities, and equipment. According to 2007 World Health Organization figures, 29 of Africa's 53 countries offer no postgraduate training in public health. Eleven countries (20.7 percent) have one program and an equal number offer more than one program (Ijsselmuiden and others 2007). Anglophone Sub-Saharan countries and North African countries have more developed postgraduate public health training programs than Francophone, Lusophone, and the one Hispanic country in Africa. The largest gap is in the Lusophone group, where 91 percent of the population lives in a country without graduate public health programs. Thirty-four percent of Francophone Africans live in a country without a graduate public health programs (Ijsselmuiden and others 2007). In Uganda most higher education teaching posts remain empty because of low salaries and unattractive benefits (INHEA). In Zimbabwe the medical faculty sought to reduce its enrollment from 120 students to 70 because of the lack of lecturers (Meldrum 2003). Low numbers of qualified teachers is one of the major reasons universities in Rwanda restrict admissions into specialized programs (Sy 2008).

As a result of both low institutional capacity to absorb the growing number of applicants and poor academic preparation of candidates, schools and faculties restrict access to safeguard quality. In Uganda the number of candidates eligible to enter university rose 12 percent annually from 1994 to 1999. The total rise in the number of candidates with two advanced passes (the mark of eligibility to enter university) in the same period was more than 50 percent. In 2000 the number of eligible candidates surged to 24,000 (INHEA. Even secondary institutions have started limiting the intake of students from lower to upper secondary. The transition rate from junior to senior secondary education declined from 72 percent to 60 percent, reflecting more selectivity in the face of a rapid increase in junior secondary graduates (UNESCO 2009).

A similar pattern occurs in health sciences. In Tanzania the Muhimbili University College of Health Sciences enrolled only 43 percent of applicants in 2004–05 (table 17.4). In Ghana too, health training institutions across different disciplines are unable to accommodate a much larger supply of qualified secondary students, which exceeds the capacity of schools to enroll, train and produce them (figure 17.2). Schools have limited fiscal capacity to invest and expand their capacities in an environment where most public institutions charge low or no tuition (Appiah

Table 17.4   Applied and Admitted Candidates for Muhimbili University College of Health Sciences, Tanzania

School	2000/01		2002/03		2003/04		2004/05	
	Applied	Admitted	Applied	Admitted	Applied	Admitted	Applied	Admitted
Medicine	269	150	357	179	336	183	388	185
Dentistry	30	30	36	6	46	44	52	47
Pharmacy	124	29	102	44	133	35	186	80
Nursing	20	23	24	25	22	19	25	25
Public health	34	21	37	22	60	35	43	30
Total	477	253	556	276	597	316	186	80
Percent admitted	53		49.6		52.9		43	

Source: Muhimbili University College of Health Sciences website, Facts and Figures.

Figure 17.2   Applicants and Enrollment at Selected Health Training Institutions in Ghana, 2008

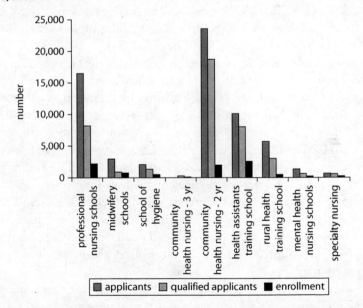

Source: Appiah, E; Herbst, C; Soucat, A, 2012: Human Resources for Health In Ghana: Towards Evidence based Interventions, 2012, Directions in Development, World Bank, forthcoming.

et al. 2012). In Benin the government halted admissions of new students to the national midwifery and nursing schools for two years, claiming concern about the declining quality of applicants (Lemière 2008). In many countries the demand for enrollment into health sciences by eligible students is greater than the capacity of institutions to absorb them.

Promising Government and Institutional Interventions

Several governments are intervening to correct the access and quality challenges in the tertiary sector, particularly in health science faculties. Some interventions achieve substantial results and can encourage similar solutions in other countries.

From the early 2000s, Ghana increased the average remuneration for all public sector employees by 44 percent to make public service more attractive. Remuneration for Ghana Education Services staff was the largest component of the wage bill, increasing by 23 percent. Remuneration of health service staff increased by 181 percent. In addition, the government is attempting to alter enrollment distributions to favor science and technology fields. Today, 70 percent of students study humanities and social sciences and only 30 percent study science and technology. The government is trying to reverse these numbers by changing the structure of programs and distribution of students to reach 70 percent enrollment in science and technology. Science and technology graduates will likely have better employment prospects and contribute more to the development process of the country (World Bank 2008e).

Countries are piloting new methods to provide greater training to medical and mid-level health students at lower costs, with a focus on localized training and contextual learning. Evidence shows that curricula should be linked to the local context in which students will practice. Although evident, this approach was not applied (Strasser and Neusy 2010). Community-based training, socially responsive education, and a range of apprenticeship models are being tested in a number of countries to reach rural areas. A focus on mid-level professionals lowers costs and supports competitive pricing (UNESCO 2008). Ghana's five-year work program stresses scaling up mid-level cadres, particularly nurses and midwives, and improving their salaries and benefits (Beciu 2010). Other countries have also intensified their mid-level health workers training.

New technologies and broadband connectivity bring innovative options for learning and knowledge sharing. Open-source and distance learning can ease coverage constraints in remote areas. Many countries are testing these options, and the benefits must still be analyzed in light of the required financial investments. The results of these innovative methods should be benchmarked to education standards.

Ethiopia's Ministry of Health, in partnership with the Open University in the United Kingdom, is piloting open and distance learning medical training with students at St. Paul's Millennium Medical School in Addis Ababa, which opened in 2008. The program consists of a "blended learning" curriculum that will combine hands-on training with study through learning resources, including printed materials, interactive DVDs and CDs, and videos of lectures and demonstrations (Open University n.d.). In Kenya the African Medical and Research Foundation offers computer-based distance education to 4,500 nurses through a network of 127 schools and E-Centers. Enrolled students work toward certification as registered nurses using a mix of computer and clinical learning. These hybrid methods provide access to students in rural areas without imposing relocation costs. They also extend specialized skills in rural areas. Countries like Kenya, Nigeria, and Tanzania, which have a high dispersion of their nursing pool, are ideally suited for this model. In Kenya and Tanzania talent is spread across six to seven major regions. These regions usually have a commercial hub or major hospital that can afford computers and instruction equipment (IFC 2008).

At the secondary level governments are intervening to include compulsory science at both junior and senior levels. Greater demand for higher level skills often drives these reforms. Countries are moving toward knowledge-based economic development, which requires higher cognitive skills. The main constraint to executing these reforms is the lack of qualified teachers, textbooks, and equipment at the secondary level. As highlighted earlier, the low test results of African countries in international benchmarking exams expose the poor implementation of these reforms.

Some countries are designing health science faculties that offer multiple subdisciplines and cross-subsidization with other faculties. Since most forms of medical education require similar fixed investments in laboratories, medical equipment, and buildings, schools that have multidisciplinary courses can become financially sustainable through cross-subsidies. By offering multiple disciplines and sharing facilities with other faculties, they can increase the overall volume of students and amortize their capital costs over a larger revenue base. There are also examples of self-standing medical institutes that provide different health programs. Herbert Kairuki University, a nonprofit, fully accredited private medical university in Dar es Salaam, offers multiple degrees in courses ranging from holistic medicine to graduate courses toward a medical degree. It even has its own teaching hospital. This type of solution requires government support through regulations that facilitate private education while maintaining strict quality standards and student loan financing systems (UNESCO 2008). Similar solutions that take advantage of economies of scale are being adopted in Swaziland.

Conclusion

Successful recruitment into education programs for health workers requires high-quality education and rewarding career pathways. In addition, graduates of these programs must have the requisite skills and inclination to provide health care to the populations with greatest needs.

With the number of applicants exceeding admission rates by 70 percent in most countries, one of the main barriers to increased medical and health science education is the limited institutional capacity of these faculties, expressed by the lack of equipment, infrastructure, and teachers.

Greater access to tertiary health science schools will depend on government regulations that broaden institutions' autonomy to pay competitive salaries, set tuition fees, and establish programs that adopt new methods of teaching and learning. Government regulations should also enable institutions to respond to economic needs through mechanisms such as short-term programs for mid-level health workers. As institutions gain autonomy, governments should assure the maintenance of quality standards and provide financing for lower socioeconomic groups. Governments should also encourage the involvement of more private education providers, which can help close the gap between applications and enrollments. A priority for governments should be facilitating the involvement of private providers while regulating and monitoring their performance since there often are more private institutions than public institutions in Sub-Saharan Africa (UNESCO 2008).

The focus on scaling up health workforce education is not just about resourcing "more of the same." In most cases, frontline health care providers in Africa are not registered nurses or doctors, but practical nurses and medical assistants. Education initiatives should focus on graduating health workers who will strengthen the local health care system—consistent with evidence showing that students recruited from rural and underserved areas, and educated in that context, are more likely to choose a career in a rural setting (Strasser and Neusy 2010). Recruitment into health worker education programs should be part of a wider system that supports health workers so they can care for their own people in rural and underserved areas.

Notes

1. The number of admissions into health training programs does not equal the number of health professionals available in the future. Health workers may leave the profession or emigrate. Because of this uncertainty, the numbers in this chapter might be skewed.

2. See SARUA (2009) for comparison, gross enrollment rates in Organisation for Economic Co-operation and Development countries average 60 percent.

3. http://epdc.org/static/Retention.pdf.

4. http://www.musph.ac.ug/programmes_mhsr.html.

5. Authors' interviews, University of Ghana.

6. Prof. Ian Couper, Chair of Rural Health in the Wits Faculty of Health Sciences, written comments.

7. Prof. Ian Couper, Chair of Rural Health in the Wits Faculty of HealthSciences, written comments.

References

Beciu, H. 2009. Capacity of health training institutions in Mozambique. Draft technical report, Washington, DC, World Bank, unpublished.

Beciu, H. 2010. "Pre-Investment Studies in Ghana, Mozambique and Sierra Leone." Draft., World Bank, Washington, DC.

Brier, M., and A. Wildschut. 2008. "Changing Gender Profile of Medical Schools in South Africa." *South African Medical Journal* 98 (7): 557–60.

IFC (International Finance Corporation). 2008. *The Business of Health in Africa: Partnering with the Private Sector to Improve People's Lives.* Washington, DC: IFC. www.ifc.org/ifcext/healthinafrica.nsf/AttachmentsByTitle/IFC_Healthin Africa_Annex5/$FILE/IFC_HealthinAfrica_Annex5.pdf.

Ijsselmuiden, C. B., T. C. Nchinda, S. Duale, N. M. Tumwesigye, and D. Serwadda. 2007. "Mapping Africa's Advanced Public Health Education Capacity: The AfriHealth Project." *Bulletin of the World Health Organization* 85 (12): 914–22.

INHEA: http://www.bc.edu/bc_org/avp/soe/cihe/inhea/profiles/Uganda.htm

Kaye, D. K., A. Mwanika, and N. Sewankambo. 2010. "Influence of the Training Experience of Makerere University Medical and Nursing Graduates on Willingness and Competence to Work in Rural Health Facilities." *Rural and Remote Health* 10: 1372.

Kotecha, P., ed. 2008. *Towards a Common Future: Higher Education in the SADC Region.* Johannesburg: Southern African Regional Universities Association.

Lemière 2008. Benin HRH analysis, working paper, Washington DC, World Bank, Unpublished.

Meldrum, A. 2003. "'Mugabe Says We Are Being Stolen. All We Want Is Better Pay': The Brain Drain Has Badly Hit Zimbabwe's Fragile Health Service." *The Observer* (United Kingdom), August 10. http://www.guardian.co.uk/uk/2003/aug/10/zimbabwe.nhs?INTCMP=SRCH.

Ministry of Education of Ghana. 2008. *Education Sector Performance Report 2008*. Accra: Ministry of Education of Ghana.

Mullan, F., and S. Frehywot. 2007. "Nonphysician Clinicians in 47 Sub-Saharan African Countries." *Lancet* 370 (9605): 2158–63.

Muhimbili university of Health and Allied Sciences: http://www.musph.ac.ug/programmes_mhsr.html

Open University. n.d. *OU in Africa: Open to and for Africa*. Milton Keynes, U.K.: Open University. www.open.ac.uk/africa/index.shtm.

SARUA (Southern African Regional Universities Association). 2009. *SARUA Handbook 2009: A Guide to the Public Universities of Southern Africa*. Johannesburg: SARUA.

Strasser, R., and A. J. Neusy. 2010. "Context Counts: Training Health Workers in and for Rural and Remote Areas." *Bulletin of the World Health Organization* 88 (10): 717–96.

Sy, A. 2008. Analysis of health reduction capacity in Rwanda, working paper, Washington DC, World Bank, Unpublished.

UNESCO (United Nations Educational, Scientific and Cultural Organization). 2008. Paris, UNESCO.

UNESCO (United Nations Educational, Scientific and Cultural Organization). 2009. *A New Dynamic: Private Higher Education*. Paris: UNESCO.

World Bank. 2007. *Developing Science, Mathematics and ICT Education in Sub-Saharan Africa*. Washington, DC: World Bank.

World Bank. 2008a. *Accelerating Catch-up: Tertiary Education for Growth in Sub-Saharan Africa*. Washington, DC: World Bank.

World Bank. 2008b. *At the Cross Roads, Choices for Secondary Education in Sub-Saharan Africa*. Washington, DC: World Bank.

World Bank. 2008c. *Costs and Financing of Higher Education in Francophone Africa*. Washington, DC: World Bank.

World Bank. 2008d. *Curricula, Examinations and Assessments in Secondary Education in Sub-Saharan Africa*. Washington, DC: World Bank.

World Bank. 2008e. *Ghana Job Creation and Skills Development*. Draft Report. Washington, DC: World Bank.

World Bank. 2008f. *Higher Education in Developing Countries: Peril and Promise.* Washington, DC: World Bank.

World Bank. 2010. *Financing Higher Education in Africa*, Draft Report. Washington, DC: World Bank.

World Health Organization. 2006. The World Health report, 2006 – Working together for Health; Geneva, World Health Organization.

CHAPTER 18

Paying for Higher Education Reform in Health

Alexander Preker, Hortenzia Beciu, Paul Jacob Robyn, Seth Ayettey, and James Antwi

This chapter reviews the economics of scaling up education for health workers in Sub-Saharan Africa. It considers four interlinked issues. First, the chapter examines the varying costs, both initial and recurrent, of increasing the number of health workers trained. Second, it explores potential sources for the additional financing needed to scale up training, including the amounts required under alternative scenarios. Third, the chapter evaluates whether it is possible for countries to get better value for their money in health worker production through different financing and aid mechanisms. Fourth, it reviews some of the regulatory constraints on improved financing of health education. The chapter lays out some policy options for reform and scenarios for future spending and financing trends. It provides regional estimates for Africa and relies on specific examples from Ghana while drawing on relevant examples from the United States and other countries.

The delivery of health care is labor intensive (Mandel and Weber 2006), and the production of a qualified health workforce is capital intensive. With major health worker shortages in both developing and developed countries, policy makers everywhere are trying to determine how to scale up the production of health workers (Scheffler 2008; Scheffler and others 2009). There is a considerable body of work on estimating health worker labor market targets (Scheffler and others 2010; Soucat and Scheffler, forthcoming; WHO 2006), but few analyses examine the recurrent and capital cost implications for training institutions and partnering ministries.[1] This chapter addresses that omission by examining the cost implications of scaled-up health education.

The Cost of Training Health Workers

Several factors are relevant to estimating the cost of scaling up health worker education. These include the training institution's recurrent operating costs and the associated investment costs before and during the scale-up. The number of students trained and the time required to graduate additional health workers also affect training costs (Preker and others 2008).

The total recurrent operating costs of scaling up health worker education are based on the average cost of training existing students, the marginal cost of training additional students, and the total number of students trained. Total capital investment costs are based on initial investment, the depreciation of assets over time, the investment cost of increased intake, and the shadow cost of access to free or highly subsidized capital. The total number of students depends on enrollment, the dropout rate, student transfers, course repeaters, and the output of students. The time frame required for scaling up health worker production will vary according to the time needed to invest in improved standards or grow production capacity, and the time to train a student in a specific program.

This section examines two variables that determine total health worker training costs: recurrent expenditures and total investment. For both analyses, Ghana is a useful case study.

Recurrent Expenditures in Training Health Workers

In many countries the cost of training is only a small part of overall health care spending (Association of American Medical Colleges 2011). Among U.S. schools, public and private, an average of 3.5 percent of schools' revenues come from tuition (Association of American Medical Colleges 2011). In Organisation for Economic Co-operation and Development countries, only 2 percent of total health expenditures is spent on the recurrent cost of educating health workers (Simoens and Hurst 2006). African countries follow a similar pattern, with one considerable difference: the cost of undergraduate education is often borne by at least one ministry (the ministry of health or education), with support from development partners and nongovernmental organizations. These contributions are rarely captured in subsequent cost analyses.

Because medical education straddles both the education and health sectors, quantifying the overall recurrent expenditure is complex. The analysis should consider how the costs of laboratories, utilities, infrastructure maintenance, teacher salaries, administrative and fixed overhead, and educational and reference material are divided between the two sectors (Beciu and others 2009; GHWA 2010). In preservice settings, some infrastructure facilities used for training or housing health students are shared with other university students. Similarly, the infrastructure for in-service training is typically shared with service delivery programs. As a result, it is difficult to separate the costs of training health workers from the costs of training other university students, or of providing health care services.

In most developing countries there is no clear picture of the cost elements and figures associated with undergraduate and postgraduate education. The authors of this chapter, in their study of Ghana, analyzed the cost of scaling up health worker education at a national level with data on capital and recurrent expenditures from a sample of training organizations, supplemented with data from Ministry of Health and Ministry of Education. The information gleaned may be useful to other countries in the region that are exploring ways to increase their output of health workers.

Recurrent expenditures in context: The Ghana case. Estimated training costs for health workers in Ghana vary according to their cadre (table 18.1). With the exception of professional training for doctors and dentists, and bachelor-level training for nurses, the estimated training costs include only the direct cost of preservice training. The costs for training doctors, dentists, and bachelor-level nurses also include the indirect overhead and operating costs shared with the institutions that provide tertiary education during the preclinical phase of the training. Lack of detailed data on indirect costs at the university level for all cadres makes it difficult to reliably attribute the indirect costs of universities' fixed overhead. To facilitate the analysis, the authors assumed a 25 percent overhead cost for each institution.

Many of the professional training institutions surveyed said that expenditures were considerably below the level needed for quality teaching. For medical schools the respondents felt that current spending was about 50 percent below necessary spending (Beciu and others 2009). When calculating training costs it is important to note that following their

Table 18.1   Expenditure on Health Training Institutions in Ghana

Profession	Years	Annual cost	Total recurrent cost (dollars)	Total capital cost	Investment ratio (percent)
Doctors	6	8,975	18,084,625	236,883	1.3
Specialists	4	10,785	3,235,500	43,000	1.3
Dental surgeons	5	7,500	1,132,500	54,307	4.8
Pharmacists	4	3,161	2,174,768	31,114	1.4
Professional nurses[a]	3	990	7,661,610	1,126,450	14.7
Midwives	3	2,376	3,466,584	72,450	2.1
Laboratory technicians	3	2,600	483,600	10,000	2.1
X-ray technologists	3	2,600	530,400	10,000	1.9
Pharmacy technicians	2	350	14,000	300	2.1
Community health nurses (certificate)	2	323	1,093,678	239,353	21.9
Health assistants	2	386	1,387,516	117,419	8.5
Medical assistants	3	500	193,000	40,000	20.7
Others	3	300	588,000	5,000	0.9
Total	n.a.	n.a.	40,045,781	1,986,276	5.0

Source: Beciu and others 2009.
Note: At the time of the study 1 Ghanaian cedi was equivalent to $1. The cost calculation is based on an average cost coming from the Ghana preinvestment study, coupled with the capital investment budget data from the Ministry of Education (National Council on Higher Education) and Ministry of Health. n.a. = not applicable
a. Combines the four categories across different costs (diploma, bachelor, and postgraduate).

preclinical education, medical students receive postgraduate in-service training at teaching hospitals and clinics. The cost of a fully trained specialist far exceeds that of his or her preclinical training. In 2008 the rector of Ghana's College of Physicians and Surgeons estimated that the average cost for postgraduate training per student a year was around $10,000.[2]

Nurse training costs vary with the level of the training institution and the number of students enrolled. It costs much more to train a nurse in a school of allied health sciences than in some of the freestanding institutions that are not part of a university. It costs less to train nurses in schools with high enrollment rates, such as those where community health nurses train.

The cost element is not the only relevant variable. Learning experiences also differ according to institution type. The real cost of training nurses and midwives at health science schools is probably higher than estimated, largely due to underspending and the indirect costs of related clinical training, which the Ghana study did not address. If hospitals pay clinical staff, as is the case for most nurse trainers, the study likely underestimates the cost of training nurses in Ghana. Physicians who work in teaching hospitals in Ghana are usually hired and paid by the university. Their costs are reflected in school expenditure sheets and thus were included in the study's estimates.

The average annual cost of training a doctor in Ghana is about nine times the cost of training a professional nurse and more than three times that of training a midwife. As Ghana moves toward middle-income status, the costs of medical education will approach those in high-income countries, though today those numbers remain far apart.

Data on aggregate trends in the cost and number of students trained in Ghana are rarely available, and those available cover only short periods. With limited data it is difficult to calculate the marginal cost of increasing enrollment. Based on selected examples, the marginal cost of increasing enrollment in settings with sufficient staffing and physical capacity should be small, because the largest costs associated with training are salaries and infrastructure. Adding a few students to a class does not raise the overall cost greatly, due to the low cost of items such as textbooks, laboratory supplies, and other variable costs. These investments do not rise commensurate with enrollment, though several directors of medical training institutions expressed views to the contrary.

The cost structure of training institutions is heavily skewed toward salaries and bonuses, especially for higher education (figure 18.1). Salaries and bonuses make up almost 90 percent of the total recurrent expenditures of medical and dental schools in Ghana. The proportion of recurrent expenditures dedicated to salaries and bonuses declines with each decrease in education level, reaching around 60 percent among schools for community health workers and health assistants. Training for health professionals is more labor intensive than other types of higher education due to the need for low teacher-student ratios, ideal for one-to-one mentoring in preclinical and clinical settings.

Ghana's health training schools rarely use foreign lecturers for training. Medical schools and schools of health sciences, which employ some full-time international teachers, were the exception. In postconflict settings universities often rely, however, on short- and long-term contracts with international teachers to cover core disciplines. Higher labor costs and smaller student numbers relative to fixed overhead combine to drive up the cost of medical education in these countries. Given the high salaries and prevalence of international teachers, and the ratio of nonteaching staff to teaching staff (in some cases 2 to 1) (Bankya and Elu 2001), the costs associated with medical education are very high.

Figure 18.1   Cost Structure of Health Training Institutions in Ghana

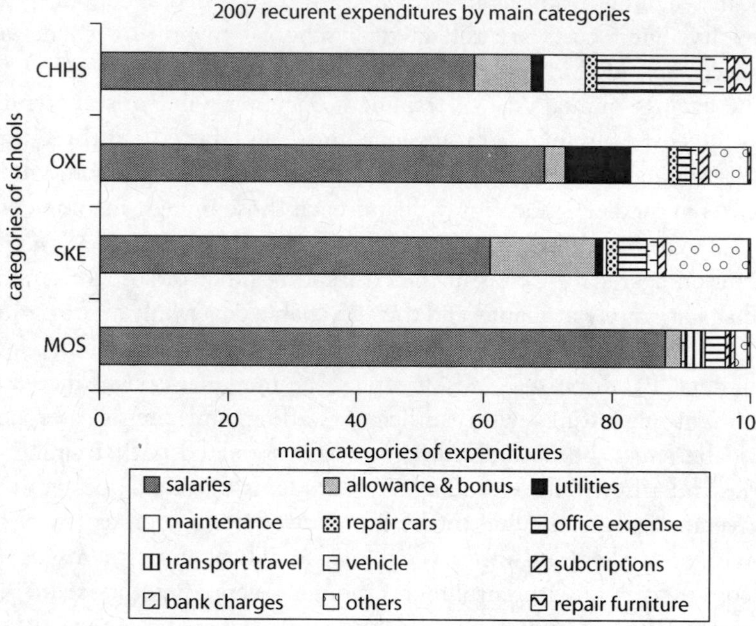

2007 recurent expenditures by main categories

Source: Beciu and others 2009.

The Investment Costs of Training Health Workers

Because medical education straddles the health and education sectors, identifying overall capital expenditures is complex. The costs of land, infrastructure, and specialized medical equipment contribute to overall capital expenditures, as do initial investments in educational and reference materials, laboratories, utilities, and subsequent depreciation costs. The infrastructure for training health workers (mainly at the university level)—particularly libraries, dorms, cafeterias, and sometimes laboratories—is often shared with other university students.

The infrastructure for in-service training is also used for service delivery. Just as it is difficult to separate the recurrent costs of health service training from the recurrent costs of health service delivery, it is equally difficult to separate the investment costs of training from the investment cost of service delivery. Capital investments in medical education traditionally include two institutional parts: an undergraduate training institution and a teaching hospital. These structures are often vertically integrated. Although some training organizations operate separately, many are associated with neighboring tertiary-level teaching facilities.

The land for training institutions is often acquired at a highly subsidized rate and not properly monetized as part of overall investment cost estimates. Initial infrastructure and equipment quantities are constrained by limited budgets and may be inferior to what is needed. Once built, infrastructure is not depreciated at the standard 20- to 30-year life (which should be shorter in the harsh climate in Sub-Saharan Africa). Likewise, once bought, teaching equipment is not depreciated at the standard 5- to 7-year lifecycle. There is often a rapid deterioration in the capital stock shortly after the institutions are built.

Capital cost estimates for scaling up the education of health workers should include rehabilitating or upgrading existing facilities and greenfield investments in new facilities. The need for rehabilitation or greenfield infrastructure investment varies within each country context. Postconflict countries like Liberia and Sierra Leone have significant greenfield investment needs due to the destruction of infrastructure and equipment during their civil wars.

Investment costs in context: The Ghana case. Recent preinvestment studies in Sub-Saharan Africa and elsewhere suggest that it costs about $40 million to build a new medical school to train an intake and output of 250 students a year. Preinvestment costs for larger schools that include medical specialties and strong research capacities may reach $160 million (Temple University, School of Medicine n.d.). Relatively stable countries like Ghana may realize improvements in capacity by rehabilitating existing training schools.

Investments by Ghana's Ministry of Health in the training of diploma nurses, community health nurses, and health assistants allowed training institutions to scale up in recent years. Continued investments have not kept up with the depreciation of infrastructure and equipment. As a result, the cost of upgrading existing facilities varies depending on the number of schools, the state of existing infrastructure and staffing, and the desired capacity of the training program.

Although the situation differs from country to country, several observations from Ghana may be relevant to other countries. First, total spending on health education training by the Ministry of Health ($25 million) is much higher than spending by the Ministry of Education ($15 million). Second, the average annual unit cost and total cost of training highly professional staff under the Ministry of Education is much higher than lower cadre training through the Ministry of Health (GHc7–8,000, or ~$7–8,000, recurrent per graduate under the Ministry of Education compared with ¢800 under the Ministry of Health). Third, capital investment by the Ministry of Education is very low as a ratio of recurrent to capital spending (1.3–4.8 percent) compared with international norms of 6 percent. Fourth, there appears to be considerable underinvestment by the Ministry of Health in programs for midwives and technicians, but much higher recent expenditure on professional nurses, community health nurses, and medical assistants (14.7–21.9 percent). Fifth, the total average annual investment per professional student is around ¢116, while the average annual investment on lower skilled workers is around ¢86.

Primary Financing Sources for Health Worker Education

The funding sources for health worker education are similar to those for health worker salaries and services. Funds from governments, student fees, nongovernmental organizations, the private sector, endowments, and domestic and foreign donors all support health worker education (figure 18.2). Although there are exceptions, health insurance funds usually are not used for training.

Figure 18.2   Sources of Financing

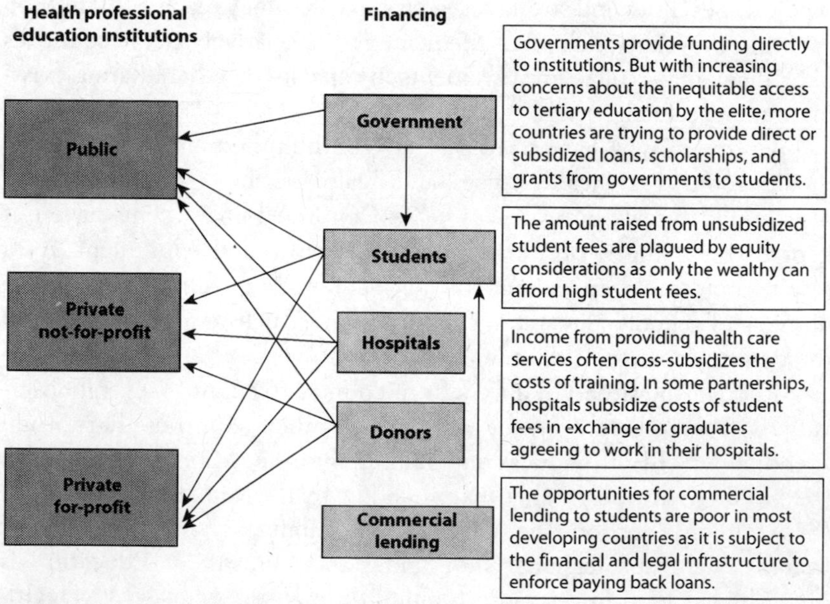

Source: Preker and others 2008.

In most low-income countries the public sector largely assumes responsibility for financing both recurrent and capital investment in health worker higher education. In the United States and Europe student fees are a nominal portion of revenues. When public sector contributions are smaller, donors and alumni play a larger financial role, especially in developed countries. In developing countries student contributions make up a higher percentage of school revenues. If teachers and teaching infrastructure remain insufficient, the financial resources generated from student tuition in developing countries can cover only investment costs. Discussions with the managers of private for-profit schools in Ghana, Kenya, Mozambique, and Tanzania reveal that the government is often reluctant to buy services or pay student tuitions at for-profit institutions. Although there may be exceptions, the private sector is largely responsible for generating its own funding.

The not-for-profit status of many training institutions limits the sources of capital available to finance their investment needs. Limited institutional capacity may also constrain higher private investment in educating health workers. According to studies on the shortage of nurses in the United States, efforts to scale up nursing education are constrained primarily by the shortage of nursing faculty (American Association of College of Nurses 2006). The shortage of nurses in the United States is so severe that federal policies actively target higher student enrollment and expanded nurse training capacity. The lack of sufficient teaching staff is also problematic in Sub-Saharan Africa. Countries such as Ghana, Liberia, Mozambique, and Sierra Leone face pressures to raise enrollment even though they lack adequate numbers of teachers.

Countries that are resource-constrained often do not have the financial and legal infrastructure that typically allows students to borrow money to finance their education. Rates of return for individuals who invest in a medical education are typically high enough to provide a financial incentive. Estimates for initial personal investment requirements such as time and access to capital are not available in many developing countries. Some information exists from Latin American countries where tertiary education has a strong private financing component.

Developed countries offer direct-to-student financing to help realize the positive returns on medical education. For the most part it is not available in developing countries. Studies on investments in medical education examine the personal expected rates of return to investing in a long and expensive education, presenting a picture of the demand forces for medical education. There are typically high rates of return to individuals who invest in medical education and thus strong demand for it. But there are significant demand constraints from limited access to financing and high opportunity costs in the general labor market.

One study estimated a private rate of return to secondary and higher education at about 20 percent, based on tuition for a medical student at the University of Witwatersrand in South Africa, and salary and cost of living for doctors in South Africa and the United States (World Bank 1998). A South African doctor can earn ten times more in the United States over 20 years than if he or she remains in South Africa.

The government is the main funding source for training health workers in Ghana, though some money is generated from student fees, grants, and donations. Domestic and foreign student fees as a percentage of total revenues are higher for schools that train lower cadres. Donations of books and laboratory equipment also contribute to in-kind revenues, but their value was not monetized for this study. With very few exceptions, the in-kind contribution was not significant, appropriate, or systematic among the schools sampled. Endowments and other innovative financing mechanisms are not widely used or routinely reported as part of overall financing.

Demand for slots in medical schools is high in low- and middle-income countries. Among the sampled schools, public nursing schools in Ghana turn away 30 percent of qualified applicants because they do not have the capacity to train them (Beciu and others 2009). In 2009 the Tubman National Institute of Medical Arts in Liberia had 101 qualified applicants for a capacity of 25 students.[3] As noted by Dr. Tabeh Freeman of the Tubman National Institute: "It is not possible to increase the number of students without capital investment. The maximum capacity of a classroom is 25 students; so to increase the number of students, we must have additional classrooms. Currently, we have a problem with enrolling more students because of classroom space."

Regulatory Constraints to Better Funding Options

Even if governments do not directly control student intake, medical schools and health worker training institutions are still highly regulated by government and self-regulating bodies. These regulatory bodies can influence the supply of medical schools and health worker output either by limiting the number of slots available in medical schools, or requiring a minimum standard for accreditation, such as student-teacher ratios or space per student requirements, which raise the costs of producing medical graduates.

Constraints on supply distort the link between spending on higher education and the number of graduates produced. There is a strong correlation between financial allocation in tertiary education and output of graduates, but due to governing bodies' influence over the supply of health professionals, this correlation is not as strong in medical education as in other areas. The financing of medical schools is not necessarily linked to physician output.

The high degree of regulation in medical education may illustrate one reason why most medical schools worldwide (both public and private) receive some public funding, even in more market-oriented environments. The high degree of supply regulation raises costs of production and limits the profitability of medical schools (box 18.1). Where medical school supply is heavily regulated, even indirectly, there are high hurdles for new entrants and limited scope for schools

Box 18.1

The Effects of Self-Regulation and Financing on Medical Education: Physician Supply in the 21st Century

In the United States physician supply is controlled through medical school accreditation, entrance requirements, and sometimes entrance caps, physician licensure requirements, and caps on available residency positions. Medical schools must be accredited by the Liaison Committee on Medical Education, which is empowered by two nongovernmental bodies: the American Medical Association and the American Association of Medical Colleges. At a minimum, medical schools must be accredited by the Liaison Committee on Medical Education to receive federal grants or partake in federal loan programs.

From 1930 to 1965 the growth in physician supply held pace with population growth of about 1 percent a year. The physician growth rate could not, however, keep up with the rising demand for health care that resulted from technological improvements and increases in prepaid group practice plans. During this time the self-regulating controls on physician supply led to a series of government interventions. In 1941 the U.S. Department of Justice accused the District of Columbia Medical Society and the American Medical Association of conspiring to monopolize trade in physician services. In 1963 the U.S. Congress passed the Health Professions Educational Assistance Act, which required medical schools to increase capacity and allow foreign doctors to practice. Under the provisions of

(continued next page)

Box 18.1 *(continued)*

this law, states built more medical schools, and existing schools received more government funding with the condition that medical student enrollment rise by at least 5 percent a year (Getzen 1997). Within two decades the number of medical school graduates more than doubled (box figure 1).

Box Figure 18.1.1   Medical School Enrollment and Revenue Patterns, 1960–95

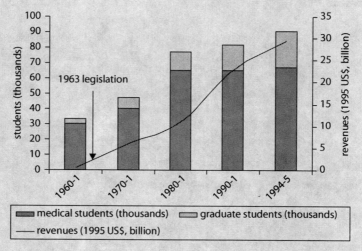

Source: Association of American Medical Colleges 1996.

The 1963 legislation had a sizable impact on medical student enrollment and output. Enrollment and graduate output increased rapidly while medical school revenues grew modestly. Medical school revenues grew fastest from 1980 to 1995, while the number of medical students remained fairly constant.

Source: Keuffel, Preker, and Ly (2010), based on Getzen (1997).

to generate revenues from increasing output from their core business of producing doctors. U.S. medical schools do not generate much revenue from student tuitions. Although tuition in the United States is the highest in the world, it covers only a small fraction of the total operating revenues (Jones and Korn 1997). Medical schools rely on income from other services to subsidize teaching.

Developing countries are less likely to have effective systems to regulate the quality of medical schools. Sub-Saharan countries usually have independent or semi-autonomous professional bodies in charge of medical licensing, accreditation, and certification but may not be able to enforce their regulations. On the other hand, some countries either do not have accreditation or certification bodies, or these bodies are not capable of conducting their certification processes in a timely and efficient manner. In addition, varying laws (or lack of laws) influence the governance of higher education institutions. The governments of Benin, Cameroon, Madagascar, and Tanzania directly oversee their universities. Other countries, such as Angola, Guinea, Ghana, Liberia, and Sierra Leone allow universities to be autonomous.

Private Contributions to Scaling Up Health Worker Training

Where public resources are constrained, the private sector may fill the void and foster opportunities to scale up health worker education (box 18.2). In the Democratic Republic of Congo the number of medical and nursing graduates doubled from 2001 to 2003, largely due to private sector-led growth in training health workers (WHO 2006).

A study by the International Finance Corporation estimates that, given the public sector's resource constraints, there is a private investment opportunity of $1.7 billion in medical education in Africa (IFC 2007). The study gives examples in Senegal and Tanzania, where the private sector offers sustainable models of nursing and medical education while innovating to solve resource constraints. The Institut Santé Services, a private nursing school in Senegal, functions with student fees as its sole revenue source. In Tanzania 90 percent of the revenues of Hubert Kariuki Memorial University come from student fees, and the rest from its hospital services.

The private sector still faces limitations in developing countries, especially in Africa. Many of the constraints applicable to promoting private industry are also relevant to medical education. Many countries lack the requisite legal and financial infrastructure to increase access to investment finance for private firms and to enable individuals to invest in their education through student loans.

Private investment in health worker education is a sensitive issue in many countries because education funding traditionally falls within the public sector's jurisdiction. Some commentators express concern that private sector involvement will compromise the quality and access to education. This does not need to be so. Private investment should be

Box 18.2

Private Medical Education in India

In India the private sector is a major provider of medical education. Over the last five decades the number of undergraduate medical institutions grew eightfold, and the number of student slots fivefold, due mostly to the private sector. Whereas private medical colleges had a small share of the market in the 1950s, they now account for more than 45 percent of all medical institutions in India.

Merit-based entrance exams determine admissions to public medical schools. Private medical schools also offer subsidized "merit seats" based on exams. The remaining private school slots are allocated through a "management" quota that considers merit but imposes substantial student fees. Despite laws requiring transparent merit-based admissions and minimum infrastructure and faculty standards for private institutions, anecdotal evidence suggests that higher tuition fees and inadequate staff and infrastructure compromise student quality.

Private allopathic medical schools are set up mainly in wealthier states, linked to the growing inequality of enrollment as the share of wealthy medical students rises. Because physicians tend to practice near where they studied, the distribution of new physicians in India favors the richer states. The emigration of some top graduates from highly ranked public institutions adds to the problems of physician distribution. Despite the significant private sector-led scale up of physician output, equity problems remain in accessing health care in India.

Box Table 18.2.1   Inequality in Access: Distribution of Seats for Bachelors of Medicine and Surgery

	Public		Private	
	Seats (number)	Share (percent)	Seats (number)	Share (percent)
Bottom 50 percent income	4,712	30	520	7.8
Top 50 percent income	8,008	63	6,115	92.2

Source: Mahal and Mohanan 2006.

accompanied by regulatory oversight to establish minimum standards and appropriate targeting of education opportunities to safeguard equitable access for low-income students. Equitable and inclusive education is key to ensuring the production of quality health workers who can serve in high-need areas.

Getting Better Value for Money

Countries should explore options to obtain better value for money in financing higher education in health. Mobilizing additional resources and using available resources more efficiently can realize better value. In recent years the international community increased aid to the health sector in developing countries. Many vertical programs, previously neglected, benefited from these resources.[4] These programs are now at risk of failing due to an insufficient and inappropriate mix of human resource cadres.

Two aspects of vertical programs undermine their impact and restrict health worker resources more broadly. First, although many vertically funded programs devote significant resources to short-term training and other capacity-building activities, few support the preservice and undergraduate education of health workers. At the same time, vertical programs compete for funding with basic education. Unless this misallocation of resources is rectified, current financing strategies will not only damage priority programs but also continue to block advances in human resource development.

Second, vertical programs lead to wage inflation and competition for staff within the health sector. This competition reduces the ability of horizontal programs, such as maternal and child health, to function effectively. Many core horizontal programs now face a severe shortage in staff because of the distortion caused by a disproportionate amount of donor money flowing into a few programs.

Countries also face internal challenges. National health worker education systems are often plagued by inefficiency. The unit costs of training can be reduced through four channels. First, governments and training institutions can stem the loss of resources by reducing the dropout rate and brain drain. Second, governments can encourage greater collaboration among schools, countries, and regions. By sharing staff and teaching facilities across different schools and among countries, training programs can reduce costs. Third, health worker education programs can reduce costs by sharing the delivery of preclinical training with the basic science programs of associated universities. Fourth, appropriate use of modern teaching aids and technology adaptation can reduce unit costs in health worker training.

Policy makers need detailed country-level information to determine the best approaches to financing the scaling-up of health worker training. Individual countries make their own decisions about appropriate tradeoffs in the numbers and types of health workers they can support. They must also define their priorities for aid expenditures with development partners and international financial institutions.

Governments and donors can enlarge the fiscal envelope for investing in plans to scale up health education through several courses of action. Governments can increase their commitments to the health and education sectors, particularly the share of these sectors dedicated to health education. They can coordinate health education programs, including those between countries, to improve efficiency through both shared faculty and facilities and integration in preclinical training between health education programs and undergraduate science training. Donors can focus on preservice education to address the supply and quality of education in the medium to long term.

Scenarios for Financing Health Worker Education

In collaboration with Results for Development, we applied a costing tool to estimate the various scenarios for scaling up health worker education in Ghana (table 18.2). We altered the scenarios by varying the assumptions about the available resource envelope; the cost of absorbing health workers into the labor force at different staffing levels, skill mixes, and remuneration; and the recurrent and capital costs of educating more health workers up to the affordable staffing level.

Best-Case Economic Scenario

For this analysis, the best-case scenario is 7 percent annual economic growth and 15 percent government spending on health. Under these conditions Ghana would affordably reach the targeted human resources staffing set out in the Ministry of Health's human resources policy by 2017. We assumed no changes in the desired skills mix or the relative

Table 18.2   Health Expenditure Scenarios, Ghana

Scenario	Annual economic growth (percent)	Public health expenditures, 2017 (percent of government expenditures)	Total public spending on health, 2007 ($, millions)	Total public spending on health, 2017 ($, millions)
Best case	7	15	600	1,200
Current trends	4–5	9	600	900
Worst case	0	4.5	600	300

Source: World Bank data.

wage bill. Before concluding that 2017 workforce targets are affordable under the best-case economic scenario, we examined training schools' abilities to scale up health worker production to reach targets and adjusted this for school dropout and workforce attrition (emigration, internal migration, retirement, deaths, and other exits from clinical practice).

Under the best-case economic scenario, at current production levels some programs would not reach the target number of health worker graduates needed to attain the desired affordable staffing levels until 2030. The problem is most acute in the high-level cadres under the Ministry of Education, such as doctors, specialists, dental surgeons, and pharmacists. The limited training capacity for midwives and pharmacy technicians under the Ministry of Health is also acute, and at the time of the study these two cadres did not receive sufficient resources to achieve the desired scale-up.

Current-Status Scenario

The costing tool defined the current scenario in Ghana as 4–5 percent annual economic growth and 9 percent government expenditure on health. Under current economic conditions and with the government's current ability to increase budget allocations to the health sector, the government would need to lower staffing targets for highly skilled staff by 25–33 percent to meet the 2017 target. Even at these lower targets, a large annual increase in training costs ($25 million) and investment costs ($20 million) under the Ministry of Education would be necessary.

Under the current economic conditions and the government's ability to increase its budget allocation, current production levels for professional nurses, community health nurses, and medical assistants under the Ministry of Health would overshoot the targets. This can be avoided if the Ministry of Health scales back these areas and shifts part of the budget to the training programs for midwifery, where there is an acute shortage.

Worst-Case Scenario

The worst-case scenario is defined as 0 percent annual economic growth and 4.5 percent government spending on health. Under these conditions, expanding the current workforce would be unaffordable, and training schools would need to retreat to replacement levels in their graduate output. There could be an erosion in the wage bill, which would force the health sector to rely on lower qualified and less expensive staff.

Conclusion

The cost implications of scaling up health worker training are significant, particularly in the health and education sectors. A realistic understanding of the initial and recurrent costs, coupled with a broader array of financing options and an easing of regulatory constraints, is key to increasing production of health workers.

The Ghana example shows that decision makers need detailed country-level analyses to support recommendations on the best policies for financing the scale-up of health worker training; each country functions within its own political, economic, and policy contexts. Individual countries must determine the tradeoffs required to support the numbers and cadres of health workers needed to meet national targets—and together with development partners and international financial institutions, determine aid priorities.

Acknowledgments

The authors are grateful for contributions from many people. In particular, Aaron Lawson (provost of the Korle-Bu College of Health Sciences) and Yaw Adu-Gyamfi (United Nations Population Fund Consultant), who provided valuable guidance. The team also collaborated with and received feedback from Agnes Soucat (World Bank), Richard Scheffler (University of California, Berkeley), and Eliot Sorel (M.D., D.L.F.A.P.A., George Washington University).

Notes

1. Partnering ministries may include ministries of health, ministries of education, ministries of industry and innovations, ministries of science and technology, and other ministries involved in stewardship of the health training schools.

2. Ghana College of Physicians and Surgeons, 2008 Postgraduate Expenditures Estimates.

3. Correspondence with Dr. Tabeh Freeman, Tubman National Institute of Medical Arts on September 7, 2007.

4. "Vertical" programs focus on a particular theme or disease. The Global Fund to Fight AIDS, Tuberculosis, and Malaria and the Global Alliance for Vaccines and Immunizations are examples of large vertical programs. In contrast, "horizontal" programs focus on broader issues within the health sector.

References

American Association of College of Nurses. 2006. "Student Enrollment Rises in US Nursing Colleges and Universities for the 6th Consecutive Year." Press Release, December 5.

Association of American Medical Colleges. 1996. "The Financing of Medical Schools." Task Force on Medical School Financing, Washington, DC.

Association of American Medical Colleges. 2011. "Financial Planning at Medical Schools Revenues." https://www.aamc.org/download/251012/data/i.reven ueofu.s.medicalscholsbysourcefiscalyear2010.pdf http://www.aamc.org/students/considering/financial.htm.

Bankya, K., and J. Elu. 2001. "The World Bank and Financing Higher Education in Sub-Saharan Africa." *Higher Education* 42: 1–34.

Beciu, H., A. Preker, S. Ayettey, J. Antwi, A. Lawson, and S. Adjei. 2009."Ghana Pre-Investment Study." Working Paper, World Bank, Washington, DC.

Getzen, T. E. 1997. *Health Economics: Fundamentals and Flow of Funds*. New York: John Wiley & Sons.

GHWA (Global Health Workforce Alliance). 2010. *Resource Requirement Tool.* Geneva: World Health Organization. http://www.who.int/workforcealliance/knowledge/publications/taskforces/ftfproducts/en/index.html

IFC (International Finance Corporation). 2007. *The Business of Health in Africa.* Washington, DC: IFC. http://www.ifc.org/ifcext/healthinafrica.nsf/Content/FullReport.

Jones, R. F., and D. Korn. 1997. "On the Cost of Educating a Medical Student." *Academic Medicine* 72 (3): 200–10.

Keuffel, E. L., A. Preker, and C. Ly. 2010. "Finance for Health Education Institutions in Africa." Working Paper, World Bank, Washington, DC.

Mahal, A., and M. Mohanan. 2006. "Medical Education in India: Implications for Quality and Access to Care." *Journal of Educational Planning and Administration* 20 (4): 173–84.

Mandel, M., and J. Weber. 2006. "What's Really Propping Up the Economy." *Business Week*, September 25.

Preker, A. S., M. Vujicic, Y. Dukhan, C. Ly, H. Beciu, and P. N. Materu. 2008. "Scaling Up Health Professional Education, Opportunities and Challenges for Africa." Working Paper, Commissioned by the Global Task Force on Health Education, World Bank, Washington, DC.

Scheffler, R. M. 2008. *How Many Physicians Are Enough?* Palo Alto, CA: Stanford University Press.

Scheffler, R. M., J. X. Liu, Y. Kinfu, and M. R. Dal Poz. 2009. "Estimates of Health Care Professional Shortages in Sub-Saharan Africa by 2015." *Health Affairs* 28 (5): w849–w862.

Simoens, S., and J. Hurst. 2006. "The Supply of Physician Services in OECD Countries." Health Working Paper 231, Organisation for Economic Co-operation and Development, Paris.

Soucat, A., R. M. Scheffler, eds. Forthcoming. "Human Resources for Health in Africa: A Fresh Look at the Crisis." World Bank, Washington, DC.

Temple University, School of Medicine. n.d. "New Medical School Building." Philadelphia, PA. www.temple.edu/medicine/about/new_building.htm.

WHO (World Health Organization). 2006. *The World Health Report 2006: Working Together for Health*. Geneva: WHO.

World Bank. 1998. *World Development Report 1998/99: Knowledge for Development*. Washington, DC: World Bank.